Religious Experience in the Hindu Tradition

Religious Experience in the Hindu Tradition

Special Issue Editor

June McDaniel

MDPI • Basel • Beijing • Wuhan • Barcelona • Belgrade

Special Issue Editor
June McDaniel
College of Charleston
USA

Editorial Office
MDPI
St. Alban-Anlage 66
4052 Basel, Switzerland

This is a reprint of articles from the Special Issue published online in the open access journal *Religions* (ISSN 2077-1444) in 2019 (available at: https://www.mdpi.com/journal/religions/special_issues/hindutradition)

For citation purposes, cite each article independently as indicated on the article page online and as indicated below:

LastName, A.A.; LastName, B.B.; LastName, C.C. Article Title. *Journal Name* **Year**, *Article Number*, Page Range.

ISBN 978-3-03921-050-3 (Pbk)
ISBN 978-3-03921-051-0 (PDF)

Cover image courtesy of Leonard Plotkin.

Contents

About the Special Issue Editor . . . . **vii**

June McDaniel
Introduction to "Religious Experience in the Hindu Tradition"
Reprinted from: *Religions* **2019**, *10*, 329, doi:10.3390/rel10050329 . . . . **1**

Jeffery D. Long
Religious Experience, Hindu Pluralism, and Hope: *Anubhava* in the Tradition of Sri Ramakrishna
Reprinted from: *Religions* **2019**, *10*, 210, doi:10.3390/rel10030210 . . . . **7**

Frederick M. Smith
The Fulcrum of Experience in Indian Yoga and Possession Trance
Reprinted from: *Religions* **2019**, *10*, 332, doi:10.3390/rel10050332 . . . . **24**

Christopher Key Chapple
Religious Experience and Yoga
Reprinted from: *Religions* **2019**, *10*, 237, doi:10.3390/rel10040237 . . . . **40**

Veena R. Howard
Divine Light and Melodies Lead the Way: The Santmat Tradition of Bihar
Reprinted from: *Religions* **2019**, *10*, 230, doi:10.3390/rel10040230 . . . . **53**

Alfred Collins
Religious Experience without an Experiencer: The 'Not I' in Sāṃkhya and Yoga
Reprinted from: *Religions* **2019**, *10*, 94, doi:10.3390/rel10020094 . . . . **67**

Antoinette DeNapoli
Earning God through the "One-Hundred Rupee Note": Nirguṇa Bhakti and Religious Experience among Hindu Renouncers in North India
Reprinted from: *Religions* **2018**, *9*, 408, doi:10.3390/rel9120408 . . . . **82**

J. E. Llewellyn
Saints, Hagiographers, and Religious Experience: The Case of Tukaram and Mahipati
Reprinted from: *Religions* **2019**, *10*, 110, doi:10.3390/rel10020110 . . . . **97**

Guy L. Beck
Sacred Music and Hindu Religious Experience: From Ancient Roots to the Modern Classical Tradition
Reprinted from: *Religions* **2019**, *10*, 85, doi:10.3390/rel10020085 . . . . **111**

Mani Rao
The Experience of Srividya at Devipuram
Reprinted from: *Religions* **2019**, *10*, 14, doi:10.3390/rel10010014 . . . . **125**

Jeffrey C. Ruff
Modern Transformations of *sādhanā* as Art, Study, and Awareness: Religious Experience and Hindu Tantric Practice
Reprinted from: *Religions* **2019**, *10*, 259, doi:10.3390/rel10040259 . . . . **135**

Perundevi Srinivasan
Sprouts of the Body, Sprouts of the Field: Identification of the Goddess with Poxes in South India
Reprinted from: *Religions* **2019**, *10*, 147, doi:10.3390/rel10030147 . . . . **151**

Sukanya Sarbadhikary
Shankh-er Shongshar, Afterlife Everyday: Religious Experience of the Evening Conch and Goddesses in Bengali Hindu Homes
Reprinted from: *Religions* **2019**, *10*, 53, doi:10.3390/rel10010053 . . . . **166**

About the Special Issue Editor

June McDaniel is Professor Emerita of the History of Religions in the Department of Religious Studies at the College of Charleston. She is the author of three books on India, a book on religious experience, a co-edited volume on mysticism, and many articles. She received her MTS in Theology from Candler Seminary at Emory University, and her Ph.D. was in the History of Religions from Divinity School at the University of Chicago. Dr. McDaniel has spent two years in India on grants from the American Institute of Indian Studies and as a Fulbright Senior Research Scholar, and she is currently investigating religion in Indonesia.

religions

MDPI

Editorial

Introduction to "Religious Experience in the Hindu Tradition"

June McDaniel

Department of Religious Studies, College of Charleston, Charleston, SC 29424, USA; mcdanielj@cofc.edu

Received: 6 May 2019; Accepted: 11 May 2019; Published: 16 May 2019

Abstract: This special issue of *Religions* brings together a talented group of international scholars who have studied and written on the Hindu tradition. The topic of religious experience is much debated in the field of Religious Studies, and here we present studies of Hindu religious experience explored from a variety of regions and perspectives. They are intended to show that religious experience has long been an important part of Hinduism, and we consider them to be important and relevant. As a body of scholarship, these articles refine our understanding of the range and variety of religious experience in Hinduism. In addition to their substantive contributions, the authors also show important new directions in the study of the third-largest religion in the world, with over one billion followers. This introduction will discuss some relevant issues in the field of Indology, some problems of language, and the difficulties faced in the study of religious experience. It will also give a brief sketch of the religious experiences described by our authors in some major types of Hinduism.

Keywords: India; Hinduism; yoga; tantra; devotion; meditation; prayer; saints; brahman; bhāva; mahābhāva; bhakti; trance; samādhi; mokṣa; darśan; bhakti

---

Religious experience in Hinduism is a challenging topic—all three terms are contested ones. 'Hinduism' is not an indigenous word, it is an umbrella term used first by outsiders, intended to cover a wide variety of systems of belief and practice in India. The term 'religion' has a wide variety of definitions, ranging from individual to social to universal. Additionally, the concept of 'experience' has come under scrutiny over the past century, with philosophical emphases on materialism, empirical proofs, and the limits of human knowledge. The opposition to the area of religious and mystical experience as a legitimate area of study has been written about many times in recent years; a good overview of the literature can be found in Leigh Eric Schmidt's article "The Making of Modern Mysticism."[1]

While Hindu philosophy also has materialist schools, there are many branches that allow for a greater range of human awareness and understanding than we see in Western philosophies. The self is structured in a more complex way than is currently acceptable in Western psychology, with forms of perception that bring different interpretations of the world (and worlds) in which we live. While these abilities may be strengthened and clarified by specific beliefs and practices, they are not understood to be created by them. For many of the meditative traditions, they might be comparable to muscles, which are present naturally but can be made stronger and more visible through exercise.

A single journal issue cannot be comprehensive on such a broad subject. This Issue is intended to show some of the range of religious experiences in Hinduism, and some academic approaches to understanding it. It includes articles on men and women, householders and renunciants, yogis and devotees, artists and musicians, and philosophers. Some forms of religious experience are blissful and positive, others are more dangerous. Some papers focus on empathy and are 'experience-near,' while

---

[1] (Schmidt 2003).

others are more skeptical and 'experience-distant'. For the practitioners described here by our authors, religious experience is a way to understand life as meaningful and worthwhile, lived in relation to a greater whole.

Each of the papers here has its own approach to the topic. Religious experience can include such ideal religious states as *mokṣa, samādhi, śāanti, darśan, bhakti, brahmajñāna, śaktipat*, and *rasa*. However, it can also include darker states, such as the presence of disease deities, as well as ways of blessing everyday life. There is no single correct religious experience in the great array of beliefs and practices included under the Hindu umbrella, though different traditions emphasize their own as preferable.

Every approach has its own concepts and terminology. However, one important general concept in this area is the term *bhāva*. It has both the breadth and ambiguity that we see in the English word 'experience.' It can refer to existence, state, condition, mental state, mood, emotion, inner significance, imagination, and ecstasy.[2] The Monier–Williams Sanskrit Dictionary has four columns of definitions for the term *bhāva*, and the *Bangalar Bhasar Abhidhan* has two columns, which include such meanings as heart, imagination, divinity, yogic powers, passion, trance, and rapture.[3] When used simply as *'bhāva'*, it often means a mood or state of mind (which can be secular), but when it is phrased as *mahābhāva* or great *bhāva*, the term refers specifically to a religious state. We sometimes see it used as *anubhāva* or direct inner experience (a legitimate source of knowledge in Indian philosophy), and *bhāvaveśa* or 'the state of possession trance', referring to a person being overwhelmed by a deity, an ancestor, or a passion. All of these papers examine different *bhāvas*, as states of being or religious experiences.

Our first article, by Jeffery Long, describes the historical origins of Hindu universalism. Rather than being a product of modern colonialism or the 'neo-Hinduism' of Vivekananda and others, Dr. Long shows that the ideas of universalism are much older and more traditional, a part of the philosophy of the Vedas, Upaniṣads, Brahma Sūtras, and Bhagavad Gītā. As expressed by the nineteenth century Bengali saint and *siddhā* Ramakrishna Paramahamsa, direct experience of ultimate reality by different paths is a valuable part of life, like different musical instruments playing together to create a symphony, or pieces of a jigsaw puzzle that work together to show us a whole. Direct experience, as shown in terms like *anubhāva* and *pratyakṣa*, is a part of Hindu philosophy and considered a legitimate source of knowledge. Dr. Long compares several Eastern and Western philosophers on the logical connections between universalism and direct religious experience. He also notes the value of such an approach for daily life, bringing tolerance and compassion to people of different religions.

Our next article by Frederick Smith compares religious experience in Sāṃkhya, yoga, and possession trance. He argues that an inner organ (*antahkarana*) is activated when the person experiences *samyama*, the fusion of the three highest yogic states according to Patanjali. This occurs after the state of *samādhi*. It is the awakening of this internal organ that impels or generates the experiences described in texts and ethnographies. He discusses Sāṃkhya and Yoga texts, and research on the state of possession. He finds that the moment of transition from ordinary body awareness to experiencing possession trance and final emergence of the deity is comparable to the yogin entering into the states of concentration, meditation, and *samādhi*, which eventually achieve a critical mass. It is at that point that he or she enters a state in which higher powers can be realized.

The article by Chris Chapple discusses the role of yoga as bringing three qualities emphasized by the philosopher William James: light, knowledge, and morality. Basing his discussion on Patanjali's Yoga Sūtra and the Bhagavad Gītā, he shows how yogic light brings both enlightenment and being 'lightened' from past karma, with inner light that purifies the mind and body. Yoga brings knowledge through the quality of *jñāna*, physical and metaphysical knowledge expressed through Vedānta and Sāṃkhya philosophical teachings. The practitioner can move from ignorance to reason, and also

---

2 These definitions come from the *Samsad Bengali-English Dictionary*, and the breadth of the meaning of the word is discussed in (McDaniel 1989, pp. 21–25).

3 Ibid, p. 21.

develop moral virtues, such as non-violence and compassion. Dr. Chapple also suggests some practices that he has personally found to encourage these states.

Veena Howard's article on the Sant Mat tradition describes a spiritual path of sound and light, involving yogic meditative practices, mantra, and visualization. Its goal of spiritual peace or *śāanti* is reached with the help of a teacher, a congregation, a moral system, and set of meditative techniques. Her focus here is the Bihari school of Santmat, led by Maharishi Mehi, whose books and discourses she has been translating. It combines Hindu teachings, especially from the Upanishads, with other religious traditions. There are both monastic and lay followers, and the meditative practices are linked to social reform in rural and tribal areas.

Alfred Collins' article explores the psychological impact of *darśan*, the encounter with ultimacy through vision, in the Hindu perspectives of Sāṃkhya and Yoga. He examines the challenges to exploration of the individual self in philosophy, as due to critiques of essentialism, supposed limits of the capitalist mind, and the 'death of God' in the modern West. Religious experience, according to the Hindu schools he examines, does not glorify the individual self but rather has that self dissolve into its realization of pure spirit (*puruṣa*). It exists through its perception of the universal; the self sees through being seen, uniting the opposites of life. Dr. Collins describes different constructions of the self in Eastern and Western psychology, focusing on the dualistic Samkhya school. As in modern 'self-psychology' where the child's psyche is developed through the mother's gaze, in Sāṃkhya we have the individual self which becomes realized through the gaze of the universal spirit.

Antoinette DeNapoli's article discusses the experience of *nirguṇa bhakti*, devotion to a formless god, among the North Indian *sādhus* with whom she has worked. The goal for these Rajasthani renunciants is peace and stillness, in the presence of an impersonal god beyond the physical senses. *Sādhus* describe this state as melting into the ocean of god consciousness, a process of surrendering individual will and ego. She shows extraordinary empathy for her informants, describing their emotions and the goals of their lives. Singing *bhajans* or hymns is a practice that encourages this state of *bhakti*, thus "keeping the diamond safe"; it is the best form of loving devotion to the god.

Jack Llewellyn's article on *bhakti* has a more experience-distant approach, and it asks the question, 'How much can we know about a devotee's religious experiences?" He examines seventeenth century hagiographies of the saint Tukaram, of the Varkari Vaiṣṇava tradition of Maharashtra. His article asks whether saint biographies are simply fictions, whitewashing life events and idealizing their subjects, or do they show what believers think is true, or what is actually true? Is the scholar able to appreciate a 'sense of presence' from historical narratives? Can modern people understand the experiences of people who might have a different sense of self and world? Dr. Llewellyn holds to the skeptical approach—that our knowledge is necessarily limited.

Guy Beck's article on religious experience evoked by music gives a fine history of sacred sound and Hindu spirituality. From Vedic chant to the Upaniṣads, from Yoga philosophy to Tantric rituals, from theistic worship in the Bhakti movements to classical Rāgas, we can see that religious states can be evoked by aesthetics as well as text and narrative. The goal of hymns and mantras was classically *śabda brahman* (realization of god as sound), and later the experience of aesthetic *rasa*, religious emotion experienced through drama and through ritual worship and *kirtan* singing. Musical religious experience can include both *nirguṇa* and *saguṇa* understandings of deity, and sacred sound is a way of linking together the various sectarian schools of Hinduism.

Mani Rao's description of Srividya religious experience at Devipuram involves tantric imagery, and discusses the uses of mantra and the ways that visionary experience is evoked. The disciples of Amritanandanatha Saraswati focus on a particular type of symbol, the Sriyantra, whose triangles represent the union of Shiva and Shakti. This yantra acts as a meditative tool, as a map of spiritual space, and as a place of embodiment; it is both a description and a location. The person's body becomes identified with the yantra as he or she enters into it. Dr. Rao describes the visionary experiences of many disciples, as well as the founding vision of the guru, and the central role of both mantra and vision in meditation.

Jeffrey Ruff's article focuses on a particular type of religious experience, the unity of art and *sādhanā* or spiritual practice. In Shākta tantra, the awakening of kundalini energy or *śaktipāt* can occur during initiation and meditation but it can also occur through appreciation of beauty. The goddess' grace shows itself in a variety of ways, with a blurring of boundaries between the religious and the aesthetic. Artists, teachers, and writers can inspire bliss in others, and modern tantric practitioners have described unconventional forms of religious experience, ranging from traumatic to ecstatic. The power of the goddess may be found in wealth and good luck, knowledge, and awareness; in artistic and scientific creativity; and in traditional tantric meditative practices.

However, what if god is an affliction, who gives you diseases and fevers? The article by Perundevi Srinivasan has a very different approach to religious experience, where the South Indian goddess Mariyamman shows her presence by illness. Like the Biblical Job with his boils, the devotee has been faithful, yet the gift of the god's presence through illness is also a curse. While the question in Job is theodicy, the origin and reason for such disasters, Dr Srinivasan explores the question of complexity through the metaphorical understandings of divine presence through disease in this article. Illness can be the 'play' of the goddess; it can act as protection from astrological dangers, and it can be understood as divine grace, as possession, and as fertility.

Our last article brings religious experience down to earth, as blowing the conch in the evening brings household happiness that is linked with life, death, and rebirth. Sukanya Sarbadhikary's article discusses Bengali domestic worship of the goddesses Lakshmi and Manasa, in a home which is understood to be the embodiment of cosmic space and time. The AUM sound of the conch evokes Lakshmi and auspiciousness, as well as Manasa, who both bring danger and rescue people from it. Daily life is immersed in sacred time, including both fertility and renunciation. The complex symbolism of the conch unites these ideas, with a home altar that brings opposites together in the religious experience of the everyday world. Rather than transcendent experiences of divinity, here we have the immanent blessing of the physical world and the family in it.

There are thus many perspectives in this Issue on religious experience in Hinduism. While some modern writers in Religious Studies argue that interest in Eastern religious experience is post-colonial and a Western imposition,[4] we can look back to arguments over its role in Hindu writings from many centuries ago.

One interesting discussion on this topic allows us to end on a lighter note, to see an early use of satire in the area of religious experience. This style can be seen in the tradition of tantra in India, which developed gradually but is usually dated from sixth to seventh century onwards.[5] While today its popular association is rebellion and sexuality, its earlier uses include military, political, and medical applications. Tantric religious experience was also associated with ecstasy, but also with health and longevity.

One famous tantric text is the *Kulārnava Tantra*, frequently cited by Bengali practitioners as the most important tantra for Shākta tantrikas.[6] It is a medieval text usually dated to the thirteenth century

---

[4] For example, Robert Sharf writes in his article on "Experience" in Mark Taylor's *Critical Terms in Religious Studies*, ideas of religious experience in Asia are "a relatively late and distinctively Western invention." This is discussed in (McDaniel 2018, pp. 235–36).

[5] The dating of the tantric tradition has been widely debated. Here I follow the dating of Geoffrey Samuel (who cites the research of Alexis Sanderson and David Gordon White). See (Samuel and Johnston 2013, p. 35).

[6] The *Kulārnava Tantra* is a major text for Shākta tantric practitioners in West Bengal. Shāktism or goddess worship is a type of sectarian Hinduism that emphasizes the role of the goddess as both creatress and savioress, and the tantras that follow this tradition discuss goddess worship in detail. Shākta tantrikas interviewed during two years of fieldwork in West Bengal told me that the *Kulārnava Tantra* was the most important Shākta tantric text written, and it was used in daily ritual. Here I use the Bengali translation of the *Kulārnava Tantra* published by Nababharat Publishers, which was the version used by most informants. The most famous translation, by Sir John Woodroffe/Arthur Avalon, leaves out large chunks of the text and does not translate the writing line by line. Instead, it gives Woodroffe's opinions on what tantra should be. It also slants many translations towards Vedānta and away from Shāktism, portraying tantra as philosophical and rational. Thus, I will not use this translation here, and go directly to the Sanskrit/Bengali text.

CE, though Goudriaan and Gupta give a wider range, from the tenth to the fifteenth century CE.[7] While some later commentators tend to emphasize the intellectual goal of tantric study and practice, and use such words for tantra's goal as *vidyā* (learning or scholarship), *tattvā* (essential nature, truth, philosophical knowledge), and *jnana* (wisdom, understanding), we see this text itself using terms like *pratyakṣa* (immediate experience), *bhāva* (mood, feeling, emotion), *upalabdhi* (realization), and *ullāsa* (blissful joy). Here, the text satirizes brahmin intellectuals and philosophers, who value theory over experience:

- 87. O Beloved! Many ignorant people fall into the deep well of the six philosophies; they are controlled by their instincts and cannot attain the highest knowledge;
- 88. They are drowning in the dreadful ocean of the Vedas and shastras, and they are driven in one direction and then another, by philosophical discussions and debates, which are like terrible waves and crocodiles;
- 89. [There are] people who have read the Vedas, Agamas, and Puranas but who do not know the highest truth. All their knowledge is like the cawing of crows, and nothing more;
- 90. O Goddess, they turn their backs on truth and read books day and night, always worrying about what they should be learning, saying this is knowledge or that is knowledge;
- 91. They know literary style, syntax, and poetry, and ways to make writing attractive, but they are fools, and they are confused and worried;
- 92. What they understand is not the ultimate truth (*paramātattvā*), and what they interpret is not the real meaning of the sacred books;
- 93. They speak of ecstatic consciousness (*unmanī-bhāva*) but they do not experience it. [This is because] some are vain and some have never been taught by a guru;
- 94. They chant the Vedas and fight among themselves, but they do not know the highest truth, as a cooking ladle does not know the taste of the food in it.[8]

Studying the Vedas and Shāstras gives knowledge of the tradition, but it does not give the seeker what is most needed, which is direct insight and ecstatic consciousness. The *Kulārnava Tantra* condemns shallow pandits and philosophers:

- 97. Discussion of ideas cannot destroy the illusions of the world, as talk of a lamp will not get rid of the darkness;
- 98. A person who studies but does not know ultimate reality is like a blind man looking at his face in a mirror.[9]

As we can see, the topic of religious experience is not a new one in Hinduism, brought in the nineteenth and twentieth centuries by colonialists, Orientalists, and Western scholars. As the articles in this issue show, it has been present and important for thousands of years. It has not only been emphasized in many Hindu religious traditions, but its lack has been both noticed and critiqued.

As we examine the role of religious experience in Hinduism, let us turn to our first article.

Funding: This research received no external funding.

Conflicts of Interest: The author declares no conflict of interest.

---

7 (Goudriaan and Gupta 1981, p. 93).

8 Upendrakumar Das, ed. 1363 B.S./1976. *Kulārnava Tantram: Mūla, Tīkā O Banganubadasaha*, Calcutta: Nababharata Pablisars. This is a Sanskrit text, with a Bengali translation and commentary. It will be abbreviated here as KT. The English translations are my own. KT I. 87–94.

9 Ibid, KT I. 97–98.

References

Schmidt, Leigh Eric. 2003. The Making of Modern Mysticism. *Journal of the American Academy of Religion* 71: 273–302. [CrossRef]

Samuel, Geoffrey, and Jay Johnston. 2013. *Religion and the Subtle Body in Asia and the West: Between Mind and Body*. Abingdon: Routledge, p. 35.

Goudriaan, Teun, and Sanjukta Gupta. 1981. Hindu Tantric and Sakta Literature. In *A History of Indian Literature*. Edited by Jan Gonda. Wiesbaden: Otto Harrassowitz, vol. II, p. 93.

McDaniel, June. 1989. *The Madness of the Saints: Ecstatic Religion in Bengal*. Chicago: University of Chicago Press, pp. 21–25.

McDaniel, June. 2018. *Lost Ecstasy: Its Decline and Transformation in Religion*. New York: Palgrave Macmillan, pp. 235–36.

religions

MDPI

Article

Religious Experience, Hindu Pluralism, and Hope: *Anubhava* in the Tradition of Sri Ramakrishna

Jeffery D. Long

Department of Religious Studies, Elizabethtown College, Elizabethtown, PA 17022, USA; longjd@etown.edu

Received: 2 February 2019; Accepted: 15 March 2019; Published: 19 March 2019

Abstract: The pluralistic turn in modern Hindu thought corresponds with the rise of an emphasis on direct experience of divine realities in this tradition. Both pluralism and a focus on experience have precedents in premodern Hindu traditions, but have become especially prominent in modern Hinduism. The paradigmatic example in the modern period of a religious subject embarking upon a pluralistic quest for direct experience of ultimate reality as mediated through multiple religious traditions is the nineteenth century Bengali sage, Sri Ramakrishna Paramahansa (1836–1886), whose most famous disciple, Swami Vivekananda (1863–1902) played a prominent role in the promotion of the idea of Hinduism as largely defined by a religious pluralism paired with an emphasis on direct experience. The focus in the teachings of Sri Ramakrishna and Swami Vivekananda on Brahman as a universal reality available, at least in principle, to being experienced by anyone, and interpreted using the categories of the experiencing subject's religion or culture, gives rise to a corresponding pluralism: a move towards seeing many religions and philosophies as conducive to the experience of a shared ultimate reality. This paper will analyze the theme of experience in the thought of these two figures, and other figures who are representative of this broad trend in modern Hindu thought, as well as in conversation with recent academic philosophers and theorists of religious experience, John Hick and William Alston. It will also argue that aspects of Hinduism, such as pluralism and an emphasis on direct experience, that are often termed as 'Neo-Vedantic' or 'Neo-Hindu' are not simply modern constructs, as these terms seem to suggest, but are reflective of much older trends in Hindu thought that become central themes in the thought of key Hindu figures in the modern period. Finally, it shall be argued that a pluralistic approach to the diversity of religions, and of worldviews more generally, is to be commended as an approach more conducive to human survival than the current global proliferation of ethno-nationalisms.

Keywords: Hinduism; religious experience; Ramakrishna; Vedanta; pluralism

1. Introduction

Two features of at least one major current of modern Hindu thought are this current's emphasis upon pluralism and the centrality of direct experience of the divine as definitive of the ultimate goal of religious practice. The prominence of pluralism in modern Hinduism is illustrated by the fact that it is a central theme in the writings and teachings of major Hindu thinkers of the modern period, including, although not limited to, Sri Ramakrishna, Swami Vivekananda, Mohandas K. Gandhi, Sarvepalli Radhakrishnan, and most of the well-known gurus who traveled to the Western world in this period, developing considerable followings. These teachers include, but again, are by no means limited to, Paramahansa Yogananda, Maharishi Mahesh Yogi, A.C. Bhaktivedanta Swami Prabhupada, Mata Amritanandamayi Devi (who is popular known as Amma), and Sadhguru Jaggi Vasudev.

The presence of pluralism in modern Hinduism is also illustrated on the popular level by such readily observable and well-attested phenomena as the sharing of sacred spaces by Hindus and the members of other religious communities, the patronage by Hindus of non-Hindu sacred spaces, like mosques, gurdwaras, and Jain temples, and the celebration by Hindus of the holidays of other religious traditions.[1]

Despite the rise of Hindu nationalism in recent years, and the tendency of some authors to identify Hindu pluralism, paradoxically, with a kind of Hindu triumphalism, the connection between these two is not a necessary or logical one, and is one which many Hindus would reject. As Elaine Fisher has written of Hindu pluralism of the kind under discussion here:

> ... Hindu pluralism, in contrast to the endemic communalism of post-independence India, itself has genuine roots in the subcontinent's precolonial heritage ... [T]he genuine theological work done by Vivekananda and his contemporaries in constructing a viable pluralistic worldview ... holds meaning for practitioners past and present. Inclusivist pluralism, for many, is a sincerely held theological commitment and can viably be promoted as a genuine emic Hindu pluralism.[2]

The extent to which scholars have tended to dismiss Hindu pluralism as an appendage of Hindu nationalism—a way for Hindus to pat themselves on the back for being inclusive even while not being so in practice—is shown by the fact that Fisher feels the need to make an argument for what would otherwise be seen as a fairly obvious point: that pluralism is a widely held Hindu position. Indeed, not only can pluralism of the kind promoted by many modern Hindu thinkers be "a sincerely held theological commitment," as Fisher affirms; but it could arguably serve to help counteract the spread of nationalism and communalism, not only in India, but globally. It would of course be naïve to argue that simply affirming a pluralistic worldview could alone serve to counteract the rise of widespread, deep-running currents of inter-religious, inter-ethnic, and international antagonism. Why, a critic might ask, has Hindu pluralism not already won the argument in India against Hindu nationalism, which is also a prominent current of modern Hindu thought? It would be cynical, though, to give up on the project of developing and promoting an alternative to ethno-nationalism: an alternative with considerably more promise to aid in the cultivation of a sustainable human civilization. Although beliefs and worldviews can certainly be overridden by other forces—socio-political, economic, and so on—beliefs do matter, and can affect reality profoundly.

The central thesis of this paper is that the co-occurrence of the themes of pluralism and direct experience in modern Hindu thought is not simply coincidental, but that pluralism and an emphasis upon direct experience are logically interlinked. This linkage can be discerned in the thought of two major contributors to modern Hindu thought in particular—namely, Sri Ramakrishna Paramahansa and Swami Vivekananda, building upon the work of earlier Hindu thinkers in the Brahmo Samaj movement of nineteenth century Bengal. In the teachings of both of these figures, pluralism and a direct experience of ultimate reality are central themes.

The logical connection between pluralism and an emphasis on direct experience is that the more traditional emphasis on a particular scriptural text as the final authority on religious matters tends to issue in the conclusion that one tradition alone is the true source of saving knowledge, whereas an emphasis on direct experience as one's final authority opens up the possibility that many traditions can lead to such experience. This can be seen as analogous to science, which is also rooted in reflection on experience. It does not matter whether the scientist is Indian, American, British, or Brazilian. There is no Indian, American, British, or Brazilian physics. There is just physics. Similarly, so the thought

---

1 There are abundant examples that could be cited in regard to this practice of what could be called 'popular pluralism' among Hindus and members of other religious communities in South Asia. To mention just a few, there are the shared Hindu-Jain celebrations of Dīvālī, or Dīpāvalī, and the shared Hindu-Jain worship of the deities Gaṇeśa, Lakṣmī, and Sarasvatī (Long 2009, p. 26). There is the Hindu employment of Muslim healers in popular village Hinduism in India, as well as Hindu worship at the tombs of Sufi saints (Flueckiger 2015, p. 194). And there are many other examples of Hindu-Muslim religious interactions in a pluralistic mode (Gottschalk 2000).

2 (Fisher 2017, p. 191).

process runs, divinity or ultimate reality is just as universally present as physical reality is, and just as universally available.

The possibility that many traditions can lead to an experience of the divine is tested in the life of Sri Ramakrishna, who will be the central focus of this study. Of course, there are also scriptural texts which enjoin, or which can easily be interpreted as enjoining, pluralism. And the lives of persons who have experiences of this kind also, themselves, can become the subject matter of texts later regarded by a tradition as scriptural (as the sources on the life of Ramakrishna have become for the tradition that is rooted in his life and teachings). One might thus believe in pluralism because this is what one's scripture teaches. The suggestion is not of a tight, logical, 'if-then' connection between scriptural authority and exclusivism, on the one hand, and between experience and pluralism, on the other, but of an affinity between the latter two. Scriptural authority tends to tie one to a particular tradition and to a particular, textually conditioned mode of experience, while experience as such is available, in principle, to anyone: just as, again, the observation of the physical world is similarly available. To be sure, discerning spiritual realities does require one to cultivate certain epistemic qualities. To say that spiritual realities are universally available does not mean that everyone experiences them to the same degree or with the same intensity. Again, though, the analogy holds with physical reality, that a certain training is also required in order to see the night sky as an astronomer sees it. But the night sky is there for all to perceive.

Beyond the discernment of these two themes in the thought of Ramakrishna, a suggestion will be made about why a strong emphasis upon a universally available religious experience might be attractive, and why it is increasingly popular among many contemporary spiritual practitioners in the Western world, particularly among the growing numbers of practitioners who define themselves as 'spiritual but not religious,' or who find themselves drawn to Asian religions precisely for their perceived openness to eclecticism and pluralism.

2. Defining Our Terms: Pluralism, Direct Experience, and Modern Hinduism

First, what do we mean when we speak of *pluralism* as a major theme of modern Hindu thought? *Pluralism*, in theological terms, refers to the idea that attainment of what one takes to be the ultimate goal of practice is not limited to members of one's own religious tradition or community, but is something which can be achieved by practitioners outside these limited boundaries. This term has both sociological and theological usages, referring descriptively to the very fact of religious diversity, as well as to the theological stance just described here, which takes religious diversity to be a positive thing, and to see access to the divine as being itself plural in nature, and not limited to any single tradition, community, text, or institutional authority.[3]

---

[3] A very well-known, and more sociological understanding of pluralism, though one which certainly has theological implications, is formulated by Diana Eck as follows:

"First, pluralism is not diversity alone, but the *energetic engagement with diversity*. Diversity can and has meant the creation of religious ghettoes with little traffic between or among them. Today, religious diversity is a given, but pluralism is not a given; it is an achievement. Mere diversity without real encounter and relationship will yield increasing tensions in our societies.

Second, pluralism is not just tolerance, but the *active seeking of understanding across lines of difference*. Tolerance is a necessary public virtue, but it does not require Christians and Muslims, Hindus, Jews, and ardent secularists to know anything about one another. Tolerance is too thin a foundation for a world of religious difference and proximity. It does nothing to remove our ignorance of one another, and leaves in place the stereotype, the half-truth, the fears that underlie old patterns of division and violence. In the world in which we live today, our ignorance of one another will be increasingly costly.

Third, pluralism is not relativism, but the *encounter of commitments*. The new paradigm of pluralism does not require us to leave our identities and our commitments behind, for pluralism is the encounter of commitments. It means holding our deepest differences, even our religious differences, not in isolation, but in relationship to one another.Fourth, pluralism is *based on dialogue*. The language of pluralism is that of dialogue and encounter, give and take, criticism and self-criticism. Dialogue means both speaking and listening, and that process reveals both common understandings and real differences. Dialogue does not mean everyone at the "table" will agree with one another. Pluralism involves the commitment to being at the table—with one's commitments." (Eck 2006).

Our central focus here is on pluralism as a theological stance—as a type of theology of religions, also referred to be Paul F. Knitter as the 'mutuality model.'[4] The two usages of this term, though, are not entirely separable, given that a common argument for a pluralistic theology of religions involves the claim that such a theology, if its implications are followed logically, should issue in a more accepting and peaceful society, where religious diversity is celebrated, and not feared. Pluralism of the theological variety is thus seen as sustaining of pluralism of the sociological variety. This is the position taken in this paper as well.

On a critical note, pluralism, as a type of theology of religions, can sometimes be said, as Francis X. Clooney explains, to "reflect ... from the perspective of one's own religion on the meaning of other religions, often considered merely in general terms."[5] Pluralism, in other words, can be a stance at which one arrives for reasons purely internal to the logic of one's own tradition, such as on the basis of a belief in a deity who loves and who desires the salvation of all living beings. This can be affirmed without any engagement whatsoever with the actual teachings or practitioners of other religions.

Pluralism can also arise, though, on the basis of an emphasis on a direct experience of ultimate reality as the final basis of religious authority, rather than a specific text or tradition. Ramakrishna's approach to divinity through an engagement with many traditions would be a particularly dramatic example of such an experientially based pluralism.

There are various types of pluralism, some of which emphasize the presence of truth in a variety of religious traditions and philosophies, and some of which emphasize the salvific efficacy of many religious paths. The Jain pluralism found in the works of such thinkers as Haribhadrasūri (c. 8th century CE) and Yaśovijaya (1624–1688), and well expressed in the *anekānta*, *naya*, and *syāt* doctrines of this tradition, is of this kind, emphasizing that aspects of truth are captured in the teachings of many systems of thought and practice.[6] Salvifically, though, these thinkers tend to view Jain practice as being essential to the attainment of the ultimate goal of mokṣa, as the Jain tradition conceives of it (though Haribhadrasūri seems to allow that non-Jain paths might also help take one to liberation).

The pluralism of the philosopher of religion John Hick (1922–2012), however, and, as we shall also see, that of Sri Ramakrishna, tends to emphasize the salvific efficacy of many paths, their ability to lead to the same ultimate salvific goal, rather than their ability to capture truth. Hick, for example, relegates religious truth claims to a realm of things that cannot be known, at least prior to death, asserting that claims of this kind will require "eschatological verification."[7] On Hick's view, one cannot really know, for example, prior to death, if the afterlife consists of an eternal paradise, or a purgatory, or rebirth in another form, and so on. For Sri Ramakrishna, who held a definite Hindu worldview, religions could vary in the degree to which they expressed the truth, but this did not inhibit them from being effective paths to the experience of ultimate reality.[8] Ultimately, all religions, according to Sri Ramakrishna, express sufficient truth to enable the personal quest for the direct experience of divinity to be successful. It is in this sense that Sri Ramakrishna claims that, "All religions are true."[9] 'True' here means 'true enough to be salvifically efficacious; not so flawed as to prevent the direct experience of ultimate reality through an embodied practice'.

Finally, there are religious pluralists who argue that there are many true and salvifically effective religions, but that salvific efficacy need not imply a singular goal that is shared by all. Thus Christians, in other words, may attain salvation as this is defined by their tradition, while Theravāda Buddhists may also attain nirvāṇa, but this does not mean that Christian salvation and Buddhist nirvāṇa coincide in some third, higher reality that includes them both, or that one of these salvations can be reduced to

4 (Knitter 2010, pp. 109–24).
5 (Clooney 2010, p. 14).
6 See (Matilal 1981; Chapple 2003).
7 (Tooley 1976, pp. 177–99).
8 (Maharaj 2018, pp. 101–9).
9 (Nikhilananda 1942, p. 1).

the other. This is the view of, for example, David Ray Griffin and John Cobb.[10] According to the view of these thinkers, informed by the thought of Alfred North Whitehead, reality includes a dimension that corresponds to the idea of a personal deity found in theistic religions and an impersonal cosmic principle found in traditions such as Buddhism, Jainism, and Daoism.

In the tradition of Sri Ramakrishna, the term that most typically refers to the pluralism this tradition affirms, on the basis of Ramakrishna's life and teachings, is *dharmasamanvaya*, which is generally translated in the tradition as "harmony of religions". By this, it is not meant that the world's religions are simply identical, nor that their differences are completely insignificant, but that, like different musical instruments playing different parts of a piece of music, they can be seen as forming a harmony, as pieces of a larger truth toward which each points beyond itself. This tradition, in the words of one representative, is as follows:

> The world's spiritual traditions are like different pieces in a giant jigsaw puzzle: each piece is different and each piece is essential to complete the whole picture. Each piece is to be honored and respected while holding firm to our own particular piece of the puzzle. We can deepen our own spirituality and learn about our own tradition by studying other faiths. Just as importantly, by studying our own tradition well, we are better able to appreciate the truth in other traditions.[11]

Another analogy used in the tradition to illustrate this concept is the famous and popular Indian folk tale of the Blind Men and the Elephant:

> Once some blind men chanced to come near an animal that someone told them was an elephant. They were asked what the elephant was like. The blind men began to feel its body. One of them said the elephant was like a pillar; he had touched only its leg. Another said it was like a winnowing-fan; he had touched only its ear. In this way the others, having touched its tail or belly, gave their different versions of the elephant. Just so, a man who has seen only one aspect of God limits God to that alone. It is his conviction that God cannot be anything else.[12]

Secondly, what do we mean when we speak of *direct experience* as an important theme of modern Hindu thought? Direct experience, or *anubhava*, is contrasted with indirect, or mediated experience: such as experience that occurs through sensory perception. In Indian philosophy, the means by which knowledge is attained are known as *pramāṇa*-s.

A pramāṇa, at its most basic, is that which justifies one in believing that one has a true belief about a given topic. In the words of B.K. Matilal, "A Pramāṇa, as the etymology of the word indicates, is a *Pramā-karaṇa*, i.e., the instrumental cause of what is known as *Pramā*."[13] *Pramā* is knowledge, and is closely related to the concept of *jñāna*, which is also often translated as 'knowledge,' but which often refers specifically to saving knowledge, the knowledge of the true nature of reality that leads to–or, in Advaita Vedānta, that constitutes–liberation.[14]

In modern Hindu thought, the strongest basis for having a belief about the nature of divinity is for one to have had a direct experience of divinity for oneself, rather than believing in divinity on the basis of other pramāṇas, such as the authoritative testimony of others, as found in the Vedic scriptures. The Vedic scriptures are authoritative because they are the records of the direct experiences of the sages to whom they were revealed, rather than on the basis of some intrinsic authority, axiomatically held to be the case. This is, again, a major theme of modern Hinduism. Swami Vivekananda, for example, claims that the scriptures of all of the world's religions are based on a universally available direct experience:

---

10 See (Griffin 2005).
11 (Vrajaprana 1999, pp. 56–57).
12 (Nikhilananda 1942, p. 191).
13 (Matilal 1985, p. 372).
14 (Chatterjea 2002, p. 29).

> Thus it is clear that all the religions of the world have been built upon that one universal and adamantine foundation of all our knowledge–direct experience. They teachers all saw God; they all saw their own souls, they saw their future, they saw their eternity, and what they saw they preached.[15]

In traditional Indian philosophy, the least controversial of the pramāṇa-s is *pratyakṣa*, or sensory experience. One is typically justified in believing something about the sensory world because one has perceived it to be so. I know there is a glass of water on my desk because I can see it. It is important to note, though, that pratyakṣa is distinct from anubhava, or direct experience, inasmuch as it is mediated through the sensory organs, and thus indirect. There is thus a potential for it to be flawed, such as if my eyesight is poor, or the lighting in the room is less than ideal. In other words, there is no *direct* contact between my center of awareness and the objects of my senses. Unless there is some such flaw, though, that can be checked against the sensory experiences of others, or with further sense experiences of my own (such as after I have turned the light on), pratyakṣa is generally viewed as a reliable guide to knowledge about those kinds of things which are susceptible to being perceived by the senses.

The Lokāyata, or Cārvāka system of Indian philosophy, which affirms a materialist view of reality, denies the validity of any pramāṇa other than sensory perception. This amounts to the claim that there are no entities beyond those which are susceptible to being perceived by the senses. The remaining systems of Indian philosophy, though, also affirm the validity of *anumāna*, or inferential reasoning. The most famous example of anumāna used in the Indian tradition is the example of fire on a mountain. I can know that there is fire on a mountain, even if I have not seen the fire myself, based on reasoning from other things that I *have* perceived, such as smoke rising from the mountaintop. I know that smoke is caused by fire. I have seen other occasions where fire and smoke have been present together. Therefore, if I see smoke rising from the mountaintop, I can infer that there is fire on the mountain.

Like sensory perception, inferential reasoning has the potential to be wrong. If the sense data on which it is based has been misinterpreted or misperceived, for example, the inference can lead to a wrong conclusion. Maybe what I think is smoke on the mountain is fog or haze, and not smoke caused by a fire. Also, perhaps the conjunction between fire and smoke has exceptions of which I am not aware, or which I am not considering. Maybe things other than fire can cause smoke, so my inference is invalid.

Probably the most controversial of the traditional Indian pramāṇa-s is *śabda*, or the word of an authoritative person. It is not controversial within Hindu schools of thought, which affirm it almost universally; but, as we shall see in a moment, it becomes controversial when these schools of thought come into conversation with non-Vedic traditions. Traditions like Jainism and Buddhism accept idea of a śabda pramāṇa, or authoritative word, but do not take the Vedas to constitute this authoritative word, but rather their own scriptural texts.

The idea of the śabda pramāṇa is that another valid basis for knowledge is the word of someone who can be trusted to communicate reliable information. Perhaps a good, trustworthy friend of mine, with good eyesight, has been to the mountain and seen that there is fire there, and he informs me that this is the case. Then, even if I have not seen the fire for myself, and even if I have not even seen any smoke rising from the mountaintop (perhaps because the mountain is too far away for me to see it), I can still be said to know, on the word of my trustworthy friend, that there is fire on the mountain.

The śabda pramāṇa is controversial because, of course, it is possible to disagree, as Indian philosophers traditionally have, about what finally constitutes a trustworthy authority. Is the best authority the words of the Vedas? The words of the Buddha? The words of the Jinas? And if we extend the conversation more broadly, beyond the traditional Indian religions, is it the words of the Bible? The words of the *Qur'an*?

---

15 (Vivekananda 1979, p. 126).

The affirmation of the word of an authoritative person as a pramāṇa, particularly regarding issues related to ultimate reality, thus raises, immediately, the issue of religious diversity. Is there any possible neutral ground on the basis of which one can adjudicate the claims of all these higher authorities—the Vedas, the canonical scriptures of Buddhism and Jainism, the *Guru Granth Sahib*, the Bible, the *Qur'an*, the *Daodejing*, the *Analects* of Confucius, and so on?

The strand of modern Hindu thought represented by Sri Ramakrishna and Vivekananda affirms that there is, indeed, a basis on which to evaluate the various authorities proposed by the world's religions as foundations for valid knowledge about ultimate reality. The way to adjudicate these claims is to experience the ultimate reality directly for oneself—as, so it is claimed by Vivekananda, the great authorities did themselves.

The category of anubhava, or direct experience, as deployed by modern Hindu thinkers, is a reference to experience of a different order either from sensory experience, from reasoning based on sensory experience, or faith in a trustworthy or authoritative source. It refers to a direct contact between one's center of consciousness and ultimate reality, or any reality which one is perceiving in a direct fashion. It is defined as perception, direct presentation, knowledge, and experience.[16]

Anubhava, as a category, though, is far from being limited to modern Hindu thought. It is a central theological category of the Śrīvaiṣṇava tradition, for example, as Archana Venkatesan notes:

> The word *anubhava* means experience, enjoyment or relish, and for Śrīvaiṣṇavas this enjoyment is special, for it is directed to Viṣṇu, his consorts and his most exemplary devotees, such as the *āḻvār* poets. *Anubhava* is activated on three major levels: poetic, narrative, and ritual, and each of these enable the devotee to access an ecstatic experience of the divine. It is a means to understand god's unfathomable nature, to enter into his world of play, and to make manifest the divine presence on the terrestrial realms.[17]

For one familiar with the life of Ramakrishna, Venkatesan's account of anubhava has resonance; for one can see a clear continuity between anubhava as understood and deployed in the Śrīvaiṣṇava tradition and many Ramakrishna's samādhi experiences, which were often evoked by his listening to religious songs or discourses.

No less a premodern Hindu authority than the *Mundaka Upaniṣad* teaches: *sa yo haiva tatparamaṃ brahma veda brahmaiva bhavati*—"One who knows Brahman becomes Brahman."[18] Brahman itself is of the nature of experience: namely, the experience of consciousness (*prajñānaṃ brahma*).[19] One who has experienced consciousness as one's own true nature has realized one's identity with Brahman, on an Advaitic understanding of Vedānta.

The concept of direct experience clearly has many precedents in premodern Indian thought, and is arguably presupposed even in systems where it is not mentioned explicitly. In the classical Yoga tradition, for example, as it is expressed in the *Yoga Sūtras* of Patañjali, the eighth and final 'limb' or stage of the practice is defined as *samādhi*, a state in which one's consciousness becomes completely absorbed in the object of contemplation. In the case of Patañjala Yoga, this object, the ultimate reality in this worldview, is the *puruṣa*, or true self, which is utterly distinct from the realm of nature, *prakṛti*, which, prior to samādhi, forms the object of one's awareness.

Sri Ramakrishna, too, and the Vedānta tradition that has developed on the basis of his teachings, deploys the concept of samādhi to refer to a state of complete absorption in ultimate reality. In the tradition of Sri Ramakrishna, the concept of religious pluralism, or universalism, or the harmony of religions, as this teaching is variously known, is rooted in the accounts of Ramakrishna's life, in which

16 (Grimes 1996, p. 40).
17 (Venkatesan 2013, p. 220).
18 *Mundaka Upaniṣad* 3.2:9.
19 *Aitareya Upaniṣad* 3.3.

it is said that he attained samādhi through the practice of numerous spiritual paths, both Hindu and non-Hindu. This is the experiential basis of the Ramakrishna tradition's universalism:

> 'I have practiced,' said he, 'all religions–Hinduism, Islām, Christianity–and I have also followed the paths of the different Hindu sects. I have found that it is the same God toward whom all are directing their steps, though along different paths . . . The substance is One under different names, and everyone is seeking the same substance; only climate, temperament, and name create differences. Let each man follow his own path. If he sincerely and ardently wishes to know God, peace be unto him! He will surely realize Him.'[20]

Thirdly, what do we mean by *modern Hinduism*, when we are speaking of a current of Hindu thought that is characterized by pluralism and direct experience as its central points of emphasis?

By modern Hinduism, we are referring to a current of Hindu thought with its historical roots in the Bengal Renaissance of the nineteenth century, beginning with Rāmmohan Roy (1772–1833). Widely known as "the father of modern India,"[21] Roy was the first of a series of Hindu reformers who responded to criticisms of Hinduism on the part of both rationalists and Christian missionaries, not by renouncing Hinduism, but by affirming that the elements of this tradition which its critics had targeted were not, in fact, reflective of the original teaching of Hinduism—which he identified with the Vedānta of the Upaniṣads—but were later corruptions of what was originally a monotheistic, and ultimately monistic, doctrine teaching the inherent divinity and dignity of all beings.

For Roy, the reform of Hinduism was not only a matter of principle, but also a matter of practicality. In a letter dated 18 January, 1828, Roy writes to a friend that:

I agree with you that in point of vices the Hindus are not worse than the generality of Christians in Europe and America; but I regret to say that the present system of religion adhered to by the Hindus is not well calculated to promote their political interest. The distinction of castes, introducing innumerable divisions and sub-divisions among them, has entirely deprived them of patriotic feeling, and the multitude of religious rites and ceremonies and the laws of purification have totally disqualified them from undertaking any difficult enterprise . . . It is, I think, necessary that some changes should take place in their religion, at least for the sake of their political advantage and social comfort.[22]

Given the connection, in Roy's mind, between the reform of Hinduism and the need for political unity and 'patriotic feeling' among Hindus, it is clear that there is some linkage between the current of Hindu thought that Roy initiated and the later phenomena of Indian and Hindu nationalism. Roy's approach is not, however, characterized by the antagonism toward non-Hindu schools of thought that one finds in Hindu nationalist writings. Indeed, Roy believed that the original teachings of Vedānta, later corrupted by Hindu ritualism and casteism, and the original teachings of Christ, later corrupted by Christian trinitarianism and the doctrine of Christ as a divine incarnation, were one and the same: that Jesus was, in effect, a great teacher of Vedānta. The very next line in the letter by Roy just cited is, "I fully agree with you that there is nothing so sublime as the precepts taught by Christ, and that there is nothing equal to the simple doctrine he inculcated."[23]

In fact, Roy, much like Thomas Jefferson, published a version of the Christian gospels, with all references to miracles and Christ's divine paternity removed, titled *The Precepts of Jesus*.

Roy's lasting legacy is largely due to the fact that, in addition to his prodigious work in promulgating his ideas through books and pamphlets, as well as his activism in bringing about the banning of the practice of widow immolation—*sati* or 'suttee'—he also established an organization to promote the ideal of a 'purified' Hinduism based on the teachings of the Upaniṣads. This organization—the *Brahmo Samāj*, or 'Community of Brahman'—attracted a large number of male

---

20 (Nikhilananda 1942, p. 35).
21 (Richards 1985, p. 1).
22 Rāmmohan Roy, cited in (Richards 1985, pp. 8–9).
23 Rāmmohan Roy, cited in (Richards 1985, p. 9).

followers from amongst the emerging English-educated middle class of Bengal, many of whom went on to become influential teachers in their own right. The first president of the Brahmo Samāj, after Roy, was Devendranath Tagore (1817–1905), who was known, among other things, for being the father of the famed Nobel laureate, playwright, songwriter, poet, essayist, and all-around Bengali cultural hero, Rabindranath Tagore (1861–1941). The long-lived elder Tagore presided over the Brahmo Samāj for the better part of the nineteenth century. He was thus in a position to exert a major influence on the current of Hindu thought that Roy had initiated before him. A man of deeply spiritual inclinations, the direct experience of divinity was a major theme of his life and his writings. His moving, frank, and painfully honest reflections upon his experiences are very well represented by the following quote:

> Then I went out and sat underneath an ashvattha tree and according to the teaching of the saints began meditating on the Spirit of God dwelling in my soul. My mind was flooded with emotion, my eyes were filled with tears. All at once I saw the shining vision of Brahma in the lotus core of my heart. A thrill passed through my whole body, I felt a joy beyond all measure. But the next moment I could see Him no more. On losing sight of that beatific vision which destroys all sorrow, I suddenly rose from the ground. A great sadness came over my spirit. Then I tried to see Him again by force of contemplation, and found Him not. I became as one stricken with disease, and would not be comforted. Meanwhile I suddenly heard a voice in the air, 'In this life thou shalt see Me no more. Those whose hearts have not been purified, who have not attained the highest Yoga, cannot see Me. It was only to stimulate thy love that I once appeared before thee.[24]

Another prominent leader of the Brahmo Samāj who was a contemporary of Tagore, Sri Ramakrishna, and Swami Vivekananda, was Keshub Chunder Sen. Sen plays a major role in the history of the pluralistic and experientially based current of modern Hindu thought as an intermediary between the Brahmo Samāj tradition and what would emerge by the end of the nineteenth century as the Vedānta tradition of Ramakrishna and Swami Vivekananda. Sen (1838–1884) emphasized even more than Roy had what he perceived as the harmonies and affinities between Hinduism and Christianity. He envisioned a 'New Dispensation,' or *Nava Vidhān*, which he described in the following terms:

> It is the harmony of all scriptures and prophets and dispensations. It is not an isolated creed, but the science which binds and explains and harmonizes all religions. It gives history a meaning, to the action of Providence a consistency, to quarrelling churches a common bond, and to successive dispensations a continuity. It shows marvelous synthesis how the different rainbow colours are one in the light of heaven. The New Dispensation is the sweet music of diverse instruments. [An echo of this image can be discerned in the modern Vedāntic teaching of 'harmony of religions,' mentioned earlier, that has clearly drawn inspiration from Sen's teaching.] It is the precious necklace in which are strung together the rubies and pearls of all ages and climes. [This echoes *Bhagavad Gītā* 7:7, in which Krishna says, "All beings are strung upon me like pearls upon a thread."] It is the celestial court where around enthroned Divinity shine the lights of all heavenly saints and prophets. [This is a pluralist take on the traditional Christian image of God as a divine sovereign enthroned in heaven.] It is the wonderful solvent, which fuses all dispensations into a new chemical compound. [Here we see Sen also bringing in scientific imagery, another characteristic of modern Hindu thought.] It is the mighty absorbent, which absorbs all that is true and good and beautiful in the objective world. Before the flag of the New Dispensation bow ye nations, and proclaim the Brotherhood of God and the Brotherhood of man.[25]

---

24 Devendranath Tagore, cited in (Richards 1985, p. 27).
25 Keshub Chunder Sen, cited in (Richards 1985, pp. 43–44).

These words of Sen, describing a new 'universal religion' drawing upon all that is good, beautiful, and true in all faiths would not be out of place in the *Complete Works* of Swami Vivekananda. The historical link between Sen, Ramakrishna, and Vivekananda is very clear, for it is found in the original source material on the life of Sri Ramakrishna, which has become akin to a scripture in the Ramakrishna movement. According to *The Gospel of Sri Ramakrishna*, Ramakrishna was a frequent visitor to Sen's home, and the two were close conversation partners. In fact, one of the three photographs taken of Ramakrishna during his lifetime was taken in Sen's house, during a Brahmo Samāj gathering which Ramakrishna attended. In the photograph, Ramakrishna is seen standing in one of his famous samādhi trances, being kept from falling by one of his disciples who is standing nearby. It is highly likely that there was mutual influence between Sen and Ramakrishna. Indeed, this is well attested. Similarly, the young Narendranath Datta, later to take the monastic name Swami Vivekananda, was also a frequent attendee of Brahmo Samāj gatherings at Sen's house. It was at Sen's house that Datta and Ramakrishna first crossed paths, with Ramakrishna hearing the young Datta sing hymns. It was later, with Sen's passing, that Ramakrishna would take on the role of Datta's guru. The religious thought of both Sen and Sri Ramakrishna can be discerned in the teachings of Swami Vivekananda.

It has become customary among scholars to refer to the current of thought represented by all of these figures as 'Neo-Hinduism' or 'Neo-Vedānta.' This convention, though, has come under recent scrutiny, as it has been shown to convey a pejorative sense that this branch of the tradition is somehow inauthentic.[26] Any tradition of sufficient age and complexity certainly exhibits both continuity and change over time. There are core themes of Vedānta which persist from this tradition's foundational texts—the *Upaniṣads, Brahma Sūtras,* and *Bhagavad Gītā*—to its current iterations, including the thought of Ramakrishna. And there are discontinuities amongst the various systems of Vedānta that have developed through the centuries: Śaṅkara's Advaita Vedānta, Rāmānuja's Viśiṣṭādvaita Vedānta, Madhva's Dvaita Vedānta, Nimbārka's Bhedābheda Vedānta, Caitanya's Acintya Bhedābheda Vedānta, and so on. Each of these systems would have been 'neo' at the time of its first expression.

The term 'Neo-Vedānta' was coined by Indologist Paul Hacker. Hacker, as James Madaio has argued, "influentially argued that Neo-Vedānta was a nationalistic movement dependent upon the 'assimilation' of Western ideals. The term 'Neo-Vedānta' thus entered mainstream academic discourse as a pejorative term–indiscriminately used in reference to a number of different Hindu thinkers who held variant theological views–and connoting a sense of inauthenticity because 'continuity with the past has been broken.'"[27] Hacker's dichotomy of 'Neo' and 'genuine' Vedānta depends upon a reification of Śaṅkara's Vedānta as definitive of authentic Vedānta, rendering all other versions of this philosophy inauthentic. If a scholar were to make an analogous move with regard to Hacker's own tradition, it would render all Roman Catholic thought coming after Thomas Aquinas as 'Neo-Catholicism'. Major Catholic thinkers of the modern period, such as Hans Urs von Balthasar and Karl Rahner, not mention Hacker himself, would thus become 'Neo-Catholic'. As Madaio argues, this artificial bifurcation of Hindu tradition into authentic Śaṅkaran Advaita and inauthentic 'Neo' Vedānta depends on an ignorance of post-Śaṅkara Vedāntic developments.

Two of the main features which differentiate modern Vedānta and modern Hindu thought generally from the premodern forms of Hinduism are those which are under consideration in this paper: the pluralism and the emphasis on direct experience of ultimate reality that are central themes in the teachings of modern Hindu teachers like Ramakrishna and Vivekananda, and many other modern Hindu teachers as well, including Sri Aurobindo and Sarvepalli Radhakrishnan, and many of the gurus with followings in the Western world, starting with Vivekananda himself. The prominence of universalism and direct experience as major themes of modern Hindu discourse, though, while

[26] (Maharaj 2018, pp. 45–50).
[27] ((Madaio 2017, p. 3).

certainly differentiating this discourse from premodern forms of Hindu thought, should not be taken to imply that modern Hindu thought marks a massive or unbridgeable rupture with the earlier tradition, as the terms 'Neo-Vedānta' and 'Neo-Hindu' might suggest. The themes of universalism and direct experience both have antecedents in premodern Hindu sources.

In regard to pluralism, particularly famous sources often cited in support of this view include the *Ṛg Veda* and the *Bhagavad Gītā*, respectively:

> Reality is one, though the wise speak of it in various ways.[28]
>
> In whatever way living beings approach me, thus do I receive them. All paths, Arjuna, lead to me.[29]

There is also the entire medieval Indian tradition of Hindu and Muslim figures, such as Kabīr, and the first Sikh Guru, Nānak, speaking in syncretic and universalistic ways, crossing the boundaries of Hindu and Islamic traditions in order to affirm the oneness of divinity, beyond sectarian divides.

In regard to the primacy of direct experience of sources such as book learning (the śabda pramāṇa), there is, in addition to the *Yoga Sūtras*, mentioned earlier, this verse from the *Bhagavad Gītā*:

> As useful as a water tank when there is flooding in all directions, that is how useful all of the Vedas are for a Brahmin who has true insight.[30]

The distinction between modern and premodern thought, while certainly real, can be, and often has been, overstated, and typically involves the invocation of Hacker's term, 'Neo-Vedānta.' Such overstatement typically stems, again, from comparing the thought of a modern Hindu thinker, such as Vivekananda, with the thought of the eighth to ninth century giant of Advaita Vedānta, Śaṅkara, while ignoring the intermediate developments that have occurred in the Vedānta tradition in the centuries between Śaṅkara's period and the present.[31]

3. The Logical Connection between Pluralism and an Emphasis on Direct Experience

The logical connection between pluralism and an emphasis on direct experience in the thought of modern Hindu figures such as Ramakrishna and Vivekananda is not simply an effect of the idea, mentioned previously, that Ramakrishna is understood to have pursued and achieved the state of samādhi, or of absorption of his consciousness in ultimate reality, through diverse practices rooted in a variety of religious paths. This could be seen, rather, as validation of a deeper axiom that makes possible a set of experiences of the kind that the Ramakrishna tradition claims him to have had: the axiom that direct experience, *anubhava*, is the most reliable guide to the nature of ultimate reality, and the further claim that what such direct experience reveals is that there is truth in all religions.

The logical connection between pluralism and direct experience is as follows. In what might be called a conventional constructivist account of religious experience, religious experience is a result of the cultivation of mental states which operate on the basis of certain assumptions and practices given to the experiencing subject by her cultural and religious environment. A Christian mystic, to put it at its simplest, might therefore engage in a series of practices that issue in a vision of Christ. They will not typically issue in a vision of Krishna or the Buddha. Similarly, a Vaiṣṇava Hindu mystic will engage in practices that issue in a vision of Krishna, not of Christ or the Buddha, and a Buddhist will engage in practices that issue in a formless nirvāṇa: the aim, precisely, for the sake of which the practice is cultivated

28 *Ṛg Veda* 1.164: 46c.
29 *Bhagavad Gītā* 4:11.
30 *Bhagavad Gītā* 2:46.
31 The work of scholars like Andrew Nicholson, Ayon Maharaj, and James Madaio has begun to help in rectifying this situation, particularly Madaio (2017) article, cited earlier; though the terms 'Neo-Vedānta' and 'Neo-Hindu' still seem to have considerably currency amongst scholars of religion. There is, in particular, a tendency to link 'Neo-Vedānta' with Hindu nationalism, which is at odds with the pluralism central to Ramakrishna's and Vivekananda's thought.

This is somewhat at odds, however, with what religious practitioners take themselves to be engaged in, very often, in the world's religious traditions. The constructivist account of religious experience need not entail, but is quite compatible with, the assumption that religious experiences are ultimately delusory; and this often does seem to be an assumption underlying constructivist accounts of religious experience. Such accounts are often reductive in nature, amounting to the claim that religious experiences can be accounted for, not merely in certain aspects, or in the forms that they take, but *in their totality*, through recourse to cultural, economic, political, psychological, and other, ultimately material, factors. According to this understanding, Christians and Vaiṣṇavas and Buddhists do not have their experiences of Jesus or Krishna or nirvāṇa because there is really a Jesus or a Krishna or a nirvāṇa that is, in some sense, really *there*, but due to the fact that, if one manipulates one's mind in a particular way, conditioned by a particular set of shared religious and cultural assumptions, then one will have experiences of this kind. However, for the Christian or the Vaiṣṇava, Christ and Krishna can be perceived because they are really real, and are bestowing this particular grace upon those of their devotees who have cultivated the proper state of mind to be receptive to this divine gift; and for the Buddhist, nirvāṇa can be experienced because it is the true nature of reality, which spontaneously becomes evident to one who has cleared away all of the mental obstructions to its true perception.

This is not to say that constructivism is a wholly incorrect or inappropriate conceptual tool for understanding religious experience, even if one is committed to a realist religious worldview of the kind that I have sketched here as characterizing the worldview of the religious practitioner. Indeed, there are many religious traditions which also emphasize the constructed nature of experience, and the fact that certain realities which are not evident to the senses are available for perception only to practitioners who have cultivated the requisite mental and moral disciplines. Advaita Vedānta and Buddhism both come readily to mind, though there are many other examples as well. 'Constructed' need not mean 'false,' though it is, again, compatible with, and can certainly lend itself to, a view of religious experience as a fundamentally delusory experiential modality. To take a side on this question, as a reductionistic skeptic or as a religiously realist believer, requires the importation of some additional philosophical assumptions.

In regard to Vedānta, a traditional or premodern conception of how the process of reaching the experience of Brahman occurs fits extremely well with a constructivist model. As Rambachan and others have shown, in the Advaita Vedānta of Śaṅkara, an essential component of cultivating the true knowledge, or *jñāna*, that issues in—and is indeed constitutive of—*mokṣa*, or liberation from the cycle of rebirth is learning about Brahman from the Vedic texts, which form the śabda pramāṇa:

> How is it possible for the words of the Upanisads to function as a direct and valid source of knowledge? Words can provide valid knowledge when the object of knowledge is readily and immediately available, not separate from the knower by a gap of time or space, and does not have to be created or brought into existence ... In the case of the story of the tenth person [in which a group of ten friends who have swum across a river fear they may be missing someone, and the leader keeps coming up with nine when doing a head count, and then realizes, when someone points it out to him, that he has been failing to count himself] ... the words 'You are the tenth person' fulfill their intention and purpose when rightly comprehended because the tenth person is immediately available and lost only in ignorance. The words in the wisdom section of the Vedas (the Upaniṣads) function like the words addressed to the tenth person.[32]

Brahman is not the kind of entity that can be perceived through the senses, so it cannot be known through sensory perception (pratyakṣa). The certain existence of Brahman also cannot be inferred through logical reasoning (anumāṇa). Brahman is a unique entity that can only be known through

[32] (Rambachan 2015, p. 44).

the words and revelations of the Vedas, directly informing one 'You are That.' The śabda pramāṇa is essential.[33]

It is not that the knowledge of Brahman is a result of simply hearing the Vedic texts. As Rambachan says, the words of these texts must be "rightly comprehended." Hearing (*śravaṇam*) is merely the essential first step in the process of, ultimately, experiencing the reality of Brahman. Hearing is followed by reflection on the meaning of the text, in order to comprehend it correctly and thoroughly, typically with the guidance of a knowledgeable, competent teacher. Rational reflection (*mananam*) is thus an important part of the process as well. The process finally culminates in *nidhidhyāsana*, or meditative reflection, which issues, at last, in the direct experience (*anubhava*) of Brahman. For Śaṅkara, anubhava is a pramāṇa, but one which is dependent, for its occurrence, upon the prior acts of hearing, reflecting, and contemplating just outlined. It does not arise independently of these, and it is not contemplated that it might arise through engagement with the teachings and practices of another tradition, like Buddhism.

This model fits well with constructivism because there is no question of, say, a Buddhist, much less a Roman Catholic from medieval France or a Sunni Muslim from the Arabian peninsula of Śaṅkara's time, experiencing Brahman. *Brahman* refers to a specific concept knowable only in the context of the Vedic literature in which it appears. A Buddhist, a Catholic, or a Muslim will not have an experience of Brahman any more than a Christian will have a vision of Krishna or a Vaisnava will experience nirvāṇa as understood in Theravāda Buddhism.

This model is compatible with a constructivism of the skeptical sort because all of these putative objects of religious experience are capable of being seen as cultural constructs of the literary, ritual, and other religious settings where they arise—and nothing more.[34]

The multi-religious practices of Sri Ramakrishna, though, would seem to sidestep the epistemic process that is described in traditional Advaita Vedānta. Ramakrishna, by most accounts and studies of his life, was not an educated person, at least in a traditional sense. He had a prodigious memory and spent a good deal of time listening to religious and philosophical texts being read to him. But he was, for the most part, not focused upon uninspired 'book learning,' uninformed by spiritual practice. Indeed, he compared such learning to the actions of carrion birds who fly in the sky of knowledge but have their attention fixed on rotting corpses on the ground.[35]

Ramakrishna was focused on cultivating experience of the divine reality. The accounts of his practices in our sources on his life describe not so much an intellectual process as an emotional one, characterized mostly by deep and intense longing. His injunctions in regard to how one can "see God" consistently emphasize the importance of desiring the divine vision above all things:

> One should cry for God that way, like a child. That is what it means to be restless for God. One doesn't enjoy play or food any longer. After one's experiences of the world are over, one feels this restlessness and weeps for God.[36]

How is it possible to experience Brahman without first cultivating the kind of knowledge that is prescribed by Śaṅkara: or, for that matter, to experience Christ without first being baptized and taking instruction in the traditional Christian fashion, or to encounter the Prophet Muhammad in a vision after only three days of practicing as a Muslim? These are precisely the achievements attributed to Sri Ramakrishna in the extant works on his life.[37]

---

33 See (Rambachan 1994).

34 June McDaniel notes that if mystics "do experience figures outside of the particular constructivist meditation, it will be understood as madness. But such experiences are not impossible. Most religions have concepts of religious madness (or heresy), including contacting the wrong deity." Personal communication.

35 (Nikhilananda 1942, p. 101).

36 (Nikhilananda 1942, p. 1011)

37 The *Śrīśrīrāmakṛṣṇakathāmṛta*, translated and already cited here as *The Gospel of Sri Ramakrishna*, translated by Swami Nikhilananda, and the *Śrīśrīrāmakṛṣṇalīlaprasaṅga*, translated by Swami Chetanananda as *Sri Ramakrishna's Divine Play* (St. Louis: Vedanta Society of St. Louis).

One response to the question, clearly, is the skeptical response: that Ramakrishna actually did none of these things, but that he suffered from a sequence of delusory experiences brought on by a combination of his own, idiosyncratic mental makeup and whatever spiritual practices he had been engaged in. Another possibility, however, suggests itself in the very textual sources that the Advaita tradition utilizes in cultivating the saving knowledge that is its goal. This is the religiously realist possibility that Ramakrishna was able to have the experiences that he did because Brahman is real, and can be experienced in the great variety of forms that Ramakrishna experienced.

The *Upaniṣads* do not teach that Brahman is a mere conceptual construct. Brahman is rather, according to these texts, the foundational reality that is at the basis of all existence. *Sarvaṃ khalvidaṃ brahman*, claims one of the 'great sentences,' or *mahāvākya*-s, which Śaṅkara takes to convey true knowledge of Brahman. "All of this, indeed, is Brahman."[38]

If Brahman is, indeed, the universal reality—or, for that matter, if Christ is the divine Word (*logos*) through whom all things were made, or if nirvāṇa is the true nature of reality, revealed to one's consciousness after all obstructions have been removed—then it is reasonable to expect that this universal reality has been experienced by persons in other cultures and traditions, albeit using the categories available to them. If Brahman is the universal reality, might it not be possible to experience Brahman in the form of the ultimate realities posited by many traditions: as the various deities, as Christ, and so on? I would argue that it was on this assumption of religious realism, the assumption of a universal reality behind all veridical experience, that Sri Ramakrishna pursued his multi-religious practices and found them validated in his various experiences of samādhi.

Of course, a skeptic could at this point argue that a pluralistic set of religious experiences is no less constructed than those pursued through the medium of a singular tradition. So, just as a devout Christian experiences Christ, a Vaisnava Hindu experiences Krishna, and so on, a pluralist like Ramakrishna experiences all of these things. According to the constructivist thesis, whatever it is that we ultimately expect of our spiritual practices, if we pursue these practices with sufficient diligence to the point where our mental make-up is transformed by them, we get just that thing. We get precisely what we expect.

It seems that there is really no way to adjudicate this issue, as it is based on whatever prior ontological commitments one brings to the discussion. But an alternative narrative to the skeptical one is possible, in which it is not that the experiences of a mystic like Ramakrishna are *solely* the constructs of the mystic's mind, composed of the elements from the mystic's cultural environment. The alternative narrative is that there is, indeed, a higher reality that is experienced by religious practitioners who cultivate the required sensitivity to have such experiences, but that this is a reality that lends itself to being experienced in multiple ways: as Christ, as Krishna, and so on.

This, famously, is the route pursued by philosopher of religion John Hick in the developing his Pluralistic Hypothesis, according to which the various realities that are experienced by religious persons of varied traditions are all grounded in a common ultimate reality to which he refers as 'the Real'.[39] Hick builds upon the work of William Alston, who develops the concept of belief-forming, or 'doxastic' practices: practices which predispose us to perceive reality in a particular way, based on the beliefs on which these practices are based and which they, in turn, support.

This sounds like constructivism—and is, to some extent. It acknowledges the role played by culture and the categories practitioners draw from their traditions in the construction of their putative experiences of divinity. But Alston is not skeptic. He is a Christian apologist. In fact, his central thesis is that Christians are justified in trusting the experiences that they have on the basis of their doxastic practices, given that such practices are not of a fundamentally different type from doxastic practices that form common beliefs about the material world based on sensory perception. As he points out,

---

38 *Chāndogya Upaniṣad* 3.14:1.
39 See (Hick 1989).

the charge of circularity that can be leveled at Christians who believe based upon the experiences that they have which are cultivated, in part, by those very same beliefs, can be leveled just as well at belief in the reliability of sensory perception. If there is no non-circular way to validate Christian mystical experiences, there is similarly no non-circular way to validate sensory perceptions; for if we doubt a particular sensory perception, the way we typically test it is through recourse to other sensory perceptions. Sensory perception as such, as a modality of knowledge, is not, itself, questioned, at least in our everyday experience, but also in higher-level secular doxastic practices, such as in the practice of modern science.[40]

While Hick utilizes Alston's work to argue for the validity of mystical experience as a way to attain knowledge of transcendental realities, Alston returns the favor by citing Hick in response to one possible objection to his theory: namely, that it is not only Christians, but people of many different religions who can, using his model, claim validity for their religious experiences. Alston responds to this objection by raising, at least as a possibility, the idea that Hick's claim of a shared ultimate reality underlying all religious experience is true. If the ultimate reality is not something that can be contained in any single concept—if it is, to cite the *Upaniṣads*, 'not this, not that,' *neti neti*–then it lends itself to being experienced in ways cultivated by diverse doxastic practices.

4. Conclusions: The Appeal of the Universalist Experientialist Approach

Why is a modern Hindu approach to religion, which combines universalism with a strong emphasis on direct experience of ultimate reality, appealing to so many contemporary spiritual practitioners, particularly amongst those who define themselves as 'spiritual but not religious,' or who are drawn to Asian religions such as Hinduism and Buddhism?

To answer this question properly would require a book-length study. No doubt the answer would have to include discussion of the growth of individualism and the concurrent disintegration of traditional religious identities in late modernity, the rise of multiculturalism, globalization, perceived ethical lapses, materialism, and hypocrisy among religious practitioners and institutions, and so on.

Briefly, though, it seems fair to say that many today recoil from the violence of a growing trend toward ethno-nationalism, often couched in religious terms, with its attendant hostility to the religious or cultural other. No religious tradition, it seems, has been exempt from this trend in the early years of the twenty-first century. Christian, Islamic, Hindu, Buddhist, and Jewish versions of it can be found. Even a critic of the claim that Ramakrishna experienced ultimate reality under the guise of a variety of forms and modalities, points out the following:

> It goes without saying ... that Ramakrishna's claim of practical God-realisation through different religions is accepted as genuine by his followers. Having such a belief can definitively infuse in them a tolerant attitude towards different religions. To that extent Ramakrishna's religious experiences can certainly be a source for peaceful coexistence and interreligious harmony.[41]

In a world of, it seems, ever-growing interreligious hostility, Ramakrishna and his multireligious experiences are an inspiration to those who wish to cultivate a more peaceful, harmonious world, while at the same time not giving up on religion altogether.

One option, clearly, for those who wish to go beyond a world of inter-religious hatred is to set aside religion as such. And yet religious narratives, for many, provide essential comfort in the face of the sufferings of life: death, disease, and loss of all kinds. Rather than opt for the idea of 'one true religion' in the face of these sufferings, and then run the risk of conflict with those who make a different choice, it is far more appealing to opt for the idea of many true religions, many effective

---

40 See (Alston 1993).
41 (Akram 2017, p. 52).

paths to salvation. We thus each make our own choices without having to clash with our neighbors over religion.

Even beyond this kind of theological rationalization, Sri Ramakrishna's experiential approach invites others to pursue their own direct experiences as well. It is thus not only that Ramakrishna's pluralism is an attractive theological stance for those seeking a *religious* alternative to religious tribalism. It is also that this approach invites and sustains an openness, not only conceptually, but experientially, to the religious other. We are thus enabled, even while adhering to whatever particular religious identity we regard as our own, to explore the practices of others, and to experience ultimate reality in the ways that others do. One can see Thomas Merton, for example, as one such pluralistic pioneer of experience, delving deeply, even while remaining a committed Catholic, into the Hindu yogic and Buddhist Zen traditions. Religious experiences do not merely differentiate. There also are powerful experiences of universal compassion, or divine love for all beings, that can sustain a life commitment to peace, social justice, and human dignity.

Those figures who have committed themselves to these dimensions of practice command multi-religious followings, beyond their home religious communities—figures such as Gandhi, King, and the Dalai Lama have universal appeal. The logical connections between religious pluralism, or universalism, and the quest for a direct experience of ultimate reality, are not only of an intellectual nature. They can run through the heart as well.

Funding: This research received no external funding.

Conflicts of Interest: The author declares no conflict of interest.

References

Akram, Muhammad. 2017. God-Realisation through Multiple Religions? A Study into Religious Experiences of Sri Ramakrishna. *Islamic Studies* 56: 1–2.

Alston, William. 1993. *Perceiving God: The Epistemology of Religious Experience*. Ithaca: Cornell University Press.

Chapple, Christopher Key. 2003. *Reconciling Yogas: Haribhadra's Collection of Views on Yoga*. Albany: State University of New York Press.

Chatterjea, Tara. 2002. *Knowledge and Freedom in Indian Philosophy*. Lanham: Lexington Books, p. 29.

Clooney, Francis Xavier. 2010. *Comparative Theology: Deep Learning across Religious Borders*. Oxford: Wiley-Blackwell, p. 14.

Eck, Diana. 2006. What Is Pluralism? Available online: http://pluralism.org/what-is-pluralism/ (accessed on 19 January 2019).

Fisher, Elaine. 2017. *Hindu Pluralism: Religion and the Public Sphere in Early Modern South India*. Oakland: University of California Press, p. 191.

Flueckiger, Joyce Burkhalter. 2015. *Everyday Hinduism*. Chichester: Wiley Blackwell, p. 194.

Gottschalk, Peter. 2000. *Beyond Hindu and Muslim: Multiple Identity Narratives from Village India*. Oxford: Oxford University Press.

Griffin, David Ray. 2005. *Deep Religious Pluralism*. Louisville: Westminster John Knox Press.

Grimes, John. 1996. *A Concise Dictionary of Indian Philosophy*. Albany: State University of New York Press, p. 40.

Hick, John. 1989. *An Interpretation of Religion: Human Responses to the Transcendent*. New Haven: Yale University Press.

Knitter, Paul. 2010. *Introducing Theologies of Religions*. Maryknoll: Orbis Books, pp. 109–24.

Long, Jeffery David. 2009. *Jainism: An Introduction*. London: IB Tauris, p. 26.

Madaio, James. 2017. Rethinking Neo-Vedānta: Swami Vivekananda and the Selective Historiography of Advaita Vedānta. *Religions* 8: 101. [CrossRef]

Maharaj, Ayon. 2018. *Infinite Paths to Infinite Reality: Sri Ramakrishna and Cross-Cultural Philosophy of Religion*. Oxford: Oxford University Press, pp. 101–9.

Matilal, Bimal Krishna. 1981. *The Central Philosophy of Jainism (Anekānta-vāda)*. Ahmedabad: L.D. Institute of Indology.

Matilal, Bimal Krishna. 1985. *Logic, Language, and Reality: Indian Philosophy and Contemporary Issues*. Delhi: Motilal Banarsidass, p. 372.

Nikhilananda, Swami. 1942. *The Gospel of Sri Ramakrishna*. New York: Ramakrishna-Vivekananda Center.

Rambachan, Anantanand. 1994. *The Limits of Scripture: Vivekananda's Reinterpretation of the Vedas*. Honolulu: University of Hawaii Press.

Rambachan, Anantanand. 2015. *A Hindu Theology of Liberation: Not-Two Is Not One*. Albany: State University of New York Press, p. 44.

Richards, Glyn. 1985. *A Source-Book of Modern Hinduism*. Richmond: Curzon Press.

Tooley, Michael. 1976. John Hick and the Concept of Eschatological Verification. *Religious Studies* 12: 177–99. [CrossRef]

Venkatesan, Archana. 2013. Ecstatic Seeing: Adorning and Enjoying the Body of the Goddess. In *Contemporary Hinduism*. Durham: Acumen, p. 220.

Vivekananda, Swami. 1979. *Complete Works*. Mayavati: Advaita Ashrama.

Vrajaprana, Pravrajika. 1999. *Vedanta: A Simple Introduction*. Hollywood: Vedanta Press, pp. 56–57.

religions

MDPI

Article

The Fulcrum of Experience in Indian Yoga and Possession Trance

Frederick M. Smith

Department of Religious Studies, University of Iowa, Iowa City, IA 52242, USA; frederick-smith@uiowa.edu

Received: 29 March 2019; Accepted: 6 May 2019; Published: 17 May 2019

Abstract: The "inner organ" (*antaḥkaraṇa*) in the Indian philosophical school called Sāṃkhya is applied in two different experiential contexts: in the act of transcendence according to the path of yoga explored in the Yogasūtras of Patañjali (ca. 350 CE) and in the process of identity shift that occurs in possession by a deity in a broader range of Indian cultural practices. The act of transcendence will be better understood if we look at the *antaḥkaraṇa* through an emic lens, which is to say as an actual organ that is activated by experiential shifts, rather than as a concept or explanation that is indicative of a collocation of characteristics of the individuating consciousness or merely by reducing it to nonepistemic objective or subjective factors.

Keywords: antaḥkaraṇa; Yogasūtras; saṃyama; possession; Balaji; Ganges; pilgrimage

---

1. Introduction

In her recent book Lost Ecstasy, June McDaniel addresses critics of the study of commonality in religious experience, specifically ecstasy. Critics argue against its very legitimacy because what is important, they maintain, are differences; nothing else is worth studying because attempts to locate convergences obscure what makes religious experiences unique, namely their differences. McDaniel understands that "[w]hile the study of religion in India lacks the comparative categories of understanding and analysis that we see in Western departments, it has also been free of the Western reduction of religion to political and economic forces" (McDaniel 2018, p. 8). Through a methodological analysis, McDaniel frees herself to study religious experience, regardless of the present intransigence of the community of critics in the West that has positioned itself against such study.

In this essay I align myself with McDaniel, whose understanding is closer to the emic; she does not impose external or etic methods of reinterpreting indigenous understandings of religious experience. Following this lead, I will draw from an array of sources to argue that an "internal or inner organ" is activated and energized at the time one undergoes certain kinds of experience that they regard as religious. Thus, what I am trying to do here is rescue an emic understanding of the subtle physiology of an internal organ. It is this organ or organ system that is awakened from its somnolence and impels or shepherds the interconnected web of cognitive and physiological processes in the direction of specific experiences that closely resemble those described in multiple reliable sources, including texts and ethnographies. The "evidence" for this, if this term is permissible here, will be drawn from Indian text and practice. The texts are from the realm of Sāṃkhya and Yoga, including, notably, the Yogasūtras, and from the "practice" of possession, which is in fact most often performed and nearly as often carefully choreographed, even if textual models from classical or even modern literature are lacking or insufficient. This is not to deny that yoga and the experiences derived from it also manifest through performance, because it surely is, even if it is performed only for oneself.

This essay will be divided into six sections: (1) introduction; (2) a description and interpretation of an inner or internal organ (*antaḥkaraṇa*); (3) examination of the description and function of what Yogasūtras 3.4 invokes as the power or, we might say, the organ that is illuminated when the three highest stages of Patañjali's eightfold path combine into a single cognitive unit, namely *saṃyama*; (4) the experiential point at which an individual's personality transitions from one to another during the process of possession (*āveśa*); (5) discussion and reflections on the three substantive sections; and (6) conclusions that in which we will examine how we might (or might not) put all of this together in order to come more closely into engagement with an "organ" that generates transcendence and motivates it to press forward into other modes of experience and consciousness. We cannot at this point correlate our findings with an ever-deepening understanding of organ systems as understood medically, or of the role of neurotransmitters in this process. The identification and understanding of neurotransmitters are rapidly expanding, and I feel confident that eventually these two areas of understanding and discourse will be brought together.[1]

At the moment, however, I would like to see two paths converge, or come asymptotically close at any rate. These are, first, the path of yoga as articulated in the Yogasūtras, and, second, the lived experience of possession as a mode of self-identification and even re-embodiment. A theoretical foundation for this may be seen in the structure of the *antaḥkaraṇa*. How then can the *antaḥkaraṇa*, drawn largely from Sāṃkhya, *saṃyama* from the Yogasūtras, and possession intersect, and how are they relevant to each other? I hope to identify within them a fulcrum of that balances worldly and transcendental experience, an organ that opens the door to ecstasy and yogic realization, one that enables individuals to experience deity or spirit possession. I will take the concept of *saṃyama* in YS 3.4 and analyze it as an organ that becomes operational only when *samādhi* is achieved, one that draws and recasts the energy of *samādhi* into what are called *siddhi*s or *vibhūti*s—"powers of perfection," in Miller's (1998) term,[2] which are only possible as concentrated and subtle experience. I would then like to examine the way in which this organ stands at the fulcrum of personal identity that is evident and transformational in states of possession.

2. The *Antaḥkaraṇa*

Let us begin with an attempt to discover what an "internal organ" that regulates experience might look like or how it might be described. The Sanskrit term that presents itself as the primary suspect is *antaḥkaraṇa*, regarded as one's emotional and perceptual center. The *antaḥkaraṇa* is classically translated as "heart," although it must be understood as a secret heart, the locus of deep emotional engagement. This overlaps with the sense of the physical heart (*hṛd*, *hṛdaya*), which also often shares these connotations. Thus, the heart was regarded as a multifaceted organ that went beyond physical, measurable, dissectible qualities. The *antaḥkaraṇa* was classically defined as the combination of *buddhi*, *ahaṃkāra*, and *manas*, or intellect, egoity, and mind (Larson and Bhattacharya 1987). These, taken together, constitute a single functioning organ that comprehends "all objects in all three worlds" (Larson and Bhattacharya 1987, p. 188), and to which the "external organ" of perception and cognition (*bāhyakaraṇa*), the composite of the five sense organs (*buddhīndriya*) and the five organs of action (*karmendriya*), is subservient (Larson and Bhattacharya 1987, pp. 52, 62, 87). Thus, the "internal organ," more powerful and consequential than the "external organ," is conceptualized as the awakened heart, the organ of consciousness and intentionality. The heart is regarded as the center of the system of five *prāṇa*s or lifebreaths in classical Indian medicine (Ayurveda). It is the locus of the union and separation of the upward moving breath (also called *prāṇa*) and the downward moving breath (*apāna*), as well as the organizing force or vector of all the lifebreaths. This is because it provides them with both magnitude and direction. It is the container and the locus of both intentionality and the cognitive self. It is, then, a substantial fulcrum that contains within it the intellect, egoity, and mind, as well as the organizer or organizing principle that moves this powerful composite towards it externalized mirror image, the physical world (*bāhyakaraṇa*, "external organ", or *lauikika*, "worldly," realm) as well as to the

1 For a brief summary, see https://www.tuck.com/neurotransmitters/.
2 See her translation of YS 3.37 and 4.1, pp. 68 & 74, respectively.

transcendental (*alaukika*) realm. As reasonable as this appears to be, however, according to Sāṃkhya, which lies at the "heart" of Indian philosophical orthodoxy,[3] both the *antaḥkaraṇa* and the *bāhyakaraṇa* irrevocably abide in the relative world, in that field of "primordial materiality" (prakṛti) (Larson and Bhattacharya 1987, p. 24, passim). Even if the various components of the internal organ and the external organ possess different densities, form, and mobility, they are substantialities nonetheless.[4] They are, therefore, forever separate from and untouched by an individual or monadic "catalytic consciousness" (puruṣa), as Elisa Freschi describes it, which is not substantial and is "distinct from intellect and primordial materiality." The *antaḥkaraṇa* is, she states, "the abode of mental events such as thinking, imagining and remembering" (Freschi 2012, p. 371). Even if this is the case, its "presence . . . is essential for the occurrence of the awareness function of intellect and the transformations of primordial materiality" (Larson and Bhattacharya 1987, p. 25).[5] This presentation is essentially adopted by the Yogaśāstra, but this is understandable because it does not tally with the correlative function of the *antaḥkaraṇa* in yoga practice as found in the Yogasūtras.

The *antaḥkaraṇa* is more expansively described by the Vaiṣṇava sectarian founder and philosopher Vallabhācārya (1479–1531?) in his brief Antaḥkaraṇaprabodha, "Awakening of the Inner Organ," the seventh treatise in the Ṣoḍaśagranthāḥ or Sixteen Works.[6] In this text of ten and a half verses, he addresses the *antaḥkaraṇa* as if one part of his inner self were speaking to another. It is this brief sense of dialogue that is important here, as if the *antaḥkaraṇa* were an intermediary between his will and his actions, between his learned and cultured sense of Krishna as the Supreme Lord and his devotional ecstasy, learned and cultured on the other side of the *antaḥkaraṇa*. He does not describe the anatomy of this inner organ, which appears to be a bridge between internal and external awareness. However, the copious commentaries on this text do explain it. It is most easily summed up by Nṛsiṃhalāljī, who composed an undated Brajbhāṣā commentary on Vallabhācārya's Ṣoḍaśagranthāḥ between 1775 and 1825. Nṛsiṃhalāljī says in his commentary on verse 4 of Vallabhācārya's Nirodhalakṣaṇa (Smith 1998) that if a devotee experiences *kīrtana* or enlightened discourse in the association of one who has attained proximity to Kṛṣṇa (*bhagavadīya*), then Kṛṣṇa appears in the *antaḥkaraṇa* of the devotee. The *antaḥkaraṇa* is defined as consciousness (*cit*), mind (*manas*), intellect (*buddhi*), and ego (*ahaṃkāra*) taken together as a single functioning organ. The extra ingredient—consciousness—is added here, thus placing it entirely within the realm of what Sāṃkhya would regard as *prakṛti*, with the

---

3 This is the case even if Sāṃkhya metaphysics is entirely different from the other orthodox schools that obtained maximum currency as religious schools, namely the various expressions of Vedānta. Thus, Sāṃkhya cosmology, minus the nettlesome duality of prakṛti and puruṣa, nature and individual consciousness, was employed as the baseline explanation of the structure of the self in Ayurveda, virtually all sectarian Purāṇas, and most philosophical schools. Similarly, it is accepted at face value, which is to say in its Sāṃkhya embodiment, by Abhinavagupta, a term on which he does not speculate. It is absent from the Tāntrikābhidānakośa, which suggests that the Tantras paid scant attention to it; it was simply a structure designed to uphold the inner constitution. Thanks to Alberta Ferrario for pointing this out to me. It is interesting that the *antaḥkaraṇa* barely plays a role in Abhinavagupta's discourse on śaktipāta (Tantrāloka, chapter 13), which brings about the kinds of transitional experience discussed below (Ferrario 2015).

4 Loriliai Biernacki writes: "Known as the *antaḥkāraṇa*, the inward sense organs, these include the intellect (*mahat/buddhi*), the ego (*ahaṁkāra*), and the mind (*manas*). These three, as evolutes of Prakṛti, fundamentally lack sentience. Thus what a contemporary Western scientist might understand as "mind", "awareness", or 'consciousness', is, to the contrary, from an Indian perspective relegated to the level of mere materiality" (Biernacki 2014, p. 4).

5 The epistemological process here is well-described recently by Walter Menezes: "Knowledge arises when there is a modification (vṛtti) of *antaḥkaraṇa* in the form of the object, assisted by the instrumental cause (karaṇa). Thus, the same basic consciousness assumes various forms through different mental modes corresponding to different objects. This clarifies why there is knowledge of varied forms, such as, knowledge of a thing, e.g., tree, house, and horse; knowledge of an attribute, e.g., redness, beauty, and roundedness; and knowledge of action, e.g., flowing, flying, and blowing. Like the varied knowledge of external objects, there is also varied knowledge of mental states, such as happiness fear, love, imagination, memory, and so on, of which mind is also the instrumental cause. By taking various forms of diverse objects, antaḥkaraṇa causes variations in knowledge or consciousness, but does not generate it" (Menezes 2016, p. 157). Note that the term *antaḥkaraṇa* also entered the stream of non-philosophical Sanskrit. Kalidāsa used it in Abhijñānaśkuntalā 1.19: *asaṃśayaṃ kṣatraparigrahakṣamā yad evam asyām abhilāṣi me manaḥ | satāṃ hi saṃdehapadeṣu vastuṣu pramāṇam antaḥkaraṇapravṛttayaḥ ||* "Doubtlessly she is fit to be wed by a warrior, since my heart [*manaḥ*] desires her so. For in matters of doubt the inclinations of their inner faculties [*antaḥkaraṇa*] are authority for the good" (Vasudeva 2017, p. 195).

6 For information on the Ṣoḍaśagranthāh, see (Smith 1998; Redington 2000). Redington has translated the Antaḥaraṇaprabodha along with a few textual notes and more extensive notes from his teacher, Shyam Manohar Goswamy from Mumbai.

Supreme Lord (*puruṣottama*) Krishna, with his *līlā* or divine play replacing *puruṣa*.[7] Thus it is that *antaḥkaraṇa*, the awakened heart as the organ of consciousness and the storehouse of intelligence and personality, can serve as the intermediary between awareness and the Supreme Lord. Elsewhere, Vallabhācārya states in the Sarvanirṇayaprakaraṇa (51–52, unpacked in the commentaries) of his massive Tattvārthadīpanibandha that only through the *antaḥkaraṇa* can one experience the true bliss of the *svāminīs* (*gopīs*) or milkmaids of Vraja, the archetypal exemplars of single-minded divinely envisioned devotion. Thus, the antaḥkaraṇa serves as the bridge between ordinary (*laukika*) and transcendental (*alaukika*) experience.[8]

In sum, we can do little better than to quote Paranjpe (1998) on advaita Vedānta (the identity of the philosophical school he is citing is unimportant), which, he says,

> "assigns the tasks of perception, cognition, recollection, and others to an entity conceived as the "inner instrument" (*antaḥkaraṇa*), [which] includes the mind (*manas*) manifesting attentivity, the intellect (*buddhi*) meaning the capacity for determination and ascertainment, and *citta*, a storehouse of past impressions and memories. The inner instrument is a crucial aspect of the embodied person that coordinates the functions of the senses and the body while in constant interaction with events within the body and its surroundings. The inner instrument is said to "reach out" to objects in the environment through the senses, and to become transformed into their shapes, so to speak. The inner instrument is constantly undergoing modifications, depending on the objects it reaches out to, and it tries to 'know' them by itself being transformed into their shapes."

This must be distinguished from the Vaiṣṇava reckoning of the inner organ as delineated by Vallabhācārya in that the latter is theistic, in which the inner organ functions within a theistic or *saguṇa* context, while the advaita Vedānta that Paranjpe describes operates within a nondual or *nirguṇa* context.[9] Let us now see how this squares with saṃyama of the Yogasūtras.

3. Saṃyama

Scholarly and popular exegesis on the Yogasūtras of Patañjali constitute a major area of focus in advocating and assessing the "spirituality" of both India and the West. The 194 *sūtras* or aphorisms are divided into four *pādas* or chapters. Since the compilation or composition of the YS in the late 3rd or early 4th century CE,[10] the first two *pādas* have received nearly all the scholarly and public

---

7 Vallabhācārya and the commentarial tradition on his work speak of *līlāvatāra*, a broader extended realm of the Supreme Lord, which includes materiality as his līlā or divine play. In this reckoning the *antaḥkaraṇa* would be regarded as part of the whole fabric of līlā, neither external nor internal, but a mere facet of a whole in which its role as connective tissue is devalued. Much has been written on līlā; see, for example, (Sax 1995).

8 Somewhat analogous to this is Elaine Fisher's quotation of Kumārasvāmin, a fifteenth century Śaivasiddhānta philosopher who has written a commentary on the Tattvaprakāśa of Bhojadeva: "For, unmediated [*aparokṣabhūta*] knowledge [*jñāna*], in fact, is the cause of su-preme beatitude [*apavarga*]. And its unmediated quality arises when the traces [*saṃskāra*] of ignorance [*avidyā*] have been concealed through intensive meditation [*nididhyāsana*]. And intensive meditation becomes possible when the knowledge of Śiva arises through listening to scripture [*śravaṇa*] and contemplation [*manana*]. And those arise because of the purification of the inner organ [*antaḥkaraṇa*]. That [purification] occurs through the practice of daily [*nitya*] and occasional [*naimittika*] ritual observance, with the abandoning of the forbidden volitional [*kāmya*] rituals" (Fisher 2017, p. 42). Again, the *antaḥkaraṇa* serves as a radio; it is a mechanism, a device with varying degrees of clarity or static, which mediates between a remote source and a listener. In a more modern context, note the words of the 20th century yogi Pattabhi Jois: "*Sira* [channel systems of the mind, otherwise labeled *srotas*] are those *nāḍī* [internal channels] that carry messages from the *antaḥkaraṇa*, a "message center" located in the region *of* the heart, throughout the body, and also provide a "vital link in the functioning of the sense organs" (Smith 2008, p. 10, fn. 11).

9 More could be said about this, particularly because the guiding forces of the *antaḥkaraṇa* in these two cases would be different. In the case of theistic *saguṇa*, it would be Supreme Lord (*puruṣottama*), while in the nondual *nirguṇa* case the *antaḥkaraṇa* would be guided more by the interior dynamic between the self or *ātman* and its conscious positioning with the abstract absolute, the *brahman*. To say more would require a separate essay.

10 (Maas 2006, 2010), and elsewhere, settles this debate. He also argues, from manuscript sources, that the YS was composed in its entirety by Vyāsa, the first commentator on the YS. Many questions can be raised about this assertion, but this is not the place for it. However, this is why efforts such as Chapple's essay "Reading Patañjali Without Vyāsa" remain valuable (Chapple 2008, pp. 219–35). Other reasons for keeping the debate alive are found in (Acri 2012; Gokhale 2015).

attention. The reasons for this are because they deal with formal categories of *samādhi*, the eightfold (*aṣṭāṅga*) path of yoga (which continues through the first three *sūtra*s, out of fifty-five, of the third *pāda*), and their discussions of the goals, ethics, and obstacles on the path of yoga.[11] The remainder of the text, nearly the entire third *pāda*, and the entire fourth *pāda* (consisting of 34 *sūtra*s), has been all but neglected. The dimensions of the Sanskrit commentaries, the secondary sources, and the weight of the teachings of virtually all yogis and yoga schools in India and the West, bear out this disregard. The reasons are clear enough: the third *pāda* consists largely of a list of transcendental powers (*siddhi*, "accomplishment", or *vibhūti*, "the power to extend everywhere" (White 2014, p. 31)) that are of little interest to the scholarly traditions in both India and the West that have been responsible for perpetuating the *yogaśāstra*, the system of knowledge of yoga that is transmitted as an intellectual project. This list of *siddhi*s and the means of achieving them is patently exotic. The *siddhi*s lack an empirical or testable basis, even if they make logical or cosmological sense. Nevertheless, recent scholarship has shown that *siddhi*s, either those mentioned in YS Chapter 3 or elsewhere,[12] were in fact the most commonly sought-after goals of yoga in the first half of the second millennium CE.[13] The fourth *pāda* presents a different set of problems: it is difficult and often elliptical, as it attempts to tie together various strands from the YS, eluding or exhausting nearly all who have dealt systematically with it. Here our concern is the method of achieving *siddhi*s described in the third chapter, called Vibhūtipāda.[14]

What I suggest here is that if we understand the first several *sūtra*s of the third *pāda*, especially the fourth *sūtra*, we will be better able to grasp the experience that the YS offers to its learned audience. The *sūtra* reads *trayam ekatra saṃyamaḥ*, "*Saṃyama* is the three taken together as one." *Saṃyama* means "holding together, restraint, complete control." The literal meaning, however, is less important than the fact that it serves as a designation for the state in which the three higher limbs of yoga described in YS 3.1–3.3—*dhāranā*, *dhyāna*, and *samādhi*—are held in a delicate stasis. The goal of yoga stated in YS 1.2 is the cessation of the oscillations of the mental processes (*yogaś cittavṛttinirodhaḥ*). Its fulfillment is articulated here, at the beginning of the third *pāda*, in the description of the three higher or "inner" limbs (*antaraṅga*) of the eightfold path. What it requires is, first, fixing the mind to an object of thought (*dhāraṇā*, 3.1). This is then allowed to flow uninterruptedly through time in a settled state of watchfulness (*dhyāna* or meditation, 3.2). Finally, the true essence of the object shines forth without

---

11 Namely the *vṛtti*s, waves or mental modifications that must be evened out through the practice of yoga (YS 1.5-1.11), obstacles (*antarāya*) to our practice (YS 1.29-1.40), and (3) afflictions (*kleśa*) with which we must all deal (YS 3.3-3.14).

12 Many of the tantric and yoga texts list eight characteristic siddhis: *aṇimā* (reducing the size of the body to molecular dimensions), *mahimā* (expanding the size of the body to enormous dimensions), *garimā* (heaviness, increasing the body weight), *laghimā* (becoming light as a feather), *prāpti* (ability to translocate), *prākāmya* (ability to acquire whatever is desired), *iṣitvā* (lordship), and *vaśitvā* (ability to control nature). These are referred to in YS 3.45, but are not listed. Indeed, this *sūtra* should serve as the link between the *siddhi*s mentioned in YS and the array of later texts. Many more than these are found in the later texts, although nowhere are they explicitly tethered to the process discussed in the YS. It is not certain that the later yoga texts thought about *siddhi*s as actualized through the same process or explanation discussed in the YS, namely through *saṃyama* as the stable collocation of *dharāṇa*, *dhyāna*, and *samādhi*, but the conceptual link leaves space for this to have been carried forward.

13 See (Mallinson 2012) and elsewhere. This is now acknowledged in the academic study of yoga. See (Vasudeva 2011) for an eighteenth century example of the early goals of yoga as articulated in the YS later on losing their dualist focus as yoga is appropriated into the realm of Vedānta.

14 All translations and editions of the YS (or PYŚ, as it's commonly called now, for Pātañjalayogaśāstra, (Maas 2006) must perforce address the topic of siddhis, but the treatments are usually briefly, with almost no learned elucidation. The infrequency of the term outside the YS may be seen in its treatment by Mallinson and Singleton (2017, pp. 286–87, 324) and Larson and Bhattacharya, where it is rarely referred to outside the YS and its commentaries. Larson and Bhattacharya present the commentarial discussions (see their index), even if they are difficult to follow due to the policy of the Encyclopedia of Indian Philosophy to include minimal Sanskrit. Precedents, however, this may be seen in the Bhagavadgītā. Cf. BhG 4.26 śrotrādīnīndriyāṇy anye saṃyamāgniṣu juhvati—One should offer senses such as hearing and others into the fires of saṃyama, viz. self-control); 2.61 (tāni sarvāṇi saṃyamya yukta āsīta matparaḥ—with the senses restrained, he should sit, disciplined focused on me); 3.6 (karmendriyāṇi saṃyamya ya āste manasā smaran—he sits, restraining his organs of action); 6.14 (manaḥ saṃyamya maccitto yukta āsīta matparaḥ—the mind restrained, collected together, etc.), 8.12 (sarvadvārāṇi saṃyamya mano hṛdi nirudhya ca—having restrained all the gates [orifices], confining the mind in the heart). These passages present the general semantic horizon for this term prior to the YS.

mediation (*samādhi*, 3.3). These taken together constitute the singular unified state of *saṃyama*. Eleven *sūtras* follow (3.5–3.15) that describe the nature of the transformation brought about by the process of cessation (*nirodhaparināma*, 3.9), which invites transformation within the expanded realm of one-pointed unmediated focus (*ekāgratāpariṇāma*, 3.12).

The list of the *siddhis* begins at 3.16 and continues with little break through 3.46.[15] They include knowledge of the past, present, and future, the movement of the stars, the interior arrangement of the parts of the body; vision of perfected beings (*siddhas*); the attainment of the four commonly listed virtues (friendliness, compassion, joyfulness, and equanimity); the ability to fly through the air; and many more. Most of these "powers of perfection" betray a formulaic rhetoric: from saṃyama on X, Y is achieved. For example, in a complex act, 3.21 reads "from *saṃyama* on the form or appearance of the body, one can become invisible by obstructing another's ability to grasp the body by blocking their eyes from the light."[16] Many are much simpler, for example 3.26 reads, "from saṃyama on the sun, one gains knowledge of the worlds."[17] Another well-known *sūtra*, 3.42 reads, "from *saṃyama* on the relationship between the body and empty space or ether (*ākāśa*), and from absorption in a state in which the body becomes as light as cotton, one can move through space."[18]

These examples are sufficient to show that *saṃyama* serves as a valve between the world of ordinary reality and discourse and the realm of transcendental or supernatural accomplishments. It may be viewed as the neck of an hourglass through which awareness must pass and become transformed. The possibility for such accomplishments exists, but it is inert until it is awakened by taking advantage of the higher operations of the path of yoga. One might say it is an organ that is activated or switched on by the singular operation of dhāraṇā, dhyāna, and *samādhi*. *Saṃyama* might then be imagined as an organ that reallocates the composite energies of *dhāraṇā*, *dhyāna*, and *samādhi*, rendering them useful in attaining exalted and unprecedented knowledge, power, and virtue. It is the heart of cognition and the cognition of the heart. In Patañjali's manner of speaking, it is the purified *antaḥkaraṇa*, because, as described above, it is the organ, the inner organ, through which the *laukika* and *alaukika*, the worldly and the transcendent, are mediated and communicated to one another. It is also the moment of dissociation when one identity overtakes another and allows an individual to manifest divinity in a state of invited or controlled possession. This leads to consideration of an inner organ that mediates this moment of dissociation.

4. Possession

Possession falls into two basic categories: voluntary and involuntary. When voluntary, in a large number of cases, it may be labeled positive and oracular.[19] When involuntary, it is nearly always negative and disease producing. The latter constitutes a formal category in classical Ayurveda, *āgantuka unmāda*, madness (Sanskrit: *unmāda*) that comes on a person from outside (Sanskrit: *āgantūka*). This is medicalized at length in the early Ayurveda literature and treated with a broad pharmacological spectrum, with ritual, and through unique psychodynamic practices and processes.[20] It is then picked up and dealt with extravagantly in a large number of tāntrik texts as well in the regional languages of India in which the earlier categories of possessing entities, which fit collectively under the name *bhūtavidyā* ("science of possessing entities") are expanded and localized.[21] What we will address here,

---

[15] The most notable break is the much discussed sūtra 3.37, te samādhāv upasargā vyutthāne siddhayaḥ, which states that if one is not careful these siddhis can become impediments to samādhi, that we can be overtaken by our own success.

[16] kāya-rūpa-saṁyamāt tat-grāhyaśakti-stambhe cakṣuḥ prakāśāsaṁprayoge 'ntardhānam.

[17] bhuvana-jñānaṁ sūrye-saṁyamāt.

[18] kāyākāśayoh sambandha-saṃyamāl laghutūlasamāpatteś cākāśagamanam.

[19] See Sax 2002, 158ff., who speaks of oracular possession in terms of "complex agency." The notion of assigning agency to non-human actors is controversial in anthropology, but my experience over the years in the Himalayas forces me to concur with Sax's observations and conclusions.

[20] This is described and analyzed at length in Smith (2006, chp. 12).

[21] Most of this is also described in (Smith 2006). Some of what appears in the next few paragraphs is drawn from various parts of that publication. See also (Smith 2010).

however, is positive oracular possession, which is, as I argued earlier (Smith 2006, chp. 1), the most frequently sought after state of transcendence in India. It is nearly always induced through ritual, and is therefore virtually always public. It is attractive and enticing, it entreats and impels the individual into an inner zone of safety, power, and authority. To the unknowing outsider or observer, including "official" representatives of priesthoods and orthodox hierarchies, it appears frightening and dangerous. But to the experiencer it is uplifting. In most cases, a gradual crescendo of emotional engagement is visible to observers, whether it is in a religious festival, a healing temple, or a devotional environment in which musical or other activity that may be identified as shamanic, such as drumming, occurs (Rouget 1985). This is distinct from siddhis in yoga, which are, by necessity, private. We are then proceeding in this section from the realm of the theoretical, the *antaḥkaraṇa*, and the private, the cultivation of *siddhi*s, to the public realm, the learned, anticipated, and manifested moment of transcendence into a divinely inspired state.[22]

Two brief ethnographic examples must suffice here. One is from a video titled Kusum (2000), filmed most prominently at and near the Balaji temple in Mehndipur, Rajasthan (Pakaslahti 1998; Dwyer 1999, 2003), a few kilometers off the main road, about halfway between Agra and Jaipur. The other is drawn from a pilgrimage to the headwaters of the Ganga, along the Bhagirathi between Gangotri, the temple town that marks the origin of the Ganga,[23] and Mukhba, 27 km south, where Gaṅgā Devī travels with her retinue for the winter (Smith 2018).[24] The evidence here, ethnography, is of a very different order than the textuality that guides the two previous sections. It is neither Sanskritic nor philosophical. But there is sufficient common experiential or emic ground for the link to be justifiable.

Balaji is a well-known pilgrimage center known for the treatment of possession, which is to say an exorcism center. Many modalities are employed here, because hundreds of healers, largely from villages in Uttar Pradesh, Delhi, Haryana, Rajasthan, and Madhya Pradesh, come from their native villages every month for perhaps a week, renting out small spaces which they use for their ritual. This is in addition to the exorcistic rites sponsored by the Balaji temple itself. In the last half century, the number of worshippers and individuals who believe themselves to be in need has dramatically expanded, from a trickle of a few hundred per day to no less than seven- or eight-thousand every day. Not everyone who comes feels they are possessed and in need of exorcism. The main reason is because it is exclusively family therapy; if one person is afflicted, then the rest of the family must be, so the narrative among healers goes. Also, afflicted individuals need family around them to withstand the often heavy-handed psychodynamic processes that occur at Balaji.

One of the afflicted was a fourteen year old girl named Kusum. Her treatment (along with many others) was tracked by Pakaslahti, and filmed by a Finnish television crew in 2000 (Aaltonen 2000). Kusum was brought to Balaji, like many if not most others, as a last resort healing center. Biomedical doctors had failed to diagnose her condition and Western psychoanalysis and psychopharmacology were unavailable, as is the case for nearly all Indians, for whom the bare facts of life render such treatment an irrelevant upper class Westernized luxury.[25] Kusum's father was an autorickshaw driver

---

22 See (Freeman 1993, 1998), on possession as learned behavior.

23 Although the actual beginning is at Gaumukh, 18 km further upriver, where the Bhagirathi emerges as a fully formed river from beneath the receding Gangotri glacier. However, it is only possible to travel there on foot. Thus, the temple, beyond which very few people go (the government imposed limit is 150 trekkers per day), is in the densely built up pilgrimage center of Gangotri.

24 The data and comments included here are based to some extent on my fieldwork at Balaji in 2001, 2002, and 2007, and participation in the Mukhba-Gangotri pilgrimages in 2007, 2013, 2015, and 2016. Much of this was conducted thanks to two senior research fellowships from the American Institute of Indian Studies in 2001 and 2006, and two from Fulbright, including a Fulbright-Hayes in 2007 and a Fulbright Nehru in 2015–2016.

25 Pakaslahti begins his important 1998 article by pointing to an article then twenty-five years old (Neki 1973), which needs to be updated, that provides an interesting statistic: "80% of the population first consult[s] religious folk healers when they seek outside help for mental health problems" (Pakaslahti 1998, p. 129). This statistic cannot have changed much in the last half century.

in a very poor area in South Delhi, her aunt folded and glued discarded newspaper pages into fragile paper bags for use in the market, and her mother was at home all day every day to prevent the tiny house in the jam-packed slum from being robbed. Without providing more details of the case than are necessary here, suffice it to say that three or four families, each with an afflicted family member, were in attendance in a moderately sized rented room that had been turned into a temple, and that entrancing music blared loudly from a CD player for a couple of hours each morning to the accompaniment of well-known exclamatory chants such as Śrī Rām Jay Rām Jay Jay Rām, Jay Śrī Mā, Jay Bābājī, and so on. At a certain point someone, not necessarily the afflicted individual, will enter a trance state. This can become contagious, but in my experience is limited to members of a single family. In this case it was Kusum's aunt that fell into a trance state.[26]

Eventually, after a few days of sitting in the back of the room, more or less staring blankly, appearing pent up and reserved, Kusum developed the comfort and confidence to express herself, and finally entered a state of possession. As is standard for such behavior in India, Kusum first unbound her tightly braided hair.[27] This is emblematic of a state of freedom; indeed, this is part of the kinesthetics of possession-based freedom for women in India. Another facet of the bodily expression of possession is rotating quickly counterclockwise with the arms flailing in the air. Kusum did not do this. She remained seated, but her eyes bulged and her tongue lolled down to the tip of her chin as she took on the visage of Kālī (Aaltonen 2000, minute 44:00 and onwards), a familiar goddess who often evokes bouts of possession (Figure 1). In fact, one of the walls of the room featured a common color poster of Kālī (Figure 2). The extent to which Kusum's tongue lolled downwards is not normal; the mimetic replication of Kālī was unmistakable. Regardless of what one's theoretical positioning might be, from that moment on Kusum's healing began to manifest, and continued on an upward swing.[28]

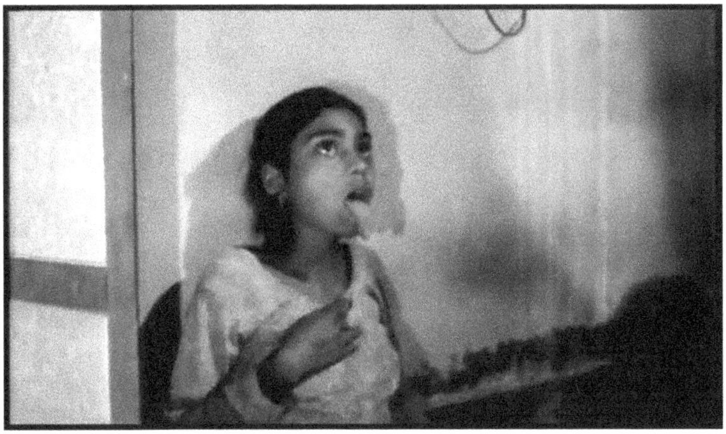

Figure 1. Kalī possessing Kusum (Kusum 45:52).

[26] It is important to note that the healers who transit through Balaji operate through very different modalities even if nearly all of them advocate family therapy. They are not certified by any outside bureau or board; their procedures are highly idiosyncratic. Among other things this is a reason for more research to be conducted there.

[27] See (Obeyesekere 1981; Erndl 1993; Hiltebeitel 1991), although some of this requires modification today.

[28] The most promising theory is Bruno Latour's actor-network theory (Latour 1996, 2005), which provides limited and contextual agency to non-human entities and objects; see (Sax 2009), for applying this to possession in the central Himalayas.

Figure 2. Kālī, poster art (in the author's collection).

So, we must ask, what happened here? What process of liberation transpired within Kusum's mind and body that began to generate her healing? What exactly is this unique, untested, and perhaps untestable healing process? The main actors were *pūjā*, the music, the singing, and the ritual actions of Bhagatji, the healer, a kindly man with a third standard education from the town of Hapur, eighty kilometers east of Delhi, and his assistant, Meena, an intelligent and compassionate woman with a sixth standard education, who had the uncanny ability to temporarily wrest invasive spirits from those in the room who were possessed. The sum of their parts allowed the creation of a small space of safety and community, even if the families did not know each other.[29] Bhagatji, dressed casually and standing off to the side, usually smoking a cigarette, confidently in charge, studiously and intently surveyed the room and observed the shifting dynamics. When a family member of an afflicted individual fell deeply into a state of possession, Meena, sitting at the front of the room with her kindly unassuming smile, suddenly entered into a state of possession and unloosened her own hair, her eyeballs disappearing upwards into her head, or so it seemed. In this ostensibly blind and cathartic visage, she nevertheless expertly wrestled the disembodied entity from the person holding it, who was not necessarily the one identified as the afflicted family member. Eventually Meena and the possessed person collapsed, exhausted from the battle, but still fully in their altered states. Bhagatji strode to the front of the room from the side and proceeded to psychoanalyze the spirit, not the individual who was afflicted. Bhagatji called out for the spirit, *bhūt* or *bhūtpret* in Hindi, to identify him or herself, ask their reason for being there. Bhagatji would plead to the spirit to cooperate with his intention of transforming the "lives" of invasive bothersome spirits, who destroy the lives of those we regard as the living, and to join the

[29] One can easily label this a shamanic scenario, and create a list of shamanic features, but the labeling is not important here.

legions of the spirits of the good, which is to say in this case the army (*phauj*) of Hanumān. In this paradigm, the good spirits were marshalled together as an effective force, the ethereal army of the chief magistrate of this court of law, namely Balaji, as the baby Hanumān is called in this part of Rajasthan. All of this helped generate an unambiguous trigger point that enabled Kusum to unfurl her hair and unburden herself to an extent unprecedented in her short life, in the closed and hardscrabble social space that was the lot of her family. Throughout much of that fateful morning, Bhagatji interrogated, sometimes brutally, the entity held within Meena's body that she had borrowed from the auntie. At a certain point this achieved a critical mass, following which Kusum let loose, crying desperately at the heart of Kālī, who was none other than herself.[30]

How, we might ask, is this trigger point different from the extreme concentrated energy that is unloosed in the post-*samādhi* state of *saṃyama*, at which the *antaḥkaraṇa* or internal organ is the fulcrum or balancing point that holds ordinary or laukika reality on one side and the transcendent or *alaukika* realm of *siddhi*s or manifestation of a deity that heals on the other side? We shall return to this shortly.

The second example is of possession during a Himalayan pilgrimage. The venue was the annual pilgrimage of the Goddess of the Ganges, Gaṅgā Devī, from Mukhba, on the north bank of the Bhagirathi, where she spends the winter resting, to Gangotri, 27 km further east, the nominal source of the Ganges. This pilgrimage occurs on akṣayya tṛtīyā, the third day of the bright half (*śuklapakṣa*) of the month of Vaiśākha, towards the end of April or beginning of May. This is widely considered an auspicious day for embarking on new beginnings. The return journey from Gangotri to Mukhba occurs on Dīpāvalī, the well-known family and community festival that falls on the new moon of the month of Kārttika, towards the end of October or beginning of November. The semiannual peregrination features Gaṅgā Devī, accompanied by her associates Sarasvatī and Annapūrṇā in a *dolī* or palanquin (lit. "a swing"), carried by seasoned and strong men, followed by pilgrims, at first perhaps five hundred, but by the end no more than twenty-five or so. The number decreases as the terrain becomes more difficult and the altitude rises, from Mukhba at approximately 8700 feet (2652 m) to Gangotri at 10,300 feet elevation (3139 m), and the cliff from the trail becomes more precipitous.

One of the primary features of this procession and festival, as is the case at festivals and pilgrimages throughout India, is possession.[31] The experience here is closer to the norm of "normal" oracular possession that is found across India (if one can, for a moment, accept possession as normal behavior reflecting a normal ontology). Usually it is women who are awakened to the presence of the deity, although it is not uncommon of to find men experiencing such "ecstatic" possession, especially in the Himalayas, where they most often serve as oracles to the deities. Gendered behavior is approximately similar. Certain behavioral manifestations of public possession, such as untying and loosening the hair, then spinning counterclockwise, are usually associated with women, although this is certainly possible for men (disregarding the unloosening of the hair), as noted in the video Kusum. The terms employed for possession in the Himalayas are *jhulānā*, "causing (the god) to swing" (Sax 2002, p. 175 n. 39); *bhāv ānā*, "to bring on a feeling or experience"; *khelnā*, "to play"; and *āveś*, "to invite entry." *Āveś* discloses the senses of "charge, agitation, intense emotion, frenzy, wrath."[32] The verb nācnā, "to dance," is also in common use because of the widespread perception that the deity is *dancing* in the body of the devotee (note the title of Sax's 2002 book, Dancing the Self). This possession, Sax says, "is brought on in by musicians' esoteric knowledge, magically powerful spells, and especially their drumming, [which] induce possession and provide the highly charged ambience of a performance. Moreover,

30 Cardeña's (1994) clear articulation of dissociation is invaluable here.
31 For example, see (Stanley 1977), for the festival at the Khaṇḍobā temple at Jejuri, fifty kilometers southeast of Pune the on the *somavatī amāvāsyā* or new moon that falls on a Monday; Hiltebeitel 1991 for the Draupadī festival in North Arcot district of Tamilnadu; (Sax 1991) for the pilgrimage to Nandadevi; and much more. See (Smith 2006, chp. 4), for further examples.
32 See (Smith 2006, p. 113) for the richness of the vocabulary of possession in North India.

what I have called "possession" is conventionally understood as dance.[33] Village gods and goddesses, along with the Pāṇḍavas, are said to enjoy 'dancing' in the bodies of human beings" (Sax 2002, p. 53).

What I observed in Gāṅgā Devī's pilgrimage was less the deities dancing, even if outbursts of it were occasionally visible, than divination performed by pilgrims for their own benefit or temple priests and other skilled brahmans communicating with the devatā, often employing easily accessible forms of divination to shed light on a pressing situation for a client. Some of the conventional possession behavior was observable, but not nearly as ubiquitous as is the case when a festival does not require walking long distances in a more or less orderly fashion, or at healing centers such as Balaji. Regardless, however, of the mobility or external physical demands on the participants, the behavior during the pilgrimage resonated with that of the Mahābhārata characters in the Pāṇḍav līlā; most if not all Garhwali public performances are related through the flexible and localized Garhwali Mahābhārata.[34] "They become possessed by the character in question and begin to tremble, roll their eyes, and exhibit other conventional signs of possession" (Sax 2002, p. 137).

5. Discussion

We must ask whether and how the experiences of Kusum in her positive or "divine" possession by the Goddess, induced specifically to counter a prior negative disease-producing possession,[35] and that of the participants on Gaṅgā Devī's pilgrimage are similar, or even related. Do they reflect a sufficiently recognizable underlying psychophysical mapping to enable us to infer that a single internal organ was guiding the process? Is there a moment, a threshold, beyond which transcendence occurs during "divine" possession, when the individual and his or her agency emerges into that of a deity (or spirit)? As noted, among the "conventional signs of possession" are unloosening the hair, trembling, rolling the eyes, and spinning counterclockwise. Some of the other symptoms are resonant with what Abhinavagupta and others in Kashmir wrote a thousand years ago in describing samāveśa or "complete immersion in the sense of ontological identity" (Ferrario 2015, p. 11), including a feeling of intoxicating devotion" (ibid.), convulsions (*ghūrṇi*, kampa), and loss of consciousness (nidrā) (Smith 2006, p. 370). At a certain point, this allows the individual to become fully identified with the deity, whether it is Śiva, Bālājī of Mehndipur, or Gaṅgā Devī. It is this point of transition that we must address in drawing conclusions.

With this in mind, it is important to note that there is no common word or term in South Asian regional languages to describe or identify the moment of identity transformation in experiences of possession, or that can be equated with the word saṃyama in the Yogasūtras. Indeed, in other yoga texts, including those that lie within the Yogaśāstra but outside the immediate realm of the Yogasūtras,

---

33 In June 2018, quite by accident, I attended a village festival at Shri Dhan Singh Devta, Aleru, Tehri Garhwal, south of Chamba, on the road to Rishikesh. It began as a simple chai stop during my taxi ride. I soon heard drums beating up the hill behind the chai shop. I asked man at the chai shop about the commotion. He said simply, *nāc, upar se mandir haiṃ*, "they're dancing up at the temple." I quickly finished my chai and climbed the hill behind the chai shop to discover perhaps 150 people, in mid-morning, dancing, many of them, both men and women, exhibiting the characteristic behavior of possession. Dhan Singh was a resident who had died suddenly from cholera, and was transformed into a rathī devatā. The reason is because he was believed to have traveled to the heavenly world in a chariot (ratha). This piqued my interest for a number of reasons. Later, I discovered the videos of a young Garhwali filmmaker who calls himself Ashish Chamoli. in which all of this is explained. It is illuminating to watch the following; https://www.youtube.com/watch?v=8SzrmaIbNqM&t=105s (subtitled in English) Ashish Chamoli's videography here is a good example of what can now be found scattered across the Youtube universe (and no doubt on social media) that is helpful in gaining access to cultural forms throughout the world. It is just as possible that I would not have seen this than that I did.

34 Presently D. R. Purohit, William Sax, and I are working to bring out an edition and translation of one version of the Garhwali Mahābhārata, the only one for which the recited text has been written down, hailing from the town of Agastmuni, along the Mandakini River north of Rudraprayag.

35 An outsider sensitive to other modes of thought might diagnose the initial possession as depression or anxiety. These concepts, at least as considered by western academics and the biomedical establishment, are not operable in rural India. The local interpretation, then, must be honored in order to abide by the dictum that the informant is always right. The notion of counter-possession is present not only in India but in Christian practice as well. Thiessen writes "Possession by the Spirit is a form of counter-possession in contrast to demon possession. If demons are dissociative phenomena, then positive possession by the Spirit is also a positive dissociative phenomenon" (Thiessen 2014, p. 183).

the word *saṃyama* is not employed in the same decisive and programmatic way that it is found in the third *pāda* of the Yogasūtras. Possession is, as I argued earlier, the most highly valued and frequently sought after form of spiritual experience in India.[36] Its devaluation by elites within India across the political spectrum that try to define Hinduism to those outside, or even inside, cannot regularize the discourse because its lexical markers differ regionally and often from one venue to another within a small area. This hampers the ability of a comparative project such as this one to achieve a definitiveness that many would seek. It is only possible to say with certainty that the moment of transcendence must remain a mystery no matter how sophisticated an argument or model can be made for lining up and equating related sets of conditions. It's less comparing apples and oranges than it is comparing varieties of apple.

A proper inquiry now is to ask whether that point or fulcrum of transitional experience is the same in positive and negative possession. Further distinctions may be made within the realm of positive possession, including (a) devotionally induced possession (*āveśa*),[37] which accounts for a preponderance of possession in Indian spiritual and ritual situations; (b) yogic and ritually induced possession, which is to say when a yogi possess another person's body (*paraśarīrāveśa, parakāyapraveśa*)[38] or possession as induced in children for divinatory purposes[39]; and (c) Śaiva initiatory possession (*samāveśa*). Another category that should probably be added here, although it possesses characteristics of (a) and (b), is possession that occurs when a singer induces positive possession in an audience. For example, in Garhwal and Kumaon in the central Himalayas, bards hold nocturnal sessions called *jāgar*, "awakening," in which a locally recognized shaman gains the ability through song and drumming to awaken the deity in others.[40] Taking all of these forms together, it is possible to say that regardless of the specific point along the scale of experience the fulcrum is balanced in these different forms of positive possession, there is no question that the conditions for each one establish the definition and nature of *laukika* and *alaukika* experience for each, and that within the framework of each experiential mode transcendence is a reality. It is their reality, and we must go with this.

It is inadvisable, in my opinion, to deny the individuals within these collocated groupings their own model of transcendence by imposing etic methodologies and standards. Our priority must be to understand the models we study and to see that each has a balancing point, which we are here labeling the *antaḥkaraṇa*, based on a widely used indigenous model of cosmological analysis and personality structure. It is neither possible nor advisable to search for an absolute point for all these modes at which the *antaḥkaraṇa* allows the individual experience to shift from the *laukika* to the *alaukika*. The very possibility of transcendence means it must be inferred. Each realm of experience contains sufficient descriptive and theoretical force to allow such an inference to become validated within its own realm. Thus, the "awakened heart" that one feels in devotional possession is qualitatively different from the visionary landscapes of initiatory possession or the moment of cessation (*nirodhapariṇāma*, YS 3.9) that allows the yogi to disappear into voyages of discovery after experiencing *saṃyama*. Even states of negative possession, in which dissociation may be wild, erratic, uncontrollable, and destructive, are characterized by a balancing point on which the *antaḥkaraṇa* rests, even if it shifts constantly up and down a dissociative scale.

---

36 "As an indigenous category in ancient and classical India, possession is not a single, simple, reducible category that describes a single, simple, reducible experience or practice, but is distinguished by extreme multivocality, involving fundamental issues of emotion, aesthetics, language, and personal identity" (Smith 2006, p. 4).

37 This is covered in (Smith 2006, chp. 4), describing ethnographies (pp. 110–72), and chapter 9 on devotion explicitly articulated (pp. 345–62). Keep in mind that nearly all of South Asian religion is devotional, and any intense experience can lead to possession. This is generally acknowledged.

38 See (Smith 2006, pp. 255–65, 286–89, 294–97; White 2004).

39 (Smith 2006, pp. 440–48).

40 Such performances are almost always performed by lower caste bards in fairly small rooms with a relatively small audience. See (Alter 2018) for discussion of the music; (Sharma 2006, 2012) for a wealth of local information on *jāgars*; and (Bhatt et al. 2014) for an illuminating depiction of the use of *jāgar* in the Garhwal Himalayas.

6. Conclusions

The *antaḥkaraṇa*, we have decided, is the collective energy of the cognitive and conscious self that rests at the balancing point between its disparate parts and their reorganization into a unified higher functioning unit; it is, in other words, as much a faculty or, to materialize it even further, an organ as it is a theory. As such, the consciousness (*cit*), mind (*manas*), intellect (*buddhi*), and [according to some, the] ego (*ahaṃkāra*) congeal and radiate more powerfully in a singular concentrated purposefulness. In this way they become a tripartite or quadripartite organ, an internal organ that abides at and as the fulcrum that balances ordinary (*laukika*) experience with the supraordinary (*alaukika*) realm. The components of the *antaḥkaraṇa* for everyone are therefore the same, but they are arrayed and organized differently for everyone, as well as differently for each person or living being constantly, as the components change from one moment or day to the next, just as other internal organs and mental and psychological processes change as they grow, flourish, and wane. Thus, the *antaḥkaraṇa* shifts along a scale of individual identity formation like a chord in a song. The chord cannot be held for too long, its nature is to change until the song is over.

We have examined two modes of transition that demonstrate this. The first is through the practice of yoga and achievement of *saṃyama*, the point that separates the developmental stages of yoga, including *samādhi*, and the higher or *alaukika* realizations, namely the *siddhi*s. This, as described in the Yogasūtras, can only be practiced by well-schooled and (more likely) initiated practitioners. The list of *siddhi*s and the details of the *saṃyama* are unique to this text, and, I suggest, were rarely presented in this systematic a manner in guru–disciple pedagogical exchange. This we can assume from the history of practice, from the division between Yoga as *śāstra* and yoga as a disciplinary practice (Yoga with a capital Y and yoga with a lower case y), which appears to have begun soon after the composition of the Yogasūtras, as James Mallinson and others have amply demonstrated.[41]

The second mode is through deity or oracular possession, which has been a widespread phenomenon in India for a very long period (Smith 2006). In this practice, which is actually a set of related practices, surely numbering in the hundreds, that were localized throughout India, the devotee learned how to come into such close contact with a deity that his or her own identity was at least partially erased as the deity and its power to assert agency came to the fore. The moment of transition from ordinary body awareness to experiencing the initial symptoms of possession to final emergence of the deity is, I am arguing, comparable with the *yogin* entering into a practice (any practice will do), developing and perfecting his or her powers of concentration, meditation and samādhi, which eventually achieve a critical mass, and finally enters a state in which higher powers can be realized. In both cases, I am proposing, the congealed power of the *antaḥkaraṇa* is transformed from habitual directedness towards the *laukika* world to a retrained focus on the *alaukika* world. These alaukika realms are envisioned differently in Pātañjala yoga and possession states. The point of transcendence is always found at a junction, balanced as if on a fulcrum. It is an inner, secret, changeable, and highly individual point where light emerges in fullness from shadow or darkness. Furthermore, as this is cultured, its effects redound upon the practitioner's life, enabling him or her to achieve, on one hand, the final result of yoga as stated in the fourth *pāda* of the Yogasūtras, namely *dharmameghasamādhi* (YS 4.29), a state beyond *siddhi*s when one's samādhi emerges as a cloud of right action. It is also, within the scope of positive possession, a realm of continuous experiential empowerment, which envelopes social empowerment, where the deity without becomes available as the deity within.

Funding: This research received no external funding.

Conflicts of Interest: The author declares no conflict of interest.

[41] See, for example (Mallinson 2011, 2012, 2016), and elsewhere; (White 2014; Vasudeva 2011) and others illustrate the bifurcation of the yoga tradition in which study of the Yogasūtras and its commentaries became limited to the paṇḍita or scholarly community while yoga practice was taken up largely by ascetics with their own very different textuality.

References

Primary Sources

Antantaḥkaraṇaprabodha with Five Sanskrit Commentaries. Edited by Gosvāmī Śyām Manohar. Baroda: Śrī Kalyāṇarāyajī kī Havelī, Saṃ. 2036 (1979).

Nṛsiṃhalāljī-*Ṣoḍaśgranth*. 1970. *Gosvāmī Śrīnṛsiṃhalāljī Mahārāj kṛt Brajbhāṣā ṭīkā sahita*. Mumbai: Śeṭh Nārāyaṇdās aur Śeṭh Jeṭhānand Āsanmal Ṭrast, pp. 108–21.

Tāntrikābhidhānakośa, vol. 1: A-AU [vowels]. By Helene Brunner, Gerhard Oberhammer, André Padoux, et al. Österreichischen Akademie der Wissenschaften, phil.-hist. Kl., Sitzungsberichte, vol. 681. Vienna: Verlag der Österreischen Akademie der Wissenschaften, 1999.

Tattvārthadīpanibandha (saprakāśaḥ): Śāstrārtha-Sarvanirṇaya-rūpa-prakaraṇa-dvayopetaḥ. Edited by Gosvāmī Śyām Manohar. Kolhapur: Śrī Vallabhavidyāpīṭha-Śrīviṭṭhaleśaprabhucaraṇāśrama Trust, Saṃ. 2039 (1982).

Secondary Sources

Aaltonen, Jouko. 2000. Kusum. Illume Co. Helsinki, 69 minutes. Available online: https://search-alexanderstreet-com.proxy.lib.uiowa.edu/view/work/bibliographic_entity%7Cvideo_work%7C1879379 (accessed on 20 March 2019).

Acri, Andrea. 2012. Yogasūtra 1.10, 1.21-23, and 2.9 in the Light of the Indo-Javanese *Dharma Pātañjala*. *Journal of Indian Philosophy* 40: 259–76. [CrossRef]

Alter, Andrew. 2018. Recasting Lok and Folk in Uttarakhand: Etymologies, Religion and Regional Musical Practice. *South Asia: Journal of South Asian Studies* 41: 483–92. [CrossRef]

Bhatt, Ram Prasad, Heinz Werner Wessler, and Claus Peter Zoller. 2014. Fairy lore in the high Himalaya Mountains of South Asia and the hymn of the Garhwali fairy 'Daughter of the Hills'. *Acta Orientalia* 75: 79–166.

Biernacki, Loriliai. 2014. A Cognitive Science View of Abhinavagupta's Understanding of Consciousness. *Religions* 5: 767–79. [CrossRef]

Cardeña, Etzel. 1994. The domain of dissociation. In *Dissociation. Clinical and Theoretical Perspectives*. Edited by S. J. Lynn and J. Rhue. New York: Guilford, pp. 15–31.

Chapple, Christopher. 2008. *Yoga and the Luminous: Patañjali's Spiritual Path to Freedom*. Albany: State University of New York Press.

Dwyer, Graham. 1999. Healing and the Transformation of Self in Exorcism at a Hindu Shrine in Rajasthan. *Social Analysis* 43: 108–37.

Dwyer, Graham. 2003. *The Divine and the Demonic: Supernatural Affliction and Its Treatment in North India*. London and New York: RoutledgeCurzon.

Erndl, Kathleen M. 1993. *Victory to the Mother: The Hindu Goddess of Northwest India in Myth, Ritual, and Symbol*. New York: Oxford University Press.

Ferrario, Alberta. 2015. Grace in Degrees: Śaktipāta, Devotion, and Religious Authority in the Śaivism of Abhinavagupta. Ph.D. dissertation, University of Pennsylvania, Philadelphia, PA, USA.

Fisher, Elaine M. 2017. *Hindu Pluralism: Religion and the Public Sphere in Early Modern South India*. Berkeley: University of California Press.

Freeman, J. Richardson. 1993. Performing Possession: Ritual and Consciousness in the Teyyam Complex of Northern Kerala. In *Flags of Flame: Studies in South Asian Folk Culture*. Edited by Heidrun Brückner, Lothar Lutze and Aditya Malik. New Delhi: Manohar, pp. 109–38.

Freeman, J. Richardson. 1998. Formalized Possession Among the Tantris and Teyyams of Malabar. *South Asia Research* 18: 73–98. [CrossRef]

Freschi, Elisa. 2012. *Duty, Language and Exegesis in Prābhākara Mīmāṃsā. Including an Edition and Translation of Rāmānujācārya's Tantrarahasya, Śāstraprameyapariccheda*. Leiden: Brill.

Gokhale, Pradeep. 2015. Interplay of Sāṅkhya and Buddhist Ideas in the Yoga of Patañjali (With Special Reference to *Yogasūtra* and *Yogabhāṣya*). *Journal of Buddhist Studies* 12: 107–22.

Hiltebeitel, Alf. 1991. *The Cult of Draupadī. Vol. 2: On Hindu Ritual and the Goddess*. Chicago: University of Chicago Press.

Kusum. 2000. Produced and directed by Jouko Aaltonen. London: Royal Anthropological Institute.

Larson, Gerald James, and Ram Shankar Bhattacharya. 1987. *Sāṁkhya: A Dualist Tradition in Indian Philosophy*. Encyclopedia of Indian Philosophies. Edited by Karl Potter. Princeton: Princeton University Press, vol.4.

Latour, Bruno. 1996. On actor-network theory: A few clarifications. *Soziale Welt* 47: 369–81.
Latour, Bruno. 2005. *Reassembling the Social: An Introduction to Actor-Network-Theory*. Oxford: Oxford University Press.
Maas, Philipp A. 2006. *Samādhipāda. Das erste Kapitel des Pātañjalayogaśāstra zum ersten Mal kritisch ediert*. Aachen: Shaker.
Maas, Philipp A. 2010. On the Written Transmission of the Pātañalayogaśāstra. In *From Vasubandhu to Caitanya. Studies in Indian Philosophy and its Textual History*. Edited by Johannes Bronkhorst and Karin Preisendanz. Delhi: Motilal Banarsidass, pp. 157–72.
Mallinson, James. 2011. Nāth Sampradāya. In *Brill Encyclopedia of Hinduism, Vol. III*. Edited by Knut A. Jacobsen, Helene Basu, Angelika Malinar and Vasudha Narayanan. Leiden and Boston: Brill.
Mallinson, James. 2012. *Siddhi* an *Mahāsiddhi* in Early *Haṭhayoga*. In *Yoga Powers. Extraordinary Capacities Attained through Meditation and Concentration*. Edited by Knut A. Jacobsen. Leiden and Boston: Brill, pp. 327–44.
Mallinson, James. 2016. The Amṛtasiddhi: Haṭhayoga's Tantric Buddhist Source Text. Draft of Paper to be Published in a festschrift for Professor Alexis Sanderson.
Mallinson, James, and Mark Singleton. 2017. *Roots of Yoga*. London: Penguin.
McDaniel, June. 2018. *Lost Ecstasy: Its Decline and Transformation in Religion*. New York: Palgrave Macmillan.
Menezes, Walter. 2016. Is Viveka a Unique Pramāṇa in the Vivekacūdāmaṇi? *Journal of Indian Philosophy* 44: 155–77. [CrossRef]
Miller, Barbara Stoler. 1998. *Yoga: Discipline of Freedom: The Yoga Sūtra Attributed to Patañjali*. New York: Bantam.
Neki, J. S. 1973. Psychiatry in South-East Asia. *British Journal of Psychiatry* 123: 257–69. [CrossRef] [PubMed]
Obeyesekere, Gananath. 1981. *Medusa's Hair: An Essay on Personal Symbols and Religious Experience*. Chicago: University of Chicago Press.
Pakaslahti, Antti. 1998. Family-Centered Treatment of Mental Health Problems at the Balaji Temple in Rajasthan. *Studia Orientalia* 84: 129–66.
Paranjpe, Anand C. 1998. *Self and Identity in Modern Psychology and Indian Thought*. New York: Plenum Press.
Redington, James D. 2000. *The Grace of Lord Krishna: The Sixteen Verse-Treatises [Ṣoḍaśagranthāḥ] of Vallabhacharya*. Delhi: Sri Satguru Publications.
Rouget, Gilbert. 1985. *Music and Trance: A Theory of the Relations between Music and Possession*. Chicago: University of Chicago Press.
Sax, William S. 1991. *Mountain Goddess: Gender and Politics in a Himalayan Pilgrimage*. New York and Oxford: Oxford University Press.
Sax, William S. 1995. *The Gods at Play: Līlā in South Asia*. New York: Oxford University Press.
Sax, William S. 2002. *Dancing the Self. Personhood and Performance in the Pāṇḍav Līlā of Garhwal*. New York: Oxford University Press.
Sax, William S. 2009. *God of Justice: Ritual Healing and Social Justice in the Central Himalayas*. New York: Oxford University Press.
Sharma, D. D. 2006. *Uttarakhand ke lok devatā*. Haldwani: Ankit Prakashan.
Sharma, D. D. 2012. *Uttarākhaṇḍ gyānkoṣ (A Compendium of Uttarakhand Related Knowledge)*. Haldwani: Ankit Prakashan.
Smith, Frederick M. 1998. *Nirodha* and the *Nirodhalakṣaṇa* of Vallabhācārya. *Journal of Indian Philosophy* 26: 589–651. [CrossRef]
Smith, Frederick M. 2006. *The Self Possessed: Deity and Spirit Possession in South Asian literature and Civilization*. New York: Columba University Press.
Smith, Benjamin Richard. 2008. "With Heat Even Iron Will Bend": Discipline and Authority in Ashtanga Yoga. In *Yoga in the Modern World: Contemporary Perspectives*. Edited by Mark Singleton and Jean Byrne. New York: Routledge.
Smith, Frederick M. 2010. Possession. Oxford Bibliography Online. doi:10.1093/OBO/9780195399318-0101. Available online: http://www.oxfordbibliographies.com/view/document/obo-9780195399318/obo-9780195399318-0101.xml (accessed on 20 March 2019).
Smith, Frederick M. 2018. Gaṅgā Devī between Worlds: Her Annual Pilgrimage between Mukhba and Gangotri. *South Asian Studies* 34: 169–85. [CrossRef]
Stanley, John M. 1977. Special Time, Special Power: The Fluidity of Power in a Popular Hindu Festival. *Journal of Asian Studies* 37: 27–43. [CrossRef]

Thiessen, Gerd. 2014. Sarx, Soma, and the Transformative Pneuma: Personal Identity Endangered and Regained in Pauline Anthropology. In *The Depth of the Human Person: A Multidisciplinary Approach*. Edited by Michael Welker. Cambridge: Wm. B. Eerdmans, pp. 166–85.

Vasudeva, Somadeva. 2011. Haṃsamiṭṭhu: 'Pātañjalayoga is Nonsense'. *Journal of Indian Philosophy* 39: 123–45. [CrossRef]

Vasudeva, Somadeva. 2017. The Inarticulate Nymph and the Eloquent King. In *Revisiting Abhijñānaśākuntalam: Love, Lineage and Language in Kālidāsa's Nāṭaka*. Edited by Saswati Sengupta and Deepika Tandon. Hyderabad: Orient Black Swan, pp. 185–205.

White, David Gordon. 2004. Early Understandings of Yoga in the Light of Three Aphorisms from the Yoga Sūtra of Patañjali. In *Du corps humain, au Carrefour de plusieurs saviors en Inde: Mèlanges offèrts à Arion Roşu par ses collègues et ses amis à l'occasion de son 80e anniversaire*. Edited by Eugen Ciurtin. Paris: De Boccard, pp. 611–27.

White, David Gordon. 2014. *The Yoga Sutra of Patanjali: A Biography*. Princeton: Princeton University Press.

religions

Article

Religious Experience and Yoga

Christopher Key Chapple

Bellarmine College of Liberal Arts, Loyola Marymount University, 1 Loyola Marymount University, Los Angeles, CA 90045, USA; cchapple@lmu.edu

Received: 16 January 2019; Accepted: 26 March 2019; Published: 30 March 2019

Abstract: Yoga practice provides access to religious experience, which has been defined by William James as "immediate luminousness, philosophical reasonableness, and moral helpfulness." In this paper the processes of Yoga will be summarized as found in the *Bhagavad Gītā* and the *Yoga Sūtra.* This article concludes with instructions on how to perform a practice that integrates Yoga breathing and movement with reflections on the Sāṃkhya descriptions of physical and emotional realities (*tattvas* and *bhāvas*).

Keywords: William James; Yoga; Gāyatrī mantra; Bhagavad Gītā; Patañjali; Sāṃkhya philosophy; Gandhi; Bhakti; Vedānta; *Yoga Sūtra*

1. Yoga and the Light

As one enters a conversation about religious experience, Yoga and Hinduism, it can be helpful to begin with images of light. Vedic mantras signaling the importance of light include the Pavamāna and Gāyatrī mantras.

asato mā sad gamaya,
tamaso mā jyotir gamaya,
mṛtyor mā amṛtaṃ gamaya,
Lead me from chaos into order.
Lead me from lethargy into the light.
Lead me from death to immortality.
—Bṛhadāraṇyaka Upaniṣad 1.3.28[1]

tatsaviturvareṇyaṃ
bhargo devasyadhīmahi
dhiyo yo naḥ prachodayāt
The sun has no rival.
We reflect on the luminosity of its power.
May it inspire our own vision.
—Ṛg Veda 3.62.10

The term light (*jyotir*) in the Pavamāna Mantra and the invocation of the rising sun (*savitur*) in the Gāyatrī Mantra both indicate a unity between the internal process of waking up the human body and the external, macrocosmic event of sunrise. Both these mantras are frequently chanted in the world of modern Yoga and lend a sense of antiquity and continuity to the contemporary practice of what

[1] All translations are by the author.

Elizabeth deMichelis has called "Modern Postural Yoga."[2] The implication of both is clear: a light can be kindled within through processes of Yoga and meditation. This inner light mirrors and connects with the power of the rising sun. To become an adept at Yoga entails moving towards light and away from darkness, to arrive at a place of spiritual enlightenment.

Two other light-referent terms central to Yoga are *sattva* and *samādhi*. The former indicates the lightest state of being that comes closest to replicating the luminosity of witness consciousness, the seer (*puruṣa, draṣṭṛ, Yoga Sūtra* II:41, III:35, 49, 55); while the latter indicates full emplacement within the state of being completely absorbed, ego-free, and free (*YS* I:20, 46, 51; II:2, 29, 45; III:3, 11, 37; IV:1, 29). Both terms indicate a state of being filled with light and lightness, no longer weighed down by the effects of past karma. Such a person is free from regrets about the past as well as content in terms of what might happen in the future.

In Hindu Yoga traditions, this experience of lightening becomes externalized and internalized, observed and witnessed as well as felt in the realm of affect. Aesthetic moments can stun a person into a silent state, a direct connection with beauty and awe. Two practices enhance the possibility of this experience: seeing images of the divine in a statue or in a living exemplar (*darśana*) and the performance of rituals that create a mood of reverence. External rituals can be elaborate Vedic sacrifices (*yajña*), simple home devotionals (*pūjā*), the veneration of a teacher (*guru-śraddhā*), or pilgrimage to a temple (*mandir*) or some other holy place (*tīrtha*).[3] Internal rituals that kindle the inner light (*jyotir*) include the practice of various forms of Yoga, including reflective attempts at self-improvement, bodily movement to generate heat (*tapas*) that purifies the body (*śuddhi-śarīra*), breath control, developing a sense of inwardness leading to concentration and meditation, culminating with the still of the minding into a state of absorption. Quite often this practice will be coupled with the more external devotions mentioned above, and the recitation of mantra and singing.

2. Yoga and Religious Experience: James and Gītā

Juxtaposing the words Yoga and religious experience, one automatically goes to William James and his book *Varieties of Religious Experience* (1902). This seminal work in many ways places Yoga at the nexus of conceptualizing a religious experience, in terms of both process and actualization. James posits three criteria for assessing genuine religious experience, which he places in italics. They include: "*immediate luminousness* ... *philosophical reasonableness*, and *moral helpfulness*"[4]. This article will explore what can be expected and achieved within these three categories through Yoga.

What is Yoga? Patañjali, in the early centuries of the common era, defined Yoga as *citta-vṛtti-nirodhaḥ*, the restraint of mental fluctuations (YS I:2). Gurāṇi Añjali (1935–2001), founder of Yoga Anand Ashram, proclaimed that "Yoga is a point in time where a sacred secret occurs. And the individual is filled with an ecstasy that stops all language."[5] This latter definition somewhat resembles William James's definition of Yoga as "training in mystical insight that has been known from time immemorial."[6] James, in his description of Yoga, quotes Swami Vivekananda's *Raja Yoga*: "There is no feeling of I, and yet the mind works, desireless, free from restlessness, objectless, bodiless. Then the Truth shines in its full effulgence."[7] From darkness, one has turned towards light.

Perhaps one of the best places to assess Yoga in terms of James's three criteria of *immediate luminousness* ... *philosophical reasonableness*, and *moral helpfulness* would be the four forms of Yoga articulated in the Bhagavad Gītā: discernment or Jñāna Yoga, action or Karma Yoga, devotion or

2 (De Michelis 2004).
3 See the works of C. J. Fuller, Axel Michaels, Diana Eck, Constantina Rhodes, James J. Preston and others for full descriptions of these practices.
4 (James [1902] 1961).
5 (Añjali forthcoming).
6 James, op. cit. p. 314.
7 Vivekananda as quoted in James, p. 325.

Bhakti Yoga, and meditation or Raja Yoga. It is only after great struggle that Arjuna, the protagonist of the Gītā, comes into a state of *luminousness*, albeit fleeting, following instruction in meditation and devotion. From the start of the text, Arjuna's preceptor Krishna brings him to a place of *philosophical reasonableness* by instructing him in the physical and metaphysical teachings of Sāṃkhya and Vedānta philosophies, through Jñāna or discernment Yoga. In various ways, Krishna instructs Arjuna on the complexities of *moral helpfulness*, specifying that Karma Yoga, with its sense of aplomb, will see one through even the most difficult of tasks, and that it is possible to hold to one's dignity whether faced with humiliation or glory.

The Yoga of the Bhagavad Gītā begins with a crisis. Arjuna, faced with the prospect of slaying family members and teachers on the Kurukshetra battlefield, falls into a state of paralysis. On their shared chariot, his cousin, Avatāra Krishna, instructs Arjuna about the ways of discernment (*jñāna*) and steady wisdom (*sthita prajñā*).

Gandhi discovered the *Bhagavad Gītā* while in England. For him it became the touchstone to states of Yoga. Through its narrative he discovered a way to think more expansively about his own story. He sought solace particularly in the last eighteen verses of the second chapter (54–72), finding inspiration in their message: be the best person you can possibly be, at all times and in all circumstances. To understand Yoga as a tool of reasonableness and moral helpfulness, this section of the text will be considered, as well as other passages that similarly describe that exemplary person who is able to maintain dignity and calm in the midst of chaos and difficulty.

Arjuna asks Krishna:

> How can the person of steady wisdom be described,
> that one accomplished in deep meditation?
> How does the person of steady vision speak?
> How does such a one sit and even move?
> The Blessed One responds:
> When a person leaves behind all desires
> that arise in the mind, Arjuna,
> and is contented in the Self with the Self,
> that one is said to be steady in wisdom.
> The person who is not agitated by suffering (*duḥkha*),
> whose yearnings for pleasures have evaporated,
> whose passions, fear, and anger have evaporated,
> that sage, it is said, has become steady in vision.
> One whose passions have been quelled on all sides
> whether encountering anything, whether pleasant or unpleasant,
> who neither rejoices or recoils,
> such a person is established in wisdom.
> And when this person can draw away from the objects of sense
> by recognizing the senses themselves
> like a tortoise who draws in all five of its limbs,
> such a person is established in wisdom.

Krishna explains how restraint of the senses allows stability, and then describes how attachment and the blind pursuit of desires can lead to one's downfall:

> Fixation on objects
> generates attachment.
> Attachment generates desire.
> Desire generates anger.

Anger generates delusion.
From delusion, mindfulness wanders.
From wandering mindfulness arises the loss of one's intelligence.
From the loss of intelligence, one perishes.
By giving up desire and hatred
even in the midst of the sense objects
through the control of the self by oneself,
person attains peace. (Translation of BG II:54–72 by the author.)

Krishna tells Arjuna that this peace equips a person with the discipline needed to practice meditation and that "Without meditation there can be no tranquility. Without tranquility, how can there be happiness?" An adept with the stabilized mind, grounded in peace, and skilled in meditation is described as one "free from possessiveness, free from ego". These qualities encapsulate the best of what is possible through Yoga. This section of the Gītā provides a definition of Yoga in accord with the Jamesian principles of reason and helpfulness. Krishna urges Arjuna to cultivate a way of being in oneself and in the world that does not fall prey to distraction, desires, and selfishness. Holding steady, one is able to cleave to what is most central and dispel all forms of delusion.

This poem-within-a-poem can be parsed into four basic messages, starting with the initial volley of Arjuna's question. Arjuna has been utterly paralyzed by his situation. He feels miserable, defeated, confused, and impotent. His world has been so radically shaken by treachery committed by his own cousin-brothers that he cannot move forward. The first message lies in the opening question: we must look for a way of being in the world that will provide peace and tranquility.

The second message of this *Gītā* portion asks for a reconsideration of the fixity of the external world. The external world "arrives" because we say it is so, because of agreed-upon conventions about right and wrong, tasty and disgusting, worthy and unworthy. Krishna provides a measured critique and analysis of this habitual way of engaging with the world. He calls into question the relationship between the senses and the objects of the senses. Krishna urges one to "dial it back", to recognize that a sense object does not exist before the sensory organ (*indriya*) "lands" upon it, seizes it, and makes it real. Careful direction of the senses can help shape one's emotional relationship with the world. By learning to step back into a place of consideration before, in Nietzsche's words "going under," in this case under the thrall of the senses, one can gain a measure of mastery that ultimately leads to self-understanding and self-control. Releasing the grip of what one wishes to be, one can face reality and respond accordingly.

Third, Krishna articulates a cascade of unfortunate consequences that can result if one does not gain self-control. Attachment leads to desire. Thwarted desire leads to anger. Anger confuses the mind. A confused mind knows no tranquility. The emotional fallout from uncontrolled desire can not only ruin one's day, but can take down entire families, villages, and nations. Affect leads to effect; emotions have consequences. Yoga advises the restraint of emotion, which can only arise from an honest assessment of one's situation. In the words of Gurāṇi Añjali, understanding leads to acceptance. Acceptance leads to peace, and in peace one finds freedom.

Fourth, Krishna emphatically declares the possibility of freedom through Yoga. If one can reverse the outflows of the senses through managing one's emotions, one can become like a still ocean. One can be wakeful in the midst of ignorance. One can move away from ego fixity and obsession into a state of no ego, no possessions, no lust for the things that bring bondage. The Prajñā Sthiti, the person established in wisdom, becomes godlike, Brahmī Sthiti, and enters the divine abode of Brahma Nirvāṇa (BG II:72), ascending to a heavenly realm characterized as a place where the winds of desire no longer blow.

Religious experience as expressed in this rendering of Yoga does not remove one from the world of the real (*sat*) but from the unreal (*asat*), echoing the Vedic verse quoted at the start of this essay: lead me from the chaos of the unreal (*asat*) to the world of truth and order (*sat*). Arjuna's freedom does not provide an escape from the world but into a place of greater responsibility, with a wisdom that arises from discernment. Arjuna moves away from fear and anger and learns to embrace his action with equanimity.

2.1. *After the Enlightenment: How to Act with Luminosity, Reason, and Helpfulness*

Krishna provides instruction on how to stabilize the body, breath, and mind through concentrated practice in the sixth chapter of the Gītā, outlining the practices of Raja Yoga or meditation, leading to a sense of *immediate luminousness.* He teaches devotional practice, Bhakti Yoga, in chapters seven through ten, wherein he instructs Arjuna to view the world as an extension of Krishna's own body, using frequently analogies of light and luminosity. In chapter eleven, where Arjuna witnesses the vast expanse of Krishna's cosmic and eternal form, into which all manifestations eventually are drawn, like moths to a flame, to their death. Here the luminous roars into a state of destructive conflagration, a fire that burns and purities. In chapter two, Krishna had taught that souls can never be destroyed. In chapter eleven he shows Arjuna that all bodies can and will be devoured in the jaws of time. This approach to Yoga in many ways elides the distinctions between philosophy, luminosity, and morality, revealing the inescapabilty of darkness and death.

The latter chapters of the Gītā provide a sustained examination of how one can learn to live a life informed and guided by the Yoga of freedom. They make an abiding appeal to adopt an attitude and philosophy of what James calls moral helpfulness. The following passages from chapter 12 (13–19) provide concrete instances of the attitude through which one can manifest moral helpfulness in the name of Yoga:

> 12.13–18 The one beyond hate who shows loving kindness
> and compassion for all beings,
> free from "mine! mine!" and free from ego,
> unruffled in suffering or happiness, patient:
> that Yogi, who is content at all times,
> whose self is controlled, whose resolve is firm,
> ... who is of even eye, pure, capable, neutral,
> free from wanting things to be a certain way,
> ... who neither elates nor hates,
> neither mourns nor hankers,
> giving up obsession over purity or impurity,
> the same whether with an enemy or a friend,
> the same in honor and disgrace,
> in heat or old, happiness or suffering,
> free from attachment,
> maintaining equipoise when blamed or praised,
> content with whatever happens,
> without fixed abode yet steady minded,
> full of devotion: that one is dear to me. (Translation by the author.)

Krishna encourages Arjuna to adapt a stance of neutrality in the midst of life's vicissitudes. To remain unruffled in the midst of difficulty communicates a stance of ease and peace that can calm the anxious. Similarly, to accept without undue elation life's happy moments can help to prevent an exuberance that can lead to an inevitable let-down.

2.2. *Philosophy and Moral Assessment through the Three Guṇas:*

The three *guṇas* comprise a core teaching of Yoga and Vedānta. They are also at the core of Sāṃkhya philosophy and account for all aspects of potential and kinetic energy (*sukṣma* and *stūla*), subtle and gross, that govern the unmanifest and manifest worlds (*avyakta* and *vyakta prakṛti*). They exist to be witnessed by consciousness (*puruṣa*) and to provide the experience that causes one to seek the understanding that leads to freedom. As introduced in the second chapter of the Gītā (II:45), the *guṇas* describe the changes and fluctuations of states of being, cycling through heaviness and lethargy (*tamas*), action (*rajas*) and buoyant illumination (*sattva*). Krishna advises Arjuna to recognize these qualities and to simply observe that whatever happens, it is "merely the *guṇas* working on the *guṇas*" (III:28). In the fourteenth chapter, Arjuna asks for details, wanting to know the "qualities of the one who has gone beyond the three *guṇas*," asking for a description of the conduct (*ācara*) of the one who goes beyond the three *guṇas* (*trīn guṇān ativartate* XIV:21). Krishna states that such a person not only goes beyond the dualities of the positive and the negative, but transcends the tripartite qualities of "illumination, activity, and delusion (*prakāśaṁ, pravṛttiṁ, moham* XIV:22)" neither hating (*dveṣṭi*) nor desiring (*kāṅkṣati*) their appearance". Knowing that it is "only the *guṇas* working" (*guṇā vartanta ity eva* XIV:23) that person "stands firm, not wavering" (*avatiṣṭhati na iṅgate* XIV:23).

Krishna calls for the negation of all dualisms, proclaiming that the Yogi remains the same in the midst of suffering and happiness, love and disdain, blame and praise. However, Krishna also includes an allusion to a threefold distinction that might correlate to the *guṇas* here as well: one is to have equal regard for a lump of earth, which may refer to *tamas*, a stone, which might refer to *rajas*, and gold, which might correlate to *sattva* (*samaloṣṭāśmakāñcanaḥ*, IV:24). Similarly, Krishna offers one more threefold description of how the person who has transcended the *guṇas* operates: equanimous in honor and dishonor (*tamas*), equanimous whether with friends or enemies (*rajas*), and renouncing all attachment to all undertakings (*sattva*) (XIV:25).

The first three verses of chapter 16 give specific qualities that characterize one with "divine endowment" (*saṁpadam dāivīm*).

> No fear, purity of *sattva*,
> standing persistently in the Yoga of knowledge,
> practicing giving, self-control, and sacrifice,
> study of Self, austerity, appropriate behavior,
> non-violence, truth, no fear,
> giving up attachment, manifesting tranquility, without ill words,
> compassion for beings, without craving,
> kind, modest, and steady,
> vigorous, patient, firm, pure,
> without malice, without excessive pride,
> this, Arjuna, is your birthright,
> this divine endowment. (Translation by the author.)

At the center we find the quality of nonviolence, *ahiṃsā*, the epitome of moral helpfulness. These qualities in the aggregate define *sattva*, the mode of being in the world that brings one closest to the pure witness, the consciousness that gives purpose to all experience. Through careful observance of these behaviors, one moves into the paradigm of the spiritual hero.

2.3. *Moral Helpfulness and the Sattva Guṇa*

Moral helpfulness can be found throughout the seventeenth chapter, which describes many salubrious qualities of the *sattva guṇa*. Krishna praises a reverential attitude (*pūjanam*) toward gods and priests and teachers of wisdom, accompanied with purity, appropriate behavior and comportment, and nonviolence. These are called bodily austerity. Next Krishna describes austerity of speech as calming words that are truthful, lovely, and beneficial, informed by the study and practice of sacred texts. Krishna concludes this triad with a discussion of austerities of the mind, which include cultivation of peace, gentleness, self-restraint, silence, and purity. All these austerities (*tapas*) of body, speech, and mind further emphasize the role of self-development in the practice of moving Arjuna's experience of the world from one of helplessness, despair, and alienation into one of constructive engagement. Chapter seventeen ends by emphasizing the meaning of truth (*sat*) as a state of being (*bhava*) that manifests in laudable actions and words (*karmani* and *śābda*), as well as in sacrifice and austerity (*yajñā* and *tapas*).

These many exhortations urge Arjuna to move toward a place that combines immediate luminousness with moral helpfulness. His descriptions of greater light and lightness are accompanied with various warnings about the results of self-interested action (*rajas*), as well as lethargy and doubt (*tamas*). By the eighteenth and final chapter, three qualities associated with luminosity and morality predominate: sacrifice, giving, and austerity. Arjuna can no longer act from a place of self-interest. Rather than stewing in memories of regret and fear of the future, he is prepared to act and to give freely. Furthermore, he is prepared to give up the fruits of his action, leaving behind all doubt. He has become freed from attachment and ego, steady, resolute, and unconcerned with success or failure (XVIII:26) which allows him to declare "I stand here now with my doubts dispelled, my delusion destroyed. I have regained my memory and am now ready to do what you command" (XVIII:73). Arjuna waged unremitting war on his cousins and suffered in hell as a consequence, having sacrificed even his own well-being for the sake of a higher good. Just as William James talks eloquently and repeatedly about the plight of the sick soul, detailing the sufferings endured by George Fox, Teresa of Avila, and many others, so also Arjuna, as part of his spiritual quest, faced his own inner fears and doubts in the first chapter of the Gītā, the terrifying face of God in the eleventh chapter, and his own purgation in the depths of hell at the end of the Mahābhārata epic before returning to his divine state.

This single heroic narrative provides a template for religious experience that entails difficulty and suffering, bravery, honesty, and the sustained practice of Yoga in its many forms. In a sense, Arjuna becomes a symbol for every person who seeks solace in the midst of troubles, small or large. The Yogas taught by Krishna, including meditation techniques, discernment, acting without attachment, and devotion, each find usefulness in the story of Arjuna and can be assimilated in their own ways by the modern Yoga practitioner. Before sharing a modern version of how this might take place, attention will now be given to another text that delineates the practice of Yoga, the *Yoga Sūtra* of Patañjali.

3. Patañjali's Eightfold Yoga

The Yoga system of Patañjali as given in the 196 statements of the *Yoga Sūtra* (ca. 250 C.E.), defines Yoga as the quelling of thought (*citta vṛtti nirodhaḥ*, YS I:2). Several techniques to attain this state are described, including the eight limbs of Yoga: discipline, observance, ease of bodily movement, control of breath, inwardness, concentration, meditation, and *samādhi*, a state of absorption. The *Yoga Sūtra* of Patañjali along with its accompanying commentary by Vyāsa (ca. 450 C.E.), comprises one of the six core philosophical treatises of Indian thought. It teaches that by gaining inner mastery one can shape one's emplacement in the realm of experience and move towards freedom (*kaivalyam*).

The *Yoga Sūtra* is divided into four chapters, focusing on meditative absorption, the practices required to achieve this state, the powers that consequently arise, and the ascent to freedom. The text begins with a definition of Yoga as quelling the fluctuations of the mind and ends with a description of what Vyāsa calls the liberated soul, freed of afflicted karmas. The Yoga tradition differs from, and remains similar to the five other schools of Indian thought. Unlike the *Brahma Sūtra* of Bādarāyaṇa, a distillation of Vedānta ideas from the Upanishads, Yoga does not claim that the world is in any way illusory and the *Yoga Sūtra* does not use the term Brahman. Like the *Sāṃkhya Kārikā* of Īśvarakṛṣṇa, the *Yoga Sūtra* posits two complementary, eternal principles, consciousness (*puruṣa*) and the events of human experience (*prakṛti*) which are characterized according to three typologies, the pure, active, or lethargic *guṇas*, described in the earlier section on the Bhagavad Gītā. Unlike the *Sāṃkhya Kārikā*, it lists dozens of practices including the efficacy of religious devotion as a possible pathway toward purification. As advocated in the Nyāya system outlined by Gautama, it follows rules of logic. It begins with the premise stated above regarding the quelling of thoughts, proceeds to examine the five categories of thought, and then provides means to purify thought and action. Like the Vaiśeṣika school, it acknowledges the presence of physical realities, and like Mīmāṃsā, Yoga sees benefit in some forms of ritual behavior, particularly in its descriptions of devoting one's attention to a chosen deity or ideal.

The Yoga system also bears traces of influence from Jainism and Buddhism. The first part of Yoga's eightfold path describes the five vows found in the *Ācārāṅga Sūtra*, the earliest extant Jain text (ca. 325 B.C.E.). Like Jainism, it describes karma as multi-colored. It also shares in common with Jainism and Sāṃkhya a concern for the individuality of each particular soul or perspective. Throughout the text it lists terms and practices associated with Theravada and Mahayana Buddhism, including the list of qualities attributed to the liberated Buddhist saint or *arhat* (loving kindness, compassion, sympathetic joy, and equanimity) and markers for spiritual accomplishment including faith, mindfulness, energy, and wisdom as well as stages including the tenth and highest attainment of the Bodhisattva, absorption in the cloud of Dharma. It also seems to engage the Buddhist position on no-self, acknowledging that the ego must be transcended, a key premise of Buddhism, while simultaneously asserting the abiding presence of a witness consciousness, tying Yoga closely to Vedānta and Sāṃkhya.

The second chapter of the *Yoga Sūtra* outlines a threefold method for achieving *samādhi*: rigor (*tapas*), study (*svadhāya*), and dedication to divinity (*īśvara praṇidhāna*). It then describes the five afflictions that obstruct *samādhi* (*avidyā, asmitā, rāga, dveṣa, abhiniveśa*), and describes in detail the first five limbs of Patanjali's eightfold path (*yama, niyama, āsana, prāṇāyāma, pratyahāra*). The threefold method, known as Kriyā Yoga, starts with austerity (which in practice often takes the form of regularly fasting and silence) and moves into study of the higher self and dedication to emulating the ideal Yogi. The afflictions to be overcome are ignorance, egotism, attraction to objects of desire, repulsion, and the desire for continuity. Each of these is said to "seed" one's bed of karmas prompting repeated experiences of change and suffering. Patañjali recommends developing discernment to overcome attachment and move into the witness consciousness, deemed to be a state of freedom. By setting aside all the afflictions rooted in ignorance, confusion ceases.

The first two of Patañjali's limbs, the disciplines and observances, require the individual Yogi to abide by a code of ethics and to cultivate positive behaviors, in the style of James's moral helpfulness. As one becomes skilled in nonviolence, enmity ceases in one's presence. By telling the truth, one becomes reliable and one's words hold great sway. By not stealing or even coveting, one finds happiness with what is at hand. By not dissipating one's focus on carnal matters, one gains vigor. By minimizing possessions, one can understand experiences more fully. The positive behaviors to be cultivated include purity, through which one prepares to move into witness consciousness. Through contentment, one becomes abidingly happy. Through austerity one brings the body and senses toward perfection. Through study of the higher self, one begins to emulate the chosen deity. Through dedication to the most accomplished of Yogis, one enters *samādhi*. This process establishes a link between moral helpfulness and immediate luminousness, all in the spirit of philosophical reasonableness.

The remaining passages from the second chapter describe the next three limbs. Yoga postures bring steadiness and ease. Mastery of the inbreath and the outbreath, including the extended hold of each, allows one's innate radiance or immediate luminousness to be revealed. With one's relationship with the world stabilized and purified through the disciplines and observances, and through mastery of body and breath, one then can enter the fifth aspect of Yoga, a place of inward calm.

The third chapter of the *Yoga Sūtra* describes the last three aspects of eightfold Yoga and the powers they generate. Concentration (*dhāraṇā*) leads to meditation (*dhyāna*) and to *samādhi*. From the place of *samādhi*, one re-enters the world with a new skill: the ability to apply focused intention. As one re-engages the world after engaging in times of deep absorption or *samādhi*, the following masteries emerge: knowledge of past and future; ability to understand foreign languages; knowledge of prior births; clairvoyance; ability to remain unseen; knowledge of the time of death; ability to manifest sympathetic joy, and equanimity; physical strength; knowledge of the movements of the sun, moon, and stars; knowledge of the energies of the belly, throat, third eye, head, and heart; ability to experience the bodily feelings of another person; the ability to remain light even in mud or muck; and beauty. This chapter ends with a warning not to become attached to any of these powers, but to always keep the eye on the prize: the state of discernment that releases one from the grip of threefold change of the *guṇas*, summarized above as pure, active, and lethargic.

The fourth and final chapter of the *Yoga Sūtra* elaborates on the operations of karma, reiterates that the state of freedom can never be claimed by the ego, and describes the pinnacle of Yoga as "steadfastness in own form and the power of higher awareness."[8] The key to this state of freedom, the cessation of afflicted action, yields absorption in a cloud of abiding virtue (*dharma megha samādhi*).

Because it includes so many different strands of thought and modes of practice drawn from various Hindu, Jain, and Buddhist traditions, and because it remains open-ended in regard to the choice of deity, or even the necessity to adopt a theological approach to achieve freedom, it became widely read and drew many commentators. It was translated into Arabic in the 10th century by the Muslim philosopher al-Biruni. Since the revitalization of interest in Yoga in the 19th century, it has been translated hundreds of times into many languages, providing a philosophical roadmap for the popular practice of Yoga. Yoga as found in the *Yogavāsiha/Mokopāya* (11th century) emphasizes the centrality of the mind in determining one's place in the world, control of breath, and the elemental meditations. The Jain Yoga of Haribhadra Virahāṅka (6th century) as found in the *Yogabindu* teaches the importance of moving beyond the binding effects of karma, while that of Haribhadra Yākinīputra in the *Yogadṛṣṭisamuccaya* (8th century) emphasizes the many paths of Yoga, correlating Patañjali's eight limbs with the 14 stages of spiritual progress (*guṇasthānas*) delineated in Jainism. The texts of Haṭha Yoga (11th century ff.) provide details on the ascent of energy through the cakras, as well as details on the performance and benefits of *āsanas* and *prāṇāyāma*. The Jain Yoga of the *Jñānārṇava* (11th century) and the *Yogaśāstra* (12th century) includes the Yoga Tantra emphasis on correlations and progressive elemental meditations. In the modern era, the scientific research of Swami Kuvalyananda at Kaivalyadham in Pune informed the Yoga as practiced and taught by Mahatma Gandhi, Swami Sivananda, and Krishnamacharya, who in turn brought the knowledge and practice of Yoga to the masses worldwide, complementing the earlier work of Swami Vivekananda and the philosophical interpretations of Yoga by Sri Aurobindo.

4. Yoga in Practice

This special issue of Religions is open to including aspects of religious experience within Hinduism beyond textual studies. Thus far, this article has fallen short of the mark, partly out of a reluctance to "own" my own positionality as a scholar-practitioner and teacher of the Yoga tradition. For five decades, Yoga and meditation have been central to my personal and professional life. For more than a dozen years I studied at Yoga Anand Ashram in Amityville, New York, learning Yoga in theory and practice, simultaneously earning undergraduate and advanced degrees focused on Buddhist and Hindu philosophies and the study of the Sanskrit and Tibetan languages and literatures. Subsequently, as a scholar of religion and a theologian, I have translated and analyzed numerous texts of Yoga, including the *Yoga Sūtra*, the *Bhagavad Gītā*, the *Yogavāsiṣṭha*, as well as Jain Yoga texts including *Yogadṛṣṭisamuccaya*, the *Yogabindu*, and the *Jñānārṇava*. Additionally, I have been indirectly and directly involved in the training of more than a thousand women and men certified by the Yoga Alliance and the International Association of Yoga Therapists, primarily through program development, teaching and supervision at Loyola Marymount University's certificate and degree programs in Yoga Studies, as well at the Hill Street Center in Santa Monica and the YogaGlo online streaming service. Along the way, I have come into the orbit of countless schools of Yoga and meditation practice, including the techniques taught by B.K.S. Iyengar, Pattabhi Jois, Bikram Choudhury, Deshikachar; Swamis Vishnudevananda, Veda Bharati, Chidvilasananda, Adhyatmananda, Bodhananda; the disciples of Swami Lakshmanjoo; Buddhist teachers Philip Kapleau and Trudy Goodman; as well as Jain teachers including Acharyas Tulsi, Mahaprajna, Vidyananda, Siva Kumar Muni, and many others. So, to close

[8] (Chapple 2008).

this essay, I would like to share a summary of two aspects from a larger Yoga practice that I developed, drawing from these experiences with an eye to how Yoga practice might be grounded philosophically in such a manner conducive to luminosity and moral helpfulness.

4.1. A Suggested Daily Practice of Yoga

As we begin the third and final section of this article, the verb mood will move into a form rarely seen in scholarly writing. Academic papers generally employ the indicative mood with an occasional sprinkling of the interrogative, conditional, or subjunctive, generally rendered in the third person to maintain distance and objectivity from the material. However, this next section will switch into a combination of direct command from the perspective of the first person (the author) telling the second person (the reader) how to move the body in a particular sequence of moves that involve breath, verticality, horizontality, motion, and rest. As such, this discourse steps out of a mood and mode of third person remove into a place of direct encounter that holds the possibility of evoking a body-felt experience even in the reading of the material. This next section invites the reader to visualize, to feel, and perhaps to perform.

For anthropologists, this might raise the question of whether the author is taking an emic or an etic approach to the Yoga tradition. Is it possible for a scholar to write about a topic in which one has an investment? Louisa May Alcott's character Jo received sound advice from her professor mentor and her mother in the children's classic *Little Women*: Write what you know. Write from your own experience.[9] As noted above, my life's work has been as a theologian and philosopher, seeking to develop tools to assist in a search for meaning. This has included the development of curricula for university courses, extension courses, and classes for the general public in the thought and practice of Yoga. Some suggestions are given below for a Yoga class that would be quite different from many of the gym-based exercise versions of Yoga. Two aspects have been identified below from my own learning and teaching of Yoga that could distinguish this form of practice from other popular styles. None of these aspects are "original". They can be found in the Yoga literature, but generally have not been featured in the teaching of mainstream modern postural Yoga. The two are focusing on the five great elements (*pañca-mahābhūta*) and cultivating four positive minds states (*bhāvas*) as delineated in the *Sāṃkhya Kārikā*.

4.2. The Five Great Elements: Pañca Mahābhūta

Earth, water, fire, air, and space comprise the basic material and ethereal substances that comprise the human body and the cosmos. Recognition of these five substances while practicing Yoga postures can create a mood of meditative connection. The Bow (Dhanurāsana), followed with the Locust (Śalabhāsana) can serve to call one's attention to the earth and water. While still supine with the stomach and chest upon the floor, one can then rise up into the Full Arm Snake Pose (Nāga) to acknowledge heat and fire, and then into the Bent Elbow Snake pose (Ardha Nāga) to connect with the air. A fifth pose, the Sphinx, wherein one props oneself up on the elbows, can evoke space, completing a fivefold sequence.

Gravity normally pulls the body downward. Every human movement stands in relation to this force. Surrender fully, belly down, to the earth, head turned to the side. In this sequence, to be repeated three or more times, the body rises up away from gravity. Just as the vertical and horizontal movement of the prior sequence inverted and extended the body, the limbs exert an outward and upward movement with similar results.

First, place the chin on the ground. Lift the feet upwards. Reach back and grasp the feet or ankles with the hands and lift the body away from the earth into the Dhānurāsana, the bow pose.

---

9 (Alcott [1869] 1987).

With shallow breath, repeat earth, earth earth, *pṛthivī*, *pṛthivī*, *pṛthivī*. Return both arms and legs to the ground and turn the head to one side.

Second, place the chin on the floor and the arms under the thighs, forming a fist with the hands. Lift the legs up into the Śalabhāsana, the Locust pose. Hold for a few seconds and with shallow breath, repeat water, water, water, *jal*, *jal*, *jal*. Bring the legs back to the earth and turn the head to the other side.

Third, place the hands, fingers facing forward, palms down on the floor under the shoulders. Lift up into the Nāgāsana, the cobra pose, with arms extended fully. Hold for a few breaths, repeating fire, fire, fire, *agni*, *agni*, *agni*. Lower the torso to the earth and turn the head to the other side.

Fourth, place the hands once again under the shoulders. Place the toes on the floor, with heels elevated. Lift up into the Ardha Nāgāsana, the half cobra pose, with elbows bent. Visualize the body as if it were a cloud being billowed forward by the wind. Hold this posture for a few seconds, repeating air, air, air, *vāyu*, *vāyu*, *vāyu*. Lower to the earth and turn the head to the other side.

Fifth, elevate the front of the body, with elbows on the floor, entering the Sphinx Pose. Gaze forward as if looking into the vast sands of the Sahara. Repeat space, space, space, *ākāśa*, *ākāśa*, *ākāśa*. Lower to the earth and turn the head to the other side.

Repeat the sequence as above, moving backward from the elements in a movement known as *pratiprasava*, this time evoking the subtle elements or *tanmātras* and their connection with the sense organs, the *buddhīndriyas*. While in Dhanurāsana, reflect on the process of smelling with the nose, *gandha* (fragrance) known through *nasa* (the nose). While in Śalabhāsana, reflect on the process of tasting with the mouth, *rasa* (flavor) known through the tongue, lips, and palate (*mukha*). While in Nāgāsana, reflect on the process of seeing with the eyes, apprehending *rūpa* or form with the eyes (*akṣa*), rotating the eyes first in one direction and then the other. While in Ardha Nāgāsana, feet perpendicular to the ground, reflect on feeling or *sparśa* through the largest organ, the skin or *tvak*. While in the Sphinx Pose, bring attention to the ears or *karṇa*, the gateway to sound or *śabda*.

In the third repetition, focus in turn on the correlations between the Dhanur Pose and the lifting of the anus away from the force of gravity; in Śalabhāsana, the lifting of the genitals away from the earth; in Nāga, the power of the hands as they push against the earth; in Ardha Nāga, the legs as they push into the earth; in Sphinx, bring attention to the voice, the throat, the larynx. These motor functions allow full engagement with all aspects of the manifest world.

This sequence completes mindfulness of the twenty *tattvas* that connect the body and the world: the five gross elements of earth, water, fire, air and space; the five subtle elements that allow smelling, tasting, seeing, touch, and hearing; the five sense organs of nose, mouth, eyes, skin, and ears; and the five motor capacities of evacuating, allowing the passage of water, grasping with the hands, walking with the arms and feet, and speaking with the voice.

4.3. The Four Bhāvas of Positivity

In the *Sāṃkhya Kārikā*, Īśvarakṛṣṇa emphasizes the disposition of one's emotional outlook in the determination of experience within the world. The intellect, according to this philosopher, finds itself constituted internally, awaking, as it were, to a world inseparable from one's emotional landscape. The term for intellect, Buddhi, derives from the verb root Budh, which means "awaken". If one awakens into weakness, attachment, ignorance, and viciousness, trouble will result. In the sequence that follows, one trains to engage the reverse.

Sit up straight extending both legs to the front. Bring the right foot inside the left thigh. Reach up toward the sky and extend outward, bringing the head toward the knee and grasping the big toe or foot if possible. Move into Paścimatānāsana. Speak the positive quality (*bhāva*) that indicates empowerment, *aiśvarya*. Release both feet forward. Bring the left foot inside the right thigh. Reach upward and then bring the head toward the right knee, grasping the big toe or foot. Speak the positive quality for non-attachment, *virāga*. Bring both feet forward. Stretch upward and outward, bringing the head toward the knees, grasping the big toes or feet if possible. Speak the word for liberative knowledge, *jñāna*. Release and bring the feet out in front once more. Bring sole to sole, moving the heels toward the perineum, moving into butterfly pose, Baddha Koṇāsana. Speak the word *dharma*. These four terms indicate the positive attitudes and states of being (*bhāvas*) that can be cultivated through yogic intention: *aiśvarya*, *virāga*, *jñāna*, and *dharma*. Repeat twice more, utilizing your own phrases for each positivity. The *bhāvas* determine one's outlook and attitude, allowing ascent into higher states of awareness and, in the words of William James, moral helpfulness. Their description can be found in the *Sāṃkhya Kārikā*, 23 and 44–46.

These two practices each serve to reposition one's sense of self away from mindless repetition of past actions into their epoche or suspension and entry into a time and space of purposeful intent. In a sense, these moments and movements bring forth the sort of reversal described in the *Bhagavad Gītā*:

> The Blessed One said:
> They speak of the changeless aśvattha tree,
> its roots above, its branches below.
> Its leaves are the Vedic hymns.
> The one who knows it knows the Vedas.
> Its branches stretch below and above, nourished by the *guṇas*.
> Its sprouts are the sense objects.
> In the world of people,
> it spreads out the roots that result in action (BG 15:1–2, translated by the author).

This metaphor suggests that actions in the world can be called back into an unmanifest space, a place of silence, not unlike the process described in the second chapter of the Gītā wherein the yogi remains unruffled in the midst of change. By focusing on the elements and the interlinkage between the senses and the objects and actions of the external world, one can develop mindfulness that allows appreciation and, when needed, a skillful remove. By cultivating emotions and attitudes of positivity as recommended in the *Sāṃkhya Kārikā*, one can create predispositions that will help overcome the inevitable difficulties that arise in the course of daily life.

These two examples of an integrated, thoughtful Yoga practice, seek to link movement with higher intent. While perhaps not hard-wired into most Yoga experiences in this exact shape and form, awareness of the five elements and the concept of improving one's disposition were undoubtedly well known to the originators of modern traditions of Yoga, many of whom were mentioned earlier. A bit like the children's game of telephone, where a phrase whispered from one to another will be altered by the time it reaches the other side of the room, yes, Yoga has undergone many changes in the processes of translation and reception. However, as Andrea Jain has noted, this adaptability has been a hallmark of the Yoga tradition over the course of several centuries.[10]

Many people associate Yoga with physical flexibility and with agnosticism when it comes to things religious or philosophical. The practices of moving toward greater lightness and increased virtue emphasized in this article serve to complement the enhanced physicality and philosophical openness of Yoga practice. Not only can it make one's body limber and strong, Yoga can effect positive change in personality.

Does the fetishization of the physique benefit a rigorous Yoga practice or detract from what some might perceive to be its "pure" message and intent? Perhaps. Can obsession with form cause a destabilization of the body and emotion? Certainly. Additionally, the potential shadow side of Yoga teacher power dynamics must be acknowledged and critiqued. Amanda Lucia insightfully analyzes the ways in which a Yoga teacher can be deified, sometimes setting the stage for scandal and abuse.[11] These all too common and unfortunate occurrences violate the precepts of Yoga which are grounded in non-violence (*ahiṃsā*) and truth (*satya*). For those who adhere to the vision of Yoga that enhances

---

10 (Jain 2015).
11 (Lucia 2018).

self-worth and self-respect leading toward "the light," Yoga can be an important gateway to places of luminous encounter, philosophical insight, as well as kind and helpful actions.

5. Conclusions

This article opens and closes with the quotation of mantras, words from the Sanskrit language that establish a mood of connection. The opening verses beckon to the sun and the inner light. The paradigm of the Yogi as described in the Gītā describes a process of inner stabilization as a ground for the Yoga experience. The *Yoga Sūtra* outlines a reciprocity between the cultivation of self and one's relationship with the world. Thoughtful daily practice of Haṭha Yoga has been described here as well, through movements and intentions that connect with the elements and uplift one's attitude and mood. The combination of all these aspects of Yoga enhance the possibility of positive transformation. Yoga makes a call, a suggestion that purpose and meaning in life can be found within and without. Through stabilizing one's body, emotions, and thoughts, one can cultivate states of luminosity, insight, and helpfulness, embracing an integrated sense of religious experience.

Funding: This research received no external funding.

Acknowledgments: In this section you can acknowledge any support given which is not covered by the author contribution or funding sections. This may include administrative and technical support, or donations in kind (e.g., materials used for experiments).

Conflicts of Interest: The author declares no conflict of interest.

References

Alcott, Louisa May. 1987. *Little Women*. New York: Children's Classics, pp. 277, 342. First published 1869.

Añjali, Guräṇi. forthcoming. *Meditations through Yoga*. Amityville: Vajra Press, p. 43.

Chapple, Christopher Key. 2008. *Yoga and the Luminous: Patañjali's Spiritual Path to Freedom*. Albany: State University of New York Press, p. 138.

De Michelis, Elizabeth. 2004. *A History of Modern Yoga: Patanjali and Western Esotericism*. London and New York: Continuum.

Jain, Andrea R. 2015. *Selling Yoga: From Counterculture to Pop Culture*. New York: Oxford University Press, p. 173.

James, William. 1961. *The Varieties of Religious Experience*. London: Collier. First published 1902.

Lucia, Amanda. 2018. Guru Sex: Charisma, Proxemic Desire, and the Haptic Logics of the Guru-Disciple Relationship. *Journal of the American Academy of Religion* 86: 953–88. [CrossRef]

religions

MDPI

Article

Divine Light and Melodies Lead the Way: The Santmat Tradition of Bihar

Veena R. Howard

Department of Philosophy, California State University, Fresno, CA 93740, USA; vehoward@csufresno.edu

Received: 22 February 2019; Accepted: 20 March 2019; Published: 27 March 2019

Abstract: This paper focuses on the branch of Santmat (thus far, unstudied by scholars of Indian religions), prevalent in the rural areas of Bihar, India. Santmat—literally meaning "the Path of Sants" or "Point of View of the Sants"—of Bihar represents a unique synthesis of the elements of the Vedic traditions, rural Hindu practices, and esoteric experiences, as recorded in the poetry of the medieval Sant Tradition. I characterize this tradition as "Santmat of Bihar" to differentiate it from the other branches of Santmat. The tradition has spread to all parts of India, but its highest concentration remains in Bihar. Maharishi Mehi, a twentieth-century Sant from Bihar State, identifies Santmat's goal as *śānti*. Maharishi Mehi defines Śānti as the state of deep stillness, equilibrium, and the unity with the Divine. He considers those individuals sants who are established in this state. The state of sublime peace is equally available to all human beings, irrespective of gender, religion, ethnicity, or status. However, it requires a systematic path. Drawing on the writings of the texts of Sanātana Dharma, teachings of the Sants and personal experiences, Maharishi Mehi lays out a systematic path that encompasses the moral observances and detailed esoteric experiences. He also provides an in-depth description of the esoteric practices of divine light (*dṛṣti yoga*) and sound (*surat śabda yoga*) in the inner meditation. After providing a brief overview of the history and distinctive features of Santmat of Bihar, this paper will focus on the specifics and unique interpretations of the four structural principles of the tradition: *Guru* (spiritual teacher), *dhyān* (inner path of mediation), *satsaṅg* (spiritual discourses or congregating practitioners for meditation or study), and *sadācār* (moral conduct). Through a close analysis of textual sources, Sants' oral discourses that I translated, as well as insights from my participant-observant experiences, I will examine how the four elements reorient the practitioner from the mundane world to the sacred inner experience of *śānti*.

Keywords: Santmat; Sants; religious experience; divine light and sound; medieval Sant tradition; moral conduct; modern gurus; śānti; dhyān; guru

---

1. Introduction

Santmat—literally meaning "the Path of Sants," "Teachings of Sants," or "Views of the Sants," —is a spiritual movement, which historically began in the twelfth or thirteenth century on the Indian subcontinent[1]. Santmat of Bihar represents a unique synthesis of the elements of the Vedic traditions, rural Hindu practices, and esoteric experiences, as recorded in the poetry of the medieval Sant Tradition[2]. Maharishi Mehi, a twentieth-century Sant from Bihar State, identifies Santmat's goal as *śānti* (stillness; the ultimate peace). In his words, "Stillness or steadiness is the essence of Śānti

---

1 Even though sant and saint are often used interchangeably, they differ in meaning. The term "sant" etymologically relates to *Sat* (Truth, Divine reality). Thus, sants are those who have realized the Divine Truth in this life. The term "saint," derived from the Latin *sanctus* (sacred), is often used for those holy men and women who are canonized by the church for their piety and deep spirituality.

2 I designate this tradition as "Santmat of Bihar" to differentiate it from the other branches of Santmat. The tradition has spread to all parts of India, but its highest concentration remains in Bihar. I draw some ideas from my 2017 article,

and those who have attained Śānti are sants[3]." Like other Sant traditions originated in the medieval times, Santmat of Bihar is egalitarian in its approach. Maharishi proclaims that this state of sublime peace (inner realization of the Truth) is equally available to all human beings, irrespective of gender, religion, ethnicity, or status; however, it requires a systematic path. Drawing on the writings of the texts of Sanātana Dharma, teachings of the Sants and personal experiences, Maharishi Mehi lays out a systematic path, and provides an in-depth description of the esoteric experiences of divine light and sound that are encountered on the inner journey during meditation.

After providing a brief a historical context and distinctive features of Santmat of Bihar, this paper will focus on the specifics of the four structural principles of the tradition: *Guru* (spiritual teacher), *dhyān* (inner path of mediation), *satsaṅg* (spiritual discourses or congregating practitioners for meditation or study), and *sadācār* (moral conduct). Through a close analysis of textual sources, Sants' oral discourses that I translated, as well as insights from my participant-observant experiences, I will examine how the four elements reorient the minds of the practitioner away from the sensory desires to the sacred experience of *śānti*. In addition, the four-fold structure also helps engender a social environment that constrains exploitative conditions.

In addition to this examination of the Santmat tradition's four elements, I will explore how its monastic leaders integrate the inner path to *śānti* with societal reform, especially with respect to caste, gender, and class inequities[4]. This represents an alternative model to popular, contemporary guru-disciple traditions, which have recently allowed for situations of abuse[5]. As a participant-observer at various ashrams and events in Bihar, Uttarpradesh, Delhi, and Kolkata since the 1980s, I have witnessed how the present-day monastic leaders make the path of light and sound accessible to men and women of all walks of life, especially those from the marginalized classes. This analysis reveals how religious experiences through an inner journey are significant for personal *śānti* (peace, spiritual freedom; realization of the Divine) and is also valuable for bringing about social harmony.

2. Historical Context

The Santmat tradition can be traced to the twelfth or thirteenth century although it may be considerably older than that as lives of many prominent female and male sants can be traced back to the seventh and eighth century. Julius Lipner states:

> Before the advent of modernity, there was an influential vernacular 'movement', or more properly, a swell that attacked the privileges and discriminations of caste 'from below', that is, from a popular base among ordinary people. This has been called *Sant-Mat*, the View of the Sants or poet-saints, who became prominent in a broad arc from east to west mostly in the central and northern regions of the subcontinent from about the late thirteenth century[6].

Lipner traces the historical factors that contributed to the rise of these vernacular systems throughout Central and Northern India. Religious orthodoxy in the prevalent forms of Hinduism—built on caste, gender, and authoritative hierarchal systems—faced fierce criticism from various vernacular Sant movements. Many sects within the Sant movement share certain characteristics with each other, such as rejecting caste and gender-based hierarchy, using a vernacular medium

---

"The modern monastic Santmat movement of Bihar: building bridges between Sanātana Dharma and Sant-Mat." https://link.springer.com/article/10.1186/s40613-017-0058-8 (accessed on 1 February 2019).

3 Maharshi Mehi, *Mokṣa Darśan* (*Philosophy of Liberation*), translated by Donald and Veena Howard (Maharshi 1998, p. 7). It is now available online: https://archive.org/details/PhilosophyOfLiberationAManualOfSantMatMysticism/page/n19 (accessed on 15 February 2019).

4 Bhagat (1976) and Bronkhorst (1998) provide great historical insights into the tradition of renouncer. Maharishi Mehi's Guru (Baba Devi Sahib) never donned ochre robs, but Maharshi Mehi by virtue of his experiences and ascetic status redefined Santmat and took it to the deep villages of Bihar and Nepal.

5 In her recent article, Amanda Lucia provides a probing analysis of the issues of charisma and logics of the Guru-disciple relationship that create situations leading to sexual abuse.

6 (Lipner 2010, p. 129).

of expression, highlighting the importance of a Guru, and emphasizing one's personal religious experience. Nevertheless, these traditions are by no means "homogeneous[7]". There is a great variety of belief with regard to philosophical thought and soteriological practices. Because of this variety, the followers of each Sant (e.g., Kabir, Dadu) have distinctly identified their sects as Kabir Panth, Dadu Panth, and more.

Since the eighteenth century, the term "Santmat" has come to signify the non-sectarian institutions in Northern India that reject religious dogma and advocate the importance of a living, true guru (*sadguru*) and the inner path of Divine light and sound[8]. Historically, many of these traditions in one way or another trace their lineage to the eighteenth or nineteenth century Sant Tulsi Shaib (1763–1843), who lived in Hatharas, Uttarpradesh. The writings of Sant Tulsi Sahib, as well as various medieval Sants, points to the path of Divine light and sound by which practitioners traverse various physical and subtle regions in an inner journey aimed at the realm of the Divine—ineffable and infinite.

Even though a variety of splinter groups have emerged, such as Rādhāsoamī, Eckankar, and Kripal Singh's Ruhani Satsang, scholars have noted that the Rādhāsoamī movement "boldly proclaims itself to be the manifestation of *sant mat* (the Sant tradition)[9]." Furthermore, while Rādhāsoamī and Eckankar have been recognized as a part of the Sant tradition in textbooks on new religious movements, Santmat of Bihar, which is a parallel tradition that traces back its lineage to Sant Tulsi Shabi of Hatharas, has escaped any scholarly attention[10]. The reason behind such oversight includes (1) a lack of writings available in English translation until recently, (2) a lack of contact with Western academia due to its remote locations in the rural areas of Bihar, and (3) a lack of interest from the Santmat leadership in travelling to foreign lands.

3. Distinctive Characteristics

The twentieth-century leader of the monastic Santmat, Maharishi Mehi (1885–1986), who was born in a small Bihar village and chose a monastic life in his youth, redefined Santmat in the modern period[11]. Maharishi Mehi did intense *sādhanā* (meditation) in the caves of Kuppaghat Bhagalpur, Bihar. After emerging from his intense meditation, he spent many years researching the history and accounts of inner experiences throughout spiritual texts of the Vedas and the writings of Sants to various religious texts. From his personal experiences and research, he concluded that Santmat was not affiliated with any particular religious sect and its path could be practiced by followers of any religion, any social strata, or any gender. Maharishi Mehi presented a distinctive, organized framework for Santmat that included the following:

(1) Uniquely defining Sant, Santmat, and the goal as *śānti* (absolute peace, unity with the Divine).
(2) Identifying Santmat as Vedic Dharma (Vedic thought without fanaticism and extremism) through new commentaries on the Hindu texts.
(3) Showing resonances among the inner spiritual path of Sants, the sages of the *Upaniṣads,* and the mystical teachings of all religions.
(4) Building the structure of monastic leadership to spread the path to the most marginalized masses, which is similar to the ministry of the Buddhist Sangha.
(5) Determining the qualifications of spiritual leaders on the basis of their own spiritual accomplishments not on the bequest but the blessings of the Guru.

---

7 (Ibid., p. 130).
8 (Partridge 2004, p. 190).
9 (Juergensmeyer 1987, p. 329).
10 Some Indian scholars have done work on this branch of Santmat including advising Ph.D. thesis on the various aspects of Santmat of Bihar.
11 Maharishi Mehi's Guru, Baba Devi Sahib, was born with the blessings of Sant Tulsi Sahib and said to have said to have received blessings from him as a child.

The Rādhāsoamī tradition has set itself apart through its unique, single-lineage-based identity, which has continued for over 200 years. Santmat of Bihar has spread through monks who are initiated and blessed by the senior monks, but not necessarily are formally enshrined as the only leaders in the lineage. In fact, the tradition lacks a formal system of lineage of one single salvific figure, who holds high power[12]. Nevertheless, all monastic leaders consider Maharishi Mehi their model and yield to his spiritual power. They do not assert their own individual charisma or accomplishments, which creates a unique atmosphere for grassroots movements to spread the teachings of Santmat. Thus, the identity of the Santmat of Bihar is grounded not in a formal lineage, but in a unique spiritual vision captured by these features of Santmat of Bihar.

4. Santmat Redefined

Historically, the terms Sant and saint have been used interchangeably even though they connote distinct meanings. It is difficult to find a text that succinctly defines "Sant" and "Santmat." In his book *Mokṣa Darsana*, Maharshi Mehi provides a detailed definition:

1. *śānti* is the state of inner tranquility and equanimity [absolute inner peace, unity with the Divine][13].
2. Those recognize as Sants have experienced the inner *śānti*[14].
3. Santmat encompasses the thoughts and way (*mat*) of Sants.
4. The desire to attain *śānti* is natural in human beings. Inspired by this inherent desire, seers of ancient times searched for the inner peace and found the path to attain it. This path has been expounded in the *Upaniṣads*[15]. Similar views have been expressed by more recent *sants* such as Guru Nanak and Kabir Sahab. They expressed their views in Punjabi and Hindi vernaculars, respectively[16]. Such expressions in native languages were meant to inspire and instruct the people of all backgrounds. The teachings of these later Sants are what is referred to as Santmat[17].

A systematic elucidation of the Santmat's principles structures the theoretical foundation for the Santmat monastic movement. For Maharishi Mehi, "the Upaniṣads must be considered the foundation of Santmat because they uniquely and copiously elucidate on the means for attaining *śānti*[18]." Drawing on the later *Upaniṣads*, such as *Nādabindopaniṣad*, *Śāṇḍilyopaniṣad*, *Dhyānabindopaniṣad*, and *Yogaśikhopaniṣad*, he argues that "the Upaniṣads explain the yogic techniques and systematic

---

12 Dimitrova (2007) demonstrates how one guru of Rādhāsoamī movement sought to appropriate the concept of Sanātana Dharma.

13 *Śānti* is a Sanskrit word with several English meanings such as "peace," "tranquility," "bliss," etc. The peace that results from some degree of Divine communion is *śānti*.

14 A *sant* in the Santat tradition is one who experiences Sat (Truth), the mystical state of divine union. It is a title conferred because of yogic achievements. A saint of the Santmat tradition is one who has achieved the realization of the Divine, and, subsequently, his behavior is moral. Clearly, many Western saints also fall into the Santmat definition of saint. The words "sant" and "saint" are used interchangeably.

15 Maharishi Mehi focuses on the select *Upaniads* in order to support this thesis. In his research on yoga and the nature of *ātman* and Brahman, he cites passages from the texts, including *The Bhagavad-Gītā* and *Śvetāśvatara Upaniṣad*. For his support for the path of Divine Light and Sound, he draws on the later *Upaniads*, including from *Nāda Bindu Upaniṣads, Dhyānabindu Upaniad*, and *Śāilyopaniad*. He does not concern himself with the academic debates on the authority and authenticity of the earlier *Upaniads*.

16 The seers of the *Upaniṣads* wrote in the Sanskrit language, which is not a language of the common people. According to Maharishi Mehi, Guru Nanak and Kabir Sahib elucidate the same Upaniṣadic wisdom in vernacular, regional languages understood by common people.

17 Maharshi Mehi, *Mokṣa Darśan* (*Philosophy of Liberation*), translated by Donald and Veena Howard (Maharshi 1998, p. 7). It is now available online: https://archive.org/details/PhilosophyOfLiberationAManualOfSantMatMysticism/page/n19 (accessed on 15 February 2019).

18 Maharshi (1998, p. 8). https://archive.org/details/PhilosophyOfLiberationAManualOfSantMatMysticism/page/n19.

views of transcending mind and attaining the Absolute through the path of Divine Sound (Yoga of *Surat-Śabd*)[19]." This move was to create a bridge between the Vedic wisdom and Sant teachings.

Not only does Maharishi Mehi locate the path of Santmat in the Vedānta literature, but he also establishes the underlying unity among the teachings of the Sants, saying:

> Often the teachings of various Sants would, on the surface, seem contradictory to each other or even contradictory to the principles of the Upaniṣads. However, there is an unbreakable unity in the spiritual path of all Sants and Sages. These variations are due to the fact that different times and in different regions Sants appear, and their followers name their tradition after the particular sant [and formulate the teachings in regional dialects][20].

According to Maharishi Mehi, the apparent differences among the Sant teachings can be attributed to the variation of regional languages and traditions. By virtue of his renunciate stature, Maharishi Mehi accepted the inner mystical truths elaborated in the texts of Sanātana Dharma while rejecting religious factionalism and extremism. Furthermore, through his careful commentaries, including *Ved Darśan Yoga* (the Philosophy of Vedas), *Śri Gītā Yoga Prakāś* (the Light of Gītā Yoga), and *Rāmcarit Mānas Sar Satīk* (The Essence of *Rāmcarit Mānas*), he sought to render the essence of these texts consistent with the principles of Santmat[21]. Most importantly, Maharishi Mehi's insights are accessible to all since Santmat of Bihar is inclusive of the non-literate religious vernaculars.

He emphasized the harmony among all religions on the basis of his personal experiences of the divine light and celestial sounds that are found in the religious writings across traditions. While his argument and deductive reasoning can appear to be an effort to create some kind of uniformity among the teachings of various Sants, Maharishi Mehi invited his followers and opponents alike to experience this truth through which factionalism fades way. Simultaneously, he recognized the differences of external practices, but emphasized the shared experiences of divine light and sound. He also drew attention to the common beliefs of the necessity of a qualified master (Guru) and observing moral conduct for treading the inner path. This is the reason he preferred the inclusive term "Santmat," instead of adopting a specific name as Rādhāsoamī or Eckankar.

Since Maharishi Mehi's passing in 1986, many monks have continued to produce literature and impart the teachings of Santmat in various regions of India. Numerous accomplished monks who were initiated by Maharishi Mehi have spread the teachings to different regions of Bihar, West Bengal, Punjab, Jammu & Kashmir, Gujarat, Nepal, and Uttarpradesh. Maharishi Mehi travelled to these regions and currently other monks spread the teachings of Sanmat in different areas. I have visited at least five different regions where Santmat's leaders have established ashrams to continue the teaching of Santmat. Despite various subgroups within Santmat of Bihar, they are consistent in abiding by the four essential principles of Santmat, as developed by Maharishi Mehi for progressing on the path to *śānti*.

5. The Four Principles: A Structure for Supporting the Path to *Śanti*

Maharishi Mehi maintained that all humans, irrespective of their religion, gender, class, or caste, can traverse the path of inner spiritual regions and attain *śānti*, which is a declaration that was made after he deeply studied sacred texts from different traditions and had his personal inner journey to the inner realms. Similar to the compositions of Kabir and Nanak, he documents his experiences in his poetry. He systematically organized Santmat's philosophy and path in numerous texts and voluminous

---

19 *Surat Śabda* (the Yoga of Divine Sound) is the practice of transcending the mind and entering the level beyond the mind, the level of Oneness. The vehicle for this inward journey is Sound. The way to employ Sound and to understand its use is the practical application of *Surat Śabda Yoga*. This is also known as *Nādānusandāna* (lit., "search of the divine sound").

20 (Maharshi 1998, pp. 7–8). For example, even though Sant Kabir was non-sectarian, his tradition is named as Kabir Panth and Guru Nanak's teachings eventually led to the formation of Sikh Dharma (Sikhism).

21 In his article, "The Bridge between Hindu Scriptures and Santmat," Pravesh Singh demonstrates how Maharishi Mehi builds bridge between Hindu scriptures and Santmat (Singh 2013).

transcribed lectures. In the last 14 years, I have translated three books of different Santmat Gurus, but most of the texts and oral teachings recorded in the monthly periodicals remain untranslated. By analyzing the translated texts and oral teachings, I will examine each of the four elements that serves as scaffolding for ascending the inner path to the Divine: *guru*, *dhyān*, *satsaṅg*, and *sadācār*[22].

Santmat of Bihar shares some of the elements with the Rādhāsoamī and other Sant traditions, but provides a unique interpretation of each. For example, in explaining the importance of the spiritual guru, Maharishi Mehi quotes various Hindu texts and synthesizes Sant and Vedic wisdom. Instead of rejecting the scriptures of Sanātana Dharma, Santmat's leadership of *sannyāsīs* show that all of these principles exist in the texts of Vedic Dharma, including the *Upanisads*, *Rāmāyaṇa*, and the *Bhagavad-Gītā*. Furthermore, Santmat of Bihar uses vernacular language to make these principles accessible to people who are steeped in the myths of Hindu religiosity. I show how these principles are reconstructed to include the tribal and people from the rural areas of Bihar, Uttarpradesh, and Nepal, which are areas that culturally and religiously relate to vernacular Hindu religiosities.

5.1. Guru

All branches of Santmat recognize the necessity of a living guru (literally "dispeller of ignorance") and many subgroups continue the tradition of transferring the guru's legacy to their disciple. Scholars[23] have analyzed historical, religious, and social reasons for the consolidation of the guru's power from the medieval period to contemporary times. The tradition of the guru-disciple can be traced back to the instances of such a relationship in the *Upaniṣads*, the *Ramāyāṇa*, and the *Mahābhārata*. In the *Bhagavad-Gītā*, Lord Kṛṣṣṇa does not use the word "guru," but alludes to the giver of knowledge.

> Learn the truth through humble submission, through inquiry, and through service. The wise one, who has realized the truth, will impart the knowledge unto you (4:34).

Many references in the *Upaniṣads* liken an enlightened Guru to Brahmā, Viṣṇnu, and Śiva. *Upaniṣads*, *Tantras*, Pūrāṇna, and the writings of Sant traditions emphasize the importance of a realized Guru on the inner path.

Most writings of Sant traditions do not cite Vedic or Hindu texts on the importance of Guru. They only refer to the writings of the medieval gurus like Kabir, Palatu, and Dadu. The tradition of Guru-disciple relationship continues to this day. Most Hindus look to blessings and guidance from holy men and women. In her recent article, Amanda Lucia analyzes the conditions that spawn abusive actions by modern gurus. She lays out the historical facts surrounding guru worship in the Indian context: "Devotion to living persons who are believed to have special wisdom and power has existed in India since antiquity[24]." Drawing on her ethnographic experiences, she provides a probing analysis of the "structural aspects" (including devotees' longing for proximity to their guru) of sexual abuse by "headline stealing hyper-gurus." Furthermore, she investigates how devotees' desire to experience the gurus' charisma and radiance and "the authoritarian power relationship between guru and disciple create social situations that are readied forums for sexual abuse[25]."

Notwithstanding the scintillating stories of the modern gurus, Santmat has embraced the tradition of a sanctified guru-disciple relationship. However, it makes a clear distinction between the outer power (charisma) and the inner power (experience of light and sound). Likewise, the writings of Santmat emphasize the *nirguṇa* (attribute-less) form of the Divine but does not reject *saguṇa bhakti* (visualization on the form of *guru*) to reach the *nirguṇa*. The inner, radiant form of the guru is the

---

22 In his research on the modern Rādhāsoamī movement, Mark Juergensmeyer (1987) shows its connections between the teachings of Sants like Kabir, Dadu, and Nanak, but, at the same time, he calls attention to its unique elements, including "the inner path of spirituality," "necessity of Guru," and "the fellowship of Satsaṅg." See Juergensmeyer (1987, pp. 329–55).

23 For example, Gold (1987); Juergensmeyer (1987); and Lucia (2018).

24 (Lucia 2018, p. 956).

25 (Ibid., 953).

focus of meditation. My observations and conversations with the gurus in the Santmat of Bihar reveal that the tradition cautions against conditions that might prompt physical or emotional abuse, while emphasizing the necessity of an accomplished guide on the inner path.

Maharishi Santsevi, a close disciple of Maharishi Mehi, writes:

> The spiritual teacher gives knowledge of the Self, reveals the true form of the Divine, and, thus, brings blessing into our lives. Therefore, the seeker of spiritual knowledge must ... seek a true spiritual guru[26].

By emphasizing that a true guru is not merely a human body, Maharishi Mehi preempts any attachment to the bodily charisma of the guru. He also differentiates between qualified and unqualified gurus when he quotes Sant Kabir: "The Guru is a manifestation of wisdom, and an aspirant should acquire this knowledge. Without the understanding of true knowledge and moral principles, there is neither a guru nor the true seeker[27]." Many Sants, including Tulsidas, Guru Nanak Dev, and Kabir sing praises of the Satguru who has experienced the Truth (*sat*). Maharishi Santsevi, who is an esteemed teacher of Santmat, quotes Saint Sundar Das who sees the guru as the purifier of worldly entanglements.

> By the grace of the Guru, our intelligence is refined and purified, and by the grace of the Guru, the sorrows of this world are removed.
>
> By the creation of God, the soul descends [into the web of this world]. However, by the teachings of the Guru, the same soul is liberated from the net of illusion and death (Yama)[28].

Santmat emphasizes that seekers must reject those spiritual leaders who lack stringent moral disciplines and warns against those gurus who mislead the practitioners by generating illusory experiences of light and sound through external means. A Guru must be a realized human being who is able to guide the followers on the inner path of light and sound. Swami Vyasanand provides examples below.

> Some even use computer generated images of various colors and stars in order to experience the Divine light. Some play music in order to focus on the Divine sound ... These kinds of practices and experiences are illusory, taught by misguided *gurus* who themselves do not know the inner path of light and sound ... Consequently, the seekers face obstacles on the path of Truth[29].

Moreover, a true Guru is compassionate and dedicated to the well-being of the society and rejects social evils that are sources of communal strife and personal anguish.

Monastic and lay followers of Santmat of Bihar consider Maharishi Mehi as a role model for the devotees. After returning from deep states of meditation in the 1930s, Maharishi Mehi dedicated himself to teaching the most marginalized groups in Bihar and sought to confront caste-based oppression and gender discrimination. He proclaimed that all human beings can tread the path of light and sound, and he threw open the gates of esoteric and guarded teachings to all by initiating hundreds of people in one sitting. The Guru's role is not simply a conduit to initiate the seeker into the path of *śānti*, which Sants have often emphasized. It was also to bring outer *śānti* (peace), social harmony. Maharishi Mehi, however, cautioned against only doing works of social service without a diligent focus on the inner path.

---

26 (Maharishi 2008, p. 322).
27 (Ibid., pp. 322–23).
28 Ibid., p. 327)
29 (Swami Vyasanand 2016).

5.2. *Dhyān (Meditation)*

Santmat offers a systematic path to self-realization and absolute inner peace through *dhyāna* (meditation). The specifics of the path and the markers of experiences of the Divine light are provided in detail, which begins with *ekāgṛ dhyān* (one-pointed focus). The path is consistent with the Yoga practice as elaborated by Patañjali, who emphasizes the practice of *ekāgratā* (concentration) for controlling the mind as "Yoga practice begins with *ekāgratā*, which dams the mental stream[30]." Santmat Gurus initiate the seekers into precise methods to cultivate one-pointed concentration to experience inner Divine light and sound. Santmat's path of yoga begins with efforts in concentration and culminates in deep focus.

According to the teachings of Sants, the inner path cannot be realized through the nine gates of the body (i.e., through the sensory organs) but only through the tenth gate (i.e., the third eye or the spiritual eye). The actual journey requires a broader and more detailed instruction in the stages of meditative experiences. Maharishi Mehi says: "Three covers of darkness, light, and sound encumber the soul. We need to lift this veil to have the vision of the Divine[31]." Thus, Santmat is often referred to as the path of Divine light and sound because both of these phenomenal elements serve as landmarks of inner experiences that culminate in the realization of the ultimate peace and union with the divine.

Swami Vyasanand who is one of the contemporary teachers of Santmat elaborates on the process of religious experiences of light and sound encountered by the practitioner.

> Initially, when practitioners close their eyes, the darkness is seen within. Then, after some time of diligent meditation practice, the light emerges. At that time, the practitioner experiences light that is similar to the sparks of light emerging from the rubbing of two stones. When the practitioner begins to focus for longer periods, then he experiences the light similar to that of lightning flashes amid the dark rain clouds. Then, the vision will be concentrated on this light bindu. At this juncture, the gaze through the power of increased concentration will transform into a very fine needle-like point. In addition, through the light bindu (the tenth gate), the practitioner enters into the realm of light. The experience of divine light in the meditation brings joy, and the progress then becomes rapid. Consequently, one's faith and conviction become stronger[32].

When a spiritual seeker sits in meditation, he/she makes an ascending journey, rising from the *Ājñā Cakra* (variously termed as the divine gate, third eye, *divya cakṣu, tīsrā til, dasham dwār, śiv netra, trinetra,* etc.) into the region of the thousand-petalled lotus, or the *Sahasrāra*. Maharshi Raman calls the third eye "the *Agni Cakra*." This is the place where the channels of *Iḍā* and *Piṅgala* converge. In this case, the subtle light-point begins to emerge. Ascending further, when entry is made into the *Trikuṭī*, the inner Sun becomes visible by seeing that the seeker acquires the supernatural or the divine vision in order to be able to see all the three worlds. Maharishi Santsevi uniquely shows a path of light and sound in the *Upaniṣads*. He quotes Yogashikhopanisad (6.6).

> The *īḍā nāḍi* is on the left and *piṅglā nāḍi* is on the right. One who focuses at the center of these two [on the *suṣmṇa*] is the true knower of the Vedas [divine knowledge][33].

The teachers of Santmat show resonance between the *Dhyāna* practice of focusing on the *suṣmṇa* and the concentration on the third eye (*tīsrā til*), as elaborated by various Sants. The experience of Divine light leads to the divine sound or melody, which, in turn, leads to the state beyond any sound and form, which is the formless state of Truth. Various Sants elaborate on the alluring nature of the

30 (Eliade 2009, p. 48).
31 (Swami Vyasanand 2016).
32 (Ibid., 2016).
33 (Maharishi 2008, p. 344).

divine melodies. In Sant Kabir's words, "The five kinds of sounds reverberate within, and thirty-six kind of divine melodies are also found within[34]." When the practitioner experiences various aspects of the light realm, consciousness initially is not drawn toward the divine sound due to its attraction to the light. In the higher light realms, the bright light of the sun destroys the residue of impurities of the mind. Purity (*sattva*) pervades the consciousness and *rajas* completely vanishes.

It is, at this time, that the scenes of the light realm that form the reality of name and form begin to fade, and merge into the formless. The divine melody of the formless realm becomes increasingly powerful, to the degree that, even though the experience of divine light subsists, the consciousness current (*surat*) does not become distracted. Similar accounts are given by both medieval and modern Sants, including in the Rādhāsoamī Sant tradition. Mark Juergensmeyer writes: "In the theology of the movement, the eternal essence of God resides in the form of pure energy: light and sound of matchless and incredible purity[35]." Admittedly, there are resonances among Rādhāsoamī writings and the teachings of the Santmat of Bihar, but Maharishi Mehi uniquely organized the stages of the path and provided markers for the inward journey, which he also illustrated in a chart of the inner region[36].

Over the last two decades, I have observed that this esoteric path, despite its subtleties, is not imparted only to a select few, nor are the experiences of light and sound limited to monastics. The modern monks impart the teaching to all people, male and female, irrespective of their status and caste, who seek guidance, especially to those in rural areas of Bihar. Furthermore, the gurus of the tradition hold week-long or month-long meditation retreats where hundreds of practitioners gather to meditate five times a day for one-hour sessions, beginning at three in the morning[37]. At one recent retreat in Prayag at the Kumbh Mela, along with the daily meditations, the Guru mantra was recited twenty-four hours each day for one month. The devotees took turns in unceasingly reciting the mantra out-loud. Such ceaseless chanting is the ritual of continuous chanting of Śiva mantra or reading of the *Rāmāyaṇa*. These retreats place great emphasis on inner experiences and such a regimented, intensive schedule helps the practitioner to tread the path of Divine light and sound.

The practitioners are instructed to disclose their experiences only with the Guru and seek further guidance on the path. In the exuberance of joy, however, some devotees share their experiences with other devotees. One female informant attended a week's long meditation retreat in a Bihar. She told me in 2005 that she sat in meditation each day for several hours. Her concentration deepened and she began to see flashes of light with beautiful colors. As she continued, her experiences generated great joy and bliss. She shared her experience with the Guru who affirmed the validity of her experiences. She was so entranced by these experiences that she desired longer time in meditation, which was unusual for her. Even after returning home from the retreat, she continued to experience the light while in meditation and feelings of joyfulness in her daily activities. The reports of such experiences generate enthusiasm in the hearts of seekers when they relate them to others. Such reports indicate that *dhyān* yields the results promised by the initiation into the path of light and sound. To make progress on the path, Santmat underscores the company of other truth-seekers, known as *satsaṅg*.

5.3. *Satsaṅg*

Satsaṅg is an essential component of all branches of Santmat. The term *satsaṅg* is the compound of two words: *sat* and *sang*, meaning "association with the Truth" or "association with the Sants" (who have realized the ultimate Truth). Although the term *satsaṅg* is used generically for a sacred gathering,

---

34 Sant Kabir variously speaks about the divine melodies: "The five-sounded melody keeps reverberating and my soul is ever attracted by It as a Sarang is ever after water." O the Formless One beyond all knowledge! I worship thee with all my heart." https://www.ruhanisatsangusa.org/naam/naam_shabd5.htm (accessed on 1 February 2019).

35 (Juergensmeyer 1987, p. 339).

36 https://www.speakingtree.in/blog/inner-cosmic-chart-as-sketched-by-maharshi-mehi-paramhans (accessed on 15 February 2019).

37 The practitioners come from different regions. This is evident from the language they speak, which include Hindi, Bihari, Nepali, Avadhi, Nepalese, Bengali, Marwari, Gharvali, and many others. Usually teachers give discourses in Hindi or Bihari.

Maharishi Mehi uniquely stratifies it into the two categories of inner and outer. First, the inner *satsaṅg* refers to association or coming into contact with *Sat* (truth) or the divine. This is the highest form of *satsaṅg*, and it connotes the deep state of meditation in which consciousness unites with the divine. It is a state beyond senses because only the soul or consciousness is capable of merging with the divine. "True *satsaṅg* is the unity of the soul with the Supreme Truth[38]." However, this highest kind of *satsaṅg*, unity with the Divine, does not occur suddenly. It requires many lifetimes of good actions resulting in good *saṃskāras* (spiritual imprints and tendencies). The second kind of *satsaṅg* signifies "association with the Sants or truth seekers." Various medieval Sants elucidate this further. For example, Sant Tulsidas Ji emphasizes the association with the saints in realizing the divine: "The association of the saints brings association with the divine, and alliance with people who are engrossed in the world leads the way back to this world again and again[39]."

The monastics and lay followers participate in weekly and annual gatherings of followers. I provide a glimpse of the nature of *satsaṅg* through my own experience in Bhagalpur, Bihar. The guru, who is a monk in ochre robes, sat on a stage with other *sādhus*, and gave the audience (*darśan*) to the followers who sat on the ground. Most followers, who were illiterate, came by foot, bullock-carts, bicycles, or any other vehicles from the nearby rural areas. The gathering consisted of monks and lay men and women of various strata of Hindu society, from both urban and rural areas. The discourse primarily focused on the importance of the right conduct for the inner esoteric path of meditation. They were strewn with stories from the *Rāmāyaṇa* and the medieval and contemporary Sants' lives. I was told that the tribal and rural people, who were initiated into the teachings of Santmat, used to perform animal sacrifices and consume intoxicating substances. But now, having been initiated into Santmat, they have become vegetarian and have stopped the tribal traditions of sacrifice and consumption of alcohol, and *bidis* (homemade cigarettes). In a recent (14 March 2019) OPED piece, Promod Mishra shares his encounters with a senior monk of Santmat in Nepal. He highlights the egalitarian and inclusive nature of *satsaṅg* of Santmat of Bihar[40]. Although the monks have chosen to live separately from society by virtue of his monastic lifestyle, they travel from village to village to offer teachings and guidance to all who wish to study and learn. Santmat of Bihar does not ask its followers to stop their own Hindu, Sikh, or other rural religiosities, but, instead, teaches the incorporation of Santmat's teachings in the daily lifestyle.

Most rural devotees do not even speak Hindi, only regional languages. They sing *bhajans* (sacred songs) in Hindi and regional dialects. Most Indian religious ceremonies often include the ritual of *ārtī* by lighting lamps and burning incense. Santmat of Bihar's *ārtī* does not incorporate the more typical *pūjā* paraphernalia of lamp and incense, but, rather, is a devotional song in which the symbolic offering of the *pūjā* is recited together to culminate a *satsaṅg*. Symbolic representation of the ritual satisfies the tradition of ceremonious performance. At the same time, it invites the followers to remember the inner spiritual states represented by the outer ritual. The devotees of Santmat, many of whom come from rural areas and have no formal education, have memorized the *ārtī* and sing it every morning and evening as a part of the daily worship.

> Perform ārtī in the body-temple ।
> Be still and the two rays of sight to meet in the mid-eyebrows ।।1।।
> An immensely illuminated point shines there ।
> Behold the Divine Light incomparable ।2।।
> Many celestial planes flash within ।
> Behold and then move ahead ।।3।।

---

38 (Maharishi 2008, pp. 322–23).
39 Ibid., p. 317.
40 Mishra, Pramod. "Practice What You Preach." Kathamandu Post, March 14, 2019. http://kathmandupost.ekantipur.com/news/2019-03-14/practice-what-you-preach.html (accessed on 18 March 2019).

More simple is the Yoga of Inner Sound ।
Practice it to clasp the Divine Sound ।।4।।
Such technique takes beyond the fort of bodies ।
Destroys worldly illusion and maladies ।।5।।
This sublime ārtī shatters the delusions of duality ।
Perform, O Mehi, and drink the elixir of immortality ।।6।।[41]

The public chanting of *ārtī* summons the devotees to tread the path of the divine light and sound, but they are asked to keep secret their individual inner experiences. This ritual practice occurs both in morning and evening in each āśram founded on the philosophy of Maharishi Mehi. In this practice, the Hindu religious sensibilities are transformed into esoteric experience through the recitation. Maharishi Mehi also composed a compendium of verses *Padavali*—a litany of supplications, warnings, and inner experiences—which are evocative of medieval *sant* poetry. Men and women sing these verses in melodious tunes during communal *satsaṅg* and in their daily practice. In the current age of social media, many young male and female followers use the digital media to share their recordings of these songs (bhajans).

Daily and weekly *satsaṅg*s are held in the local ashrams or in the followers' homes. I was told by one of the current leaders that there are about 1000 ashrams of Santmat of Bihar all over India, primarily in rural areas. Both monks and laity of all castes, genders, and social status equally participate in *satsaṅg* and *dhyān*. The *sādhu*'s monastic lifestyle and the locale of the ashram community form "communitas" to use Turner's (1995) language, which transcends the socially imposed structures of caste and gender. Turner says,

> This comradeship transcends distinctions of race, age, kinship position, and, in some kinds of cultic group, even of sex[42].

Furthermore, Santmat's monastic leaders negotiate the customs of Hinduism by providing esoteric interpretations of rituals and customs. This helps them guide the followers to the highest state of truth, while simultaneously defying the deceptive social fragmentations of caste and gender inequities. The tradition also seeks to strengthen the moral backbone of the seekers and society through precise instructions of ethical conduct.

5.4. *Sadācār*

Sadācār, which means "moral conduct," is considered essential to the journey on the path of light and sound. The gurus of Santmat give specific instruction on conduct for embarking on the inner path[43]. Despite some variations, the five restraints prescribed by Santmat broadly correspond to the five Yamas (Yogic restraints) and Pañc Śīla (Five Ethical precepts) of Buddhism, which are oriented to purify the seekers' conduct and prepare them for the path[44]. The monastic leaders of Santmat of Bihar draw on the teachings of various Sants who deem moral conduct as a necessary precondition for the inward path. Guru Nanak Dev Maharaj stresses the need for purifying the body and mind: "It is only in a pure, clean vessel that truth can stay. Those who lead a pure (moral) life are rare. I seek refuge in God: Lord, merge my essence into your Supreme Essence[45]!"

---

[41] Maharishi Mehi, Maharishi Mehi Padavali (Verses of Maharishi Mehi). Translation is my own. Maharshi Mehi Padavali's translation has not been published. The verses are written in Bihari vernacular, but they also include words from Hindi and Sanskrit.

[42] Turner (1995, p. 100).

[43] The initiates are asked to abstain from five vices: lying, stealing, use of intoxicating substance, violence, and sexual misconduct. The practitioner also takes the vow of observing vegetarian lifestyle.

[44] The five prohibitions are similar to those in the Yoga, Buddhist, and Jain traditions. There are some differences in all three. For example, Yogic and Jain vow to avoid greed and Buddhist disciplines and will abstain from intoxication. Often abstaining from killing also includes not consuming an animal diet.

[45] (Maharishi 2008, p. 329).

In his lectures, Maharishi Santsevi compared an immoral mind and body to a heap of dirt or waste and advised mental and physical self-control. He quotes the *Kaṭha Upaniṣad* below.

> The one who has not abstained from sinful acts, whose senses are not in control, and whose mind is not serene cannot attain the Supreme Reality by the practice of self-realization[46].

With these views in mind, Maharishi Mehi as a renouncer, incorporated morality into the initiation by creating a mandate for five vows: abstaining from lying, stealing, intoxication, violence, and adultery. Louis Dumont observes that in Indian religion renouncer has been a "creator of values[47]." Maharishi Mehi argued for the value of moral vows in religious, social, and political contexts. The initiated individuals who commit to these prohibitions report transformation in their personal and social lives. Maharishi Mehi once proclaimed: "If we are able to rid ourselves of these five sins, then how could other sins trouble us?" It implies that these five vows protect the seekers from various immoral actions.

Santmat of Bihar includes a vegetarian lifestyle as part of abstaining from violence. In Maharishi Santsevi's words,

> The saints have addressed the sin of violence with particular attention to the foods that are eaten. Foods produced by killing living beings, as well as foods that are not pure and fresh, are considered tamasic (causing inertia). Consumption of these types of foods is prohibited by the teachings of the saints[48].

Animal products such as meat, fish, and eggs are said to inhibit the clarity of the mind and the health of the body. There is an old saying: "Whatever kind of food we take in, its properties will also fill our mind[49]." Through my conversations with the devotees, I learned that the seekers are asked to follow a vegetarian diet and abstain from any intoxicating substances for at least six months before their initiation into the path of light and sound. Such restrictions ensure the seeker's commitment to the ethical lifestyle prerequisite for the inward journey.

A firm emphasis on morality and rules to circumscribe physical contact between the monastic and the lay community also obviate the possibility of corruption. Such restrictions prevent immoral conduct and scandalous episodes that make the headlines. Maharishi Mehi not only gave precise instructions for moral conduct, but he also provided stringent restrictions on the display of supernatural powers. He affirmed that the progress on the inward path also yields supernatural powers to the practitioner. Many hagiographic accounts of medieval Sants and the Sants of Rādhāsoamī also attest to such accomplishments. However, Maharishi Mehi warned against any display or misuse of religious experience or accomplishments. He prohibited any display of *siddhis* (supernatural powers) and prescribed even more strict rules for the monks, including avoiding any personal contact with the followers for imparting *śakti* and paying close attention to all five vows. In one of his talks, Maharishi Mehi related his conversation with a newcomer who asked whether he had the power to make miracles. He responded with great serenity: "In our tradition, we make the miracle of morality." Scholars and supporters alike bemoan the fact that many gurus boast miracles, but lack morality, which is a crucial component to tread the spiritual path. Sanmat of Bihar addresses the issues of social reform by integrating it with personal spiritual progress.

6. Santmat: Linking Personal Spiritual Development with Social Reform

The monastic movement Santmat of Bihar uniquely connects inner *Śānti* with outer peace and harmony. Many Santmat monks travel to rural and tribal areas of Bihar, Uttarpradesh, and Nepal to

46 (Maharishi 2008, p. 330).
47 In Howard (2013, p. 134)
48 (Maharishi 2008, p. 329).
49 Ibid., p. 330.

teach the inner path to the people who lack adequate means to travel. Many of these communities have traditionally been immersed in orthodox customs of caste-based purity laws, gender biases, and even the performance of animal sacrifices due to the fear of deities. Many followers report the transformation after being initiated by the gurus. The renouncer gurus address both the spiritual and social well-being of their followers. The renunciate Santmat leaders' active involvement with social reform differs from the lifestyle of traditional renouncers of India's religious traditions[50]. In India's pre-colonial past, although the renouncer was viewed as the catalyst for the progression of new ideas, conventionally a *mahātmā* or *sādhu* was typically identified by his renunciation of worldly ties in the pursuit of ultimate freedom (*mokṣa*). This is the predominant vision of renouncers endorsed by many colonial writings and, to a large extent, featured in Brahmanical textual models of *sannyāsa* (cf. DeNapoli 2014a, 2014b). However, renouncer-monastics like Maharishi Mehi, and those within his lineage, challenge this simplistic and detached view of *sannyāsa*, which is consistent with the twentieth-century model of engaged spirituality.

During the twentieth century (in which Maharishi Mehi assumed leadership of Santmat), religious and Indian religious and social reformers, including Swami Vivekananda and Mahatma Gandhi, disapproved of the world-denying philosophy (*nivṛtti*), so visibly represented by *sādhus* and *sannyāsīs*, for India's colonization. As John Campbell Oman has argued: "It is largely due to the subtle effects of the spirit of *sadhuism* upon the character of the people of India that the country is so easily governed by a handful of foreign officials and a few thousand white soldiers[51]." The outsiders' colonial dominance and critiques of Indian culture and religious life engendered critical discourse among elite native Indians "toward their own traditions[52]." Eventually, according to Kirin Narayan, he indigenous response to foreign criticism during the colonial era led to a reinterpretation of the value of renunciation and a revolution in the role of the *sādhus*, which "usher[ed] in the image of the socially involved renouncer[53]." Swami Vivekananada proclaimed, "Love and charity for the whole human race, that's the test of true religiousness[54]." Maharishi Mehi was moved by the suffering of the rural people, especially from lower social and economic strata, who did not have access to any spiritual path. Throughout this life, he travelled to the deep villages to deliver the path of light and sound to the common people.

Mahatma Gandhi, contemporary of Maharishi Mehi, appealed to *sādhus* to become more engaged in society. Although uniquely monastic, the concern for the total well-being of the followers is the hallmark of Santmat. Therefore, Maharshi Mehi emphasized self-supporting (living by one's own earning), socially concerned industrious followers. By virtue of its unique monastic leadership, Santmat of Bihar negotiates both the acceptance of select ideologies of the Vedic Dharma and the rejection of religious factionalism and extremism. Most importantly, it includes the non-literate religious vernaculars. Additionally, it openly accepts all, regardless of caste, creed, sex, or even nationality. Notably, despite large female followers, only male monastics held roles of leadership. However, more recently, I have observed female monastic groups emerge that have been supported by male leaders. Perhaps this the final step in leveling the playing field between genders.

In conclusion, Santmat of Bihar encompasses a systematic inward path with specific landmarks for the religious experience. Even though spontaneous euphoric states or sudden experiences are seldom reported, the tradition details that Divine light and sound are the vehicles to reach the door of *śānti* (Divine Union). Unlike other branches of Santmat, Santmat of Bihar traces the path to the *Upaniṣads* while drawing inspiration from the Sants of the medieval times. Through his native Bihar poetic vernacular, Maharishi Mehi illustrates the stages and experiences on the path. The four-fold structure of the path guides the followers on the inward path to *śānti* and guards them from immorality

---

50 In his ethnographic study, (Gross [1992] 2001) seeks to understand the persistent tradition of asceticism in India.
51 (Oman 1903, p. 275).
52 Ibid.
53 Quoted from Howard (2013, pp. 134–35).
54 In her book, *Political Philosophy of Swami Vivekananda*, Kalpana Mohapatra quotes Swami Vivekananda emphasizing his views of incorporating religion in all aspects of life (Mohapatra 1996, p. 48).

and the allures of *siddhi*. Furthermore, the walls of moral conduct (e.g., vows of not lying, stealing, killing, sexual misconduct, and avoiding intoxicating substances) and Santmat's egalitarian philosophy offer a promise for a harmonious and just society. The goal is *śānti* not *siddhi*. The one who attains the experience of *śānti* is the Sant, proclaims Maharishi Mehi. The other objectives lead the soul astray into the deeper darkness of immorality (even though the light of popular media now shines on the defectors). However, the religious experience of divine light and sound both leads to inner *śānti* and shines the light of truth and justice.

Funding: This research received no external funding.

Conflicts of Interest: The author declares no conflict of interest.

References

Bhagat, M. G. 1976. *Ancient Indian Asceticism*. New Delhi: Motilal Banarsidass.

Bronkhorst, Johannes. 1998. *Two Sources on Indian Asceticism*. Delhi: Motilal Banarsidass.

DeNapoli, Antoinette. 2014a. Our own two hands create our destiny: Narrative strategies and patterns in male sadhus' stories. *Contributions to Indian Sociology* 48: 333–56. [CrossRef]

DeNapoli, Antoinette. 2014b. *Real Sadhus Sing to God: Gender, Asceticism, and Vernacular Religion in Rajasthan*. Oxford: Oxford University Press.

Dimitrova, Diana. 2007. The development of Sanatana Dharma in the twentieth century. *International Journal of Dharma Studies* 11: 89–98.

Eliade, Mircea. 2009. *Yoga: Immortality and Freedom*. Princeton: Princeton University Press.

Gold, Daniel. 1987. Clan and lineage among the Sants: Seeds, service, substance. In *The Sants: Studies in a Devotional Tradition of India*. Edited by Katherine Schomer and William Hewat McLeod. Berkeley: Berkeley Religious Studies Series, pp. 305–28.

Gross, Robert L. 2001. *The Sadhus of India: A Study of Hindu Asceticism*. Jaipur: Rawat Publications. First published 1992.

Howard, Veena. 2013. *Gandhi's Ascetic Activism: Renunciation and Social Action*. New York: State University of New York Press.

Juergensmeyer, Mark. 1987. The Radhasoami revival of the Sant tradition. In *The Sants: Studies in a Devotional Tradition of India*. Edited by Katherine Schomer and William Hewat McLeod. Berkeley: Berkeley Religious Studies Series, pp. 338–42.

Lipner, Julius. 2010. *Hindus: Their Religious Beliefs and Practices*, 2nd ed. New York: Routledge.

Lucia, Amanda. 2018. Guru Sex: Charisma, Proxemic Desire, and the Haptic Logics of the Guru-Disciple Relationship. *Journal of the American Academy of Religion* 86: 953–88. [CrossRef]

Maharishi, Santsevi. 2008. The Harmony of all Religions. p. 322. Available online: http://www.spiritualawakeningradio.com/Harmony12-ChapterSeven-santmat.pdf (accessed on 22 March 2019).

Maharshi, Mehi. 1998. *Mokṣa-Darśan. The Philosophy of Liberation*. Translated by Don, and Veena Howard. Santmat Society of North America: Available online: https://archive.org/details/PhilosophyOfLiberationAManualOfSantMatMysticism/page/n19 (accessed on 21 March2019).

Mohapatra, Kalpana. 1996. *Political Philosophy of Vivekananda*. New Delhi: Northern Book Center.

Oman, John Campbell. 1903. *The Mystics, Ascetics, and Saints of India: A Study of Sadhuism, with an Account of the Yogis, Sanyasis, Bairagis, and Other Strange Hindu Sectarians*. London: T.F. Unwin.

Partridge, Christopher. 2004. *New Religions: A Guide*. Oxford: Oxford University Press.

Singh, Pravesh K. 2013. The Bridge between Hindu Scriptures and Santmat. Available online: https://medium.com/sant-mat-meditation-and-spirituality/maharshi-mehi-the-bridge-between-hindu-scriptures-and-sant-mat-by-pravesh-k-singh-2fadde15060d#.gyw6odt6m (accessed on 14 December 2018).

Swami Vyasanand, Ji Maharaj. 2016. *The Inward Journey of the Soul: Chal Hansa Nij Desh*, Kindle Edition ed. Seattle: Amazon Publishing.

Turner, Victor. 1995. *The Ritual Process: Structure and Anti-Structure*. Piscataway: Aldine Transactions.

religions

MDPI

Article

Religious Experience without an Experiencer: The 'Not I' in Sāṃkhya and Yoga

Alfred Collins

Alaska Neuro/Therapy Center, 615 E 82nd Ave. #102, Anchorage, AK 99518, USA; nasadasin@gmail.com

Received: 2 January 2019; Accepted: 24 January 2019; Published: 2 February 2019

Abstract: "Experience" is a category that seems to have developed new meaning in European thought after the Enlightenment when personal inwardness took on the weight of an absent God. The inner self (including, a little later, a sub- or unconscious mind) rose to prominence about 200–300 years ago, around the time of the "Counter-Enlightenment" and Romanticism, and enjoyed a rich and long life in philosophy (including Lebensphilosophie) and religious studies, but began a steep descent under fire around 1970. The critique of "essentialism" (the claim that experience is self-validating and impervious to historical and scientific explanation or challenge) was probably the main point of attack, but there were others. The Frankfurt School (Adorno, Benjamin, et al.) claimed that authentic experience was difficult or impossible in the modern capitalist era. The question of the reality of the individual self to which experience happens also threatened to undermine the concept. This paper argues that the religious experience characteristic of Sāṃkhya and Yoga, while in some ways paralleling Romanticism and Lebensphilosophies, differs from them in one essential way. Sāṃkhyan/Yogic experience is not something that happens to, or in, an individual person. It does not occur to or for oneself (in the usual sense) but rather *puruṣārtha*, "for the sake of [*artha*] an innermost consciousness/self"[*puruṣa*] which must be distinguished from the "solitude" of "individual men" (the recipient, for William James, of religious experience) which would be called *ahaṃkāra*, or "ego assertion" in the Indian perspectives. The distinction found in European Lebensphilosophie between two kinds of experience, *Erlebnis* (a present-focused lived moment) and *Erfahrung* (a constructed, time-binding thread of life, involving memory and often constituting a story) helps to understand what is happening in Sāṃkhya and Yoga. The concept closest to experience in Sāṃkhya/Yoga is named by the Sanskrit root *dṛś-*, "seeing," which is a process actualized through long meditative practice and close philosophical reasoning. The *Erfahrung* "story" enacted in Sāṃkhya/Yoga practice is a sort of dance-drama in which psychomaterial Nature (*prakṛti*) reveals to her inner consciousness and possessor (*puruṣa*) that she "is not, has nothing of her own, and does not have the quality of being an 'I'" (*nāsmi na me nāham*). This self exposure as "not I" apophatically reveals *puruṣa*, and lets him shine for them both, as pure consciousness. *Prakṛti*'s long quest for *puruṣa*, seeking him with the finest insight (*jñāna*), culminates in realization that she is not the seer in this process but the seen, and that her failure has been to assert *aham* ("I") rather than realize *nāham*, "Not I." Her meditation and insight have led to an experience which was always for an Other, though that was not recognized until the story's end. Rather like McLuhan's "the medium is the message," the nature or structure of experience in Sāṃkhya and Yoga is also its content, what religious experience is about in these philosophies and practices. In Western terms, we have religious experience only when we recognize what (all) experience (already) is: the unfolding story of *puruṣārtha*. Experience deepens the more we see that it is not ours; the recognition of non-I, in fact, is what makes genuine experience possible at all.

Keywords: religious experience; *Erfahrung*; *Erlebnis*; seeing; being seen; I; not I; Sāṃkhya; Yoga; *puruṣa*; *prakṛti*; *puruṣārtha*

---

1. Introduction

Gerald Larson (1969) insightfully described the Indian philosophical system Sāṃkhya[1] as an "eccentric dualism," its two parts—*prakṛti* (Nature) and *puruṣa* (pure consciousness)—mutually cooperative, but also fundamentally "other" (*para*) to one another (*Sāṃkhya Kārikā* [*SK*] 61). Only *prakṛti* acts, but *puruṣa* alone provides the consciousness for action and owns it. Made of "strands" (*guṇas*), or deep affective "strivings" (*bhāvas*), there is only one, universal *prakṛti* (often associated in mythology with the Great Goddess, Devi) but a multitude of scintillae of consciousness (*puruṣas*). The body (including sense faculties and objects) and mind of each person are portions of *prakṛti*'s work or action (root *kṛ-*) for the sake of the experience or pleasure (*bhoga*), and simultaneously for the release (*mokṣa*), of the particular *puruṣa* around which that body–mind–object complex is organized. The default state of *prakṛti*'s experience (at least in her human instantiations) is misery or suffering (*duḥkha* [*SK* 1]) but her efforts are aimed at overcoming suffering—i.e., gaining positive affect and achieving release (the difference between or unity of these two goals has been a major topic for reflection on Sāṃkhya and I will return to it later). Patañjali's Yoga is a closely related system of thought which differs somewhat from Sāṃkhya—which focuses on insight, *buddhi* or *jñāna*, as the path to happiness and release—by emphasizing deep meditation (*dhyāna*) leading to enstasy (*samādhi*)[2]. As a first approximation, we may say that *bhoga* corresponds to ordinary experience, especially of the pleasant sort, while *mokṣa* (and higher states of *samādhi*) are the realm of religious experience. Further reflection, however, will challenge this simple opposition. In the end, Sāṃkhya and Yoga are complex forms of mystical gnosis in which *prakṛti*, or the insightful and self-established mind which is her highest form, recognizes that she has been seen (*dṛṣta*) by *puruṣa* as wholly empty except for her focus on him (her *puruṣārtha*), and is so able to shine in his reflected light, for the first time as she truly is.

To write in 2019 on religious experience in Sāṃkhya and Yoga it is unavoidable to ask first how the general topic of "religious experience" should be understood, given the recent controversies over the reality of the phenomenon (Martin and McCutcheon 2014; McDaniel 2018; Jay 2005) which have called into question the very legitimacy of the field of "History of Religions," a realm of inquiry partially based on the study of religious experiences (and which have, in the process, systematically devaluated its most prominent practitioner, Mircea Eliade, [Jonathan Z. Smith 2004]).[3] We must also consider differences in how India and the West understand both religious "experience" and the nature of the person to whom experience occurs. Finally, to give religious experience context both in India and in the West, we must go beyond religion proper, into the broader understanding of experience in culture, especially the higher stages of cultural reflection called philosophy.

To begin with the third question, in the West experience became a central theme following the "Counter-Enlightenment" (Berlin 2000), particularly in 19th- and 20th-century European and American philosophies such as Pragmtism and Lebensphilosophie (Nietzsche, Bergson, Dilthey, Collingwood, Benjamin, Dewey, Peirce, etc. [Jay 2005]), and later became equally fundamental in religious studies (Schleiermacher, James, Eliade, Otto, van der Leeuw, etc. [Taves 2011, McDaniel 2018]). Dilthey and others had distinguished between Geisteswissenschaften (human sciences) which had to do with what is experienced, and Naturwissenschaften (natural sciences), which concerned objective, outer realities, following Descartes' res cogitans (thinking entities) and *res extensa* (things taking up space, dimensional entities). The insight—and one could suggest the *hope*—in what might be called the "experiential turn" in philosophy and religion over a few hundred years was the possibility of sustaining a realm of human

---

1 I will be discussing the *Sāṃkhya Kārika* of Īśvarakṛṣṇa, which is generally considered the primary source for the doctrine. Secondary sources besides Larson (1969) include Johnston (1937), Burley (2012), and Larson (2018). For the Patanjali Yoga Sutras, I have primarily used Bryant (2009), White (2014), and Hauer (1958).

2 "Enstasy" is a term used by Mircea Eliade (2009) to describe yogic experience but was not original with him; it may have been borrowed from Olivier Lacombe (1937).

3 June McDaniel reports that the "wreck of the good ship Eliade" was celebrated at a panel at the American Academy of Religion in 2017 (McDaniel 2018).

value, agency, culture, meaning, and life—in a word, of "experience"—after the "death of God" and beyond the corrosive reach of materialism, and particularly immune, later, to the acid of Darwinian evolutionary theory. Recently (beginning around 1970), the possibility of an independent territory of experience in religion which could be the privileged subject matter of a discipline of religious studies has come under intensive critique and revision as part of the general "linguistic turn" in the humanities and the ascendency of postmodernism (J.Z. Smith, Sharf, Proudfoot, McCutcheon, etc. [Taves 2011), partly because it seemed to imply "essentialism," positing an unexamined category of "religious experience" as a *sui generis* reality immune to criticism and walled off from history and the social (and other) sciences. Besides essentialism, the Western view of religion as experience also was vulnerable to the charge that it saw religion as individualist, the momentary "self authenticating experience of the individual" (ibid, p. 5). This implied removing religious experience from history, politics, class, and power relations. William James defined religious experience in this way as "the feelings, acts, and experiences of individual men in their solitude, so far as they apprehend themselves to stand in relation to whatever they may consider divine." (James [1902] 1985, p. 34). Momentary, sometimes mystical flashes of feeling or knowing come upon men (sic) "in their solitude." Religion was seen as "numinous" (Otto) and sublime because it shook the security of a putatively stable individual with "sudden, discrete" (Taves 2011, p. 5) moments of something radically Other ("revelations, visions, dramatic conversion experiences" [ibid]).

To locate a category of "religious experience" in Hinduism, and specifically Sāṃkhya and Yoga, requires inquiry into how "experience" in general is understood there. Sāṃkhya and Yoga have a number of terms that overlap with Western "experience." *Bhoga* names either enjoyable experience or experience generally, but most often with an implication of immediate perception with positive or negative hedonic valence. It does not generally name a religious experience, though I will try to show that Sāṃkhya does integrate *bhoga* into religious experience. At an explicitly religious level, that of *mokṣa*, spiritual release or enlightenment, the closest Sanskrit parallel to experience is the concept of "seeing" (*dṛś-*), and I will explore religious experience in Sāṃkhya and Yoga through this perspective. Although seeing in its usual, perceptual sense would seem to describe the immediate, sensory side of experience, *darśana*[4] is conceived quite differently in Hinduism as a higher or deeper sort of insight/seeing, the product of long training (philosophical study and meditation: *abhyāsa, dhyāna*). An unquestioned, perception-like understanding of experience (the "self authenticating" [Taves 2011] perceptions of "individual men in their solitude" [W. James] or (more broadly) the "naked, primitive, self evident experience of the Enlightenment" [Benjamin [1918] 2004]) might fit *bhoga* in its usual sense, but does not cover the semantic range of *dṛś-*. A distinction present in German, and important to a number of German thinkers, may help to see what is missing. *Erlebnis* (the kind of present-focused lived moment that the above citations describe) is distinguished from experience as *Erfahrung* (a constructed, time-binding thread of life, involving memory and often constituting a story). We will find that Sāṃkhya/Yoga experience is generally closer to *Erfahrung* than to the self-validating *Erlebnis* sort of experience. *Darśana* (seeing) is something constructed or worked out in practice (*abhyāsa*) although paradoxically it is also revealed, in the end, to be self-evidently visible—reflected by a seeing Other who shares it with one's (lower) "self." The *Erlebnis/Erfahrung* distinction, however, while useful, is not enough. Sāṃkhya/Yoga *darśana* finds the putative seer to be, in fact, *seen*, (the apparent experienc*er* is actually experienc*ed*) and aims to develop in the practitioner the insight (*jñāna*) and meditative focus (*dhyāna*) to realize this. Specifically, Sāṃkhya and Yoga ask us to realize personally, and integrate into life, a principle called *puruṣārtha*, "for the sake of consciousness" (*Sāṃkhya Kārikā* 69). Briefly, this concept—which I believe to be the central idea of Sāṃkhya and Yoga—asserts that all the action of sentient beings (and everything that happens in the universe is action—*karma*) is done "in

[4] The term *darśana* ("seeing") is used in both the *Sāṃkhya Kārikā* and *Yoga Sūtra* as are many other words made from the root *dṛś-*. I use *darśana* here because it is the Sanskrit term for *darshan*, the usual spelling in anthropological and religious studies works for a related concept in contemporary Hinduism that will be discussed later. (Eck 1998, etc.)

order to" (*artha*) give *puruṣa* pleasure or experience (*bhoga*) and release (*mokṣa*) from the suffering of bondage to the struggle for satisfaction of desire (*autsukya*, *Sāṃkhya Kārikā* [*SK*] 58). Actions are done by the body and mind so as to give consciousness these two kinds of experience: pleasure of the eye (and other senses) and enlightenment through seeing. It is the latter that is closest to what is generally understood as "religious experience," but we will find that the eye's pleasure also becomes religious when understood rightly.

2. Western Heuristics and the Indian Understanding of Self

Several Western ways of understanding experience will be of help in this enquiry: among them, Freudian psychoanalysis, Jungian analytical psychology, Heinz Kohut's self psychology, and Walter Benjamin's attempts to root experience in "aura" and the "dialectical image." The fluidity and permeability of the Indian self explored by Frederick Smith (2006), Alan Roland (1989), and Prakash Desai and myself (Collins and Desai 1999) also help to understand a sort of experience that is not based in an individual's momentary life (*Erlebnis*) or even solely in his constructed story (*Erfahrung*). First, in Freud, we find in ordinary pleasure (satisfaction of the drives) the key to understanding the deep and final release he calls the death instinct or nirvana principle (thanatos). I suggest that Freud's drive reduction is like Sāṃkhyan *bhoga* (specifically what is called the latter's *autsukya* quality at *SK* 58) and that Freudian thanatos is akin to the release (*mokṣa*) that is termed *ānanda* in the Upaniṣads and elsewhere, and which in Sāṃkhya and Yoga is associated with complete satisfaction and wholeness (*kaivalya*). Experience (*darśana*, seeing), is the doorway to *mokṣa*. While integral and in a way unified, *darśana* is also complex. To summarize what will take some effort to explicate, the *Sāṃkhya Kārika* asserts that *prakṛti*, or the *jnāña bhāva* or *sattvic buddhi* (both essentially refer to discriminating insight) that is her true or highest part, realizes that "I am seen as '*nāham*', not I", *by* and *for the sake of puruṣa* who, she realizes, simultaneously recognizes that "I have seen her" (*prakṛti*). Even a cursory glance shows that "religious experience" like this cannot be only a unique, momentary flash of insight into the cognitive/affective/volitional apparatus of an individual person, who is only a construct made of elements of *prakṛti* (i.e., it cannot be just a satisfaction of drives or reduction of *duḥkha*), because *darśana* sees across the division between the two principles, *prakṛti* and *puruṣa*, that are wholly "other" (*para*) to each other. *Darśana* bridges between the halves of Larson's "eccentric dualism," a psychomaterial part or aspect and a part that is pure consciousness. Religious experience involves a subtle and hard-to-comprehend relationship connecting them. To anticipate once again, *the nature or structure of experience in Sāṃkhya and Yoga (prakṛti's puruṣa orientation) is also, in the end, its fundamental content;*[5] it is what religious experience is about in these philosophies. In Western terms, we have religious experience when we recognize (see) what (all) experience (already) is.[6]

3. The Self as Composite

Psychoanalysis since Lacan in 1936, but most significantly in Winnicott (Winnicott [1971] 1971/2005) and Kohut (1977), has recognized that the sense of self is not entirely a primordial or *sui generis* fact in the personality, or at least that it is not a singular one. Alan Roland (1989) showed that what he called a "familial self" or "self-we regard" is more fundamental in Indian (and to some extent Japanese) psychology than is an individual "I." Winnicott and Kohut, to some degree following Lacan, found that Roland's insight does not apply exclusively to foreign societies and ethnicities but also, if we go deep enough, to Western European and American personality. As Winnicott showed, the Teddy Bear is part of the child who plays with it—part of his family, part of his society and world, and part of his psychodynamics. Kohut named the inner images

---

5 We may be reminded here of Marshall McLuhan's observation that "the medium is the message."

6 The ultimate experience for a person (prakṛtic construction, *liṅga*) endowed with *puruṣārtha* is precisely to realize that *puruṣārtha* is his own inmost nature.

of aspects of the world that complete us "self objects," which he defined as parts of the outer world that we treat as if they were aspects of ourselves over which we have the same sort of control and ownership as we do over parts of our own bodies and minds (Kohut 1977). In Bengali fieldwork, Inden and Nicholas (1973) discovered the concept of the *kartā*, the "seed person" within a family, village, larger land area, or region (i.e., a sort of bigger or smaller king) whose family members (wives, sons, servants, etc.) are part of him and are better felt as aspects of his life rather than as independent beings. Similarly, in Vedic thought, "when the father dies, he transfers his vital breaths (*prāṇas*) into the son and gives him the sacred knowledge. . . ." (Collins and Desai 1999, p. 379). In this way he "extends himself through offspring" (*taneyebhiḥ tanute*, ibid, p. 378). Smith's extensive analysis of the possession phenomenon in India (which can be either negative/destructive or positive/enhancing) finds that possession is more possible because the boundaries of the persons who are to possess and to be possessed are relatively permeable and not as sharp as they are in the Western individual. (Smith 2006). The relatively fluid inner workings of the personality of concern to Sāṃkhya are continuous with its outward permeability or "dividuality" (Marriott 1976). (I am proposing, in other words, that the flowing of cause into effect—*satkārya*—within a person makes possible the flowing of one person into another—*praveśa*.)

4. Experience (*Erfahrung*) in Walter Benjamin

Walter Benjamin, following Krakauer and many *Lebensphilosophie* predecessors, sought a way to true experience (*Erfahrung*, rather than *Erlebnis*) in modernity. "Benjamin never abandoned his efforts to reconceptualize the conditions of possibility for experience in modernity. In an unpublished note of 1929, he writes that 'the word [experience, *Erfahrung*] has now become a fundamental term in many of my projects.'" (Hansen 2012).

> The concept of experience (*Erfahrung*) . . . [is emphatically elaborated] in the writings of Benjamin and Adorno. . . . Benjamin, theorizing the conditions of possibility of *Erfahrung* in modernity, had linked its historic decline with the proliferation of *Erlebnis* (immediate but isolated experience) under the conditions of industrial capitalism; in this context, *Erfahrung* crucially came to entail the capacity of memory—individual and collective, involuntary as well as cognitive—and the ability to imagine a different future. (Hansen 2012, p. xiv).

One of Benjamin's central concepts is that of the "dialectical image," an image connecting past and present that can make genuine *Erfahrung* experience possible in modernity.

> It's not that what is past casts its light on what is present, or what is present its light on the past; rather, the image is that wherein what has been comes together in a flash with the now to form a constellation. In other words, image is dialectics at a standstill. For while the relation of the present to the past is a purely temporal, continuous one, the relation of what-has-been to the now is dialectical: it is not progression but image, suddenly emergent. (Benjamin 2002).[7]

Benjamin's complex intellectual development—paradoxically both messianic and materialist—from his twenties until his early death at 48 repeatedly returned to an essentially mystical sense of recognition of similarity between two moments that ignite when they come together. The image created lives between (forms a bond—in Sanskrit a *bandhu*—linking) past and present, like *prakṛti*'s life devoted to *puruṣārtha*, the giving of pleasure and release to *puruṣa*. Benjamin's understanding of how the dialectical image makes (mystical) experience possible is analogous to the experience shared between *puruṣa* and *prakrti* in *mokṣa*. The image does not live either in the past (for Benjamin, 19th-century Paris) nor the present (Weimar and post-Weimar Germany), just as

[7] Benjamin (2002), Arcades "Awakening" (Arcades, 462; n2a, 3).

kaivalya—the experience of release into pure consciousness (*citiśakti*)—does not consist of either *puruṣa* alone or of the dissolution of the fluctuations (*vṛtti*) of *prakṛti*, (*citta-vṛtti-nirodha YS* 2), but rather of both as it were together, "constellated" but not touching, because at the moment of the experience *prakrti* "is not" (*nāsmi*) and *purusa*'s vision of her has been completed; it is not something that happens only in a moment (like *Erlebnis* experience) but rather "has" been done (as it were in the perfect tense: "I have been seen;" *drstāham*, is a past-perfect participle). At the complex moment of "being seen" (*dṛṣṭāham*), the eternal fact of *puruṣārtha* as the essence of the one seen (*prakṛti*) shines forth.

5. Puruṣārtha: The Two Aims of Action in *Sāṃkhya* and Yoga

As we have seen, the ultimate purpose of the psycho-cosmology called Sāṃkhya, and the meditative practices and theory of higher states of consciousness named Yoga, is to liberate the self (*puruṣa*), which is posited to be pure, objectless consciousness, from the suffering (*duḥkha*) that forms the basic or "default" state of existence in the world. Along the way, however, Sāṃkhya reveals an extraordinarily rich perspective on virtually every aspect of life, maintaining a paradoxical but consistent balance between the aims of release from and fulfillment of the psychomaterial qualities and strivings. Sāṃkhya proceeds by analyzing natural (principally human) being, finding at the basis of action—strikingly like Freudian psychoanalysis—an implicit urge to satisfy desires, which it understands to mean bringing them to a close[8]; it aims to show that fulfillment of desire for enjoyment (*bhoga*) is similar, or even equivalent, to releasing consciousness from its apparent imprisonment in material experience (*mokṣa, kaivalya*) (*SK* 58). Yoga lays out a moral-ascetic and meditative practice that it claims will move the human mind–body entity in the direction of a less-fragmented, ignorant, overly active, and unfree state (all aspects of suffering, *duḥkha*), towards a new way of being in which the person is able to follow and realize the argument of Sāṃkhya's ontological analysis (*jñāna*). Religion, for Yoga, is meditation in service of a salvific insight or gnosis. Culture, which cannot be separated from religion, properly (though not commonly) enacts and celebrates this insight (Collins 1991, 2006). Sāṃkhya/Yoga are therefore fundamentally ways of understanding and living intelligently in the world. While commentators on Sāṃkhya/Yoga[9] from Buddhist and other Hindu perspectives (referring to its emphasis on suffering [*duḥkha*], etc.), and many Western interpreters view it as ascetic and life-denying, a worldlier, life-affirming view of Yoga[10] (at least) has been recognized in recent years (Chapple 2003; Whicher 2003). Lloyd Pflueger, who is partially aligned with this trend, sees Yoga, along with Sāṃkhya, as walking the razor's edge between a desired release (final insight into the radical difference between *puruṣa* and *prakṛti*; i.e., *jñāna*) and an inexorable reality: that one can approach the goal of release asymptotically but never fully reach it. The never-quite-achieved *jñāna* or *bhoga* is "glorified" by the meditative practice of yoga and by performance of the other arts and practices of life that can be viewed as lower or less-conscious forms of Yoga. "The real work is the work of treading the path to liberation. In an unexpected sense, the path can be seen as a goal in itself." (Pflueger 2003, p. 79). In a way, Yoga is a *Bildung*, a practice of spiritual and cultural education. As such, Yogic (and Sankhyan) experience is gradual, growing through the slow diminution of "afflictions" (*kleśas*) and ignorance of the true nature of experience itself (*ajñāna*). The practice of Sāṃkhya and Yoga is like Benjamin's dialectic, a wearing away without end of *kleśas*. *Mokṣa* is, as Benjamin put it, "dialectics at a standstill," or perhaps we could go a little farther and say it is dialectics resolved into its essence.

---

8 Clearly expressed in *SK* 2, *yogaś cittavṛtti nirodhaḥ*, "yoga is the suppression of the twists and turns of the mind."

9 The extent to which Sāṃkhya and Yoga form parts of what is essentially one perspective is disputed. Larson (1969, 2018), Burley (2012), and Pflueger (2003) are among those who have argued that Patañjali's *Yogasūtra* belongs to a school or subschool of Sāṃkhya. Others have tried to show that Yoga is different from Sāṃkhya in important ways. This paper assumes that Larson and Pflueger are basically correct, at least in their conclusion that Patāñjali's Yoga agrees with the fundamental theses of the *Sāṃkhya Kārika*, that *prakṛti* acts solely for the sake of pleasing and releasing *puruṣa*, and that her increasing knowledge of her difference from *puruṣa* paradoxically moves her closer to him and is salvific for her as well.

10 In order to view Yoga as a way of life in the world, Whicher and Chapple separate it from Sāṃkhya more than I find justified.

6. The World of the Self

I will attempt to describe the person and his world as understood by Sāṃkhya/Yoga, emphasizing that the word "his" is not intended to name persons in general; this is a gendered system concerned primarily with the male self, though one caught in an ineluctable relationship with a female environment. In Sāṃkhya's "eccentric dualism," one of the two fundamental principles, *prakṛti*, represents almost everything and the other, *puruṣa*, almost nothing. *Prakṛti* is psychomaterial substance of which body and mind both consist, the two differing only in subtlety or degree of density. Everything "from Brahma to a blade of grass" (*SK* 54) consists of *prakṛti*, which is always implicitly personified and explicitly or implicitly female. *Puruṣa*, literally a male person, is in Sāṃkhya the name of bare awareness, or perhaps better of an instance of bare awareness, a pure consciousness free from intentionality (in the sense of being "about" something, specifically, about *prakṛti*). This is a fundamental fact for Sāmkhya/Yoga that explains its "eccentricity": *prakṛti* is about *puruṣa* but *puruṣa* is not about *prakṛti*.[11] In her higher or earlier, undifferentiated state, *prakṛti* is called *avyakta*, *mūlaprakṛti*, and *pradhāna*.[12] She evolves through a process called *pravṛtti* (development) or *pariṇāma* (devolution), falling into successively lower states of being in an emanational (d)evolutionary course in which the effect is always implicit in its earlier states or cause (*satkārya*). This is very similar to Buddhist "conditioned origination" (*pratītyasamutpada*), and also like the devolution of the world process imagined in the later Hindu succession of "ages" (*yugas*) leading from the perfect past (*kṛta yuga*, the Golden Age) to the demonic present (*kali yuga*). In another way, however, *prakṛti* is inherently teleological, acting for the sake of *puruṣa* (*puruṣārtha* = *puruṣa* + *artha*). I emphasize the word "act" (Sanskrit root *kṛ*-), for *prakṛti* is never impelled by "efficient" (in Aristotle's sense) or purely mechanical causation. Whatever happens in the world is always an *action*, something *done*, never unmotivated or random movement, always behavior infused by what we could call character, the sediment or residue of past acts (*karma*, *vāsana*, *saṁskāra*, etc.) that partially or mainly motivates new action.

Prakṛti acts, yet, paradoxically, is not an actor, for she does not own what she does. As noted above, there are two sides of *puruṣārtha*, the action of *prakṛti* for *puruṣa*'s sake: first, there is the desire or impulsion to give *puruṣa* enjoyment, which is understood, much as with Freud, as the cessation of a desire. Second, there is the desire to liberate *puruṣa* from bondage in the "threefold suffering" (*duḥkhatraya*, *SK* 1) of the human condition, a goal that in psychoanalytic terms corresponds to Freud's "death instinct" (*thanatos*) or "Nirvana principle."[13] The *Sāṃkhya Kārikā* claims that these two, apparently very different, aims are intrinsically similar or even identical.

> As (in the world) (a man) engages in actions for the sake of the cessation of a desire; so also does the *prakṛti* function for the sake of the release of the *puruṣa*. (SK 58, Larson's translation [Larson 1969, p. 273].[14]

Suffering, the distance from happiness named by the word "desire"(*audsukya*, from *ud* + *suka*, literally "away from pleasure"), is found by both Sāṃkhya and Yoga to arise from a certain kind of selfhood, called *ahaṁkāra* in Sāṃkhya and *asmitā* in Yoga. This sort of self asserts itself (*ahaṁkāra*) and its "I am-ness" (*asmitā*) in a way that can and often does lead in the direction of the demonic. One of the clearest classical examples of this is the career of the demon Rāvaṇa in the epic texts. Grandson of the god Brahmā, Rāvaṇa refuses to accept his place in the proper order (*dharma*) of the world, and inflates his ego (*ahaṃkāra*) through ascetic practices, aiming to become lord of the whole

---

11 For a discussion of this eccentricity in feminist terms, see Collins (2000). In the language of (recent) "twenty-somethings," *puruṣa* is "not into" *prakṛti* as she is "into" him.

12 And *mūlaprakṛti* and *avyakta*.

13 Collins (forthcominga). Also Freud [1930] (Freud [1930] 2010) and Laplanche and Pontalis (1974).

14 *autsukyanivṛttyartham yathā*
kriyāsu pravartate lokaḥ,
puruṣasya vimokṣārtham
pravartate tadvad avyaktam (SK 58).

cosmos. This leads him to cause maximum suffering to himself and others. But Rāvaṇa, far from being unique, is best understood as an "ideal type" (in Weber's sense) for the world of action (*karmas*) that he wants to rule. His great enemy (and Lord), Rāma, can be seen similarly, as an antitype to Rāvaṇa, overcoming suffering and the cravings of egoism through insight (sattvic *buddhi, prajñā*) that realizes the fundamental difference between our unrolling karmic process (*pariṇāma, pravṛtti*) and the principle of pure consciousness (*puruṣa*) that witnesses *prakṛti*'s evolution. Suffering is thus correlated with ignorance (and demons are typically revealed as witless fools),[15] insight with release from ego.

7. "I Have Been Seen": Darshan in the Sāṃkhya Kārikā and the Yoga Sutra

While Yoga and philosophical Sāṃkhya are not generally understood as artistic or cultural performances, the texts suggest that this may be a good way of understanding what they are. Indeed, the anthropologist McKim Marriott (1989) has found that much of Indian culture and society can be seen as expressions or embodiments of the three Sāṃkhyan *guṇas*.[16] We will address the trope of Nature (*prakṛti*) imagined as a female dancer (*nartakī*) performing for the eyes of an implicitly royal witness, consciousness (*puruṣa*). Correct thinking (Sāṃkhya) and deep meditation (Yoga) are compared to a dance performed by an unsurpassably refined performer (*sukumārataram na kiṁcid asti, SK* 61) whose (mental and physical) movements enact a sort of apophatic theology, negating herself more and more until, at a moment of supreme poise, she recognizes her own emptiness and thereby opens herself to be seen by the unobstructed eye of consciousness: "I am not, I own nothing, there is no I in me" (*nāsmi na me nāham, SK* 64). This "not I" realization is at the same time a recognition of *being seen as* fully self-negating, which permits her to pass into a state of empty, but complete, fulfillment in which she need not continue to perform for *puruṣa* (*SK* 61) but only to recognize, through his eyes reflecting hers seeing his, that all is "pure essential knowledge" (*viśuddham kevalam jñānam, SK* 64).

Puruṣārtha means that all worldly action is already a dance choreographed around giving enjoyment and release to *puruṣa*. It is only so that the dance can reach a satisfactory fulfillment, can finally end, that correct thinking (Sāṃkhya) and meditation (Yoga) need be added to the performance. Yoga and Sāṃkhyan philosophy are refinements, implicit from the beginning in the principle of *puruṣārtha*, but nevertheless requiring careful practice of *jñāna bhāva*, the mental faculty or "fundamental striving" (as Gerald Larson translates *bhāva*) of "insight." All experience is religious experience when properly understood (with the *jñāna bhāva*).

In fact, the desire to cultivate *jñāna* is suggested in verse 1 of the *Sāṁkhya Kārikā*, and that text ends with insights that only pure *jñāna* can reach. Already the first verse tells us that the desire for *jñāna* (i.e., *jijñāsa*) is the basis for the quest for a "singular" (*aikānta*) and "eternal" (*atyanta*) reality beyond the "threefold suffering" (*duḥkhatraya*) of ordinary life. Near the end of the *SK* (verse 68), the *prakṛtic* person has become focused on pure *jñāna*, after turning away from the other seven *bhāvas* (mastery, attachment, etc.). This *jñāna* shows *kaivalya* (singular and essential being), which is characterized in the same words we found used aspirationally in verse 1, *aikāntika* and *atyantika*. The *SK* ends in the achievement of what it sought in the beginning.[17]

Sāṃkhya and Yoga are forms of cultivation, higher sorts of "*Bildung*," culture. They are ways of self-development, of making life a practice of the art of living insight (and so of "religious experience"), moving from the yearning for *jñāna* to the fullness of *jñāna* itself. Both Sāṃkhya and Yoga are aware that their insights and practices can never quite reach, in all its fullness, what they aim for. Imagination and metaphor are the only way to get a sense of the goal, called *kaivalya* (oneness or integrity), and the practitioner of Yoga or thinker of Sāṃkhya enacts a trope, an intricate and subtle

---

15 e.g., Kumbakarna.

16 Also Collins (forthcomingb).

17 A translation of verse 1 might be: "Because of the impact [*abhighāta*] of the 3-fold suffering there arises the desire to understand how to knock it away or make it rebound [*abhighāta*, the same word, is used again]. If you say 'there is no reason' [to seek such a radical solution] we say 'No, [other means of dealing with it] are not eternal and complete.'"

way of imagining satisfaction and release (*bhoga* and *mokṣa*). Perhaps the two best metaphors are those of the dancer performing before a spectator (*SK* 59) and the chanting of the syllable *OM* (*YS* 1.28). More than metaphors, both are better understood as *symbols*, images that evoke something ineffable, allow communication between the sensible or intelligible and a transcendent reality. The communion between the symbols of dancer and *OM*, and their ultimate referent, the fact of *puruṣārtha*, is similar to "darshan" in later Hinduism,[18] the two-way reflective gaze between human and divine (Eck 1998, Babb 1981, 1984; Elison 2014).

Seeing and being seen are the principal images the *SK* uses to describe the process by which *prakṛti* gives experience (suffering or pleasure) to *puruṣa* and also releases him. It is in seeing *prakṛti* in her different states that *puruṣa* seems to experience pain and enjoyment, and it is in seeing her at the moment of her complete recognition of selflessness that *puruṣa* approaches release (in her eye). This recognition of being seen allows *prakṛti* to stop her frantic search for the quenching of desire (*autsukya nivṛtti SK* 58) that has motivated her action previously. In letting go, she realizes that she lacks all selfhood, agency, and ownership. Standing rapt before the mirror of *puruṣa*, *prakṛti* becomes empty and shows *puruṣa* her realization that she shines as a perfect zero in his unstained eye. He no longer reflects pleasurable or painful action from her back to her cognitive faculties (only to receive it again from her in the unsatisfying mirror play that is the ordinary *prakṛtic* mentality). *Puruṣa* and *prakṛti*, through the latter's realization of *nāsmi* ("not I"), spiral towards a play of intervision (darshan) that explodes in a taste of *bhoga* when each faces their essential nature: integrity (*kaivalya*) in seeing (for *puruṣa*) and integrity in being seen (for *prakṛti*); *dṛṣṭāham* ("I am seen") and *dṛṣṭā māyā* ("I have seen her"). The two sides of *kaivalya* are also evoked at YS 4.34 where *prakṛti*'s *kaivalya* is characterized by the emptying of the *guṇa*s of their urgency to be seen by *puruṣa*, and *puruṣa*'s *kaivalya* is described as *svarūpa-pratiṣṭha citiśakti*, the "power of consciousness established in its own nature."[19]

Tropes of seeing are also central in the *Yoga Sūtra*. *Prakṛti* is referred to as the realm of the "seen" (*dṛśya*) and the two *artha*s of *bhoga* (experience, enjoyment) and *apavarga* (release) are referred to *prakṛti* in her form as "seen," *dṛśya* (*YS* 2.18). Spiritual progress is understood as improved "seeing" (*darśana*) and removal of "non-seeing" (*adarśana*). YS 2.26 refers to the purified mind as like a dust-free mirror reflecting clearly the light of *puruṣa*. *Samādhi*s (meditative ecstasies) are named by their quality of "insight" or even transcendence of insight (*jña*, i.e., *samprajñāta* and *asamprajñāta*). *Puruṣa* is characterized as the "Seer" (*dṛśi*).

Let us pursue our metaphor of the dancer (*nartakī*, SK 59) whose beautiful steps and grace allow her to express her real nature, and, as it were, to tell the story of herself and her "spectator" (*prekṣa*) from both their points of view. The image of *prakṛti*, as she moves towards realization *for puruṣa*, which she receives back from him, shows us the Sāṃkhyan practitioner as performing artist. I believe the same is true in the *Yoga Sūtra* (1.27), where utterance of the *praṇava*, the syllable *OM*, symbolizes the ineffable in a more continuous way[20] that allows *prakṛti* in her *kaivalya* state to become a kind of *puruṣa* (*puruṣa-viśeṣa*, a term used to describe Iśvara, the Lord of yoga [*YS* 1.24]).[21] The circular motion implied in darshan (seeing her seeing me seeing her. . .) is held by *OM* in a single, integral symbol that binds time in a realized whole. The artist lives or enacts the "secret" (*guhya*, *SK* 69) and enigmatic relationship between *puruṣa* and *prakṛti* in a unified image, identified in the *YS* as the Lord of yoga, Iśvara, the personification of OM.

18 And Buddhism and Jainism.

19 The same two-sided vision of spiritual realization is suggested in the first two verses of the *Yoga Sūtra*: "Yoga is the stilling of the fluctuations of thought and emotion." [1]. Then the seer (the conscious being, *puruṣa*) rests in its own form." [2] (Phillips 2009, p. 207).

20 *OM*'s omnipresence, its ability to bind time, is why chanting it immediately invokes its deep sense of the Lord (Iśvara) and makes it (whenever it is uttered) the teacher of the ancients (*YS* 1.26–1.28).

21 The idea of *puruṣa viśeṣa*, which could be construed either as a "specific *puruṣa*" or as a "likeness or sort of *puruṣa*" (along the lines of the use of the same word in Rāmānuja's *viśiṣṭādvaita*, "qualified, or a sort of, non-dualism") anticipates the goal of *prakṛti*'s (as opposed to *puruṣa*'s) *kaivalya*. *YS* 4.34.

The syllable *OM* (a-u-m) expresses at once the state of suffering or ignorance (a), yogic or philosophical practice (u) and recognition of *nāham* = "not I" (m). As an integral whole, *OM* represents the source of universal wisdom (*sarvajña*). The practice of *OM* and its meaning are one experience (*taj japas tad artha-bhāvanam* [*YS* 1.28], "reciting *OM* is to experience its meaning"). There is no separation between word and meaning, no seeking after something unattained, a *puruṣārtha* located in the future. *Puruṣārtha* is still the central idea, but now becomes something timelessly *found* rather than a goal to be sought. We are perhaps returning in the direction of a redeemed *Erlebnis*. There is a fulfillment in the practice of *OM*, not a dead or rigid stasis but a nimble and flexible state of readiness-cum-attainment, perhaps expressed in the *YS* by the highest meditative state called *dharma-megha-samādhi* or "raincloud of *dharma*" integrity. At YS 4.34, the final verse of the text, the fulfillment of *puruṣārtha* is described as *pratiprasāva*, a turning around or back of the *guṇa*s, the exact opposite of the turnings (forward into greater suffering) of the mind (*cittavṛtti*) that yoga is declared in *YS* 2 to stop.

The dance between *puruṣa* and *prakṛti* is thus the dance of the Lord of Yoga, whom we might imagine as Śiva *taṇḍava*, dancing upon a remorseful, but now enlightened, demon of Forgetfulness (Apasmara) representing the unenlightened state of *prakṛti*. This is the life of spiritual art, which we receive in the darshan of the god or goddess, in a relationship that reveals to us the union of suffering and release.

To illustrate this paradoxical vision of seeing and seen as a single fact, we will detour to the reflections of the Swiss psychologist C.G. Jung during his mystical months of 1913–1914, most adequately expressed in the short text from 1916, "Seven Sermons to the Dead." (Jung 2009). The context is Jung's visionary guru, the imaginal figure "Philemon," teaching a group of Christian "dead" a truth that they did not find in their pilgrimage to the Holy Land of Jerusalem (essentially this truth is the necessity to expand God to include evil as well as good). At the same time, the figure of Jung himself within the story queries Philemon about the truth of what he says, asking whether what "Jung," and the dead, see through Philemon's teachings is really true. "Jung" (the imaginal figure) asks, "are you certain that things really are as you say?" Philemon replies, "I am certain these things are as I say. . . . my knowledge is precisely these things themselves." (*Red Book*, p. 515). Forty years later, in a television interview, Jung was asked whether he believed in God. He answered, famously, "I don't need to believe, I know." Philemon's (and Jung's) teachings—as we see also in Sāṃkhya/Yoga—cannot be understood but can be (at least partially) known in performance, practice, *sādhana*, life—symbolically. As Jung quotes Philemon, "This God is to be known but not understood." (ibid 522). Knowledge, for Jung and Samkhya/Yoga, is not separate from being. What we know (experience, our Erfahrung) is what we are (and already were, at least virtually).

Sāṃkhya and Yoga teach what the thinkers and meditators experience in their practice, the fact of two complementary I-positions (*dṛṣṭāsmi*—the "I" of *prakṛti* in Sāṃkhya, corresponding to *dṛśya* in Yoga; and *dṛṣṭā māyā*—the "I" of *puruṣa* in Sāṃkhya, in Yoga called *dṛśi*) that approach oneness in being performed together. Seeking to give *puruṣa* enjoyment means to give him the experience of one's *prakṛtic* self. It is the quality of this self that determines whether *puruṣa*'s experience is one of suffering (*duḥkha*) or pleasant repose (*avasthāna svastha*).[22] Yet. in truth, it is always *prakṛti* who experiences *puruṣa*'s experience *for* him.[23] *Puruṣa* is imagined as a necessary "existent" (the term is

[22] The practice of Yoga passes through positive rather than painful experience. *Bhoga*, as a *puruṣārtha*, thus emphasizes the quest for pleasant experience rather than experience in general. *YS* 1.18, for instance, locates one kind of *samādhi* as following focus on the pleasant (Phillips 2009, p. 208, as "contentment").

[23] This "'for' *puruṣa*" follows from and extends the sense of *artha* in *puruṣārtha*. *Prakṛti* lives vicariously, as though she were *puruṣa*, as if she were giving *herself* enjoyment and liberation (this is Whicher's (2013) "self as seen"); but it is only when she realizes the "as if," and sees that she is actually doing it for *puruṣa* (who is an Other), that she can reach her goal, be released, achieve realization. *Prakṛti* becomes enlightened "for" *puruṣa* but in the end only she is enlightened, achieves release, as *SK* 62 clearly states. YS 2.6 "Egoity (asmitā) is when it seems as if the powers of seeing and the seen are of the same nature." (dṛg darśana śaktyor ekātmatā ivā 'smitā, my translation.) This is a very clear statement of the idea of "the self as seen." Also see *SK* 56: "This creation . . . functions for the sake of the release of each *puruṣa*; (this is done) for the sake of another [*parārtha*] as if it were for her own (benefit) [*svārtha*]." Larson translation (Larson 1969, p. 272).

from Stephen Collins' [Collins 2010] discussion of Buddhist nirvana), the observer who reflects back *prakṛti*'s affliction (suffering) or takes and passes back her "not-I" realization in a darshan that dances indefinitely closer to oneness (*jñāna, SK* 54). The ineffable is performed in *prakṛti*'s dance of apophasis: *nāsmi na me nāham*. Do Sāṃkhya and Yoga "believe" what they say? We might answer, with Jung, that they do not need to believe, because they are what they experience. *Nāsmi* is not a factual assertion; it is a mystical realization or apotheosis.

8. Darshan in Contemporary Hinduism

Lawrence A. Babb (1981, 1984) and Diana Eck (1998) some years ago studied the role of darshan in a number of Indian religious groups including the Radhasoami sects, the Brahma Kumaris, the modern saint Satya Sai Baba, and the film Jai Santoshi Ma and its religious aftermath. William Ellison (2014, 2018) later investigated darshan in the street shrines focused on the other (Shirdi) Sai Baba in Bombay, while Patrick McCartney (2018) looked at darshan-related phenomena in the Shanti Mandir, a very recent and still active offshoot of the "meditation revolution" instigated by Swami Muktananda and his guru Swami Nityananda (senior). Ellison, citing Katherine Katherine (1997), makes use of Jacques Lacan's psychoanalytic theories to explain darshan, with the fundamental idea being Lacan's seminal concept from 1936, the "mirror stage" and the subsequent creation and transformation of the image the child has of itself. Lacan's basic thought is that the self of the baby is given to her by how the mother (or other caregivers) see her. The world in which the growing child will subsequently live, the so-called "symbolic order" of constraint and unfreedom, is close to Heidegger's "calculative" and "inauthentic" realm of fallen, and "thrown," *dasein*, and perhaps even Max Weber's "iron cage" of industrial life or Adorno's view of culture as indoctrination and anesthesia. It is also close to Sāṁkhyan *ahamkāra* and Yogic *asmitā*. Although Ewing and Ellison disagree with Lacan's extreme cultural pessimism, they find value in his insight that the object of darshan (say a lithographic image of Sai Baba in a Bombay street shrine) reaches out to the passerby and visually lays hold of his consciousness; i.e., it "sees" him and causes him to look back.[24] Child research has consistently found that the reciprocal looking and smiling responses of mother and child are fundamental to the child's growing ability to regulate emotions and of the mother's to educate her child into the realities of living. (Infants who are later diagnosed with Autism show reduced sensitivity to direct gaze by the parent). Psychoanalytic self psychology (especially Winnicott and Kohut) trace the development of the self to the child's ambition to be seen as valuable by the mother and the mother's willingness to allow the child to merge with her idealized, much more powerful, adult identity. The child is constituted as a self by being perceived as one. The nature of that self can be one of suffering and disregulation or freedom and creative life.[25]

A mystery lies at the heart of this self recognized by the mother in the baby, and it is one that Indian thought has worked to understand, and locate within the ritual structure of worship. As Babb points out, darshan is reciprocal between worshipper and god, with visual and other kinds of substance flowing both ways. But in this exchange, the god is clearly the more important source, and the power behind the image is ultimately where the energy of darshan originates. A good way to see this is to consider not one image but a whole "mountainside" of them, i.e., the images carved into the outer surface of a Hindu temple, which is considered to represent a cosmos consisting of a mountain range with many terraces (foothills) occupied by celestial beings (Eck 1998, p. 61). All this rich variety of life and cosmos comes from deep within the mountain-temple, from a cave in its heart called the *garbhagrha* or "womb chamber" (ibid, p. 63). In the same way, every individual image on and in the

24 "Shrines, in the prescribed telling, are the concrete manifestation of a divine agency that is heeded by human subjects. Immanent divinity can reveal itself at some places in the form of a symptom, a material clue like a swelling in the ground or a whorl in a tree that triggers recognition in the right person. This is the logic of the *svayambhu*, or 'self-manifested,' icon, which anchors the origin stories of many of the famous sites of Brahminical Hinduism. At other sites, God—in one of His or Her myriad forms—may appear to the right person through the medium of a dream." (Elison 2018, p. 64).

25 Unfreedom for Lacan, authentic selfhood and creativity for Winnicott and Kohut.

temple can be seen as a projection into our everyday world of an "aniconic" (Eck) divine force that takes shape as it solidifies via the complex rules governing its construction by the artisan (*shilpin*) who makes it according to traditional formulas.

Many Hindu, Buddhist, and Jain images express a similar visual logic.[26] For example, the eyes of the three-faced image of Sadaśiva at Elephanta are closed. The pilgrim, or modern-day tourist, arrives in front of the statue after crossing the water, climbing up a hill to the entry of the rock temple in which the image rests, and passing through a series of doors (Berkson et al. 1983). They are there to see the god, and are rewarded with a *trimurti* expressive of three moods of the deity erupting into space from the living stone within which is supposed to live a fourth image still encased in rock. The god has projected these images outward, like the forms on the surface of a temple, from a secret inner space, the *guhya* level of the image, which is implied to be buried deep in the stone. We take darshan of the image, not in this case by gazing into his eyes, but rather, we might say, by seeing the image he projects with *his* eyes.

A series of verses in the *Sāṃkhya Kārikā* (*SK* 58, 59, 61, 64, 65, 66, 68, 69) lays out how *puruṣa* and *prakṛti* are united in enjoyment and how they mirror the state of enlightenment that follows complete satisfaction or insight. Let us return once again to the image of a female dancer (*nartakī*), the unsurpassably maidenly creature (*sukumārataram na kiṁcid asti*, *SK* 61). The *bhoga* aspect of *puruṣārtha* is expressed through *seeing*, very much like the later idea of darshan discussed above. In *SK* 61 and 66, *prakṛti* announces that "I have been seen" (*drāṣṭāsmi, dṛṣṭāham*) and in *SK* 66 *puruṣa* states the correlative, "I have seen [her]" (*dṛṣṭā māyā*). This recognition ends the work of *prakṛti* for *puruṣa*'s sake, leading to enlightenment/release, which likewise is viewed from both points of view. *Prakṛti* utters (*SK* 64) her great apophatic realization of non-being or non-self: *nāsmi na me nāham*, "I am not, nothing belongs to me, and there is no "I" [in me]." This is apophatic mysticism because *prakṛti*'s non-self-recognition is *puruṣa*'s moment of full, unafflicted selfhood. *Puruṣa*'s vision of the not-I *prakṛti*, in the next verse (65), is the view from *kaivalya*: *prakṛtim paśyati puruṣaḥ . . . avasthitaḥ svasthaḥ*, "*Puruṣa* gazes upon [the nay-saying] *prakṛti* while comfortably established in his own place." Enjoyment, seeing something utterly beautiful transpire before his eyes, i.e., *prakṛti*'s completion of all action and recognition of having no selfhood or possession, leads immediately to release from struggle against suffering. Seeing and being seen are equivalent to enjoying and being enjoyed. Full enjoyment is the end of the seeking of enjoyment and leads at once to the "superior kind of death" that S. Collins ascribes to nirvana (and Freud to *thanatos*) and that we find also in Sāṁkhya in the idea of *kaivalya*. The darshan of *puruṣa* and *prakṛti* is a mystical realization that both fulfills and transcends their absolute otherness.

9. Darshan and Intentionality

Prakṛti's life trajectory in Sāṁkhya/Yoga is quite strange: while her nature is to act "for the sake of *puruṣa*," the text further specifies that this purpose includes *to be seen by puruṣa as "not I."* It would appear that *prakṛti* exists in order to reveal her non-being, she sees in order to reveal that she does not see, or sees for *puruṣa* rather than for herself. Perhaps her life could be viewed as the enactment of a sort of close reading of intentionality, getting at and overcoming the "consciousness of" things that is fundamental to ahaṃāric existence. What for Brentano and much of European philosophy is the basic condition of the working mind—consciousness of—is split by Sāṁkhya and Yoga into two sides, one of consciousness: i.e., *puruṣa*, and one of of (sic!): i.e., *prakṛti*. The practice of close reading the mind to make this split real is both philosophy (Sāṁkhya) and meditation (Yoga). What it leads to is a transformation of the mind (*buddhi*, or the mental system *of buddhi-manas-ahamkāra* = *antaḥkāraṇa* of which it is the key element). The key to suffering is the conflation of the two sides of experience, so that something seen (something that consciousness is of) proclaims, in the act of *ahamkāra* (understood, as van Buitenen said in 1957 (Van Buitenen 1957), as "utterance of the word

[26] For Jain darshan, see the work of John Cort, e.g., Cort (2001).

'I'"), that it is the seer. A limited darshan, the whole functioning of *prakṛti* has sought *bhoga* but obtained *duḥkha* because it substituted *ahamkāra* for *nāhamkāra* (saying "I am," *aham*, rather than *nāham*, "not I"). *Ahamkāra*-infused *buddhi* says (to *puruṣa*) "I act for myself" and so actions (*karmas*), point downward into the world of suffering, i.e., lose their *puruṣa* focus. It is this that leads to the closed but still unfolding *pariṇāma* or *nivṛtti* existence that is named "3-fold suffering" (*duḥkhatraya*) in *SK* 1. Locked in the "of" and unconscious of consciousness (the *dṛśi* of *darśana*), *buddhi* nevertheless aims unknowingly at serving *puruṣa*-consciousness. As *SK* 58 says, in ordinary life we act for the sake of quenching unfulfilled cravings. In Sanskrit, the implication of this is sharper: *pravṛtti* is for the sake of *nivṛtti*, action aims to transcend action. The second half of verse 58 tells us that this really means that already, in our "normal" suffering existence, we are seeking nothing different from what *prakṛti* was doing primordially, before *ahamkāra* (i.e., in her *avyakta* state): acting for the sake of the liberation of consciousness (*puruṣasya vimokṣārtham*).

Sāṃkhya and Yoga, then, move from darshan to darshan, from a lower to a higher form of vision, where the seer in the first darshan is revealed, in the second, to be the seen and, in service to the real seer (or to the seer-ness, *sākṣitva*, of the seer), negates herself and opens the world both for consciousness and for herself.[27] This mystical opening, which the word *mokṣa* names, precisely, as "release," changes both life and death.

10. Intentionality and Experience

Religious experience as analyzed in Western terms, both the *Erlebnis* and the *Erfahrung* types, is intentional. It is about something, a moment in the case of *Erlebnis*, and bound time (or a story) in the case of *Erfahrung*. In Sāṃkhya and Yoga, a similar distinction is drawn between "afflicted" (*kḷṣṭa*) or ordinary seeing, where the psychomental apparatus (the *liṅgaśarīra*—the Indian parallel to the Western individual) sees (and hears, etc.), but also integrates, sensory data, memories, etc.; and *akḷṣṭa* experience which is characterized (in Yoga) as *samādhi* of various types, which approach, or completely are, unintentional, not about something. In these states, the prakrtic entity or person (*liṅga*) is consciously recognized as being seen (*dṛṣṭa*) rather than seeing (*dṛśi*, etc.). *Prakṛti*, or her highest evolute, *buddhi*, becomes enlightened, attains *mokṣa*, for the sake of *puruṣa*. Conversely, it is the recognition of being "for the sake of *puruṣa*" (*puruṣārtha*) that brings *mokṣa*. Religious experience *is* experience for another (*parārtha*, *SK* 17), the other that is one's true self which can only be realized apophatically, in the negation of the lower self: in fully realizing, as *SK* 64 tells us, to repeat once more, that "I am not, I have nothing, and there is no 'I' in me." (*Nāham na me nāsmi*). In realizing the I-lessness of ordinary experience (*bhoga*), religious experience (*darśana*) begins. To be not-I is to be seen (*dṛṣta)* as such, and to realize that one has been seen wholly and finally (*aikantika, atyantika*).

In conclusion, Sāṃkhya and Yoga embody—and hold out as a possibility for the practitioner—a complex, endlessly evolving mystical experience that is best understood in its own language as *darśana*, the slowly explosive self-recognition within *prakṛti* of being seen by a *puruṣa* who—she knows, in the moment she finally knows herself—sees her.

Funding: This research received no external funding.

Conflicts of Interest: The author declares no conflict of interest.

References

Babb, Lawrence Alan. 1981. Glancing: Visual Interactions in Hinduism. *Journal of Anthropological Research* 37: 387–401. [CrossRef]

[27] Ian Whicher (1998) and Christopher Chapple (2008) have discussed Patañjali's Yoga in similar terms, especially recognizing that yoga implies a transformation of life, not its negation as is often asserted.

Babb, Lawrence Alan. 1984. *Redemptive Encounters: Three Modern Styles in the Hindu Tradition*. Berkeley: University of California Press.

Benjamin, Walter. 2004. Program of the Coming Philosophy. In *Selected Writings*. vol. 1, Cambridge: Harvard University Press. First published 1918.

Benjamin, Walter. 2002. *The Arcades Project*. Cambridge: Harvard University Press.

Berkson, Carmel, Wendy Doniger Flaherty, and George Michell. 1983. *Elephanta: The Cave of Siva*. Princeton: Princeton University Press.

Berlin, Isaiah. 2000. The Counter-Enlightenment. In *The Proper Study of Mankind: An Anthology of Essays*. New York: Farrar, Strauss, and Giroux.

Bryant, Edwin F. 2009. *The Yoga Sūtras of Patañjali: A New Edition, Translation, and Commentary*. New York: North Point Press.

Burley, Mikel. 2012. *Classical Samkhya and Yoga: An Indian Metaphysics of Experience. London: Routledge*. London: Routledge.

Chapple, Christopher Key. 2003. Yoga and the Luminous. In *Yoga: The Indian Tradition*. Edited by David Carpenter and Ian Whicher. New York: Routledge.

Chapple, Christopher Key. 2008. *Yoga and the Luminous: Patanjali's Spiritual Path to Freedom*. Albany: State University of New York Press.

Collins, Alfred. 1991. From Brahma to a Blade of Grass: Toward an Indian Self Psychology. *Journal of Indian Philosophy* 19: 143–89. [CrossRef]

Collins, Alfred. 2000. Dancing with Puruṣa: The Samhyan Goddess as *pativrata* and *guru*. In *Is the Goddess a Feminist? The Politics of South Asian Goddesses*. Edited by Alf Hiltebeitel and Kathleen M. Erndl. New York: New York University Press.

Collins, Alfred. 2006. Dharmamegha Samadhi and the Two Sides of Kaivalya. Paper presented at Dharma Association of North America annual meeting, Washington, DC, 17 November 2006.

Collins, Alfred, and Prakash Desai. 1999. Selfhood in the Indian context: A psychoanalytic perspective. In *Vishnu on Freud's Desk: A Reader in Psychoanalysis and Hinduism*. Edited by Jeffrey Kripal and T.G. Vaidyanathan. London: Routledge, pp. 367–98.

Collins, Alfred. Forthcominga. "I have been seen": *Darshan* in the *Sāṃkhya Kārikā* and *Yoga Sūtra*. Edited by Chapple Christopher Key.

Collins, Alfred. Forthcomingb. Sāṃkhya/Yoga as an Indian Religious and Cultural Science. In *The Bloomsbury Research Handbook of Indian Philosophical Theories of Religion*. Edited by Pankaj Jain. London: Bloomsbury Academic.

Collins, Steven. 2010. *Nirvana: Concept, Imagery, Narrative*. Cambridge: Cambridge University Press.

Cort, John. 2001. *Jains in the World: Religious Values and Ideology in India*. Oxford: Oxford University Press.

Eck, Diana. 1998. *Darshan: Seeing the Divine Image in India*. New York: Columbia University Press.

Elison, William. 2014. Sai Baba of Bombay: A saint, his icon, and the urban geography of *Darshan*. *History of Religions* 54: 151–87. [CrossRef]

Elison, William. 2018. Site, Sight, Cite: Conceptualizing Wayside Shrines as Visual Culture. *SAMAJ* 18. [CrossRef]

Eliade, Mircea. 2009. *Yoga Immortality and Freedom. Princeton University Press*. Princeton University Press.

Katherine, Ewing. 1997. *Arguing Sainthood: Modernity, Psychoanalysis, and Islam*. Durham: Duke University Press.

Freud, Sigmund. 2010. *Civilization and Its Discontents*. New York: W. W. Norton. First published 1930.

Hansen, Miriam. 2012. *Cinema and Experience*. Berkeley: University of California Press.

Hauer, J. W. 1958. *Der Yoga*. Stuttgard: W. Kohnhammer.

Inden, Ronald, and Ralph Nicholas. 1973. *Kinship in Bengali Culture*. Chicago: University of Chicago Press.

James, William. 1985. *The Varieties of Religioius Experience*. London: Penguin Classics. First published 1902.

Jay, Martin. 2005. *Songs of Experience: Modern American and European Variations on a Universal Theme*. Berkeley: University of California Press.

Johnston, Edward Hamilton. 1937. *Early Sāṃkhya*. Delhi: Motilal Banarsidass.

Jung, Carl Gustav. 2009. *The Red Book (Liber Novus)*. New York: W. W. Norton.

Kohut, Heinz. 1977. *The Restoration of the Self*. New York: International Universities Press.

Lacombe, Olivier. 1937. *L'Absolu selon le Vedanta*. Paris: Guethner.

Laplanche, Jean, and J.-B. Pontalis. 1974. *The Language of Psychoanalysis*. New York: W. W. Norton.

Larson, Gerald. 1969. *Classical Sāṃkhya*. Delhi: Motilal Banarsidas.

Larson, Gerald. 2018. *Classical Yoga Philosophy and the Legacy of Sāṃkhya*. Delhi: Motilal Banarsidass.
Martin, Craig, and Russell T. McCutcheon, eds. 2014. *Religious Experience: A Reader*. London: Routledge.
Marriott, McKim. 1976. *Hindu Transactions: Diversity without Dualism*. Chicago: University of Chicago Press.
Marriott, McKim. 1989. Constructing an Indian Ethnosociology. *Contributions to Indian Sociology (n.s.)* 23: 1–39. [CrossRef]
McCartney, Patrick. 2018. *Suggesting Śāntamūrti and Śāntarasavāda: A Sociological Study of Shanti Mandir's Social Network in the context Of Global Yoga*. Kyoto: RINDAS, Ryukoku University, Available online: https://medium.com/@psdmccartney/suggesting-%C5%9B%C4%81ntam%C5%ABrti-and-%C5%9B%C4%81ntarasav%C4%81da-a-sociological-study-of-shanti-mandirs-social-network-and-80137d8a8cce (accessed on 1 February 2019).
McDaniel, June. 2018. *Lost Ecstasy: Its Decline and Transformation in Religion*. New York: Palgrave Macmillan.
Pflueger, Lloyd. 2003. Dealing with dualism: Revisioning the paradox of spirit (puruṣa) and matter (prakṛti) in the Yoga Sūtra. In *Yoga: The Indian Tradition*. Edited by David Carpenter and Ian Whicher. New York: Routledge.
Phillips, Stephen. 2009. *Yoga, Karma, and Rebirth*. New York: Columbia University Press.
Roland, Alan. 1989. *In Search of the Self in India and Japan*. Princeton: Princeton University Press.
Smith, Frederick. 2006. *The Self Possessed: Deity and Spirit Possession in South Asian Literature and Civilization*. New York: Columbia University Press.
Smith, Jonathan Z. 2004. *Relating Religion: Essays in the Study of Religion*. Chicago: University of Chicago Press.
Taves, Ann. 2011. *Religious Experience Reconsidered: A Building-Block Approach to the Study of Religion and Other Special Things*. Princeton: Princeton University Press.
Van Buitenen, Johannes A.B. 1957. Studies in Sāṃkhya (II). *JAOS* 77: 15–25. [CrossRef]
Whicher, Ian. 1998. *The Integrity of the Yoga Darśana: A Reconsideration of Classical Yoga*. New York: State University of New York Press.
Whicher, Ian. 2003. *Yoga: The Indian Tradition*. Edited by David Carpenter and Ian Whicher. New York: Routledge.
White, David Gordon. 2014. *The Yoga Sutra: A Biography*. Princeton, New Jersey: Princeton University Press.
Winnicott, Donald W. 1971/2005. *Playing and Reality*. London: Routledge. First published 1971.

religions

MDPI

Article

Earning God through the "One-Hundred Rupee Note": *Nirguṇa Bhakti* and Religious Experience among Hindu Renouncers in North India

Antoinette DeNapoli

Department of Religion, Texas Christian University, 2800 S University Dr, Fort Worth, TX 76129, USA; a.denapoli@tcu.edu

Received: 9 November 2018; Accepted: 6 December 2018; Published: 11 December 2018

Abstract: This article examines the everyday religious phenomenon of *nirguṇa bhakti* as it is experienced by Hindu renouncers (*sādhus*) in North India. As an Indian language concept, *nirguṇa bhakti* characterizes a type of devotion (*bhakti*) that is expressed in relation to a divinity who is said to be without (*nir*) the worldly characteristics and attributes of sex and gender, name and form, race and ethnicity, class and caste. Although *bhakti* requires a relationship between the devotee and the deity, the *nirguṇa* kind transcends the boundaries of relational experience, dissolving concepts of "self" and "other", and, in effect, accentuating the experience of union in the divine absolute. In comparison to *saguṇa bhakti* (devotion to a deity with attributes), *nirguṇa bhakti* is considered to be difficult to realize in human birth. Yet, the poetry, songs, and practices of uncommon humans who have not only left behind social norms, but also, devoting their lives to the worship of the divine, achieved forms of divine realization, people like the mystics, saints and *sādhus* of Hindu traditions, laud the liberating power and insights of *nirguṇa bhakti*. The Hindu *sādhus* featured in this article describe their experiences of *nirguṇa bhakti* through the use of the idiom of a "one-hundred rupee note" to distinguish its superior value and, as significantly, to indicate that humans "earn" God (Brahman) through the practice of *nirguṇa* devotion. As a "precious" spiritual asset on the path of liberation, *nirguṇa bhakti* establishes the religious authority and authenticity of *sādhus*, while setting them apart from other *sādhus* and holy figures in a vibrant North Indian religious landscape.

Keywords: Hinduism; renunciation; Nirguna Bhakti; devotion; performance; Sadhus; India

---

> *Wherever you look, God is there. But we can't see God. We can't do anything without God. We can't move our limbs, or blink our eyes, or even breathe without God. Only God does everything. Only God moves everything. Only God causes us to speak and to see. God feeds us and quenches our thirst. God wakes us up in the morning and puts us to sleep at night. God raises us. Only God does everything. These bodies of ours are like stones. And when these bodies die, God emerges. God is the most precious thing we have in this world. Whether you bury it or burn it, the body has no worth. It is not even worth a single rupee. If you want to meet God, then you have to offer God the devotion that is worth a single one-hundred rupee note. And God will meet us, for sure.*
>
> Ganga Giri Maharaj, March 29, 2005, India

This article explores the religious phenomenon known as *nirguṇa bhakti* in the Hindu traditions through the religious experiences and devotional practices of the Hindu mystics and holy people (*sādhus*) with whom I have worked in North India for almost two decades.[1] The research for this article

1 The research was funded by a Junior Scholars Dissertation Research Fellowship with the American Institute of Indian Studies (AIIS). The AIIS also awarded me an advanced Hindi language fellowship for the academic year 2002–2003, which made it possible for me to return a year later to Rajasthan and conduct ethnographic field research with the *sādhus*.

is based on ethnographic fieldwork that I conducted with a population sample of thirty-nine Hindu *sādhus* (24 women and 15 men) in five districts of the former princely state of Mewar in southern Rajasthan.[2] While the *sādhus* speak Hindi (or a local Rajasthani dialect mixed with modern Hindi), to make this article's transliteration practices systematic with the rest of the articles also featured in this special issue, and user-friendly for non-Indian language speakers, I follow the more common academic convention of using the Sanskrit spelling of Indian language terms, such as *nirguṇa* (rather than the Hindi version, *nirgun*), *mokṣa* (H: *mokṣ*), *sannyāsa* (H: *sannyās*), *guṇa* (H: *gun*), and so forth.[3] The exception to this standard concerns the names of Hindu deities, which correspond to the *sādhus'* Hindi pronunciation. Here, the *sādhus* say "Ram", and not Rama; "Shiv", and not Shiva, etc.

Bhakti translates to mean "loving devotion", and the concept of *nirguṇa* calls attention to a unique kind of *bhakti* that centers on the worship of a God who is said to have no defining characteristics, qualities, or traits (*guṇa*). Although *bhakti* implies relationship between the devotee and the deity, the *nirguṇa* kind transcends the parameters of relational experience, dissolving concepts of "self" and "other", and, in effect, accentuating an experience of union with the impersonal divine. As illustrated in the epigraph to this article, Ganga Giri, a woman *sādhu* with whom I worked, and whom the other *sādhus* considered an exemplary *sādhu* by virtue of her realizing (non-dual) Brahman consciousness, describes a *nirguṇa* understanding of the divine.[4] As Brahman has no shape or form, it cannot be seen. Yet, the impersonal divine can, indeed, be known. It not only "drives" everything in the universe, but it also exists within all forms of creation, waiting to be experienced. We will return to this idea shortly.

Historically, *nirguṇa bhakti* dates back approximately to the 15th century in North India in connection with the devotion exemplified by spiritually realized people known as the "sants" (literally, the "good people"), who gathered in fellowship (*satsang*) to sing to a nameless and formless God. Its practice runs across Indic religious traditions and it is featured in the *bhakti* poetry of Hindus, Sikhs, and (Sufi) Muslims. Take examples like Guru Nanak (ca. 1469), who founded the Sikh tradition. In teachings (*guru-vāṇī*) that have been enshrined in the *Guru Granth Sāhib*, the Sikh scripture, Guru Nanak says that chanting the "indestructible" name (*śabda*) of the "timeless", "colorless", and "formless" God brings peace to the heart. Subsequently, there is Kabir (ca. 1440), the "exemplar of *nirguṇa* religion".[5] As a *sant* claimed by Hindus and Muslims, and casting his vitriol at oppressive social structures and institutions, Kabir sings of the brilliance of the formless God (Ram), while cautioning against becoming absorbed in meaningless labels like "Hindu" or "Muslim". In a poem attributed to him, Kabir says:

> If God had wanted to make me a Muslim,
> why didn't he make the incision?
> You cut away the foreskin, and then you have a Muslim;
> so what about your women?
> What are they?
> Women, so they say, are only half-formed men:
> I guess they must stay Hindus to the end.
>
> Hindus, Muslims—where did they come from?
> Who got them started down this road?
> Search inside, search your heart and look:
> Who made heaven come to be?

---

2 (DeNapoli 2014).
3 As readers can see, In the Hindi pronunciation of Sanskrit terms, the final 'a' of a word remains unpronounced.
4 To accentuate narrative voice, in this article, I use the ethnographic present to describe the practices and lives of the *sādhus* with whom I worked. By doing so, I hope to evoke for readers the ethnographic presence of their teachings and the ways that their words/songs emerged in my interactions with them.
5 (Hawley and Juergensmeyer [1998] 2008), p. 41.

Fool,
Throw away that book, and sing of Ram.
What you're doing has nothing to do with him.
Kabir has caught hold of Ram for his refrain,
And the Qazi[6]?
He spends his life in vain.[7]

Nirguṇa bhakti characterizes one of two types of devotion in the Hindu traditions. The other type is known as *saguṇa*, which describes loving devotion to a deity who is imagined to have any and every kind of attribute conceivable with respect to name, form, and gender. *Saguṇa* forms of deity range from the anthropomorphic (imagining God as human) to the theriomorphic (imagining God as an animal). In *saguṇa* traditions, like Vaishnvaism, the great Hindu god Vishnu, around whom Vaishnava worship revolves, is said to have ten descent-forms (*avatāra*) by which the god incarnates in the world to save it from destruction and evil (*adharma*). Among Vishnu's *avatāras* are humans (e.g., Ram, Parashuram, Krishna), a dwarf, a half-man/half-lion, a boar, a tortoise, a fish, and one final form, Kalki, which has yet to appear, but, according to Hindu texts and popular religious understandings, will come during the end times.[8]

Unlike *saguṇa* worship, however, *nirguṇa* experience transcends the familiar epistemological boundaries of human thought, including those of space and time, to propel the devotee into sacred experience that is unimaginable to the human mind. Therein lies its appeal and its goal: the total transcendence of all (human-created and socially sanctioned) distinctions of self and other, right and wrong, the beautiful and the grotesque, pure and impure, young and old, rich and young, male and female. The list goes on and on. Not surprisingly, as the Kabir poem attests, *nirguṇa bhakti* voices through the poetry of the *sants* and, in our times, through the practices of the *sādhus* who sing the songs of the *sants*, socially uplifting messages about transcending social differences, because, "in light of the experience of sharing in God, all social distinctions lose their importance".[9] Furthermore, as the voluminous *nirguṇa bhakti* literature suggests, transcendence experienced as the dissolution of differences forges the union of the devotee's self (*ātmā*) with God-Self (Brahman), which the *sādhus* call "melting into God", to bring about an ultimate state of peace (*śānti*), equanimity, and stillness. To clarify: many of the following *bhajans* sung by the *sādhus* refer to the divine as "Ram", which characterizes *nirguṇa* understandings of the nameless, formless, and genderless absolute, and not *saguṇa* interpretations of Vishnu's *avatāra*, Ram.

We will examine the ways in which the Hindu *sādhus* talk about, and, more precisely, sing about *nirguṇa bhakti*, and why they prefer this *bhakti* over the *saguṇa* kind. We approach our analysis of *nirguṇa bhakti* through the lens of the lives and teachings of the *sādhus* because these individuals spend their days striving to realize the impersonal absolute through the *nirguṇa bhakti* path in order to attain the ultimate goal of liberation (*mokṣa*) from the endless cycle of birth, life, and death, known as *samsāra*. While there are many kinds of *sādhus* in South Asia, this articles draws the reader's attention to a specific class of *sādhus* known as renouncers. The Indian language term for a male renouncer is *sannyāsī*, and *sannyāsinī* is used for the female renouncer (the latter are also called "māī", "māī-rām", or "mātā-rām", all of which translate to mean "holy mother"). Despite the terminological specificity by which renouncers as a class are characterized in South Asia, those with whom I worked preferred the generic term "sādhu" to represent themselves (some called themselves *sants*, or "good people") and this preference cuts across gender, class, and caste.

---

6 "Qazi" translates to mean a Muslim religious professional who specializes in legal interpretations of the *Quran*.
7 Ibid., p. 52.
8 See (Dimmitt and van Buitenen 1978).
9 Ibid., p. 17.

There are two major types of Hindu renunciation in India, namely Shaiva and Vaishnava forms. The Shaiva traditions traditionally accept the great Hindu god Shiv as the divine absolute, whereas the Vaishnava traditions acknowledge Vishnu in this role. The *sādhus* with whom I worked belong to one of two Shaiva traditions of renunciation: The Dashanami (literally, "ten names") tradition of *sādhus*, which is thought to have been organized by the Hindu renouncer (and reformer) Adi Shankara (ca. 9th century), who established monasteries throughout India; the Gorakhnath Kanphata Yogi tradition (henceforth, Nath), attributed to the Hindu mystic-saint, Gorakhnath (ca. 11th century).

As renouncers, the *sādhus* practice an unconventional way of life in India, called *sannyāsa* ("world renunciation"). It demonstrates a radical religious option in South Asia as well as illuminates an alternative to the dominant social norm of householding. The *sādhus* have left behind the normative societal expectations of marriage and family, socio-economic obligations of work and career, class and caste (and the social status and privilege that are associated with different caste communities), and their broader social responsibilities to the community (*samāj*) or society in which they lived, participated, and mapped their everyday lives. As they are required to relinquish making money, the *sādhus* are not wage earners. They rely on the kindness and generosity of their householder devotees to sustain themselves physically in the world, and the *sādhus* return that generosity by giving teachings, counsel, healing, guidance, and blessings.

After taking their vows, which involve voluntary simplicity, poverty, and life-long celibacy (*brahmacārya*), and after undergoing the ritual ceremony (*sanskāra*) and initiation (*dīkṣā*) by which they sever their socio-biological ties to their former social worlds, the *sādhus* embark on a religious path that is dedicated to the salvific goal of "getting God", so as to stop any further journeying in *samsāra*. As the term denotes "endless wandering" from lifetime to lifetime due to infinite numbers of rebirths, the *sādhus* view *samsāra* in a negative way. They perceive *samsāra* as a transitory realm of "death", "pain", and "suffering", and they hope to exit from it not only as quickly as possible, but also with the liberating insight (*jnāna*) that ensures they will never return to the world.

A way of life that requires its practitioners to "die and then live" is by no means for the faint of heart. *Sādhus* are commonly revered and respected on account of the physical, mental, and spiritual hardships that are associated with *sannyāsa* (but *sādhus* can also evoke suspicion and doubt because, as they relinquish their ties to the world, no one knows who they are, where they come from, or what their intentions are). As the *sādhus* told me, *sannyāsa* is "difficult" and it requires a lifetime of patience, persistence, and perseverance. Some of the *sādhus* recognize that they may "return" to *samsāra* the next time around; however, through the good works (*karma*) that they have accumulated from the current life of discipline (*sādhanā*), these *sādhus* also feel that they will be reborn as *sādhus* and realize *mokṣa* in a future birth. Others, though, are less thrilled by that possibility and remain determined to realize *mokṣa* in this lifetime.

The central renunciant virtues around which the *sādhus* weave their worlds concern those of detachment (*vairāgya*), solitude (*ekānta*), and simplicity (*saraltā*). Of these, detachment figures prominently. In the dominant view of the "rhetoric of renunciation", as "performed" by the *sādhus* through the means of song, story, and sacred text, detachment distinguishes the "real" (*aslī*) from the "fake" (*naklī*) *sādhus*; the dilettantes from the earnest. Detachment makes possible *sādhus*' expected cutting of ties with family, community, society, and world, and leads them, as one Hindu mystical text describes, from "death to immortality".[10] Thus, viewing their lives as a sacred offering of prayer and loving devotion to God, the *sādhus* engage in practices through which they generate detachment from worldly concerns, needs, and desires. For many of the *sādhus*, *nirguṇa bhakti* provides a powerful conduit with which to engender detachment and realize the impersonal divine absolute in the current birth.

[10] *Brihadāranyaka Upaniṣad*, 1.3.28, cited from (Olivelle 1996), pp. 12–13.

In comparison to the *saguṇa* variety, *nirguṇa bhakti* commands the adoration of the *sādhus* (and the householders) whom I knew. It can do what these *sādhus* say no other practice can do: dissolve all social distinctions into emptiness, distinctions like caste (*jātī*), class (*varna*), and sex (*linga*), which have been used by the dominant Brahmanical religious power structure in the history of Hindu traditions to oppress and disclaim the full humanity of women and low-castes. Along with dissolving worldly dualities, *nirguṇa bhakti* is said to reduce the human ego to ashes. Its perceived power to bring *sādhus* to an ultimate (and fiercely coveted) state of human transcendence in which the divine is revealed to and experienced by the devotee creates the "symbolic capital" of *nirguṇa bhakti* for the *sādhus*.[11] That is, the *sādhus* who engage in forms of *nirguṇa* devotion are thought to be more accomplished and spiritually evolved by other *sādhus* and householders than the *sādhus* who do not. The *nirguṇa* worshipping *sādhus* have high spiritual prestige, as they are seen to be immersed in the God-consciousness that their *nirguṇa bhakti* is said to create. Through their performance of the rhetoric of renunciation, the *sādhus* heighten the significance of *nirguṇa bhakti* to *sannyāsa* by calling it a "one-hundred rupee note", distinguishing it from *saguṇa bhakti*, which is often termed a "single one rupee note". Ganga Giri, whose teachings are described earlier in the article, emphasizes the "priceless" value of *nirguṇa bhakti*. She sings the following *bhajan* to foreground her understanding of the primacy of *nirguṇa* worship:

> O *sants*, my tongue is singing *bhajans*.
> The bright diamond shining in the body is my satisfaction.
> If it shines in you, the diamond will make both your body and mind bright.
>
> We've met the *sadguru* (true guru) in the form of Ram (nameless/formless God).
> We've got the *sadguru* in the form of *bhajans*.
> We join hands to those walking on the path of *bhakti*.
> My tongue is singing *bhajans*.
>
> In the seven seas, the water is very deep
> In the seven seas, the water is very deep
>
> The real [*sūgrā*] devotees are filling their glasses and drinking a lot;
> The fake [*nūgrā*] devotees are standing on the shore, thirsty.
>
> My tongue is earning *bhajans*.
>
> O *sants*, this is what Gorakh and Kabir have said.
> The real devotees are walking on the path of *bhakti*.
>
> In the fort of Chittor, Mira Bai is worshipping Kali
> In the fort of Chittor, Mira Bai is worshipping Kali
> She had a water pot on her head and released it in the river.
>
> O sants, my tongue is earning *bhakti*.
> O sants, Gorakh and Kabir have said that
> The real devotees are walking on the path of *bhakti*.
> O sants, my tongue is earning *bhajans*.
>
> Don't escape from your body;
> It will be filled with diamonds some day
> It will be filled with diamonds some day

[11] I draw on the work of French sociologist Pierre Bourdieu to describe the idea of the spiritual merit in the form of *nirguṇa* knowledge as produced and accumulated by *sādhus* who practice *nirguṇa* devotion as "symbolic capital". Their *nirguṇa* knowledge represents a spiritual resource by which the *sādhus* create and establish their perceived high status and prestige in their communities. See (Bourdieu 1985).

O sants, my tongue is earning *bhajans*.[12]

After singing the *bhajan*, Ganga Giri shares this commentary on *nirguṇa bhakti*:

> There is no power in this body. The power of this body, the power within all bodies, is God. But God has no shape [*ākāra*]. God has no form. We call this knowledge *Brahma-jnāna* [*nirguṇa* knowledge of God]. In India, we have a single one-hundred rupee note. You don't have to count it. If it's small change, then you have to count it one by one. Knowledge should be like this—only a single note of one-hundred rupees. This knowledge is precious. It's not so easy to come by. *Nirguṇa bhakti* is like that. It's not so easy to live. It's not lying on the side of the road. It is very precious. The name of God [Ram] is very precious. It's the most expensive thing and yet it doesn't cost anything.[13]

As Ganga Giri indicates in her teaching, *nirguṇa bhakti,* as realized through devotional singing (*bhajans*) fills the devotee with the liberating knowledge that enables religious experience of the divine impersonal absolute. To that extent, singing *bhajans* that illuminate the "precious" *nirguṇa* knowledge of the *Brahma-jnāna* (literally, "ultimate knowledge of the impersonal God") symbolizes the valued religious "currency", in which the *sādhus* of Rajasthan, and elsewhere in India as the work of other scholars has shown, deal in their daily efforts to "get" God and attain mystical transcendence.

So that the reader may get a rhetorical "taste", or sense, of the religious texture of *nirguṇa bhakti* and develop an understanding of how, and the extent to which, the *bhajans* describe an "impersonal" experience of the divine and why it matters to the *sādhus*, in the rest of our discussion, we will examine their *nirguṇa bhajans*, the themes and motifs accentuated in their songs, and the implications of *nirguṇa* worship on the social lives and experiences of the *sādhus*. The question that frames the following analysis is this: Is an experience of an impersonal absolute possible given first, the ineffability that is implied by that experience (how do we describe that which reaches beyond human conceivability), and second, the dissolving of ego-consciousness (the awareness that "I" exist morphs into something that defies subjectivity). It seems initially a logical contradiction to experience something that has no attributes or qualities to experience. Let us now see what the *sādhus* and their songs have to say about this perplexing idea.

1. *Singing the Best Bhakti to God: Nirguṇa Bhajan* Songs and Themes

1.1. *Theme #1: Slipping into God: Cultivating an Attitude of Surrender for Nirguṇa Devotion*

Mystics across religious traditions have often emphasized the ineffability of their personal experiences of union with the divine. Words, symbols, images, metaphors, and emotions fail to accurately and concretely communicate what the divine *is* and, more precisely, what it feels like to merge with divine consciousness. The *sādhus*, too, make similar proclamations about experiencing the *nirguṇa Brahman*. Be that as it may, as with the writings of mystics throughout time and space, the *sādhus* never fail to articulate their *nirguṇa* experiences in a variety of ways. If pressed to define God, they simply say, "God is love". Most of the time, though, they speak about the *nirguṇa* God through the use of religious symbols and metaphors. For example, Ganga Giri says that "meeting" Brahman is "slippery"—meaning that it is neither easily attainable nor easily sustainable in ordinary waking consciousness. The devotee has to work "very hard" to "get" God and maintain God-consciousness. At the same time, the effort the devotee pours into her practice is not a guarantee that she will meet God. It slips from her grasp as soon as she "finds" God. Likewise, the devotee cannot "hold" God, for that would imply that God fits in her hands and can be known by her limited physical senses of

[12] March 29, 2005.
[13] March 29, 2005.

touch, sight, sound, taste, and smell. Meeting the *nirguṇa* Brahman seems to be a lot like a game of hide and seek. "God", as Ganga Giri says, "is everywhere and nowhere".

Yet, she claims to have experienced through *bhajan* singing the *nirguṇa* reality of Brahman. She says that she has felt God (Brahman; Sain; Parabrahman), but not with her physical senses. Rather, like many of the other *sādhus*, Ganga Giri says she has experienced God with her "heart-mind" (*man*). She stresses that the way to "find" Brahman is through the heart-mind, which, as I understand, is akin to the sensory apparatus of the soul (*ātmā*). "Brahman", Ganga Giri explains, "sits in the heart-mind". Even if it transcends sensory experience, there has to be a means, albeit preliminary, by which the devotee can know Brahman. The heart-mind serves that function. It represents the gateway (*dwāra*) to the self (*ātmā*) and to Brahman, and like any door, the heart-mind, too, requires a key to be opened. That key, according to Ganga Giri, lies with cultivating an attitude of surrender to and dependence (*adīntā*) on the divine.

Thus, on the one hand, meeting God demands constant and painstaking effort on the part of the devotee. One never knows, as Ganga Giri suggests, when she will find God, or *when God will find her*. On the other hand, because experiencing God is "slippery", that effort may be as simple as "letting go" and "surrendering" to God. In this way, Ganga Giri indicates that meeting the *nirguṇa* Brahman requires "slipping" into the "ocean" (*bhavsāgara*) of God-consciousness, of letting go of everything a person often struggles to hold on to, and to which one is attached (e.g., status, name, fame, fortune, ideas) by surrendering to a divine power and presence that is "everywhere and nowhere". Ganga Giri sings this *bhajan* to explain how to "get God":

> Live as God keeps you
> Mira Bai would say to the King [Mira's brother-in-law],
> Mira Bai said [to the King, her brother-in-law]
> Live as Ram keeps you.
> 'O, King, Live as Ram keeps you'.
>
> Some days there is *halvā* (sweets) and *pūrī* (fried bread) to eat.
> [And] some days you have to go hungry.
> 'O, King, live as Ram keeps you'.
>
> Some days you have a pillow and mattress
> [And] some days you have to sleep on the floor.
> 'O, King, live as Ram keeps you'.
>
> Some days you have gardens to wander in.
> [And] some days you have to live in the jungle.
> 'O, King, live as Ram keeps you'.[14]

This *bhajan* contains the signature (*cāp*) that is attributed to the woman *sant* known as Mira Bai. She was born into a royal Hindu (Rajput) household as a princess in the late 15th century in eastern Rajasthan. Mira Bai is said to have left behind not only the comforts and privileges of her royal status, but also her husband, the prince of the Sisodiya clan who hailed from western Rajasthan, and to whom, according to Rajasthani oral traditions, Mira was forced in marriage in order to devote herself to worshiping God through song. For Ganga Giri and many of the *sādhus*, Mira Bai models the intensity and commitment of loving devotion with respect to surrendering oneself to the divine. To make oneself utterly dependent on the *nirguṇa* Lord enacts a superior method for worshiping the impersonal divine absolute. When Mira Bai set out from the castle (she left after her in-laws tried to take her life on multiple occasions, as she refused to make her devotion to God secondary to her role as the wife and

[14] April 13, 2005.

princess of the Sisodiya ruler), she neither had food, nor water; neither a bed to sleep in, nor a place to live. She was alone and on her own. As the *bhajan* indicates, Mira understood the nameless and formless "Ram" to be her "real" security and basis for existence. Mira Bai is often associated with *saguṇa bhakti* in connection with her worship of Krishna. Yet, the *sādhus'* performance repertoires demonstrate that *nirguṇa* versions of Mira *bhakti* (in this *bhajan*, Mira worships the formless "Ram" and not the form of Krishna) circulate among renouncer communities in North India, and thus, illuminate the fluidity of the boundaries of these categories of devotional experience in lived Hindu traditions.

"Without God", as Ganga Giri teaches, "we are nothing". While we tend to think that we steer the course of our lives and destinies, in the *sādhus'* views, God remains the inner and outer-controller of everything in this world. The *bhajan* makes this idea explicit through Mira's repeated pleas to the king (her former husband's brother) to "live as God keeps him". That is, Mira implores her brother-in-law to relinquish his attachments to his wealth, his royal status, his kingdom, and perhaps his expectations of Mira as the daughter-in-law of the Sisodiyas, and surrender to the impersonal Ram, as nothing in this world compares to the "real" security that only God can provide.

Women *sādhus*, like Ganga Giri, locate Mira Bai within a *nirguṇa* tradition to claim a female religious heroine who "performs" the power and capacity of women to unite with the *nirguṇa* Lord, and as such, to illustrate that women are as eligible as men for experiencing non-dual Brahman consciousness. The poetry of Kabir, Guru Nanak, and Ravi Das, who came from a formerly "untouchable" caste group, have clearly made the case that anyone can experience the *nirguṇa* Lord. Much like the poetry that is attributed to Mira Bai, these *sants* similarly extol the power of surrendering to the *nirguṇa* Ram. However, the historical examples tend to privilege male exemplars, rather than women exemplars, in representing *nirguṇa* devotion. The song traditions of the women *sādhus* balance this representation out by bringing the voices of female *sants* to the center of the *nirguṇa* tradition. As Ganga Giri says after she sang this *bhajan*, Mira Bai's attitude of surrender enabled her to know what she calls the "precious diamond" of Brahman-consciousness.

1.2. Theme #2: "Keeping the Precious Diamond": The Brahma-jnāna of Nirguṇa Devotion

Another common metaphor on which the *sādhus* draw to describe their religious experiences of the *nirguṇa Brahman* involves the notion that knowledge of the impersonal absolute (*Brahma-jnāna*), as gained through *nirguṇa* practice, signifies the "precious diamond" by which they "earn" the authority (*adhikār*) to unite with God. In comparison to studying sacred texts or practicing austerities like fasting, for instance, singing *nirguṇa* songs constitutes the preferred method for "melting into God" among the *sādhus* with whom I worked, because singing transforms their bodies into sacred instruments receptive to divine revelation, of which the liberating insight of the *Brahma-jnāna* ranks supreme.[15] The *sādhus* liken *nirguṇa bhajan* performance to the chanting of Vedic *mantras* (sacred hymns and prayers containing liberating insight), which, in the history of Hindu traditions, has been a practice reserved for high-caste Brahmin men, and hence, off limits to women and low-castes. Many of the *sādhus* never learned the *Vedas*, and many of the women *sādhus* and some of the male *sādhus* never learned to read or write at all. Not having access to Vedic traditions of knowledge, however, was not an obstacle to their experiencing the *nirguṇa* Brahman, as the *nirguṇa* traditions not only accept "everyone" into its fold, but also challenge the so-called "high" authority of Vedic learning to determine the parameters for what "counts" as the *Brahma-jnāna*.

Regardless of their (former) caste status, most of the *sādhus* speak at length about the *nirguṇa bhajan* in terms of the sublime word (*śabda*), equivalent in power to the words of the *Vedas* ("Veda-vacana"). On a summer afternoon in 2005 while Ganga Giri, her disciple Tulsi Giri, and I paid a visit to the

---

[15] The cultural idiom of the body as receptive to divine inspiration, and thus, as an instrument of God is found in Hindu religious texts, such as the *Bhagavad Gita*. See (Patton 2008). It is also used by scholars to describe the "possessed" person's body who becomes a "receptive" instrument on which divine will works its power. See (Keller 2001).

hermitage of another woman *sādhu* named Devi Nath, the *sādhus* broke out in a singing session to teach the significance of the *nirguṇa bhajan* for attaining Brahma-*jnāna*. Here is a song that they performed:

> Listen my crazy [*bāvlā*] mind,
> Without *bhajans*, you lose the diamond [*hīrā*]. Keep [the diamond] safe.
>
> Listen my crazy [*bāvlā*] mind,
> Without *bhajans*, you lose the diamond. Keep it safe.
> In this story, immortal *rasas* [juices] are filled.
> Don't let your heart get attached with [worldly] things.
> Listen my crazy mind,
> In this story, immortal *rasas* are filled.
> Don't let your heart get attached to [worldly] things.
>
> Listen my crazy mind,
> Without *bhajans*, you lose the diamond. Keep it safe.
> Listen my crazy mind,
> In this story, there is a quarry of diamonds.
> Don't mix pebbles with the diamonds.
>
> Listen my crazy mind,
> In this story, there is a quarry of diamonds.
> Don't mix pebbles with the diamonds.
> Listen my crazy mind,
> Without *bhajans*, you lose the diamond. Keep it safe.
> In this story, unlimited water is filled.
> Don't wash your clothes in mud.
>
> Listen my crazy mind,
> Without *bhajans*, you lose the diamond. Keep it safe.
>
> Kabir says: 'Listen brother *sādhus*'.
> Kabir says: 'Listen brother *sādhus*'.
> It's only the *sants* who string one diamond after another.
> Kabir says: 'Listen brother *sādhus*!'
> It's only the *sants* who string one diamond after another.
>
> Listen my crazy mind,
> Without *bhajans*, you lose the diamond. Keep it safe.[16]

This *bhajan* contains a signature line attributed to Kabir who warns of losing the "precious diamond". As with most symbols, the diamond evokes multiple significations to suggest the notion of the *ātmā*, the *Brahma-jnāna*, and the attainment of *nirguṇa* Brahman-consciousness. Each of these represents a "precious" and "priceless" asset for the *sādhu* who seeks to transcend the transitory world of name and form. Perhaps the *nirguṇa* Lord itself requires such symbolic capital from the devotee in exchange for the priceless experience of transcendence. As Ganga Giri says in this singing session, "one cannot get the best thing without the authority to have it". Singing *nirguṇa bhajans* (as opposed to studying the Vedas) grants the devotee the prized authority to meet God.

Addressing the "crazy mind", the *bhajan* calls attention to the devotee who has immersed herself in the intoxicating "juice" ("rasa") of *bhajans* by which she knows the *ātmā*, the *Brahma-jnāna*, and the

[16] March 29, 2005.

nirguṇa Lord. Since *bhajans* provide access to the absolute, they, too, signify the precious diamond that the *sādhu* must guard with her life if she intends to meet Brahman. Focusing on *nirguṇa* worship rather than on worldly distractions and attachments helps the devotee to guard against losing the precious diamond. With that diamond the devotee disentangles herself from the web of *samsāra,* while advancing nearer to God. As the *bhajan* indicates, to savor the *rasa* of Brahman through the medium of the *nirguṇa* song amounts to an experience of transcendence. Thus, the *bhajan* makes a case for the primacy of *nirguṇa bhakti* as well as the importance of singing *nirguṇa* songs as often as possible every single day. For the devotee who keeps the practice of *nirguṇa bhakti*, the taste of God is sweet, indeed.

1.3. Theme #3: "The Taste of God Is Sweet": Nirguṇa Experience as Divine Bliss

So far, we have learned that, along with cultivating the necessary devotional attitude of surrender, singing *nirguṇa bhajans* joins the devotee with the *nirguṇa* Lord. However, what is that union like? How does the experience of the impersonal Brahman feel? Does it evoke ecstasy or agony for the devotee? Is it a positive experience or a negative one? Hindu mystical texts such as the *Upaniṣads,* which are part of the (late) Vedic corpus of revealed literature, tend to talk about Brahman by adopting a "via negativa" approach. The Indian (Sanskrit) language idiom of "neti, neti" recurs throughout the Upaniṣadic narratives, which means "neither this, nor that", to emphasize that no finite human concept can describe or evoke understanding of what God is. Whatever is said about the impersonal Lord illustrates an approximate representation, which, in turn, only communicates a concept; ideas hardly substitute for actually experiencing the divine.

While the *sādhus* do not disagree with this notion (recall Ganga Giri's description of God as "slippery"—no idea encompasses the "reality" of divine experience), they opt for a "via positiva" approach for describing the qualities that they correlate with their experiences of Brahman. After all, their claim that God is knowable implies that God has qualities by which God can be known, and thus, experienced by the devotee. They also suggest that by knowing God's qualities through the means of religious experience something happens to the devotee, something occurs that changes her deep from within and inspires the devotee to plunge the depths of the ocean of divine experience even further, at least until the transcendence that is sought becomes a permanent state of consciousness. Psychologically speaking, if God could never be known through, albeit limited, human thought, why would anyone want to experience God in the first place?

Studying the *nirguṇa bhajans* of the *sādhus,* it becomes clear that their songs offer glimpses of hope and the satisfaction that derives from knowing Brahman. To that extent, the *sādhus* say either on the basis of the evidence of their songs (for many of them, *nirguṇa* songs articulate the divine experiences of the *sants*), or their own personal experiences, as evoked through *bhajan* singing, which the "taste of God" (*Ramrasa*) is "sweet" (*mīthā*), like "sugar", and yet infinitely better than sugar; that the experience produces a "blissful" (*ānanda-mayī*) consciousness, in which the *sādhu* steps beyond her ego-self and expands into the divine horizon of God-self. Their descriptions point to mystical union with Brahman as a sublime experience of divine ecstasy (the agony, as I am told, occurs when its over). The devotee becomes "high" on God without moving "up" or "down" in her emotional state. As a male *sādhu* by named Prem Nath explains to me while holding *satsang* at his ashram in the company of Tulsi Giri and Ganga Giri, the ecstasy (*ānanda*) that he feels in those moments in which he "melts into" God-consciousness can be called "peace" (*śānti*). After he makes this provocative statement, Ganga Giri leads a singing session and performs these two *bhajans*:

Song #1

I offer food before [you, O Lord]
I forgot my house
I sacrificed good food,
O, my brother,
If you drink you will become immortal
The 'juice' of Ram is sweet, my brother

The whole world drinks sweet things
No one drinks bitter things
The whole world drinks sweet things
No one drinks bitter things

The ones who will drink the bitter things
The ones who will drink the bitter things
They shall become the sweetest

The juice of Ram is sweet, my brother
If you drink this, you will become immortal.
The juice of Ram is like this, my brother

The whole world goes up,
Nobody goes down.
The whole world goes up,
Nobody goes down.

The one who goes down
The one who goes down
S/He shall become the highest
The juice of Ram is sweet, my brother.
Drink the knowledge and become immortal.
The juice of Ram is like this, my brother

Dhruv drank it [Ramras]
Prahlad drank it
The butcher drank it

Dhruv drank it
Prahlad drank it
The butcher drank it

The servant, Kabir, drank it fully
The servant, Kabir, drank it fully.

And they still have the desire of drinking more
The juice of Ram is sweet, my brother
Whoever drinks shall become immortal
The juice of Ramras is like this.

Song #2

The urge to sing *bhajans* has really taken possession [over me.]
The Supreme Guru, Hari, is inside of my heart.

Yes, the great words have taken possession [over me].
The Supreme Guru, Hari, is inside of my heart.

Oh, yes, great words have taken possession [over me].
The Supreme Guru, Hari, is inside of my heart.

Everybody is saying it has taken possession.
And, nobody is saying it has not.

Everybody is saying it has taken possession.
And, nobody is saying it has not.

But when it takes possession of a knowing person,
S/he forgets about her body.
The Supreme Guru, Hari, is inside of my heart.

Yes, the urge to sing *bhajans* has really taken possession [of me].
The Supreme Guru, Hari, is inside of my heart.

It took possession over Dhruva,
It took possession over Prahlad,
And it took over the butcher.
It took possession over Dhruva
It took possession over Prahlad
And it took over the Prostitute,
Who was not having qualities.

And it possessed Mira Bai in such a way [that]
She left the comforts of the palace.

The Supreme Guru is inside of my heart.

It possessed Rama
It possessed Lakshmana
It possessed mother, Sita.
It possessed Hanuman in such a way [that]
He jumped into the water.

The Supreme Guru is inside of my heart.
The Supreme Hari is inside of my heart.

The urge to sing *bhajans* has really possessed [me].
The Supreme Guru, Hari, is inside of my heart.

It possessed Bharathari in such a way [that]
He left the comforts of the palace.
And Gopichand left sixteen [wives].

The Supreme Guru, Hari, is inside of my heart.

It possessed Dhanna, Pipa, Ravidas, and Pumba.
And, it possessed the barber, Senva.

It possessed Dhanna, Pipa, Ravidas, and Pumba.
And, it possessed Senva.

The Supreme Guru, Hari, is inside of my heart.[17]

After Ganga Giri sings the first few lines of the *bhajans*, Tulsi Giri joins in the *bhajan* session. While Prem Nath does not sing along with Ganga Giri and Tulsi Giri (though he sings other songs that he knew), he closes his eyes and allows his body to move to the rhythm of their performance, at times calling out "Hey Bhagvan" (Oh Lord) in response to the *bhajans'* refrains, particularly, as I recall, the refrain illustrated in the second song with the line, "The Supreme Guru, Hari, is inside of my heart". Their singing squeezes out the elixir that, like the devotees named in the songs, Prem Nath "drinks" by listening to the *bhajan*, filling him with the bliss that these *sādhus* suggest resembles the infinite power of Brahman to engulf the devotee rapt in mystical union.

Both *bhajans* speak of devotees who attained the "immortal" consciousness of the *nirguṇa* Lord by singing to God. The names of the devotees featured in these *bhajans* similarly appear in Hindu mythological texts, such as the *Purāṇas*, and texts that are linked to *nirguṇa* authors, like Jan Gopal.[18] In the songs, we encounter the names of famous *sants*, such as Kabir and Mira Bai, and other devotees, too, like Dhruva, Prahlad, Gopichand, and Bharathari. Even figures featured in *Rāmāyaṇa* narrative traditions like Ram and Sita, *avatāras* of Vishnu and his wife Lakshmi, and Lakshman (Ram's brother) and the monkey-god Hanuman, are mentioned to press on the intoxicating power of *bhajan* on deities, too. That such an impressive number of great personalities have attained transcendence suggests that the experience is available to anyone who longs for it and that *nirguṇa bhakti* makes it happen. As the first song says, "the urge to sing" *bhajans* generates an ecstatic state of awareness that compares to being possessed, or "taken over" by Brahman. That is, the force of Brahman-consciousness consumes the consciousness of the devotee so much so that she loses all sense of ego-self ("I" awareness), forgets her body, leaves the comforts of food, home, safety, and status to realize a state of transcendence in which dualities collapse into the unity of Brahman.

By the same token, merging into Brahman-consciousness seems to produce something else besides ecstasy. It seems that the intensity that is associated with transcendence engenders the concomitant excess of power, a spiritual residue, so to speak, which lingers in the devotee's awareness, reminding her of Brahman, even as it drives her to "drink" more of Brahman. In the views of the *bhajans*, to be swept away by the immaterial Brahman produces material effects on the body and the mind. Those material effects, as the *sādhus* teach, represent spiritual transformation caused by *nirguṇa* worship. Similarly, self-transformation results, in part, because the excess acts upon human consciousness, chiseling away destructive layers of ego-self until the gateway to the *ātmā*, that is, Brahman shines brilliantly. Could it be that the excess generated by *nirguṇa* devotion contains something of Brahman itself? Like the sea foam that is made from the churning of the ocean. Could that excess possess shades of the qualities of Brahman that register in the devotee's consciousness as "sweet" and "sublime"? The *sādhus* and their *bhajans* respond in kind with an emphatic "yes!"

2. Conclusions: "Wake up, Traveler!"—The Transcendence of *Nirguṇa Bhakti*

From the perspectives of the *sādhus*, the "difficult" path of *nirguṇa bhakti* leads a person to experience an unusual world in which the attributes of gender (or sex), name, form, status, and wealth, and whatever else a society deems as worthy of importance mean nothing in the divine encounter with the impersonal Brahman. Rather, the symbolic currency accepted by the nameless and formless divine absolute concerns cultivating qualities that can neither be seen nor measured, such as "love", "devotion", "commitment", "surrender", and "perseverance", and by which the *Brahma-jnāna* is revealed. Developing these traits molds the devotee into a receptive instrument of God who is prepared to understand and apply the liberating knowledge that not only makes self-transformation (and release from rebirth) possible, but it also brings the transcendence that is characterized by divine

[17] November 19, 2005.
[18] See (Lorenzen 1996).

mystical union to bear on human consciousness. I would imagine that for people who have been denied by religious orthodoxy the right to meet God because of their gender or perceived low status, transcending social differences illustrative of the mundane must come as a great relief. Many times over the course of my research I have observed women *sādhus* refuse to be seen and understood through the constricting lens of dominant patriarchal ideas of womanhood, and low-caste *sādhus* overturn high-caste notions of "purity" and "pollution", by singing of the *nirguṇa* devotion that disdains social hierarchies with every fiber of its being.

As the *bhajans* of the *sādhus* suggest, singing songs to (and about) the *nirguṇa* Lord endows them with the salvific power, authority, and insight to know and become God. The religious prestige ascribed to *sādhus* like Ganga Giri, Tulsi Giri, Devi Nath, and Prem Nath by devotees and non-devotees alike is in large part derived from their perceived expertise in *nirguṇa* knowledge, which they have acquired from the many long years they spent singing *nirguṇa bhajans*. Their songs inspire the courage that, according to the *sādhus*, remains necessary for the radical life of *sannyāsa*. At the same time, through the use of metaphors, symbols, and idioms, their *bhajans* describe an "upside-down"[19] form of language consistent with the religious poetics of *nirguṇa* traditions (i.e., a language that defies conventional logic) that the impersonal Lord can be understood and experienced. Resorting to a via *positiva* approach, their songs talk of "tasting" and "drinking" the unlimited "sweetness" of the sublime "bliss" of the absolute Brahman; of being overtaken by the infinite wave of God-consciousness; and, of "dissolving into" an eternal ocean of God-self that drowns out individual awareness.

And yet, as the *sādhus* and their songs remind us, no word, symbol, or idea substitutes for actual experience of Brahman. The "prize" of "earning" Brahman comes to those who combine good old-fashioned effort with a sincere attitude of dependence on God. As significantly, for the *sādhus*, experiencing *nirguṇa* as opposed to *saguṇa* worship really is not the "truth" of the matter for why they do what they do. The point is to transcend all human categories—including those that scholars (such as this author) emphasize in the effort to earn academic capital—that mire people in the trappings of *saṃsāra* and "get God". *Nirguṇa* worship brings the *sādhus* to that impersonal level of divine experience, and so they take this "boat", which is costlier than others, to cross over the ocean of worldly existence. Much like Kabir implores in the *bhajan* featured in the beginning of the article, "Hindus, Muslims, where did they come from", the *sādhus* also say "pay no attention to categories" as they lack "real" meaning for the one who wants God. To "win" the *nirguṇa* Lord means, in the words of the *sādhus'* *bhajans*, to "wake up" at last from the deep slumber that represents human existence in *saṃsāra*. Thus, I leave my readers with one last *bhajan* as sung by Tulsi Giri at her ashram in the year 2005. Its title is "Wake up, Traveler! Morning has come". Here is that *bhajan*.

> Wake up, traveler, morning has come
> It's morning now. Nevertheless, [the traveler] still sleeps.
>
> Wake up, traveler, morning has come.+*
>
> The one who sleeps [is] the one who loses everything
> The one who sleeps [is] the one who loses everything
> The one who remains awake, s/he gets everything
> The one who remains awake, s/he gets everything.
>
> Without *satsang*, there is no insight
> Without *satsang*, there is no insight
> From where will you find knowledge?
> From where will you find knowledge?
> Wake Up traveler, morning has come.[20]

---

19 See (Hawley and Juergensmeyer [1998] 2008), p. 41.
20 July 21, 2005.

Funding: This research was funded by a Junior Scholar Dissertation Research Fellowship by the American Institute of Indian Studies between 2004 and 2006.

Conflicts of Interest: The authors declare no conflict of interest.

References

Bourdieu, Pierre. 1985. Forms of Capital. In *The Handbook of Theory and Research for the Sociology of Education*. Edited by John Richardson. Westport: Greenwood Publishers, pp. 46–58.

DeNapoli, Antoinette E. 2014. *Real Sadhus Sing to God: Gender, Asceticism, and Vernacular Religion in Rajasthan*. New York: Oxford University Press.

Dimmitt, Cornelia, and J. A. B. van Buitenen, eds. 1978. *Classical Hindu Mythology: A Reader in the Sanskrit Puranas*. Philadelphia: Temple University Press.

Hawley, John Stratton, and Mark Juergensmeyer. 2008. *Songs of the Saints of India*. Oxford: Oxford University Press. First published 1998.

Keller, Mary. 2001. *The Hammer and The Flute: Women, Power, and Spirit Possession*. Baltimore: The Johns Hopkins University Press.

Lorenzen, David. 1996. *Praises to a Formless God: Nirguṇī Texts from North India*. Albany: State University of New York Press.

Olivelle, Patrick, trans. 1996. *Upaniṣads: A New Translation*. Oxford: Oxford University Press.

Patton, Laurie L., trans. 2008. *The Bhagavad Gita*. New York: Penguin Books.

religions

MDPI

Article

Saints, Hagiographers, and Religious Experience: The Case of Tukaram and Mahipati

J. E. Llewellyn

Department of Religious Studies, Missouri State University, 901 South National Avenue, Springfield, MO 65897, USA; jllewellyn@missouristate.edu

Received: 27 December 2018; Accepted: 12 February 2019; Published: 15 February 2019

Abstract: One of the most important developments in Hinduism in the Common Era has been the rise of devotionalism or *bhakti*. Though theologians and others have contributed to this development, the primary motive force behind it has been poets, who have composed songs celebrating their love for God, and sometimes lamenting their distance from Her. From early in their history, *bhakti* traditions have praised not only the various gods, but also the devotional poets as well. And so hagiographies have been written about the lives of those exceptional devotees. It could be argued that we find the religious experience of these devotees in their own compositions and in these hagiographies. This article will raise questions about the reliability of our access to the poets' religious experience through these sources, taking as a test case the seventeenth century devotional poet Tukaram and the hagiographer Mahipati. Tukaram is a particularly apt case for a study of devotional poetry and hagiography as the means to access the religious experience of a Hindu saint, since scholars have argued that his works are unusual in the degree to which he reflects on his own life. We will see why, for reasons of textual history, and for more theoretical reasons, the experience of saints such as Tukaram must remain elusive.

Keywords: religious experience; bhakti; Tukaram; Mahipati

One of the most important developments in Hinduism in the Common Era has been the rise of devotionalism or *bhakti*. Though theologians and others have contributed to this development, the primary motive force behind it has been poets, who have composed songs celebrating their love for God, and sometimes lamenting their distance from Her. From early in their history, *bhakti* traditions have praised not only the various gods, but also the devotional poets as well. And so hagiographies have been written about the lives of those exceptional devotees. It could be argued that we find the religious experience of these devotees in their own compositions and in these hagiographies.

This article will raise questions about the reliability of our access to the poets' religious experience through these sources, taking as a test case Tukaram (1608–1649; Tukaram 1991, p. vii). Though Tukaram is remembered for poems that dramatically describe his encounters with God, we will focus here on his conflictful relationship with his wife. It may seem as if this is something that does not belong in an article about religious experience. Yet we will see that in the hagiographies, Tukaram's conflict with his wife is presented as the result of his devotion to God, as she upbraids him for failing to provide for his family because of this devotion. So this article is at least about the social impact of Tukaram's religious experience. And even if Tukaram's marriage is categorized as a secular matter, it is still a good place to begin a discussion about how confidently we know *any* aspect of his experience.

Tukaram was one of the four great poets in the Varkari tradition, which is the most popular *bhakti* movement in the Indian state of Maharashtra. In the Marathi language, a "Varkari" is a person who performs a specific type of pilgrimage. And this label is appropriate for this movement, since its central ritual is a twice annual pilgrimage. Devotees from around Maharashtra travel on foot, sometimes for more than a hundred miles, to the town of Pandharpur to worship at the temple of Vitthal (more informally known as Vithoba), who is understood to be a form of Krishna. As they walk, the pilgrims sing the poems of Tukaram and the other Varkari saints in praise of Vitthal.

After his own poems, for Varkaris, the most important sources about Tukaram are the works of Mahipati (1715–1790; Tulpule 1979, p. 430). As indicated by the work of Christian Lee Novetzke and Jon Keune, Mahipati was the magisterial hagiographer of the Varkari tradition (Novetzke 2008; Keune 2011). The geographical range of Mahipati's works is not limited to Maharashtra, as he includes profiles of north Indian devotees as well, and acknowledges a debt to the great Ramanandi hagiographer Nabhadas and his Gaudiya commentator Priyadas (Tulpule 1979, p. 430; and see Hare 2011). One of those north Indian saints whose life is described at length, Kabir, was the subject of Kabirpanthi and Dadupanthi hagiographies that have been studied by David Lorenzen (Lorenzen 1991). About Tukaram, substantial accounts are found in at least two of Mahipati's four lengthy hagiographical compendia, the *Bhaktavijay* (1762) and the *Bhaktalilamrt* (1774; Tulpule 1979, p. 431).

Tukaram is a particularly apt case for a study of devotional poetry and hagiography as the means to access the religious experience of a Hindu saint, since scholars have argued that his works are unusual in the degree to which he reflects on his own life. His is "personal confessional poetry" (Tukaram 1991, p. xx). In his songs, he "expresses his own subjectivity" (Tukaram 2012, p. 27). This article will begin with hagiography in general, before moving on to take up Tukaram and Mahipati, and finally landing on more theoretical questions about religious experience.

1. Encountering Saints through Hagiography

A recent book about the comparative study of hagiography includes an article about another Varkari saint, Jnaneshvar, that describes a temple dedicated to him in his home village of Alandi. This is said to be the location of Jnaneshvar's *samjivan samadhi*, that is, the place where the saint voluntarily had himself entombed while still alive in 1296. Contemporary devotees hope to obtain blessings by worshiping at this site, Mark McLaughlin says in this article, as they believe that Jnaneshvar is still present here. This belief is illustrated strongly in an earlier century by a story that is told about yet a third Varkari saint, Eknath. A hagiography reports that Eknath had a dream in which Jnaneshvar called to him to come and restore the shrine of his *samadhi*. McLaughlin writes that "He entered the cavern and there he found Jnanesvar seated in meditation, as young and alive as the day that he had entered the cavern nearly three hundred years before" (McLaughlin 2016, p. 77). And even now, some four centuries after Eknath, here Jnaneshvar still sits.

At the end of his analysis of the contemporary worship at Jnaneshvar's temple, McLaughlin takes a detour in the direction of theory. He writes: "The compound does not simply memorialize past events. The ritual activities of the space are not simply forms of remembrance of something that has gone. To perceive this space through a lens of absence, as the historiography of modern discourse offers us, is a mistake. This is a culture of presence—a presence anchored by the perceived occurrence of Jnanesvar having taken *samjivan samadhi* in the space. Such happenings Orsi calls abundant events because the foundation event that establishes the presence in the space informs all subsequent events there" (pp. 87–88). There may be a naïve positivist historiography that would describe this temple as only a memorial, since the historian's metaphysics cannot accommodate a saint meditating in a subterranean room for the better part of a millennium. But the metaphysics of contemporary devotees are more capacious, or so McLaughlin argues.

In making this argument about presence, and even in invoking Robert Orsi, Mark McLaughlin is following the editors of the book in which his article appears. In their introduction, the editors write that they seek to move beyond a framework in which hagiography is disparaged as "mere myth or legend" (Monge et al. 2016, p. 1). In a separate theoretical chapter, one of the editors, Rico G. Monge, attacks a dichotomy between hagiography and history, in which "history is construed as representing objective truth. Hagiography, on the other hand, is that which dissembles, whitewashes, and idealizes, and thus carries with it the connotation of falsehood" (Monge 2016, p. 9). Citing the work of Hayden

White, Monge highlights "the fundamentally fictive character of historiography," as historians rely on some of the same devices to construct their narratives as novelists. Monge argues that just as "Marxists, feminists, deconstructionists, psychoanalytic theorists, queer theorists, and the like" all compose accounts of past events according to the canons each of her own methodology, so does the hagiographer (p. 17). Monge insists that "hagiographies in fact *do* what any historian does—they interpret the data about their subject's lives in a way that is intended to provide real, meaningful knowledge about them" (p. 18). At least Monge is arguing that believers can find hagiographies meaningful even if they recount tales about which historians are skeptical—that the analysis of the historian may not capture the power of the hagiography for the believer. But then at the end of his article, Monge recommends an approach that follows on the work of Robert Orsi in which "hagiographic modes of discourse would no longer be simply demythologized or mined for their anthropological value; rather, they would be allowed to speak truths on their own terms as manifestations of an 'abundance' that exceeds the limitations of modern historical-critical methodology" (p. 20). Here, I believe that Monge is going beyond my earlier second-hand academic formulation that hagiographies recount things that believers take to be true, or that even believers take to be the Truth, but that they also convey truth to the scholarly analyst as well.

As they make the case for a metaphysics of presence, both Mark McLaughlin and Rico Monge cite an article by Robert A. Orsi, "Abundant History: Marian Apparitions as Alternative Modernity." There, Orsi argues that in the west before the modern period, "the woods, homes, and forests of Europe, its churches, statues, relics, holy oils, and waters, and its shrines were filled with the presence of saints" (Orsi 2009, p. 218). By contrast, "Western modernity exists under the sign of absence. Time and space are emptied of presence" (p. 219). Yet a sense of presence persists at the site of Marian apparitions, even in our modern age, and this is something that should challenge modernity's exclusions. These are the sites of what Orsi calls "abundant events," where believers are transformed by their face-to-face encounter with Mary's power, which "radiates out from the really-real event along a network of routes, a kind of capillary of presence, filling water, relics, images, things, and memories" (p. 223). Orsi argues at least that the scholar must take into account this sense of presence in her analysis of Marian sites. But he also suggests that for the scholar (and here, he writes about a historian, but it could be an anthropologist, a sociologist, and so forth), abundant events "may very well draw the historian himself or herself, too, into an unexpectedly immediate and intimate encounter with the past" (p. 225). As with Monge, for Orsi, too, it seems an encounter with the saint's presence is not only possible for the believer but also for the scholar.

Perhaps these themes are carried to their logical conclusion, or perhaps they are pushed beyond breaking point, at the end of the "Afterword," by the comparative theologian Francis X. Clooney. The very last sentence of *Hagiography and Religious Truth* reads: "If, as the volume tells us, boundaries among the several important understandings of truth and value ought now to be recognized as in fact permeable, it seems plausible, even if not explicitly stated in the volume, that collecting in one place these studies in hagiography might also draw readers (along with authors) into a kind of interfaith communion of the saints that is indebted to each saint's tradition but reducible to no one community, religious or academic" (Clooney 2016, pp. 203–4). Of course, "the communion of saints," a phrase found in the Apostles' Creed, is generally understood to refer to the church, especially as it includes not only those Christians now living, but to those in heaven and even in purgatory. As *Hagiography and Religious Truth* is about saints in the "Abrahamic Traditions" (here, Islam and Christianity) and the "Dharmic Traditions" (here, Hinduism and Buddhism), clearly the communion Clooney conjures is "interfaith," "reducible to no one community, religious." And to the extent that scholars are invited to share in this communion, as well as believers, it is also "reducible to no one community, ... academic." It is the church of the Islamic/Christian/Hindu/Buddhist/believer/scholar.

Practically speaking, our encounter with a saint, regardless of whether as believers or scholars or some hybrid of the two, is dependent upon the sources that give us access to the saint. The next section is about the problems with those sources, particularly for Tukaram.

2. Tukaram and His "Cantakerous Wife"

Good people will have a great regard for you;
And the world will view you with growing respect.
Think of your cattle as dead
And of your pots and pans as stolen by a thief.
Think of your children as though they were never born.
Give up all desires and make your mind
Hard as Indra's warhead.
Spit out all mean pleasures
And receive pure bliss.
Says Tuka, you will be rid of great turmoil
Once you break free from the bonds of this world. (Tukaram 1991, p. 48)

This appears in the collection of poems by Tukaram translated by Dilip Chitre. Though most of the poems in this book do not have a title, this is the ninth of ten headed "Advice to an Angry Wife." In the first five of this set, the speaker is mostly not Tukaram, but his wife, who complains about his failure to provide for his family. For example, in the first poem, she asks rhetorically, "What can I feed these starving children?" (p. 42). Each poem ends with a response by Tukaram, which is either angrily or ironically dismissive. In the sixth through the eighth poem in this series, the tone changes, as the poet himself appears to complain that he is the victim of God's heavy demands, for example, asking, "Who would protect me from Him?/Where else can we go to escape Him?" (p. 47). Finally in the ninth poem, the one quoted above, there is yet another shift, as the poet seems to embrace a life "free from the bonds of this world," and urges his wife to do the same. Here, the poet's attitude seems to be more positive both toward his own self-denial and toward his wife, though the sacrifice he asks of her is extreme. His wife must regard her own "children as though they were never born."

In his earliest and most important hagiographical compendium, the *Bhaktavijay,* Mahipati appears to paraphrase this poem, including using many of the same words.[1] This hagiographer offers a much longer biography of Tukaram in a later compendium, the *Bhaktalilamrt,* and there, too, he seems to summarize this poem.[2] As Mahipati tells the story, this preaching was remarkably effective. According to both the hagiographies, this dialogue occurs when Tukaram's wife, Jijai, confronts him and demands that he return home. Though Tukaram would regularly come to their village to sing the praises of Vitthal, he spent the rest of his time out in the forest. Tukaram accedes to Jijai's demand, but with a condition. He says, "If you listen to my advice, and if you give me your word for it, then I will now come home at once" (Abbott and Godbole 1999, vol. 2, p. 222). As soon as Jijai agrees to this and they return home, Tukaram gives her a lengthy sermon about detachment from the things of this world, which includes the paraphrase of the poem that I quoted in its entirety above. The wife is so moved by Tukaram's teaching that she invites Brahmans to her home to take whatever they want and they pick the place clean. But then Jijai immediately begins to regret that she has done this. When Tukaram gives away her last piece of clothing to a woman from the untouchable Mahar caste who comes begging, Jijai "flew into a rage" (Abbott and Godbole 1999, vol. 2, p. 229). Actually the *Bhaktavijay* says that Krishna's wife, the goddess Rukmini, merely dons the disguise of a Mahar (vol. 2, p. 228).

Mahipati praises Tukaram's lack of concern with worldly life, and this is repeatedly dramatized by conflicts with his wife such as the one just described. Tukaram receives a sack of grain, which he

---

1 Compare (Chitre 2001, p. 55)) (poem 1987) with Mahipati (1974, p. 383) (49.92–96), available in English in (Abbott and Godbole 1999, vol. 2, p. 225)).

2 Mahipati (1988, p. 295) (34.44–45), in English Abbott 2000 (2000, p. 184).

immediately gives away, and his wife "flew into a rage" (Abbott and Godbole 1999, vol. 2, p. 215). Jijai miraculously receives a handful of silver coins, but then donates them to Brahmans at her husband's urging (vol. 2, p. 237). When the saint is given a load of sugarcane, all of it but one stalk is taken from him by the children of the village—he does not bother to save more for his own children. When Jijai sees that, she, once again, "flew into a rage," and hits Tukaram with the cane so hard that it breaks into pieces (vol. 2, p. 242). It may be that Jijai really was quarrelsome, but it is also true that Mahipati admits that her worldliness is a lesson for Tukaram and for his reader. In his later hagiography the *Bhaktalilamrt*, which is also full of such conflicts, Mahipati praises God's providence: "When Thou lookest on Thy *bhaktas* with the look of mercy, they at once break friendship with their worldly affairs, and Thou dost break the net that binds them to this earthly life. If Thou shouldst give to any *bhakta*, a wife who was all goodness, his love would bind him to her. So Thou dost give him as companion a cantankerous wife" (Abbott 2000, pp. 162–63).

And Jijai is not the only "cantankerous wife" that we find in the lives of the saints that Mahipati recounts. In terms of the length of his biography, the chief saint in the *Bhaktavijay* is the fourteenth-century poet Namdev. He is criticized for failing to provide for his family both by his mother Gonai, and by his wife Rajai, who complains to her mother-in-law, "my garments are torn and exceedingly old. I have not enough to eat. I have come, therefore, to your house to live my poverty-stricken life" (Abbott and Godbole 1999, vol. 1, p. 65). In an incident that seems to be clearly composed to parallel a story about Tukaram's wife mentioned earlier in this article, gold coins are given to Rajai by no less than Krishna himself, when he visits her disguised as a wealthy merchant. But then Namdev cannot keep this wealth, despite its divine source, and he "called the Brahmans of the town and gave to these twice-born the money, garments, and the ornaments" (vol. 1, p. 76). It is not the case that all of the male saints in Mahipati's books struggled with worldly wives. For example, in his Ph.D. dissertation about the Varkari poet and saint Eknath, Jon Keune notes, "In stark contrast to the wives of the Marathi sants Namdev and Tukaram, Girija is remembered to have supported and encouraged Eknath's activities with unwavering enthusiasm" (Keune 2011, p. 27). But some of the saints did struggle with their wives.

Perhaps it is obvious, but it is worth noting that there is a certain gender bias in these stories. Though one encounters women saints in India today, and even women who have renounced the world, this is something that is relatively uncommon historically, with the classical law codes only permitting renunciation for men. The authors of the law codes probably could not brook the idea of women enjoying that much independence, but they may have also assumed that the religious life was not something that women would even aspire to, mired as they were in their attachment to their children and other things of this world. If these gender prejudices helped to shape Mahipati's stories of domestic conflict, it should also be pointed out that he does tell tales of women saints as well as men, though these are relatively uncommon. Of the fifty-four saints whose stories are prominent enough to appear in the chapter titles of the English translation of the *Bhaktavijay*, only six are women.

It may have been the case that Tukaram's wife was coincidentally vehemently opposed to his way of living out devotion. However, it is also certainly the case there is a broader motif of spiritual saints fighting with worldly wives that recurs in Mahipati's hagiographies. If this motif was common at the time that Tukaram lived, we might even argue that, driven by this understanding, he chose a "cantankerous wife." However, the details of Tukaram's life story militate against this, if we are to accept Mahipati's accounts. In both the *Bhaktavijay* and in the *Bhaktalilamrt*, Tukaram seems relatively satisfied with worldly life when he marries Jijai. It is only some time later, when Tukaram sees his first wife die during a famine, and then he endures a series of business failures, that he realizes that there is no lasting joy to be found in this world.[3] It is then that Tukaram says to himself, "This earthly life is

3 The *Bhaktalilamrt* actually says that Tukaram lost not only his wife, but also a son in the famine (Abbott 2000, p. 80; 28.123). The *Bhaktavijay* does not mention the son's death.

unreal. It is the outcome of *maya* (illusion). The human body is perishable, I have spent my life for nothing, and I have forgotten the Lord of Pandhari [that is, the god Vitthal, worshiped in Pandharpur]" (Abbott and Godbole 1999, vol. 2, p. 204).

In his book *Religion and Public Memory,* which is a study of the historical development of the biography of another Varkari poet-saint, the aforementioned Namdev, Christian Novetzke contrasts hagiography and history. He describes works such as the key north Indian hagiographical compendium the *Bhaktamala* (whose title could be translated as "The Garland of Devotees"), as "splendidly circular compositions, like a necklace" (Novetzke 2008, p. 36). It is no surprise to find themes reiterated in a hagiographical compendium, as the stories of various saints are assimilated to a common model of saintliness. The reader might even find whole incidents recurring in the life of more than one character.[4] History, by contrast, Novetzke says, aims "to ward off the nonrational, replicative, and mimetic" (p. 36). Seeing the same incident repeated is something that is liable to make a historian suspicious of the veracity of the hagiographer's account.

Yet there is evidence that Tukaram had a conflictful relationship with Jijai, not only in Mahipati's hagiographies, but also in Tukaram's poems themselves, as in the poem quoted earlier. While they *may* be a reliable indicator of the saint's experience, there is no guarantee of that. In the introduction to a translation of some of his poems, Dilip Chitre admits that Tukaram's oeuvre has dramatically expanded over time. Chitre begins his introduction by describing a manuscript in Tukaram's home village of Dehu, which is said to be in the poet's own hand, and which contained, at the beginning of the twentieth century, "about 700 poems." By the time of Chitre's writing, "[s]ome scholars believe Tukaram's available work to be in the region of about 8000 poems" (Tukaram 1991, p. vii). If those seven hundred poems are the only ones certainly by Tukaram, that would mean that over 90 per cent of the poems now attributed to the seventeenth century saint were not written by him. In the history of devotional poetry in India, it is quite common for later followers to write in the style of a revered saint, even explicitly claiming that their work is by their illustrious forebear (Hawley 1988). As was the practice by the Varkaris, and in devotion poetry in Hindi and in other Indian vernaculars, each poem by Tukaram ends with his name written into the last verse. However, it appears to be the case that later followers would style themselves as Tukaram, working his name into the close of their poems.

As *Religion and Public Memory* describes it, the study of this process is particularly compelling for Namdev. Scholars have theorized that they have put their finger on later poets who identified themselves with Namdev in their poems, but who also left traces of their individual identity. So, for example, at the end of some of the poems, the author is identified as Vishnudas Nama. This could simply be the Namdev of the fourteenth century, since it is conceivable that he might call himself a "servant of Vishnu," which is what Vishnudas means. And this is probably how most devotees have understood this signature. But Vishnudas could also be a personal name, and there are some scholars who believe that this was a poet in the sixteenth century who wrote in the fashion of Namdev. Styling himself Vishnudas Nama, he was simultaneously claiming that he was the same Namdev and telegraphing that he was different. And Vishnudas Nama is not the only separate author that scholars believe they have isolated in the Namdev corpus. So Novetzke heads his chapter about this "Namdev and the Namas." This is a tradition of "remembering through imitation with variation" (Novetzke 2008, p. 137). *Religion and Public Memory* further clarifies: "This is not a case simply of borrowing a portion of a previously famous author, but a method of tapping into a complex cultural system of public memory that uses authorship to maintain a performative genealogy, and interconnection of authors over centuries" (p. 150). So later authors, steeped in the stream of Namdev's compositions, drew poems from it, but also poured their own compositions back into it, compositions

---

[4] An anonymous reviewer of this article suggested that there may be hints here of a darker South Asian conception of repetition in history, as articulated in David Shulman's analysis of the *Mahabharata,* in "which time cooks all creatures, and time crushes them" (Shulman 2001, p. 26).

that would be recognized as appropriately labeled Namdev's because they were in his style. And the same has apparently happened in the case of Tukaram.

Crucial to Namdev's legacy, and that of other Varkari saints such as Tukaram, according to *Religion and Public Memory*, is the practice of *kirtan*, described as follows: "A *kirtan* performance in Marathi involves a lead performer, a *kirtankar*, who invokes one or two famous songs or stories and gives a narrative philosophical interpretation of selected texts. This is combined with music, dance, theatrical flourishes, and often a call and response with the audience" (Novetzke 2008, p. 81). To range backward chronologically, Novetzke notes that modern printed editions of Namdev's songs have been compiled from notebooks of *kirtan* performers. Before those printed versions (and even since), it is primarily through *kirtan* that devotees would have come to know of Namdev. And Namdev himself was a *kirtankar*—he composed for performance and was the originator of this genre of performance. *Kirtan* is largely the medium that has shaped the saint's public memory. Like Namdev, for Tukaram *kirtankars* learn his poems from other performers, sometimes adding their own compositions. The primary limit to the creativity of the *kirtankar* would be a general sense of the kind of poetry that Tukaram wrote, including a sense of who Tukaram was.

For most devotional saints, the poetry they wrote or at least the poetry attributed to them is constitutive of their hagiography. Mahipati's accounts include frequent reference to his subjects' compositions—he sometimes admits that he is paraphrasing their poems. It is significant that when he introduces Mahipati, Christian Novetzke labels him first a "*kirtan* performer" and then an "author" (Novetzke 2008, p. xii). Mahipati often depicts the Marathi saints in performance. *Religion and Public Memory* argues that Mahipati's hagiographies not only contain *kirtan*, but that they were composed to be presented as *kirtan*. It is certainly the case, as Novetzke notes, that Mahipati frequently addresses his audience directly. He ends each chapter in the *Bhaktavijay* with an exhortation to pay attention, for example: "Therefore listen, O pious ones, to the deeply delightful forty-eighth chapter; it is an offering to Shri Krishna" (Abbott and Godbole 1999, vol. 2, p. 217). Novetzke even claims that Mahipati's text "appear[s] to be a transcribed *kirtan*, word for word" (Novetzke 2008, p. 121). Regardless of whether Novetzke is right about the extent to which the written text preserves an original performance, it is certainly the case that, once Mahipati's hagiographies were written about Tukaram, they would have provided one of the criterion by which the later tradition would have judged the appositeness of poems attributed to him.

There is a particularly suggestive analysis of the circular relationship between the compositions of the poet saints and their hagiographies in John Stratton Hawley's book about the sixteenth century north Indian devotee Surdas. To a Krishna worshiper today, there is something poignant about the rich imagery of Surdas's poems, as he is remembered to have been blind from birth. And there are poems attributed to Surdas in which he speaks of his blindness. However, Hawley's conclusion is that there is no unambiguous evidence of this condition in the earliest collections of Surdas's work. There are early poems in which the author calls himself blind, but in them "the blindness the poet bemoans in himself is of a spiritual, not physical nature" (Hawley 1984, p. 29). It may have been the case that "the historical Surdas" was not blind, but that his sight was taken away by the later tradition, both in hagiographies about him and even in poetry attributed to him, which read his metaphors too literally.

To return to Tukaram, we cannot know for certain that his wife Jijai was "cantankerous," even though Mahipati says so, especially given that this is a theme in the lives of some of his other saints, as noted previously in this article. And we cannot know this for sure, even though Tukaram's own poems say this, since it *is* almost certain that many of the poems now attributed to him were written after his time. Perhaps the compositions that excoriate his wife are the product of a certain gender bias in the greater Varkari tradition, which is also found in Mahipati.

This is a particularly interesting problem for Tukaram, because his poetry is often characterized as marked by a certain modern self-expressiveness. In the critical introduction that precedes his translation of a selection of Tukaram's poems, Dilip Chitre writes:

> Tukaram gave *Bhakti* itself new existential dimensions. In this he was anticipating the spiritual anguish of modern man two centuries ahead of his time. He was also anticipating a form of personal confessional poetry that seeks articulate liberation from the deepest traumas man experiences and represses out of fear. Tukaram's poetry expresses pain and bewilderment, fear and anxiety, exasperation and desperateness, boredom and meaninglessness—in fact all the feelings that characterize modern self-awareness. (Tukaram 1991, p. xx)

For our purposes, particularly interesting is Chitre's claim that we find in Tukaram's work a new "form of personal confessional poetry." Perhaps it would be appropriate in Tukaram's case to speak of his poetry as conveying his experience, at least according to Chitre's analysis, since we find in that poetry an expression of the poet's individuality, a reflection upon his inner life. One thing that is problematic in this usage is that Chitre himself admits that Tukaram's oeuvre has dramatically expanded over time, as we have noted. When Chitre claims that he finds in this tradition "personal confessional poetry," he may mean that he has developed the hermeneutical skills to identify the works that were really by the seventeenth century devotee. But I doubt that he means this, as he implies that even the experts have not had much success in isolating the historical core of Tukaram's work. On the other hand, Chitre may mean that there is a kind of confessional tone to many of the poems attributed to Tukaram, whether an individual work is by him or not. However, if this is what Chitre intends, it seems to stretch what might be called "personal confessional poetry," since that may have become self-conscious adherence to a style that is only apparently personal, expressing the anxiety and desperateness that the audience has come to regard as characteristic of Tukaram, whoever is the author of specific poems.

Like Dilip Chitre, in their translation of a selection of the poems of Tukaram, Gail Omvedt and Bharat Patankar credit the devotee with a certain modern sensibility. They write, "Tuka, however—perhaps as befitting a poet of the seventeenth century, a century emerging into modernity—gives his own extended commentaries on his life. More than any other *sant,* his song-poems are personal and compelling" (Tukaram 2012, pp. 21–22). Later, they say that Tukaram "expresses his own subjectivity, something that might be taken as a sign of modernism and a new concern with the individual" (p. 27). *The Songs of Tukoba* describes the poet as from "an age entering into modernity," a time of "rational questioning," which here is "turned into themes of questioning the divine" (pp. 35–36). The book goes on to note that this was during the same period when traditions in Europe were shaken up by Descartes, Galileo, Hobbes, and Locke. Omvedt and Patankar assert that "[t]hese trends had their correlates in India, though we find more of the themes emerging from the subalterns rather than from a dissident elite, and being cut-off by their conflict with an establishment" (pp. 36–37).

Central to Omvedt and Patankar's argument here is that they present Tukaram as a strong critic of caste oppression. In fact, he is only the most prominent representative of what Omvedt and Patankar argue is a tradition of "radical bhakti," that also included other poet-saints such as Basava, Namdev, Kabir, Nanak, and Ravidas. Within the context of this article, it should be noted that Omvedt and Patankar argue that the eighteenth century was a time of "conservative consolidation" in Maharashtra, and they see Mahipati's hagiographies as significant evidence of this (p. 44). "Mahipati's Tukaram tells Shivaji to follow *varnashrama dharma*" and return to his royal responsibilities, for example, while in his own poems, Tukaram wants nothing to do with kings, Omvedt and Patankar argue. And Tukaram humbly accepts the chastisement of the Brahman Rameshvar Bhat (p. 18).

In *The Songs of Tukoba,* Dilip Chitre comes in for criticism similar to Mahipati. Omvedt and Patankar argue that Tukaram not only criticizes caste, but also rejects "the traditional goals of Brahminism of absorption in the divine" (p. 37). Then they add in an endnote, "Here we are disagreeing with most of the interpretations of Tuka by scholars including Chitre and More. The fact is that to maintain their position of Brahminized orthodoxy, the Brahminic scholars simply have to ignore a large number of songs" (p. 50n6, and see also p. 19). So Chitre represents, according to this, a category of "Brahminic scholars" who advance "Brahminized" interpretations of Tukaram.

Within the context of an article about hagiography, an interesting example of the conflict among Tukaram's biographers is the story of the end of the saint's earthly existence. In the *Bhaktavijay*, the hagiographer Mahipati recounts that Tukaram was miraculously taken to heaven even while still alive: "Then (later) Tuka went to *Vaikunth* (Vishnu's heaven) with his body" (Abbott and Godbole 1999, vol. 2, p. 294). In his later work, the *Bhaktalilamrt*, Mahipati tells this story in much greater and more dramatic detail, as God calls Tukaram to "the luxurious Pushpak chariot of light" (Abbott 2000, p. 313). Chitre admits that "*Varkaris* believe that Vitthal Himself carried Tukaram away to heaven in a 'chariot of light'" (Tukaram 1991, pp. xiii–xiv), and he lists some other opinions about the poet's end. He concludes: "Reading his farewell poems, however, one is inclined to imagine that Tukaram bade a proper farewell to his close friends and fellow-devotees and left his native village for some unknown destination with no intention of returning" (p. xiv).

When Omvedt and Patankar take up the question of Tukaram's end, they present three alternatives. The first is the "orthodox account," "that he was carried off to heaven directly" (Tukaram 2012, p. 41). The second alternative, for which they cite Chitre's book, is "the modern Brahminic secularist explanation," "that he simply bid everyone good-by and wandered off on some unnamed pilgrimage" (p. 41, citing Tukaram 1991, pp. xiii–xiv). It is apparent why *The Songs of Tukoba* labels Chitre's account "secularist," since it seeks to offer a stand-in for Mahipati's miracle story. Why Chitre's position is "Brahminic" is only clear when Omvedt and Patankar present their third alternative: "Non-brahmins believe that he was murdered by his enemies." This seems to be the conclusion that Omvedt and Patankar lean toward. They refer to a book by A. H. Salunkhe, which "cites many bits of circumstantial evidence in favour of this" (Tukaram 2012, p. 41). Omvedt and Patankar stigmatize Chitre's position as "Brahminic," as he seeks to absolve the Brahmans of the crime of Tukaram's murder.[5]

For his part, Chitre mentions the theory that Tukaram was murdered, but dismisses it. He was "phenomenally popular," such that his assassination "would not have escaped the keen and constant attention of his many followers." Since they did not pass down any account of this, Chitre concludes that "such speculations seem wild and sensational" (Tukaram 1991, p. ix).

On the issue of the end of Tukaram's earthly existence, Chitre and Omvedt and Patankar have something important in common: they are secularists, in that they seek a nonmiraculous explanation. But there is also a substantial difference between them, which turns on Omvedt and Patankar's more basic critique that Chitre's Tukaram is too "Brahminic," that Chitre does not sufficiently emphasize the devotional poet's radical critique of caste. And there is something similar and characteristically different in how *Says Tuka* and *The Songs of Tukoba* deal with the question of the modernism of Tukaram's poetry. Though there is no sign of Chitre's existentialist "anxiety" and "desperateness" and "meaningless" in Omvedt and Patankar, they do allow that Tukaram "expresses his own subjectivity" in his poetry. However, they argue that this subjectivity includes a strong caste consciousness that is watered down in *Says Tuka*. In other words, in both of these readings, something that is characteristic of Tukaram's work is its self-expression, but it seems that the selves expressed are somewhat different, one with a greater sense of anti-Brahman resentment. Or, to shift to the rhetoric of experience, it would seem that for Omvedt and Patankar, Tukaram's experience was more strongly marked by caste oppression and opposition to it. This is something that you will not find in Mahipati's hagiographies, according to *The Songs of Tukoba*, because the hagiographer's work represented "The Conservative Consolidation of the Eighteen Century" (Tukaram 2012, p. 40). And this is something that you will not even find in Chitre's translation of a selection of Tukaram's own poems, since he "ignore[s] a large number of

[5] The opposition between the "Brahminic" view and that of "Non-brahmans" serves Omvedt and Patankar's overall activist agenda, but also lumps people together into groups that they might not otherwise choose to join. Certainly, that Tukaram was murdered is not a view that is subscribed to by all non-Brahmans. There is evidence of conflict with sanctimonious Brahmans throughout Varkari history. Tussles with Brahmans are common in Mahipati's hagiographies, though they generally lead to a reconciliation in the end. Omvedt and Patankar's more radical view of this may be in part a product of the development of a more militant Dalit consciousness in Maharashtra in the late twentieth century.

songs" (p. 50n6). It seems that in a corpus of thousands of poems, the translator enjoys some latitude to constitute the self and experience of the poet.[6]

3. Religious Experience as a Problem

One of the tricks to getting at the religious experience of Tukaram is that we do not have reliable sources. But another trick may concern the nature of experience itself. An influential critique of experience is a 1998 article by Robert H. Sharf. Before turning to that article directly, we might take a moment to consider a point that he makes, that "experience" as an analytical category has a history. In his book *Shelter Blues*, Robert Desjarlais provides a brief genealogy of "experience." It is something that is not only internal, but also personal and unique to the individual. It is authentic and true, as opposed to artificial. Within a self that is understood to be composed of a complex of multiple interior layers, experience is deep and meaningful, subject to reflective interpretation by the experiencer. At a time in recent history marked by the rise of the modernist novel and of psychoanalysis, experience is assigned its meaning in a narrative of the development of the person. So, Desjarlais concludes, "In much the same way that the truth of sexuality grew out of an economy of discourses that took hold in seventeenth-century Europe, so discourses of depth, interiority, and authenticity, sensibilities of holism and transcendence, and practices of reading, writing, and storytelling have helped to craft a mode of being known in the modern West as experience: that is, an inwardly reflexive, hermeneutically rich process that coheres through time by way of narrative" (Desjarlais 1997, p. 17).[7] My account of the progress of this notion of experience implies something that Desjarlais argues explicitly: there is nothing about this understanding of the self, or of a life narrative, or of experience itself that is universal across cultures. This is a conclusion that is significant for Desjarlais as an anthropologist. Writing about "experience" in the analysis of another culture, the ethnographer may be unwittingly imposing an alien life world.

Let us now return to the critique of religious experience expressed by Robert H. Sharf. The rhetoric of experience, his essay begins, valorizes the "the subjective, the personal, the private," over "the 'objective' or the 'empirical'" (Sharf 1998, p. 94). This is a particularly appealing rhetorical move, since it saves both religious people and scholars of religion from an empiricism, which deconstructs religion, and a cultural pluralism, which delegitimizes parochial western claims. However, Sharf comes to the conclusion that it is a mistake for scholars to rely on this rhetoric. For Sharf, it is not just that "Scholars of religion are not presented with experiences that stand in need of interpretation, but rather with texts, narratives, performances, and so forth" (p. 111). So we do not have access to the experience, but only to discourse about it. And it is not just that "a given individual's understanding and articulation of ... an experience will be conditioned by the tradition to which he or she belongs" (p. 96). So there is no such thing as a "raw experience" that is not culturally mediated. It is not even just that the contemporary discourse of religious experience only developed since the beginning of the nineteenth century, so that this rhetoric "anachronistically imposes the recent and ideologically laden notion of 'religious experience' on our interpretations of premodern phenomena" (p. 98). Rather, for Sharf, the problem with the rhetoric of religious experience is that it is incoherent. "The word 'experience,' in so far as it refers to that which is given to us in the immediacy of perception, signifies that which by definition is nonobjective, that which resists all signification" (p. 113). So the rhetoric of experience is "a mere place-holder that entails a substantive if indeterminate terminus for the relentless deferral of meaning" (p. 113).

6 It is noteworthy in this context that Omvedt and Patankar do not include any of Chitre's "Advice to an Angry Wife" poems in their collection, though they do note in passing that she is "depicted ... as an almost complete shrew" (Tukaram 2012, p. 32).

7 In the sentence quoted, Desjarlais cites Foucault (1978). Though I refer to Desjarlais's original here, I initially found this anthologized in Martin and McCutcheon (2012).

June McDaniel takes on Sharf's critique of experience in her very recent book, *Lost Ecstasy: Its Decline and Transformation in Religion.* Here, McDaniel argues that experience and, especially, ecstatic and mystical experiences have been marginalized in both religious studies and theology. One consequence of this is that people in the modern west have come to seek ecstasy outside religious channels, even in ways that are self-destructive, such as through violence, or so McDaniel states. *Lost Ecstasy* deals with Sharf most directly in the eighth chapter, "The Case of Hinduism: Ecstasy and Denial." McDaniel opens the discussion by boiling down Sharf's critique to three points:

1. Ideas of religious experience are not really indigenous ideas—they are "a relatively late and distinctively Western invention."
2. What earlier ideas exist in Asia about religious experience show that it is unimportant. There is no pre-colonial emphasis on experience; its importance only comes from Western-trained writers such as Radhakrishnan. Religious authority is rarely based on "exalted experiential states."
3. There are false, inconsistent or dubious claims about religious experience, such as claims of alien abduction. Since some claims of subjective religious experience are false, therefore, all claims on the topic are false. (McDaniel 2018, p. 235; citing Sharf 1998)

Most of the chapter is given over to a refutation of the second point, with McDaniel presenting accounts of authoritative mystical experience from a broad range of Hindu literature from the Vedic period to the present. In a section about "The Dharma Tradition," the author admits that there is little room for mysticism in works about one's worldly obligations based on caste and stage of life, but this is presented as being exceptional. The phrase "exalted spiritual states" appears in Sharf's article in a brief discussion of Buddhist works about meditation, which concludes, "the authority of exegetes such as Kamalasila, Buddhaghosa, and Chih-i [who wrote such works] lay not in their access to exalted spiritual states but in their mastery of, and rigorous adherence to, sacred scripture" (Sharf 1998, p. 99; citing Sharf 1995). Here, the critic admits that the Buddhist tradition has preserved accounts of meditative states, but that those accounts are represented in works that depend on a kind of scholastic authority. This kind of interdependence of spiritual experience and scholastic authority is not a very clear subject of McDaniel's Chapter 8, though throughout the book she charges that contemporary Christian theology has worked to narrow the range of accepted experience.

About McDaniel's third point summarizing Sharf's article, it is certainly true that it includes accounts of alien abductions. Sharf does not claim that these are religious experiences, but he does treat them as analogous. John Mack and other scholars argue that these accounts are so consistent that this is proof that something close to the events described did take place. However, Sharf is skeptical about this. It is more likely that there is no "experience" at all at the basis of these accounts. After citing this example, Sharf critiques the conclusion of a book about possession by Felicitas D. Goodman. That author agnostically admits that she cannot know whether her research subjects were actually possessed: "No one can either prove or disprove that the obvious changes in the brain map in possession ... are produced by psychological processes or by an invading alien being" (Sharf 1998, p. 112; quoting Goodman 1988, p. 126). About this tergiversation, Sharf comments derisively, "Goodman's agnosticism is but a small step away from John Mack's qualified acceptance of existence of alien abductors" (Sharf 1998, p. 112). Here, it seems that Sharf is attaching to Goodman's possession the opprobrium that seems to go with the accounts of alien abductions—we all know that these things did not happen. Perhaps Sharf reaches this conclusion because he is a thoroughgoing materialist, beginning his analysis with the assumption that there are no supernatural beings, so all the tales of encounters with them must be subject to some other kind of explanation. If that is Sharf's starting point, I cannot follow him that far. As a professor of religious studies in a state university in the United States, I am not prepared to issue a universal declaration of my own view about the existence or nonexistence of supernatural beings. However, it is not clear if that is Sharf's starting point—he does not make that explicit.

In my reading of McDaniel's book, there is little in Chapter 8 about the first point in her summary of Sharf. *Lost Ecstasy* does claim that "As we compare understandings of religious experience in Hinduism and in the Judaeo-Christian West, what is striking is their similarity" (McDaniel 2018, p. 251). But nowhere here or elsewhere is there a discussion of the kind of genealogy of experience in the modern west that we find in Sharf and Desjarlais. I assume that this is because McDaniel does not find such a genealogical analysis to be necessary to compare accounts of ecstatic experience across cultures, accounts that are manifestly similar.

Though I do not agree with all of Sharf's critiques of religious experience, I do think that there is at least one that is worthy of serious consideration. If Sharf and Desjarlais's genealogy of experience is correct, we should be careful about imposing our own cultural framework on Tukaram, if we seek access to his experience. Since the claim is made that Tukaram's poetry is particularly modern, it might seem as if this problem should not arise, that this collapses the cultural difference between the seventeenth century poet and the contemporary scholarly analyst. Yet, as noted in the second section of this essay, there are problems with this claim. Omvedt and Patankar do briefly discuss the emergence of a kind of modern critique in seventeenth century Europe, but provide no analysis of how this development occurred in South Asia. In Chitre's book, the context in cultural history becomes irrelevant, since he argues that in its "new existential dimensions," Tukaram's poetry "was anticipating the spiritual anguish of modern man two centuries ahead of his time" (Tukaram 1991, p. xx). Tukaram has apparently somehow leaped over the cultural changes that have led in the west to a modern sensibility. Of course, the historical rupture that Chitre suggests is cast into some doubt by the fact that the body of Tukaram's poetry has been added to over the centuries. More fundamentally, as discussed above, it seems that the modern self that Chitre finds in Tukaram is substantially different from the one that Omvedt and Patankar uncover.

The contemporary devotee's encounter with Tukaram, through his poetry and through the hagiographies of Mahipati, particularly during the Varkari pilgrimage, deserves to be labelled an "abundant event," in the language of Robert Orsi, as described in the first section of this essay. It is certainly the case that the devotee believes that she knows Tukaram and his experience. Orsi and Monge insist that such an encounter can have a transformative effect on the scholar as well. But it seems to me that whether the scholar is encountering Tukaram at all must depend at least to some extent on the sources that provide access to him. As noted above, we cannot rely entirely on Mahipati's hagiographies, since they were written a century after Tukaram lived, on the basis of uncertain sources, and by an author who did not have a contemporary historian's concern about his sources. We cannot even depend on Tukaram's own poems to get back to him, at least without a successful critical study of their history, since it is likely that many of the poems that are now attributed to him were written later. At best, Tukaram's oeuvre as it currently exists only gives us access to how the Varkari community has represented his experience over time. At the beginning of this essay, I argued that we find in the story of Tukaram's relationship with Jijai an account of the social impact of his religious experience. This is a story that celebrates indifference to worldly concerns, embodied by Tukaram, however much that may provoke the censure of the worldly, represented by his wife. However, because of the nature of the sources that (may or may not) take us back to the seventeenth century, we cannot be sure that this social teaching is really based on Tukaram's experience.

There have been devotional poet-saints in the history of Hinduism whose compositions were fixed in their own lifetime, but this has been relatively unusual. More common is that a saint's output has expanded over the centuries. For some poets, there are manuscripts that can be studied to analyze this development. But even this will not lead to certain knowledge of the original works of most saints. So, for reasons of textual history, if not for more theoretical reasons, the experience of saints such as Tukaram must remain elusive.

Funding: This research received no external funding.

Acknowledgments: The author gratefully acknowledges suggestions about an earlier draft of this article from Jon Keune, Russell McCutcheon, June McDaniel, and Christian Novetzke.

Conflicts of Interest: The author declares no conflict of interest.

References

Abbott, Justin E. 2000. *Life of Tukaram: Translation from Mahipati's Bhaktalilamrita, Chapter 25 to 40*. This Is a Reprint of the First Edition of 1930. Delhi: Motilal Banarsidass. First published 1930.

Abbott, Justin E., and Narhar R. Godbole. 1999. *Stories of Indian Saints: Translation of Mahipati's Marathi Bhaktavijaya*. This Is a Reprint of the Fourth Edition of 1933. Delhi: Motilal Banarsidass. First published 1933.

Chitre, Dilip Purushottam. 2001. *Punha Tukaram*. Mumbai: Popular Prakashan.

Clooney, Francis X. 2016. Afterword: Truth, Scholarship, and Hagiography in the Study of Our Saints. In *Hagiography and Religious Truth: Case Studies in the Abrahamic and Dharmic Traditions*. Edited by Rico G. Monge, Kerry P. C. San Chirico and Rachel J. Smith. London: Bloomsbury Academic, pp. 199–204.

Desjarlais, Robert. 1997. *Shelter Blues: Sanity and Selfhood Among the Homeless*. Philadelphia: University of Pennsylvania Press.

Foucault, Michel. 1978. *The History of Sexuality. Vol. 1. An Introduction*. Translated by R. Hurley. New York: Pantheon.

Goodman, Felicitas. 1988. *How about Demons? Possession and Exorcism in the Modern World*. Bloomington: Indiana University Press.

Hare, James P. 2011. Garland of Devotees: Nabhadas' *Bhaktamal* and Modern Hinduism. Ph.D. dissertation, Columbia University, New York, NY, USA.

Hawley, John Stratton. 1984. *Sur Das: Poet, Singer, Saint*. Seattle: University of Washington Press.

Hawley, John Stratton. 1988. Author and Authority in the *Bhakti* Poetry of North India. *Journal of Asian Studies* 47: 269–90. [CrossRef]

Keune, Jon Milton. 2011. Eknath Remembered and Reformed: Bhakti, Brahmans, and Untouchables in Marathi Historiography. Ph.D. dissertation, Columbia University, New York, NY, USA.

Lorenzen, David N. 1991. *Kabir Legends and Ananta-das's Kabir Parchai*. Albany: State University of New York Press.

Mahipati. 1974. *Sribhakta Vijay*. Edited by Visvanath Kesav Phadke. Pune: Yasvamt Prakasan.

Mahipati. 1988. *Sribhakta Lilamrt*. Edited by Visvanath Kesav Phadke. Pune: Yasvamt Prakasan.

Martin, Craig, and Russell T. McCutcheon, eds. 2012. *Religious Experience: A Reader*. With Leslie Dorrough Smith. Sheffield: Equinox.

McDaniel, June. 2018. *Lost Ecstasy: Its Decline and Transformation in Religion*. Cham: Palgrave Macmillan.

McLaughlin, Mark J. 2016. Turning Tomb into Temple: Hagiography, Sacred Space, and Ritual Activity in a Thirteenth-Century Hindu Shrine. In *Hagiography and Religious Truth: Case Studies in the Abrahamic and Dharmic Traditions*. Edited by Rico G. Monge, Kerry P. C. San Chirico and Rachel J. Smith. London: Bloomsbury Academic, pp. 70–88.

Monge, Rico G. 2016. Saints, Truth, and the "Use and Abuse" of Hagiography. In *Hagiography and Religious Truth: Case Studies in the Abrahamic and Dharmic Traditions*. Edited by Rico G. Monge, Kerry P. C. San Chirico and Rachel J. Smith. London: Bloomsbury Academic, pp. 7–22.

Monge, Rico G., Kerry P. C. San Chirico, and Rachel J. Smith. 2016. Introduction. In *Hagiography and Religious Truth: Case Studies in the Abrahamic and Dharmic Traditions*. Edited by Rico G. Monge, Kerry P. C. San Chirico and Rachel J. Smith. London: Bloomsbury Academic, pp. 1–4.

Novetzke, Christian Lee. 2008. *Religion and Public Memory: A Cultural History of Saint Namdev in India*. New York: Columbia University Press.

Orsi, Robert A. 2009. Abundant History: Marian Apparitions as Alternative Modernity. In *Moved by Mary: The Power of Pilgrimage in the Modern World*. Edited by Anna-Karina Hermkens, Willy Jansen and Catrien Notermans. Farnham: Ashgate.

Sharf, Robert H. 1995. Buddhist Modernism and the Rhetoric of Meditative Experience. *Numen* 42: 228–83. [CrossRef]

Sharf, Robert H. 1998. Experience. In *Critical Terms for Religious Studies*. Edited by Mark C. Taylor. Chicago: University of Chicago Press, pp. 94–116.

Shulman, David. 2001. *The Wisdom of Poets: Studies in Tamil, Telugu, and Sanskrit*. Delhi: Oxford University Press.

Tukaram. 1991. *Says Tuka: Selected Poetry of Tukaram*. Translated by Dilip Chitre. Delhi: Penguin Books.
Tukaram. 2012. *Songs of Tukoba*. Translated by Gail Omvedt, and Bharat Patankar. Delhi: Manohar.
Tulpule, Shankar Gopal. 1979. *Classical Marathi Literature: From the Beginning to A. D. 1818*. History of Indian Literature 9, 4. Wiesbaden: Otto Harrassowitz.

religions

MDPI

Article

Sacred Music and Hindu Religious Experience: From Ancient Roots to the Modern Classical Tradition

Guy L. Beck

Asian Studies and Philosophy, Tulane University, New Orleans, LA 70118, USA; beckg@tulane.edu

Received: 22 December 2018; Accepted: 24 January 2019; Published: 29 January 2019

Abstract: While music plays a significant role in many of the world's religions, it is in the Hindu religion that one finds one of the closest bonds between music and religious experience extending for millennia. The recitation of the syllable OM and the chanting of Sanskrit Mantras and hymns from the Vedas formed the core of ancient fire sacrifices. The Upanishads articulated OM as Śabda-Brahman, the Sound-Absolute that became the object of meditation in Yoga. First described by Bharata in the *Nātya-Śāstra* as a sacred art with reference to Rasa (emotional states), ancient music or Sangīta was a vehicle of liberation (Mokṣa) founded in the worship of deities such as Brahmā, Vishnu, Śiva, and Goddess Sarasvatī. Medieval Tantra and music texts introduced the concept of Nāda-Brahman as the source of sacred music that was understood in terms of Rāgas, melodic formulas, and Tālas, rhythms, forming the basis of Indian music today. Nearly all genres of Indian music, whether the classical Dhrupad and Khayal, or the devotional Bhajan and Kīrtan, share a common theoretical and practical understanding, and are bound together in a mystical spirituality based on the experience of sacred sound. Drawing upon ancient and medieval texts and Bhakti traditions, this article describes how music enables Hindu religious experience in fundamental ways. By citing several examples from the modern Hindustani classical vocal tradition of Khayal, including text and audio/video weblinks, it is revealed how the classical songs contain the wisdom of Hinduism and provide a deeper appreciation of the many musical styles that currently permeate the Hindu and Yoga landscapes of the West.

Keywords: Indian music; sacred sound; Hinduism; Kīrtan; Bhajan; Nāda-Brahman; Dhrupad; Khayal; Bhakti; Rasa; Sangīta; Rāga; Tāla

---

> Our tradition teaches us that sound is God—Nāda Brahma. That is, musical sound and the musical experience are steps to the realization of the Self. We view music as a kind of spiritual discipline that raises one's inner being to divine peacefulness and bliss. The highest aim of our music is to reveal the essence of the universe it reflects, and the Rāgas are among the means by which this essence can be apprehended. Thus, through music, one can reach God.
>
> —Ravi Shankar, Sitar maestro (Shankar 1968, p. 17)

The above statement is one of the first public expressions in the West of the spirituality of Indian music by a renowned Indian musician. Beginning in the 1960s, many Westerners were exposed to Hindu religion and culture in the form of Yoga and Indian classical music. Due to the relaxation of American immigration rules in 1965, an infusion of Indian religious teachers and musicians paved the way for the adoption of Hinduism by Americans, as well as the formal instruction in Indian music on instruments such as the Sitar and Tabla. As a result, scholars and practitioners began the careful study of ancient Sanskrit texts that revealed the close links between Hindu religious thought and Indian music. From Vedic chant to the Upanishads, from Yoga philosophy to Tantric rituals, from theistic worship to the Bhakti movements, from classical Dhrupad and Khayal songs in Rāgas (melodic patterns) and Tālas (rhythms) to lighter forms of Bhajan and Kīrtan, many seemingly disparate sectors of Indian tradition are found to be bound together in a mystical spirituality grounded in the experience of sacred sound. This essay first outlines the theoretical roots of sacred sound in India, and then explains the connections between these and sacred music, aesthetics, the traditions of devotion, and finally to the modern Hindustani classical tradition. The presentation demonstrates a continuity between the ancient and modern traditions by means of several examples of classical vocal compositions known as Khayal, including text and audio/video weblinks. The result is a deeper appreciation of the underlying spiritual unity of Indian music as well as a more accurate understanding of the variety of classical and devotional songs that permeate the Hindu and Yoga landscapes of the West.

To many Westerners, Ravi Shankar was their first exposure to Indian music. Yet two predecessors, one in America and one in India, had already set the stage for the acceptance of the spirituality of Indian music by aligning it with Yoga. Considered one of the first Yoga teachers to settle in America, Paramahansa Yogānanda (1893–1952), in his bestselling work, *Autobiography of a Yogi: The Classic Story of One of India's Greatest Spiritual Thinkers* (Yogānanda [1946] 2016, p. 131), suggested an alliance between the syllable OM (AUM) and the music or sound that can be heard through faculties taught in Yoga: "The ancient Rishis discovered these laws of sound alliance between nature and man. Because nature is an objectification of AUM, the Primal Sound or Vibratory Word, man can obtain control over all natural manifestations through the use of certain mantras or chants. The deeper aim of the early Rishi-musicians was to blend the singer with the Cosmic Song which can be heard through awakening of man's occult spinal centers."

Swami Śivānanda (1887–1963), also a key transmitter of Yoga, did not travel to the West. However, Śivānanda's teachings were a noteworthy influence through disciples who brought his message to America and the Western world, including Swami Vishnudevānanda, Swami Satchidānanda, Swami Chidānanda, and Swami Nādabrahmānanda. In his seminal book, *Music as Yoga* (Śivānanda 1956, pp. 6–7), Sivananda explained the relation between Yoga and music by means of OM: "What distinguished Indian music ... It was always held to be but an extension and outward symbolization of the Omnipresent Praṇava Sound—OM—and utilized only for purposes of God attainment—a feature it has retained to the present-day, as will be evident from the fact that, up to the end of the last century, the subject of musical compositions has rarely been anything but God and his glories." In terms of Yoga terminology, he identifies the physical Yoga with music (ibid., p. 18): "Music is a synthesis of the various Yogas or paths to God-realization. Music itself is Hatha Yoga Sadhana." These provocative statements beckon us to look further by exploring the ancient Sanskrit sources on Indian music and the spirituality of Hindu religion. Since vocal music is the root of all music, this essay will focus primarily on the vocal classical tradition.

1. Sacred Sound: OM and Nāda-Brahman

Traditionally, the Indian experience of music has been bound to the apprehension of the divine in the context of religious activities, first through ancient fire sacrifices and then through Pūjā or devotional worship of various gods and goddesses. From the singing of the ancient Vedic hymns to the devotional chants and songs of modern-day devotees, Indian music is deeply grounded in the theological principles of sacred sound as contained in Hindu scriptures. The Vedas and Upanishads (ca. 2000–1000 BCE) contain information about the practice of chant and vocal utterance in relation to fire sacrifices to the gods. These ancient Indo-Āryan texts are believed to embody the eternal primeval sound that generated the universe, symbolized by the syllable OM, the power of which is manifest through oral chant. Recent research on the origins and history of the syllable OM has revealed that OM was closely associated with tonal chant and music from the beginning of its use.in ancient India. According to Gerety (2015, p. 461), "The bottom line is that the first thousand years of OM constitute a Sāmavedic movement within the broader religious culture of Vedism. Amidst concurrent contributions by experts from the other Vedas, it was the singer-theologians of first the Jaiminīya, and then the Kauthuma, branches of Sāma-Veda who did the most to foster OM's emergence. In my view, this is the single most important finding of the present study: that the history of the sacred syllable resounds with music and song." Additionally, Wilke and Moebus (2011) explores the linguistic aspects of sound as communication in the context of Sanskritic culture. All this research helps us to understand the function of OM and why the chanting of OM is almost always tonal, unless muttered in near-silence. That is, OM is normally executed in a kind of monotone on the tonic note of a scale. This method is still the foundation of Hindu worship and the basis for opening classical vocal music performances.

The Vedic fire sacrifice always included chant and meditation on sound, such that ritual chanting was viewed as an effective means to interact with the cosmos and to obtain unseen spiritual merit toward a heavenly afterlife. Verses from the Rig Veda were chanted in roughly three distinct musical tones or accents, which were expanded to seven notes in the singing of hymns (Sāmans) from the Sāma Veda (ca. 1000 BCE). Utilized during elaborate sacrifices involving the offering of Soma juice, the Sāma Veda hymns comprise the earliest hymnal in world religion. They were believed to possess supernatural powers capable of petitioning and supporting the deities that controlled the forces of the universe, indicating to us that music was mysteriously linked to the divine at this early stage of Hindu ritual practice. Thite (1997, p. 68) described the attractive and powerful nature of the Sāma Veda hymns: "the poet-singers call, invoke, and invite the gods with the help of musical elements. In so doing they seem to be aware of the magnetic power of music and therefore they seem to be using that power in calling the gods." The connections between chant, music, and the gods in Vedic culture formed the basis of both the earliest classical music known as Gandharva Sangīta, and the later devotional music or Bhakti Sangit which formed part of the Bhakti movements. And while music in India formed part of both public worship and drama, it was viewed not only as entertainment, but as a vehicle toward liberation (Mokṣa) and immortality.

As discussed in Beck (1993), musical sound in Hindu tradition is linked to the divine Absolute known as Brahman through the concepts of Śabda-Brahman and especially Nāda-Brahman ("Sacred sound as God"), comprising Nāda-Śakti (sound energy) and Brahman (divine Absolute). Brahman, first articulated in the Upanishads, is also conceived in two ways: Nirguṇa (without attributes), and Saguṇa (with attributes). The followers of Nirguṇa-Brahman worship the Absolute beyond all material qualities, which can be approached without the use or need of icons or deities. The followers of Saguṇa-Brahman, on the other hand, prefer the use of images and statues as more effective means of meditation on the divine. The developing notion of Nāda-Brahman (sacred sound) is described in the Āgamas and Tantras as well as in Yoga commentaries and musicological texts such as the *Sangīta-Ratnākara*, encompassing both Nirguṇa and Saguṇa approaches to the Absolute. The term Nāda-Brahman refers to sacred sound that may be either unmanifest (Anāhata, "unstruck," existing in the divine realm) or manifest (Āhata, "struck," existing in the human realm, i.e., music). Although both perspectives of Nirguṇa and Saguṇa are discoverable in the Upanishads, the underlying philosophy is shared, namely, that the material world is temporary and illusory, and one should attempt to transgress the cycle of rebirth known as Samsāra by decreasing material attachment to family, friends, and possessions. This philosophy is also conveyed in the lyrics of classical songs known as Khayal.

Most Hindu practitioners follow the Saguṇa tradition. Whether as Vaishnavism (Vishnu or Krishna worship), Śaivism (Śiva worship), or Śaktism (goddess worship), the concept of Nāda-Brahman ('sacred sound') is employed to affirm that God or the Supreme Being contains the elemental of primal sound and can be approached in its deity form through sound and music. Regarding the Saguṇa aspect, Hopkins (1971, p. 20) has described how the names and epithets of deities were the sonic counterparts to the visual dimensions: "Sanskrit words were not just arbitrary labels assigned to phenomena; they were the sound forms of objects, actions, and attributes, related to the corresponding reality in the same way as visual forms, and different only in being perceived by the ear and not by the eye." True meditation on an icon thus involves both sound and image, leading us to the important role of music in Hindu religious experience. Moreover, the name of a deity was understood to contain all the spiritual potencies of the deity. Hence the well-known axiom, "Mantra (name) and Devatā (deity) are the same," that is affirmed throughout the Hindu tradition, lending credence to Nām-Kīrtan, the chanting of divine names.

2. Sacred Music: Sangīta

Indian music, known as Sangīta, is considered divine in origin and very closely identified with the Hindu gods and goddesses. The Goddess Sarasvatī, depicted with the Vina instrument in hand, is believed to be the divine patroness of music. Brahmā, the creator of the universe, fashioned Indian music out of the ingredients of the Sāma Veda and plays the hand cymbals. Vishnu the Preserver sounds the conch shell and plays the flute in the form of the incarnation known as Krishna. Śiva as Naṭarāja plays the Damaru drum during the dance of cosmic dissolution. Sangita has three divisions: vocal, instrumental, and dance.

Described in Beck (2012, chp. 2), Gandharva Sangīta was the ancient non-sacrificial counterpart to the sacrificial Sāma Veda hymns and considered a replica of the music performed and enjoyed in Lord Indra's heavenly court. Brought down to earth by the sage Nārada, this essentially vocal music included instruments such as the Vina, flutes, drums, and cymbals. The oldest surviving texts of Gandharva Sangīta, the *Nāṭya-Śāstra* by Bharata Muni and the *Dattilam* by Dattila (ca. 400–200 BCE), provide glimpses of this music as it was performed in sacred dramas, festivals, courtly ceremonies, and temple rituals in honor of the emerging great gods and goddesses such as Śiva, Vishnu, Brahmā, and Ganeṣa. Gandharva Sangīta was linked to the practice of Pūjā (worship of images) which gradually replaced the fire sacrifice as the center of Hindu religious activity.

In Sangīta, the musical note is wedded to a beat and a word. The inclusion of a lyric in the definition of music also underscores the centrality of vocal music in the ancient world. In the third verse of *Dattilam* (Nijenhuis 1970, p. 17), Sangīta is, "A collection of notes (Svara), which is based on words (Pada), which is well-measured by time-measurement (Tāla) and which is executed with attentiveness." This statement is basically the same as that found in *Nāṭya-Śāstra* (28.8). While Vedic chants and Sāma Veda hymns were punctuated by metrical divisions that generated distinct units of unseen merit that accrued to the priest or sacrificer, similar metrical units were marked by the playing of hand cymbals and drums in Gandharva music. The ancient theorists held that the musicians and audience earned Mokṣa through accumulation of unseen merit through the marking of ritual (musical) time in the form of Tāla. The significance of rhythm or Tāla can thus be traced to the earliest texts on music. Liberation within the theistic and devotional traditions was also dependent on the emotion feelings of love that the practitioners held in terms of the developing personal relationship with their deity, including the proper Rasa sentiments.

3. Aesthetics of Rasa

In the Saguṇa approach to the divine, the deity is physically visible to the devotee in the form of an icon or statue. Believed to be more accessible to human devotion, the deities became the objects of aesthetic sentiments as expressed through the musical arts. The Upanishads describe Brahman (Absolute or God) as *raso vai sah*, full of the essence of aesthetic delight or Rasa (*Taittirīya Upanishad* 2.7.1). The association between Rasa and music began to appear in the earliest Sanskrit musical treatises and texts on Pūjā and the dramatic arts. Bharata Muni, in *Nāṭya-Śāstra,* was the first to outline the basic features of Indian music as well as the various aesthetic experiences (Rasas) associated with drama and the worship of icons. Rasas are the artistic or aesthetic expressions of emotional experiences that are believed to be universal traits of humanity, such as love, compassion, and heroism. In the *Nāṭya-Śāstra* (6.15, 39–45), Bharata Muni presents the original eight Rasas: Śringāra—erotic, Hāsya—comic, Karuṇā—compassion, Raudra—terror, Vīra—heroic, Bhayānaka—fear, Bībhatsa—disgust, and Adbhuta—wonder (Rangacharya 2003, pp. 54–56). The *Nāṭya-Śāstra* (19.38-40) ties the eight Rasas with the seven individual notes of the musical scale known for the first time as Sa Re Ga Ma Pa Dha Ni (cf. do re mi fa so la ti): erotic—Pa (fifth), comic—Ma (fourth), compassion—Ga (third) and Ni (seventh), disgust and fear—Dha (sixth), heroic, terror, and wonder—Sa (tonic) and Re (second) (Rangacharya 2003, pp. 142–43).

Covering six chapters (*Nāṭya-Śāstra* 28–33), Bharata discussed vocal and instrumental music, musical instruments, and theoretical issues of scale (Grāma), mode (Jāti), meter (Mātrā), and rhythm

(Tāla). The ancient musical scales are known as Grāmas, of which there were three. Out of the notes of the Grāmas, sixteen Jātis or modes were formed which included some basic defining characteristics, such as notes of emphasis, phrase-like patterns, and so forth. The early notion of Jāti developed into the Rāga by the eighth century CE, as known from the famous text, *Brihaddeśī*, by Matanga. This text also connected the Rāga with sacred sound as Nāda-Brahman. The Rāga, as a special set of notes, was more distinct as a melodic pattern than the Jāti, and had unique structural characteristics, emotional content (Rasa), and methods of performance. All Rāgas comprise ascending and descending patterns of from five to seven notes derived from the seven-note scale above, with the additional lowering or raising of specific notes to enlarge the gamut. The Rāga quickly became the preferred form of expression for the classical and devotional songs coming out of the medieval Bhakti movements. Nānyadeva, in his twelfth-century *Bharata-bhāshya*, developed the relation between Rasas and Rāgas such that these associations were expressed in poetic form known Dhyāna-Mantras, and in the paintings (Rāgamālā) that further linked them with a season, time of day, and gender (male Rāga and female Rāginī).

As classical music was gradually separated from drama, four of the original eight Rasas—Śringāra, Karuṇā, Vīra, and Adbhuta—retained their association with music, with Śringāra Rasa holding its pride of place through the centuries. Śringāra Rasa was described as having two types: union (sambhoga) and separation (vipralambha). The first celebrates the joy and exhilaration of lovers meeting, the second endures the pangs of separation, including anxiety, yearning, and some jealousy. The universal human quality (sthāyi-bhāva) of Śringāra is romantic passion (ratī). Associated with white, pure, bright, beautiful and elegant attire, and the fullness of youth, Śringāra Rasa was also expressly affiliated with the god Vishnu, whose incarnation of Krishna became the nexus of divine love-play in later poetry and music. A ninth Rasa, Śānta Rasa (peace) was added by the Kashmiri philosopher Abhinavagupta in the tenth century CE. Śānta Rasa was the appropriate musical aesthetic in response to the formless nature of the divine, or Nirguṇa-Brahman, as endorsed by the non-dualist school of Advaita Vedanta propounded in Kashmiri Śaivism. Śringāra Rasa, however, was believed to transcend the formless or impersonal conception and was more suitable for the Saguṇa approach to the divine.

4. Bhakti and Music: Kīrtan and Bhajan

The Bhakti devotional movements began in southern India in the sixth century CE. At that time, separate Bhakti groups emerged as powerful forces favoring a devotion-centered Hinduism with song-texts composed primarily in vernacular, in this case Tamil, Telugu, and Kannada. Many new styles of regional devotional music were duly formalized to accompany liturgies in the temples of medieval times. These styles followed a simple aesthetic reflecting the perspective of music as an offering as well as a means toward communion with a chosen deity. In the evolving personal theism, Brahman was conceived as the supreme personal deity, whether Vishnu, Śiva, or Śakti, and believed to be the fountainhead of all Rasa (aesthetic pleasure or taste). The emotional experience of love and devotion produced by musicians in the minds of the listeners was linked to the divine by virtue of it being a part of the Bhakti tradition.

In support of the growing Bhakti movements, a tenth Rasa, Bhakti Rasa (devotional love), was introduced by the Vaishnava theologian Rūpa Goswami in the sixteenth century. Bhakti Rasa was widely adopted as the superior Rasa among religious groups and practitioners of the Saguṇa traditions and was believed to encompass and transform all the other Rasas. In the *Nārada-Bhakti-Sūtra* (ca. 100 BCE–400 CE) and the *Bhāgavata-Purāṇa* (ninth century CE), five types of devotional love are described, namely, Śānta (meditational), Dāsya (servitude), Sākhya (friendship), Vātsalya (parental), Kāntā (conjugal), with the highest being the latter as love between man and woman, which came to symbolize the love between the human and the divine. The *Bhāgavata-Purāṇa* outlined the path of devotion or Bhakti Mārga as being superior to the path of knowledge (Jñāna Mārga) and action (Karma Mārga). Moreover, the *Bhagavad-Gītā* and the *Bhāgavata-Purāṇa* stressed that Bhakti was the culmination of all religious experiences and included the other paths in the truest sense. Under the influence of these texts and medieval scholars of Rasa such as Bhoja of Rajasthan (eleventh century),

Rūpa Goswami held that Śringāra, within the locus of Bhakti Rasa, was synonymous with the selfless love of the Gopīs (handmaidens) for Krishna, an ecstatic affection known as Krishna-ratī or Premā (highest love). As part of temple worship, Śringāra came to refer to the early morning decoration of the deities of Rādhā and Krishna as they are 'dressed for conjugal love.'

The spread of the Bhakti traditions stimulated many new forms of architectural, literary, and artistic expression. In terms of music, the Medieval Period (ca. fourth to seventeenth century CE) is characterized by the rise of Bhakti Sangīt ("devotional music"), much of which followed the classical form of Rāga (melodic pattern) and Tāla (rhythmic cycle) and contained lyrics expressive of love and devotion toward a chosen deity. Unlike Vedic chant and Sāma Veda hymns, which are rendered in Sanskrit, Bhakti Sangīt is primarily sung in vernacular dialects such as Hindi and Braj Bhāṣā in the North, and Tamil, Telugu, and Kannada in the South. Various types of Bhakti Sangīt came to be referred to as either Kīrtan or Bhajan.

Kīrtan appears similar in definition to the Western hymn (*hymnus*, "song of praise") or psalm (*psalmos*, "plucked song of praise") as found in Biblical traditions, and in the Sufi Islamic songs of praise. The term Bhajan suggests a more interactive nature, since it shares with the word Bhakti and Bhagavān ('Lord') the common Sanskrit root *bhaj*, "to share, to partake of" (as in a rite). Bhagavān means the Lord who possesses *bhaga*, good fortune, opulence. Kīrtan and Bhajan, as terms for religious or devotional music apart from Vedic chant and the purely classical traditions, are directly linked to the growing Bhakti movements, and are performed so that God, 'Bhagavān,' is praised, worshipped, or appealed to in a mutual exchange of Bhakti. An interesting comparative study of Bhajan, Kirtan, and psalm is found in Muck (2001).

Several important scriptures in Sanskrit have endorsed Kīrtan and Bhajan in Hindu practice. These include the *Bhagavad-Gītā* and the *Bhāgavata-Purāṇa*. The *Bhagavad-Gītā* 9.13–14 provides two sequential verses that contain all three of the key terms—Kīrtan, Bhajan, Bhakti—with a shared objective. The terms Kīrtan (*kīrtayanto*) and Bhajan (*bhajanty*) refer to any act of worship or loving devotion, including music. The *Bhāgavata-Purāṇa* (6th to 9th century CE) endorses both Kīrtan and Gītī (song) as near-statutory practices within Pūjā. Kīrtan and Pūjā are inextricably linked in *Bhāgavata-Purāṇa* 11.19.20. In *Bhāgavata-Purāṇa* 11.11.36, song, dance, and instrumental music are mentioned as equal components of the divine service in the temple. Kīrtan is also understood to be expressed musically in the form of song, represented here with the Sanskrit term *gayan* ("singing") in *Bhāgavata-Purāṇa* 11.11.23. Singing in vernacular languages is an equally effective vehicle according to *Bhāgavata-Purāṇa* 11.27.45, leading to the widespread composition of vernacular songs in various regions of India.

A session of Kīrtan or Bhajan normally begins with chanting OM, and then proceeds with invocations in Sanskrit in honor of a guru, master or deity, followed by sequences of vernacular songs that reflect the group's distinct or eclectic religious outlook; these are sometimes punctuated by short sermons or meditative recitations of Sanskrit verses from scripture. In closing, a special ceremony called Ārati is conducted as part of the Pūjā ("worship service") which includes offerings of food, flowers, incense and lamps, and blowing of conches. The distribution of food, flowers, lamp wicks, and holy water concludes the session.

As musical compositions, Kīrtan and Bhajan songs range from complex structures to simple refrains or litanies containing divine names. Most have their own distinctive tune and rhythm that are easily followed by the audience. The most common Tālas are up-tempo, such as Keherva which has eight beats roughly corresponding to a Western cut time in 4/4. Another common rhythm is Dadra, a six-beat Tāla corresponding to Western 3/4 or 6/8 time. An example of a Bhajan by the poet Sūr Dās in Hindi is found in both textual and audio version in Beck (2006, p. 134). Set in the popular rhythm of Keherva, it nonetheless reflects the ancient philosophical view of the *Bhagavad-Gītā*, whereby attachment to material things can be only relieved by surrender and devotion to God. In the penultimate lyric, Sūr Dās says (in translation), "Due to over-attachment for wife, children and wealth

I have lost all of my clear intelligence. Sur Das implores, "Lord, please relieve me of this great load, for now my ship (this body) has set sail."

The collective singing of the names of God has always been very popular everywhere in India and is called Nām-Kīrtan, Nām-Sankīrtan or Nām-Bhajan. Sung to simple melodies and accompanied by drums and cymbals, Nām-Kīrtan expresses fervent devotion and serves as a means of spiritual release. Primarily a congregational practice, Nām-Kīrtan enables ordinary persons a sense of musical elation. Examples of three chants are:

(1) Hare Krishna Hare Krishna Krishna Krishna Hare Hare Hare Rāma Hare Rāma Rāma Rāma Hare Hare. This is the famous Hare Krishna chant known as the Mahāmantra, Great Mantra for Deliverance as first propounded by Caitanya and other Bhakti saints that has continued in India by pious Hindus and more recently by members of the Hare Krishna Movement (ISKCON). It is a petition to Rādhā ("Harā"), the energy of Krishna, and to Krishna who is also full of pleasure ("Rāma").
(2) Sītā Rām Sītā Rām Sītā Rām Jaya Sītā Rām. This is a chant to Rāma and Sītā: "All Glories to Lord Rāma and his consort Sītā."
(3) OM namah Śivāya. This is a chant to Śiva: "I bow to Lord Śiva."

The practice of Nām-Kīrtan is advocated in the lyrics of the classical songs of Khayal discussed below under the name of "Hari Nām" or "Rām Nām."

Bhajan, Kīrtan, and Nām-Kīrtan are mostly performed as an informal group enterprise of call-and-response, with participants seated on the floor in proximity to a lead singer, standing in temples, or walking in procession. Generally, a separate area in the temple facing or adjacent to a deity or picture is designated for music. Reading from an anthology of verses, lead singers often accompany themselves on a harmonium, a floor version of the upright, portable reed organ used by nineteenth-century Christian missionaries. The metal reed used in the harmonium, however, is Asiatic in origin. Linked to mouth organs used in the subcontinent, it is the basis for the western harmonica and accordion. Group members generally repeat the lines in unison after the leader. However, the leader may also sing solo or with occasional refrains sung by the group. Bhajan and Kīrtan musical ensembles, like almost all types of Indian music, include musical instruments. Percussion instruments, membranophones and idiophones, include pairs of hand cymbals called Kartal or Jhānjh, drums such as the Tabla, Pakhāvaj, Dholak or Khol, and occasionally bells, clappers or tambourines. A background drone may be provided by a Tanpura, if not by the harmonium or a Śruti Box, a small pumped instrument used in Carnatic music.

5. Dhrupad and Temple Music

During the thirteenth century, the classical music traditions separated into northern Hindustani and southern Carnatic. What developed as Hindustani music in northern regions stemmed from the devotional temple music that was performed by musicians in Mathurā, Vrindāvan, Braj, Gwalior, Rajasthan, Maharashtra, Gujarat, and Uttar Pradesh. For many years in the North, the musical style of Dhrupad was the principal classical vehicle for vernacular Bhakti lyrics, and was rendered in a slow, four-section format using the pure form of a Rāga, along with the strict rhythms of mainly Cautal (twelve beats) or Dhamār (fourteen beats). Dhrupad spread as a classical genre wherever it was patronized by the ruling elite, both in temples and ruling Hindu and Mughal courts. Important devotional styles that are related to Dhrupad are Havelī Sangīt and Samāj Gāyan, both originating in Vaishnava temples in the region of Braj. For specialized studies of Dhrupad, see Srivastava (1980) and Sanyal and Widdess (2004).

As the development of Bhakti included service, adoration and decoration of icons in temples, a central part of the Pūjā or worship service in temples was the rendering of songs addressed to various deities. As already explained, Hindu religion in the form of Saguṇa worship lends great importance to the image of the deity as an object of devotion and veneration. As such, many songs include lyrics that describe a god or deity as part of the meditation process of the singer and listener in visualizing the divine. The lyrics of these compositions, whether in Sanskrit or vernacular, generate a vivid description of the gods and goddesses in what may be termed a verbal icon. Meditation on this "verbal icon" enables the aspirant to effectively focus his or her mind on the form and activities of the chosen deity. As a primary Bhakti text, the *Bhagavad-Gītā* (8.6) has explained that the image in one's mind at the time of death affects one's future birth. Hence the musical experience of devotional love is not abstract but reconciled with the establishment of an image in the mind of the practitioner for purposes of gaining access to a soteriological outcome.

The three examples of traditional Dhrupad compositions below will demonstrate how the lyric creates an image in the mind of the devotee for purposes of liberation (Mokṣa) from the cycle of rebirth (Samsāra). The evolving classical style known as Khayal also served the same purpose. Expressing veneration for three Hindu deities, Sarasvatī, Śiva, and Krishna, each poem utilizes key words and phrases which invoke the visual image of the form of the deity to facilitate meditation. The songs, part of oral tradition and thus unpublished, are composed in the Braj Bhāṣā dialect of Hindi and translated by the author. The first composition is directed toward Sarasvatī, the Goddess of Learning and Music. The epithets and verbal descriptions of the Goddess serve to create an image in the mind for meditation:

Śāradā ko dharata dhyāna, Brahmā Vishnu karata gāna,
vīṇa-dhāri mayurāsana, Sāma-veda hasta dharata

Sarasvatī, who is Śāradā, is praised with song and meditated upon by Brahmā and Vishnu, is seen playing the Vina (vīṇa-dhāri), seated on a peacock throne (mayurāsana), and holding the Sāma Veda (Sāma-veda hasta dharata).

Second, a standard composition in honor of Śiva is replete with iconographic detail associated with the image of Śiva and his pastimes:

Śankara Śiva Mahādeva, nīla-kaṇṭha śūlapāṇi,
gale nāga damaru kara, lepa anga vibhu tana

Śiva, who is Śankara and Mahādeva (the Great God), is blue-throated (nīla-kaṇṭha) from drinking the ocean of poison, holds a trident in his hand (śūlapāṇi), plays the hourglass drum (damaru kara), and sports a cobra snake around his neck (gale nāga). His body is smeared with divine ashes (lepa anga vibhu tana).

The third composition is sung during the early morning hours to wake the child Krishna:

Jāgiye Gopāla Lāla, ānanda-nidhi Nanda Bāla,
Yaśomati kahe bāra bāra, bhora bhayo pyāre.

O Darling Cowherd Son (Gopāla Lāla) Krishna, Child of Nanda (Nanda Bāla), storehouse of bliss (ānanda-nidhi), morning has come and so please wake up. Your mother Yaśodā (Yaśomati) is calling you again and again.

By the sixteenth century, Dhrupad was influential in the temple music styles of several Vaishnava traditions of Krishna worship that were established in Braj, Krishna's home. These primarily include the Vallabha Sampradāya or Puṣṭi Mārg tradition, founded by saint Vallabha in the early sixteenth century, and the Rādhāvallabha Sampradāya founded in the mid-sixteenth century by saint Hita Harivamśa.

The Dhrupad songs of Puṣṭi Mārg, called Havelī Sangīt, are drawn from the Braj Bhāṣā lyrics of their poets that describe the childhood pastimes of Krishna, including the festivals of Holi in the spring season and the Rāsa Dance in autumn. Originally established in Braj, where a group of eight singer-saints (Aṣṭachāp) including the famous poet Sūr Dās performed their musical worship of Krishna, Havelī Sangīt is now widely practiced in Rajasthan and Gujarat. The Rāgas that were sung as early as the sixteenth century by the Vaishnava movements in Vrindāvan and are still sung in roughly the same manner today, are known to modern musicians through the manuscripts of hymnals that have come down to us over the centuries. These Rāgas reveal to us the range of devotional feelings and aesthetic Rasas that were common during worship services to Krishna. Many Rāgas still in use are mentioned in the hymnals of the Puṣṭi Mārg tradition, including Bhairav, Ramkali, Vilaval, Bibhas, Lalit, Malkauns, Todi, Malar, Vasant Purvi, Kalyan, Bihag, and Kafi. Unlike classical Dhrupad, Havelī Sangīt uses cymbals. As in Dhrupad, there are many compositions in Cautal of twelve beats and Dhamār of fourteen beats.

In the mid-sixteenth century, the Vaishnava saint, Hita Harivamśa, founded the Rādhāvallabha Sampradāya in Vrindāvan. This tradition established the devotional singing style known as Samāj Gāyan, which was also modeled upon Dhrupad. Focusing exclusively on the intimate love-play of Rādhā and Krishna, this sect gradually built up a unique repertoire of poetry that is saturated with Śringāra Rasa, culminating in a massive three-volume hymnal, *Śrī Śrī Rādhāvallabhajī kā Varṣotsava*. Set to various Rāgas, most of its poems describe the union and separation of Krishna and his beloved Rādhā and have been sung to musical accompaniment for nearly five-hundred years in the Rādhāvallabha temples. Within the Rādhāvallabha Sampradāaya, there are several Rāgas that are still prevalent, such as Sarang, Kanhara, Vilaval, Kalyan, Bhupali, Bibhas, Malhar, Kedar, and Todi. One hundred and eight songs from the above hymnal are preserved in text and audio format in Beck (2011). Samāj Gāyan is also practiced by members of the Nimbārka and the Haridāsī sampradāyas, two other Vaishnava traditions in the Braj area that pursue the musical interpretations of the relations between Rādhā and Krishna. Additional information on the Vaishnava genres is found in Thielemann (1996, 1999, 2000).

6. Classical Music of Khayal

The Dhrupad music of Vaishnavism described above flourished largely in isolation from the general public, catering exclusively to the devotees and pilgrims at holy shrines. Yet Dhrupad also provided the foundation for the Hindustani classical vocal music genre known as Khayal that flourished in the northern Hindu and Muslim courts. Many Muslim musicians became proficient in Khayal and contributed greatly to its repertoire and success. By the nineteenth century, Khayal virtually replaced Dhrupad as the predominant form of Hindustani vocal music, and by the twentieth century, it had shifted from the court to the concert arena. While expanding in new creative directions, Khayal, also sung in the vernacular Braj Bhāṣā dialect, nonetheless retained an affinity with the substance of the Dhrupad songs. A Khayal song is known as a 'bandish,' a carefully constructed musical composition with a balance of note, beat, and word that creates an image or idea in the mind that is greater than the sum of the individual parts. The modern Khayal performance on the concert stage has become an opportunity for musical virtuosity and showmanship with greater emphasis on creativity and free expression. Audiences of today expect to be overwhelmed by a dazzling display of stylistic elements: shimmering cascades of Tānas (note patterns comprising vowels), Mūrkīs (grace notes), Khuṭkās (rapid turns of phrases), speedy Sargams (Sa Re Ga Ma, etc.), rhythmic interchanges with the Tabla including Tihais (triplets). While many in the public sphere consider these modern innovations, they are found in the ancient texts. Khayal has been studied extensively by Wade (1984) and Raja (2009).

Despite the emphasis on vocal stylings in Khayal, and its large clientele of Muslim singers, the content depicted in the Khayal song lyrics, such as Dhrupad, continue to refer to spiritual messages, including philosophical ideas found in ancient texts, the description of deities, the praise of God through emphasis on Nām-Kīrtan, or simply the human longing for the Almighty. Many Khayal songs depict situations involving the god Krishna and his favorite goddess Rādhā, sometimes in the context of the seasons such as spring and monsoon, while other songs reveal Indian spiritual wisdom such as found in the Upanishads, including the illusory nature of material existence, the misery associated with greed and gluttony, the prospect of repeated births in the cycle of Samsāra or rebirth, and the need for assistance in crossing over to the other side, a place of permanent peace and tranquility.

The solution to these problems is often presented in the songs themselves: chanting divine names, meditation on the Lord, and engaging in devotional worship.

We now present a series of nine Khayal songs from the recording *Wisdom of the Khayal Song* (Beck 2016). Reflecting the Hindu religious experience, they establish continuity between the ancient and medieval traditions of Indian philosophy and devotion and the classical music of today. They are placed in one of four categories: (1) philosophical teachings, (2) praise of God, (3) descriptions of the divine pastimes, and (4) prescriptions of chanting divine names. The compositions are rendered in the rhythm of Tintal (sixteen beats). The lyrics and notations are published in the standard songbooks of Khayal (noted at the end of this subsection). The weblinks are given for the audio of each song, with three links to video performances.

The first two songs reflect the first category. In the first Khayal selection, the lyric expresses the notion of the divine source of music, reminding musicians and listeners that musical experience contributes toward spiritual attainments in this life and the next. This composition in Rāga Yaman reinforces the principle that music is directly connected to the notion of Nāda-Brahman or sacred sound. The lyrics contain the standard reference to Nāda as divided into Anāhata (unstruck sound) and Āhata (struck sound) and as being the source or fountainhead of the Svaras or musical notes, which are sung in this composition as part of the lyrics with reference to parts of the body and the 22 microtones.

One: Rāga Yaman (KPM 2.31–32). Audio online: https://www.saavn.com/song/ahata-anahata-bheda-nade-ke---raag-yaman/GDcxRDkGcls Video online: https://www.youtube.com/watch?v=gLOjOl5AvAM

Āhata anāhata bheda nāda ke
Prathama bheda śrutiyana so hove
Anāhata munijana dhyāna dharata jaba
Nābhi kaṇṭha aura mūrdha sthāna son
Mandra madhya aura tāra hovata
Sapta surana ke nāma bakhāne
Sa re ga ma pa dha ni sa ni dha pa ma ga re sa

Translation with annotation:

The fountainhead of sound in Indian music, Nāda-Brahman, is divided into two realms: Āhata or 'struck' sound (manifest), and Anāhata, or 'unstruck' sound (unmanifest). The struck sound is then divided into 22 Śrutis or microtones. The ancient sages meditated on the Anāhata dimensión of Nāda-Brahman, being in touch with Divine Truth. The seven notes of music, Sa Re Ga Ma Pa Dha Ni, are described as spread over three octaves, lower (Mandra), middle (Madhya), and higher (Tāra), which correspond to the three levels of the body; navel, throat, and head.

The next Khayal song in the first category is in Rāga Malkauns, and reflects the philosophy of the Upanishads and the *Bhagavad-Gītā.* This conveys the view that life is suffering and under the control of illusion or Māyā. One needs to recognize the futility of material possessions and family attachments, and earnestly try to cross-over to the other side of existence as the only remedy for permanent relief from countless rebirths in this material world.

Two: Rāga Malkauns (KPM 3.708–709). Audio online: https://www.saavn.com/song/suna-re-mana-murakha-ajnani---raag-malkauns/FRsJYB9vdFU

Suna re mana mūrakha ajñānī
Bhāī bandhu saba kuṭama kabīlā
Sanga calata kou nāhī
Moha jāla men bilama raho hai
Kauna kisī ko mānī

Eka dina panchī nikasa jā bego
Ye nece kara jānī

Translation with annotation:

Listen! Oh foolish and ignorant Mind! Brothers, friends, family, relatives, wife—none of these will accompany you at the time of death. You are mired in the false illusion of affection, when in fact no one is there for you. One day a bird will come to you and say it is time to go–will you be ready? One must concentrate on the Lord to avoid dire results at the time of death.

The next three Khayal compositions reflect the second category, whereby the lyric offers praise affirms the truth of the unity of God, who nonetheless has many names. Some songs portray a non-sectarian or 'Generic God' comprising an inclusive range of names or epithets, such as Prabhu ("Lord"), Sattār ("Divine Truth"), Karatār ("Creator"), Dātā ("Divine Giver"), who is offered prayer and a petition for liberation. The next three compositions express this notion fully. The first two are in Rāga Bhairav, an early morning Rāga for solemn meditation, and the third one in Rāga Kafi is for the daytime hours especially in the afternoon.

Three: Rāga Bhairav (RV 3.123–124). Audio online: https://www.saavn.com/song/prabhu-data-re---raag-bhairav/BlECWiN8YHQ

Prabhu dātā re, bhaja re mana jīvana ghari pala china
Jo tu cāhe ana dhana lacchamī
Dūdha pūta bahu terā
Vāko nāma bhaja guru ko nāma

Translation:

The Supreme Lord is the Giver of everything! Therefore worship Him every moment of your life. One who desires from you the blessings of this life and the next should heed this call and sincerely worship the Lord and take the name of one's Guru.

Four: Rāga Bhairav (KPM 2.181–182).

Prabhu dātā sabana ke, tū rata le mana ghari pala china
Jo tū cāhe dūdha pūta ana
Dhana lacchami imāna vāko nāma
Le vāke raba ko nāma le, prabhu dātā sabana ke

Translation:

Oh Lord! You are the Giver of everything.
Let my mind recall you at every moment.
Whatever one desires from you, material or spiritual, the highest blessing is the pleasure of chanting your name in good faith.

Five: Rāga Kafi (KPM 1.46–47). Audio online: https://www.saavn.com/song/prabhu-teri-daya-hai-apar---raag-kafi/OBkeVC0CQHU

Prabhu terī dayā hai apār
Tu agama agocara avikala cara acara sakalaka
Tu ādhār patitana ko uddhār
Dīna anātha patīta aru durabala
Mahad aparādhī śaraṇāgata hūn
Catura tihār mohe pāra utār

Translation:

Oh Lord, Your mercy knows no boundaries.

Though you are inaccesible and unknowable in your fullness, you uplift the fallen and are the foundation of everything moving and non-moving. Poor, helpless, fallen, and weak, I am a sinner, full of offenses, yet I surrender to you. The poet Catur says "Please carry me across to the other side."

In the third category, the lyric enhances meditation on a specific deity, whether Krishna, Śiva, or a Goddess, by describing the characteristics of the deity. The song formulates a "verbal icon" in the mind which assists the devotee to focus attention on a specific deity. Two examples are given. The first example is a song in Rāga Bihag that describes Krishna playing his flute by the side of the Yamunā River in his hometown of Vrindāvan. The second song in Rāga Yaman-Kalyan is a hymn to Śiva requesting him to reveal himself to the sincere devotee.

Six: Rāga Bihag (AG 38–40). Audio online: https://www.saavn.com/song/bamsi-kaisi-baji-nanda-lala---raag-bihag/BwpaAyEAYws

Bansī kaisī bajī nanda lāla
Tumarī jamunā jī ke ghāṭa
Dhuna mana men more bamsī suna sudha budha bisrānī
Jaga nistāraṇa bhakta nivāraṇa
Brija kī bhūmi para sarasa janama līno
Kālindī men nātho tuma nāga so prāṇī

Translation:

Oh Lord Krishna (Nanda Lāla), the sound of your flute by the side of the Yamunā River has captured my mind and made me lose all sense of comportment. You are the upholder of the universe and the shelter of devotees, yet you took birth in Braj, and pleased the wives of the Nāgas while defeating the demon Kaliya.

Seven: Rāga Yaman Kalyan (AG 1–2). Audio online: https://www.saavn.com/song/darasana-deho-sankara-mahadeva---raag-yaman-kalyan/Rg4kdz9yQUE Video online: https://www.youtube.com/watch?v=r76hXnGWxoA

Daraśana deho śankara mahādeva
Mahādeva tihāre daraśa binā mohe
Kala na parata gharī pala chīna dīna
Āna parī hūn śaraṇa tihāre
Tuma bīna kauna bandhāve dhīra
Bipatā parī mope mahā kaṭhina

Translation:

Oh Śankara, Mahādeva (Śiva), please give me your darśaṇa (visión) without which there is no peace even for a moment. I approach you Lord, and surrender to you. Without you there is no stability in life, only danger and distress.

The next two songs in the fourth category prescribe the chanting of divine names as a remedy for the ills and misfortunes of life. In these cases, the lyric presents an urgent call for the singer or listener to take up the chanting of the divine name of God, most especially Rāma, as in 'Rām Nām,' or Vishnu or Krishna as in 'Hari Nām.'

Eight: Rāga Vrindabani Sarang (KPM 3.503–504). Audio online: https://www.saavn.com/song/rata-kara-rasana-rama-ko---raag-vrindabani-sarang/BQ0yVzdfeGc Video online: https://www.youtube.com/watch?v=su_7Pdgdpos

Raṭākara rasanā rāma ko nāma
Raṭākara rasanā rāma ko nāma
Rāma rāma raghupati raghu-nāyaka

Krishna krishna karuṇā kara śyāma
Gopī pati gopāla gadādhara
Rādhā vara locana abhirāma

Translation:

Recite the name of Rāma with joy, Rāma who is Lord and leader of the Raghus, by whose mercy also appears as Krishna or Śyāma. Krishna is Gopāla, Lord of the Gopīs yet holds a club as Vishnu. More beautiful still is Rādhā whose eyes enchant.

Nine: Rāga Lalit (AG 112). Audio online: https://www.saavn.com/song/hari-ka-nama-sumarale---raag-lalit/BBEeVzpRVnw

Hari ka nāma sumara le tere
Dukha dalādala jāya manuvā
Jo hī terī dhyāve so hī phala pāve
Nāma sumrana sukha dāī manuvā

Translation:

Always remember the name of Lord Hari (Krishna) who takes away all pains. Whatever you desire from God, you will receive the fruits, but meditation on the Name brings the highest bliss.

Printed sources for the Khayal songs, with notations:

KPM. Bhatkhande, V. N. 1953–1964. *Kramika-Pustaka-Mālikā.* Vols. 1–6. Hathras, India.
RV. Patvardhan, V. N. 1962–1970. *Rāga-Vijñāna.* Vols. 1–7. Pune, India.
AG. Mehta, R. C. 1969. *Āgrā Gharānā: Paramparā, Gāyakī aur Cījen.* Baroda, India.

7. Conclusions

The comprehensive description and analysis of music in the major sectors of Hinduism is yet to be conducted by scholars, due in part to the enormous task it entails. Nonetheless, there have been targeted studies of religious and devotional music in ritual and temple settings over recent decades. Modern scholarship has also noted that despite differences in theology or philosophy among Hindu sects, a common factor in all these is the experience of vocal chant and music. Religious leaders widely consider devotional songs to be essential for the propagation of their faiths in order to make them more attractive, and though there may be differences in the content of the lyrics, there is no distinction in principle in the style of singing or performance. There are thousands of compositions that reflect this ideal among a diversity of sectarian traditions. The same Rāga or Tāla may be employed in songs that express love and devotion to Vishnu, Krishna, Śiva, the Goddess, or any deity. The vernacular classical songs of Khayal are an excellent focal point for the study of sacred music in Hindu religious experience because they encompass the entire range of Hindu philosophical and emotional content, reaching back to the ancient Sanskrit texts, as well as the diverse experiences of worship and reflection in the modern world. The beauty and depth of Indian classical music is also evident in the number of non-Hindu traditions that have absorbed it into their own worship experiences. There are Indian classical songs set to Rāgas and Tālas in Sikhism, in Sufi Islam, in Buddhism and Jainism, and among Indian Christians. As such, the universal experiences of love, surrender, and compassion are beautifully expressed and experienced through the medium of Indian classical music.

A clever axiom that is offered by Indian musicians themselves is that musical notes, when accompanied with the proper devotional sentiments of love, pertain to God or Īśvara, a generic name for the Supreme Being—*from svara ('musical notes') to Īśvara.*

In closing, Saxena (1997, p. 440) reiterates the case for the connection between the divine Absolute and sacred music in India: "If it is granted that the concept of the Absolute as sound is true and that music is a possible way to the final Reality, it would follow that the musician must cultivate sound in all its aspects and infinite variety." And the question of the spirituality of Indian music remains in the affirmative (ibid., p. 437): "In the theory and contemporary practice of traditional Indian music itself there is ample room to perceive one's concern and involvement with the art such that it becomes a definite help to spiritual growth."

Funding: This research received no external funding.

Conflicts of Interest: The author declares no conflict of interest.

References

Beck, Guy L. 1993. *Sonic Theology: Hinduism and Sacred Sound*. Columbia: University of South Carolina Press.

Beck, Guy L., ed. 2006. *Sacred Sound: Experiencing Music in World Religions*. Waterloo: Wilfrid Laurier University Press (with CD).

Beck, Guy L., ed. 2011. *Vaishnava Temple Music in Vrindaban: The Rādhāvallabha Songbook*. Kirksville: Blazing Sapphire Press, With 18 CD-compact discs.

Beck, Guy L. 2012. *Sonic Liturgy: Ritual and Music in Hindu Tradition*. Columbia: University of South Carolina Press.

Beck, Guy L. 2016. *Wisdom of the Khayal Song*. Kolkata: Bihaan Music, 2 CD-compact discs. Guy L. Beck, vocals and harmonium; Avijit Kastha, Tabla; Debasish Halder, Sarangi.

Gerety, Finnian McKean Moore. 2015. This Whole World is OM: Song, Soteriology, and the Emergence of the Sacred Syllable. Ph.D. thesis, Harvard University, Cambridge, MA, USA.

Hopkins, Thomas J. 1971. *The Hindu Religious Tradition*. Encino: Dickinson.

Muck, Terry. 2001. Psalm, Bhajan, and Kirtan: Songs of the Soul in Comparative Perspective. In *Psalms and Practice: Worship, Virtue, and Authority*. Edited by Stephen Breck Reid. Collegeville: The Liturgical Press, pp. 7–27.

Nijenhuis, E. Wiersma-te, trans. 1970, *Dattilam: A Compendium of Ancient Indian Music*. Leiden: E. J. Brill.

Raja, Deepak. 2009. *Khayal Vocalism: Continuity within Change*. New Delhi: D. K. Printworld.

Rangacharya, Adya, trans. 2003, *Nāṭya-Śāstra: English Translation with Critical Notes*. New Delhi: Munshiram Manoharlal.

Sanyal, Ritwik, and Richard Widdess. 2004. *Dhrupad: Tradition and Performance in Indian Music*. SOAS Musicology Series; London: Ashgate Publishing.

Saxena, Sushil Kumar. 1997. Spirituality and the Music of India. In *Hindu Spirituality: Postclassical and Modern*. Edited by K. R. Sundararajan and Bithika Mukerji. New York: The Crossroad Publishing Company, pp. 437–49.

Shankar, Ravi. 1968. *My Music, My Life*. New York: Simon and Schuster.

Śivānanda, Swami. 1956. *Music as Yoga*. Garhwal: Divine Life Society.

Srivastava, Induram. 1980. *Dhrupada: A Study of its Origin, Historical Development, Structure, and Present State*. New Delhi: Motilal Banarsidass.

Thielemann, Selina. 1996. Samaja, Haveli Samgita and Dhrupada: The Musical Manifestation of Bhakti. *Journal of Vaishnava Studies* 4: 157–77.

Thielemann, Selina. 1999. *The Music of South Asia*. New Delhi: APH Publishing Group.

Thielemann, Selina. 2000. *Singing the Praises Divine: Music in the Hindu Tradition*. New Delhi: APH Publishing Group.

Thite, G. U. 1997. *Music in the Vedas: Its Magico-Religious Significance*. Delhi: Sharada Publishing House.

Wade, Bonnie C. 1984. *Khyāl [Khayal]: Creativity within North India's Classical Music Tradition*. Cambridge: University of Cambridge Press.

Wilke, Annette, and Oliver Moebus. 2011. *Sound and Communication: An Aesthetic Cultural History of Sanskrit Hinduism*. Berlin: Walter de Gruyter.

Yogānanda, Paramahansa. 2016. *Autobiography of a Yogi: The Classic Story of One of India's Greatest Spiritual Thinkers*. London: Arcturus Publishing Ltd. First published 1946.

religions

MDPI

Article

The Experience of Srividya at Devipuram

Mani Rao

Independent Scholar; emailmanirao@gmail.com; Tel.: +91-8861891807

Received: 14 November 2018; Accepted: 24 December 2018; Published: 28 December 2018

Abstract: This essay discusses the religious experience of Srividya practices at Devipuram in Andhra Pradesh, South India, based on ethnographic studies conducted in 2014 and 2015. A summary of phenomena described by Amritanandanatha Saraswati in his memoirs situates the background. Interviews with three disciples of Amritananda probe their visionary experiences, practical methodologies and relationships with the Goddess. An inter-textual study of interviews, memoirs and narratives helps identify a theme of vision and embodiment—in particular, the aniconic graphic form of the Goddess, the Sriyantra, which is experienced as embodied within the practitioner.

Keywords: Indian Religions; religious experience; Ethnography; tantra; yantra; Srividya

1. Introduction

"Srividya" may be translated as "Auspicious Knowledge;" it refers to a tantric religious tradition in which the primary deity is Goddess Lalita Tripurasundari, a form of the primordial feminine principle also referred to as "Shakti." Srividya is practiced at Devipuram in South India, where Amritanandanatha Saraswati (1934–2015) founded a temple to Goddess Lalita based on a visionary experience. Historically, Srividya is regarded one of the four transmissions (*āmnāya*) of the Kula within the non-dualist tradtion of Kashmir Shaivism (Padoux 2013, p. 2). A number of sources in Sanskrit such as *Yoginīhṛdaya*, *Nityāṣoḍaśikārṇava* or *Paraśurāma Kalpasūtra*, and such secondary sources as Padoux (1990, 2011), Sanderson (1988, 2006), Brooks (1990), Goudriaan (1981), Gupta (1979) and Khanna (1986) help understand both the metaphysical underpinnings and ritual procedures of Srividya. More recently, Yelle (2003) studies tantric mantras through Peircean semiotics and Sthaneswar Timalsina (2015) uses cognitive theory as well as Indian aesthetics to discuss the imagery of tantric deities.

However, whereas descriptions of tantric rituals tell us what practitioners do—such as chant mantras, or worship yantras (for definitions, see Section 1.1)—they do not give us insight into *why*, nor indicate *how* actual practice articulates and innovates upon given frameworks. And the theoretical lenses of modern scholarship offer explanations which are not derived from and disconnected to the world of practice. My ethnographic research in *Living Mantra: Mantra, Deity and Visionary Experience* (Rao 2019) brings a new area, that of practice, into scholarship. Along with questions about the nature of a mantra and its relationship to deities in this book, I probed the visionary experiences of contemporary practitioners in Andhra-Telangana, especially at three communities including Devipuram.

Compared to western phenomenology of religion about the *sui generis* nature and ineffability of religious experience, the narratives I documented in my fieldwork had particulars and rich details that were effable as well as seemed repeatable. Practitioners described bodily sensations, development of extraordinary faculties, visions of deities, communications with deities, reception and perception of mantras (including *new* mantras). For them, experience was evidence of progress in *sadhana* (spiritual practice). Derived from the Sanskrit "*siddh*" (to achieve), sadhana refers to earnest effort that results in achievement, and a practitioner who does sadhana is a "*sadhaka*." Advanced sadhakas tend to become gurus for other sadhakas, and function as primary sources—they author books, disseminate guides for practice and their interpretations and editions of source texts often displace previous versions.

Additionally, a visionary guru functions as a "mandala" (circle of influence) within which a process of transformation occurs for his/her followers. Sadhakas seem to mirror the experiential themes and values held in esteem by their gurus. The authority of a guru is usually also ratified on the basis of the sadhaka's experience during practice; thus, experience is a crucible where we witness the formation of authoritative sources.

My fieldwork for *Living Mantra* (Rao 2019) amply illustrates how it is experience that motivates sadhakas to undertake arduous disciplines, not intellectual considerations. Because contemplation of a deity calls for imagination, it is offset, or anchored by the body, which becomes the site of empirical, sensory evidence. From the scholar's perspective, bodily techniques do not always have to be abstracted into principles, nor considered only symbolic of some other meanings. As Michael Jackson has argued in "Knowledge of the Body" (Jackson 1983), semiotic and linguistic analysis cannot substitute for experience (pp. 327–45). Commenting on a Kuranko ritual, Jackson upholds "the practical and embodied nature of Kuranko thought [...] as an ethical preference, not a mark of primitiveness or speculative failure" (p. 341).

1.1. Mantra and Yantra in Srividya

In addition to an iconic form (*murti*), the Goddess also has aniconic forms—a phonic form (*mantra*), and a graphic form (*yantra*). Mantras and yantras are regarded as ontological forms associated with deities and perceived by *rishis* (seers) in revelations.

In common parlance, a yantra means an instrument or weapon; in tantra, a yantra is a mystical diagram considered a revelation. In Srividya, the graphic form of the Goddess is called *Sriyantra* or *Srichakra*. Literally, a "chakra" means "wheel" and in tantra, a chakra is an enclosed space within which a ritual activity occurs. The Sriyantra consists of a *bindu* (represented by a point, or dot) at the center of five inverted and four upright triangles that are interlocked. The apexes of these nine triangles are in a line, and together this creates forty-three triangles (see Figure 1). This triangular grid is set within eight- and sixteen- petaled lotuses surrounded by three circles enclosed in a square with four openings (see Figure 1). This periphery is enclosed by three concentric lines with four 'T' shaped portals like thresholds facing four directions. When in a three-dimensional form, the Sriyantra is called a "*meru*" ("mountain" in Sanskrit). In the Navarana (nine-enclosures) puja, mantras and substances are offered to Khadgamala deities at specific locations upon the yantra—Khadgamala goddesses are the retinue of the Goddess and are also her forms.

A fundamental idea in tantra is that of the dyad of Shiva and Shakti, wherein Shiva is cosmic consciousness and Shakti is the activating power that generates the material world. (This is similar to the dyad of Purusha-Prakriti in Samkhya-darshana (school of thought) wherein Purusha is consciousness and Prakriti, matter). In the Sriyantra, five downward pointing triangles emanate from the Shakti principle and four upward pointing triangles emanate from the Shiva principle—the *Yoginīhṛdaya* explains that the chakra as creation has five energies (inverted triangles) and as dissolution has four fires (triangles with apexes upwards)—the chakra is the union of five energies and four fires (Padoux 1990). The nine interlacing triangles are described as the *navayonis,* or the primal cause (*mulakarana*) of the universe (*prapancha*). Shakti resides in the bindu at the center. When practitioners worship or/and contemplate the Sriyantra, they move their attention from the outer perimeter to the center bindu and enter deeper meditative states.

Figure 1. Sriyantra.[1]

Srividya mantras are also referred to as "vidya" or "Srividya"—i.e., they are synonymous with the mystical knowledge that a practitioner seeks. Mantra plays a vital role in tantric worship. Not only do mantras invoke deities, but they are also identified with deities. Because the purpose of tantric worship is identification, even the worshipper's body must be made of mantras. As a part of the ritual procedures, the worshipper mentally dries, burns and destroys his or her own body, and then reconstitutes it using mantras. The process of placing a mantra in the body is called *nyasa*. Individual syllables are prominent in tantric mantras, and adding the nasal *ṃ* sound (*anusvara*) to each letter/syllable turns the entire alphabet into the Aksharamala mantra. There are a number of mantras in Srividya including the Bala mantra to invoke nine-year old Goddess Bala, the fifteen-syllable Panchadashi mantra and the sixteen-syllable Shodashi mantra. Hymns to the Goddess addressing Her different forms and with Her various names include Soundarya Lahiri, (Ocean of Beauty), Lalita Sahasranamam (Thousand Names of Lalita), and Khadgamala Stotram (Garland of the Sword)—these are regarded as *mālā*-mantras (garland-mantras) due to their length. The benefits of a mantra are said to accrue only upon initiation by the guru, and mantras initiated by the guru are guarded with utmost secrecy. For example, the syllables of the Panchadashi mantra are no secret—*Ka E I La Hriṃ, Ha Sa Ka Ha La Hriṃ, Sa Ka La Hriṃ*—but unless the mantra has been given by a guru, its practice is considered ineffective by traditional practitioners.

The Srividya *puja* (worship ritual) involves a purification and consecration of both the space and the worshipper, and it is then that the deity is invited to be present. The puja is addressed or offered to the specific yantra of the Goddess being worshipped (e.g., Shyama, Bala, Varahi, Lalita), along with the specific mantra. The puja follows the basic scheme of any tantric puja (see Gupta (1979) for a detailed description).

This essay discusses the religious experience of Srividya practices at Devipuram. Visionary experiences described by the guru Amritanandanatha Saraswati situates the background. Interviews with three of his disciples probe their experiences, practical methodologies and relationships with the Goddess. An inter-textual study of interviews, memoirs and narratives helps identify a theme of vision and embodiment.

1 By N. Manytchkine [CC BY-SA 3.0 (https://creativecommons.org/licenses/by-sa/3.0)], via Wikimedia Commons.

1.2. Body and Temple at Devipuram

The experience of Srividya discussed in this essay is associated with Devipuram near Anakapalle in Andhra, South India. Devipuram was founded by a nuclear physicist called Prahlada Sastry, who became a visionary guru called Amritanandanatha Saraswati (1934–2015).[2] In a journal that he maintained online during his lifetime, Amritananda recalls that he had a questioning, empirical approach during his youth.[3] During meditation, he experienced "humming sounds" and "300 Hz sounds" within himself ("Guruji's Experiences"). An early vision that he had was that of mantras from the Ishavasya Upanishad. He also experienced sensations typical of kundalini activation along his spinal column. The kundalini refers to Shakti incarnate dormant at the base of the spine in every person. In treatises of yoga such as Purnananda Giri's *Shadchakranirupana*, kundalini shakti is described as rising along the spinal path and activating different energy centers (chakras) along the way, eventually resulting in a spiritual awakening (Woodroffe 2012).

When Amritananda conducted an elaborate Devi-*yajña*, he received a piece of land as a ritual gift. Located in Anakapalle near Visakhapatnam, and surrounded by nine mountains, this land as if embodied the nine enclosures (*navarana*) of Sriyantra. Meditating on a hillock here one day in 1983, Amritananda experienced *himself* as the ritual offering of a yajna being conducted by four others, and felt that a heavy object had been placed in his heart. After meditation, he dug at the site, and found a Sriyantra Meru buried there, made of *pancha-loha*, an alloy of five metals conventionally used in icons of deities. With a *svayambhu* (self-manifested, or natural) *yoni* as the deity, this became the location for a Kamakhya temple. Visitors can ask to *receive* the Kalavahana puja here, a puja where the *kalas* or aspects of the Goddess are invited into oneself. For this puja, one has to sit at the *yoni*, taking the place of the deity, and is formally worshipped along with oblations and mantras. 'Yoni' which means the generative center, is in the image of female genitalia.

Directly across the Kamakhya pitham, as if replicating the Meru unearthed at the pitham, Amritananda established a temple to Goddess Lalita in the shape of a Sriyantra (see Figure 2). The name, Sahasrakshi Meru temple, literally means "thousand-eyed," but it is really a trope for omnivoyance, or omniscience of the Goddess. Measuring 108 ft $\times$ 108 ft and 54 ft high, this is literally a Sriyantra one can walk into. Three levels must be climbed to arrive at the inner sanctum, and as you enter and exit the temple using different flights of stairs, you would also have circumambulated the deity. Just as a bindu is at the center of a Sriyantra, Goddess Lalita is at the center of Her temple. Additionally, She is surrounded by all the goddesses named in the Khadgamala stotram. Amritananda's followers told me that each of the Khadgamala goddesses was sculpted based on the visions and visualizations of Amritananda, a process which took several years. Thus, Devipuram was not only a manifestation of the Goddess but also an extension of Amritananda's self.

---

2 Renaming marks a transition from one phase of life to another; in religious orders and spiritual practice, it marks a life-long commitment to the order or/and practice. Prahlada Sastry and his wife Annapurna trained in Srividya with B.S. Krishna Murthy in Mumbai, and were initiated (and renamed) after a yajna in Kollur, Karnataka. Devipuram official website, under "Srividya," http://www.devipuram.com/about-devipuram (accessed on 1 April 2015).

3 During my fieldwork in 2014 and 2015, I had referred to journal entries by Amritanandanatha Saraswathi (Amritanandanatha Saraswathi Blogspot 2018) on the Devipuram Official Website www.devipuram.com under the section "Guruji's Experiences." I accessed and made a copy of these for my reference on 1 April 2015, and continued to refer to them offline during the writing of *Living Mantra* (Rao 2019). After Amritananda's demise in October 2015, the Devipuram official website was revised. The old journal entries are now available on Vira Chandra's blog. (Chandra, Vira. "Guruji's Life Experiences," *Amritananda-Natha-Saraswati* (blog), accessed on 2 May 2018).

Figure 2. Sahasrakshi Meru temple, Devipuram. Photo by Mani Rao.

2. Srividya Practitioners at Devipuram

2.1. Seeing Yantra Within

Mani Prasanna's apartment in Ameerpet, Hyderabad, is also a "pitham" (sacred seat, temple) where Srividya rituals are conducted on a daily basis. The altar and *homa-kunda* (fire-pit for rituals) were in a small room at the back, and which could accommodate, perhaps, not more than fifteen people. After showing me around, she ushered me into an adjacent room where we talked. Answering my questions without hesitation, she told me that she did Srividya rituals twice a day, and attributed her visionary experiences as well as a sense of contentment to Srividya *sadhana*.

Mani Prasanna's first vision of, and conversation with, the Goddess was in her teen years; at the time, she did not know the identity of the visitor. It was only over a decade later, in 2003, that she realized the identity of her visitor. She had attended a *homa* (ritual, *yajña*) for Goddess Chandi at Devipuram, and felt a sensation of movement in her womb during the homa. When she anxiously asked Amritananda what it meant, he told her that she was pregnant and would have a daughter. When pregnancy tests confirmed this prediction, Mani Prasanna began to believe in Amritananda. She also received the Bala-mantra from Amritananda on that visit, and began to do the mantra for Goddess Bala (the Goddess in the form of a little girl). Soon, she was visited by Goddess Bala, who spoke to her at length. Mani Prasanna recounted Goddess Bala's talk. She had said that although every part of the body was a seat of Shakti, the mind did not "know" that to be so. However, when every part of the body was "affected by mantra," the mind would become aware of that, and one would be able to "see" the inside of the body. Mani Prasanna said she had wondered how a little girl knew so much (and such a remark also, for the skeptical part of me, cued in authenticity).

I did not understand how Mani Prasanna (and Goddess Bala) meant "seeing inside" the body? As we continued to talk, Mani Prasanna gave me specific examples:

> Mani Prasanna: Once when I was reciting Khadgamala, I saw my body cut into nine pieces. Like a piece here, one here, and here, in a row, like a yantra. So then I got scared and I asked Guruji [Amritananda] and wondered what that was. He said "it appeared that way to tell you that there is no difference between you and the Sri-Vidya. That is why She [the Goddess] did it like that.

Mani Prasanna then realized the equivalence, or identification, between the Sriyantra and herself. She understood that the nine enclosures of the Sriyantra were also present in the body. When she recited the *aksharamala*, which is a mantra that names all the letters of the Sanskrit alphabet as individual deities, she saw the syllables in her body. This vision recurred when she recited the Khadgamala stotram, when she invoked the Vagdevatas. Vagdevatas are the goddesses of Speech, and regarded as the *rishis* (seers, sages) of the Lalitasahasranamam mantra. Every mantra has a rishi, who is the first to perceive that mantra and transmit it to the world; here, the rishis are the goddesses of Speech. After three months of sadhana, when she invited a deity, she felt that deity entering her body. Her puja, then, was to the deities established in her own body, and Srividya helped her realize that her own body was a Sriyantra. The detail described by Mani Prasanna suggested that this was a vision based upon which she came to the conclusion of identification with the Sriyantra and Goddess.

2.2. *Yantra As A Rosary*

Another advanced Devipuram *sadhaka* whom I interviewed was Donald McKenna. An architect by profession, he was a part of Devipuram's project to provide economical geodesic homes to the local community. We chatted at the yajna-shala in Devipuram a few steps away from the Sahasrakshi Meru temple. Don had been introduced to the Devipuram community through a colleague at Rochester, N.Y., called Chaitanyananda, aka "Aiya." He began to attend the gatherings at Aiya's home, and was impressed by the relationship between the sadhakas and the Goddess, and at how tangible it seemed. In 1993, he went to Devipuram and was initiated by Amritananda and given the Maha-Shodashi mantra (the Great Sixteen-syllabled mantra),[4] a mantra guarded with utmost secrecy and said to grant liberation to the sadhaka in this lifetime. When we spoke, Don had been reciting this mantra (among other mantras) for over twenty years.

Fascinated by the Sriyantra, Don began to learn how to draw it, and then understood the precise location of the Khadgamala goddesses.

> Don: having some understanding that the *avaranas* [enclosures] were the layers of the meru, coincided with the physical plane and celestial plane, but it also mapped out the various chakra locations of the body, for instance. So I said—ok! I am just going to stand inside the meru and I am going to put my mantra on every single location, all the way up, all the way up. And if they fell close to the right place, I was going to be happy.

Charts of Sriyantra and deities along with ritual procedures are widely available today, and while they may be drawn from sources such as the Parashurama Kalpa Sutra, it is ultimately the guru of a community of sadhakas who approves them. At Devipuram, the locations of the Khadgamala deities at the Sahasrakshi Meru Temple and in the manuals are based on notes circulated among his disciples by Amritananda. Don's methodology seemed like he was using the yantra like a rosary (*japamala*)—he "put" the mantra on each location just as one repeats the mantra with the movement of each bead of a rosary during *japa*. Don not only agreed with my analogy, but also told me that he turned around when he reached the top. This too was a typical japamala move, where one switches directions at/before the outer bead called meru. The Sriyantra had ninety-eight locations for the Khadgamala deities, and Don placed or offered his mantra at each location—on the way up and on the way down from the meru.

Next, Don felt that the mantra was like a "chord" that was already within him, and that he was not uttering it, but echoing it. When he recited mantra, it seemed to "take over," and the sounds and vibrations were so profound that he did not notice the passage of time. Don called it a

---

4 Some traditions including the Dattatreya tradition of Amritananda consider that this mantra has 28 syllables; however, fifteen syllables at its core are considered as three (sets), thus justifying the name of Maha-shodashi (sixteen-syllabled) mantra. While the Shodashi mantra is the sixteen year old deity Tripurasundari, the Maha-shodashi mantra includes the ten Dashamahavidya deities and the five deities of the Parashurama Kalpasutra—this is also why it is regarded as a very powerful mantra.

"three-dimensionality," and said that it was more than visual. When I asked if by that he meant visual imagination, in the mind, he replied, "inside the body!"

> Don: Inside the body! Your body almost ceases to exist. Your body all of a sudden is a location. And in something much larger. And all of a sudden, in a location, you are a speck. You are like an atom. And this *Hrīṃ-Hrīṃ-Hrīṃ* sounds sending out and echoing back. I mean there are aspects that are very similar to sonar ... all of a sudden I am getting these perceptions of sonar, there is a blackness.

This also coincided for him with the periods of time he was reciting Panchadashi mantra, and he found himself receiving what he called "packets of information." Don gave me some examples: these packets of information were cognitive and precognitive, and they could be about someone's illness, or a thought in their mind. Don also talked at length about how the Panchadashi mantra had given him an ability to maintain equanimity in the midst of hectic projects that involved multi-tasking. Since Don recited more than one mantra, I asked if he found any differences in the practice or results of the different mantras. Here's a summary of what Don told me: His perceptions had been improved by Chandi, he had gained clairvoyance with Maha-Shodashi, and had better physical aptitude as well as an influence over the weather due to Panchadashi mantra. Don explained that Chandi mantra was invoked *automatically* if he sent "energy" to friends in need. Typically, he would receive a confirmation by way of a phone call the next day to thank him.

2.3. Yantra As Sacred Seat

Gopichand Balla and I talked on the first floor of the Sahasrakshi Meru temple, surrounded by Khadgamala deities. At the time, Gopi and his wife had been practicing Srividya for six years. His great grandfather lived with Aghoras in Kerala, and his grandfather was a tantric who worshipped Goddess Kali. He said he had a great "zeal and attraction" for Mother from a very young age and followed the traditions taught him by his great grandfather and grandfather. He had learned the complete set of mantras for Kali, Durga, Varahi, Lalita, Syama, and Ganapati yantras—no mean achievement. In 2008, he met Amritananda who initiated him into Srividya. I summarize two specific anecdotes, and then excerpt from our conversation to convey the flavor of his expression.

In 2009, Gopi's wife was pregnant, and astrologers told Gopi that ideally, he should have a daughter: "One astrologer said that if I had another son, I would perish. If you get a daughter, then you have life." To add, he lost his job, and was in financial difficulties. This was when he made a bold move to do the chakra puja, by learning how to draw the yantra from a pdf file Amritananda had uploaded on the internet. Gopi and his wife converted their 12 × 12 ft bedroom into a space for the chakra puja, and Gopi drew the yantra in the center of the room. Next, he consecrated the various forms of the Goddess in the yantra. Gopi says, "I don't know how I did it too! [Goddesses] Varahi, Mahendri, Chamundi, Vaishnavi, Mahalakshmi, ... Everyone! I do not know, where in Srichakra [the Sriyantra] they should be placed too. This is the truth! Believe it or not!" Gopi learned how to draw the yantra on the internet, but he was intuitively able to conduct the ritual and place all the ritual paraphernalia such as betel leaves with rice and peeled coconuts in appropriate locations within the yantra. He and his wife—who was then seven months pregnant—then sat upon the yantra and chanted mantras ten million times. Gopi does not remember how many days this took—"21 days, or maybe 41" he says—but upon completion of a cycle (*purascharana*) he "got a vision! And a date and a time! that I will get a daughter." After some more twists and turns in the narrative, their daughter was born on the (en)visioned time and date. After this, his career took off and he became a very successful man in Vishakapatnam.

Gopi told me that his experience of the mantras was physical, and he felt the vibrations in the corresponding chakras. When Gopi recited the Ganapati mantra, he felt the vibration in the *muladhara* chakra (root chakra). Similarly, Shyama mantra generated vibrations in the *anahata* chakra (heart chakra); Guru mantra in the *sahasrara* chakra, and Chandi corresponded to the *manipura* chakra (solar plexus). Gopi recounted a number of anecdotes from his life of worshipping Mother and then getting results—"all is done by HER. I know she is doing it."

3. Conclusions: Embodiment and Vision

One may not extrapolate from Devipuram narratives to *all* experience of Srividya, and it would take a much wider study to think about discernable patterns of experience we can identify as Srividya experience. Therefore, I limit my conclusions to the experience of Srividya at Devipuram. "Puram" in "Devi-puram" means place, abode, or even city—in these narratives, we find how the practitioner's body is also a Devipuram, an abode of the Goddess. The experience of Srividya for all four practitioners involves the Sriyantra, the aniconic graphic form of the Goddess. Practitioners locate themselves in the Sriyantra, or the Sriyantra within themselves, and firmly link their practice to the Sriyantra. The Sriyantra is both location and map, inner meaning as well as reality, and this is a necessary step in the process wherein the practitioners arrive at a visionary experience and reaffirm their relationship with the Goddess.

The correspondence between the practitioner and the Goddess is a theme in the very foundational story of Devipuram. Amritananda feels as if a heavy object has been placed in his heart and immediately discovers a meru buried at the site of his meditation. The implication is that the two events are connected, and even though the first event occurs in Amritananda's mind, the physical discovery of a meru suggests that the event was not imaginary. The discovery of the meru is a manifestation of the sacred in a profane space, and an event that makes a sensory experience of the sacred possible; it is a classic example of hierophany as posited by Eliade (1961). The immolation described by Amritananda also recalls the scene from the Purusha-suktam, where the universe is created from the yajna where the offering is a cosmic Purusha.[5] At this yajna-like event in Devipuram, Amritananda *is* the "Purusha."[6] In the PS it is the *sapta-rishis* (seven seers) who conduct the yajna; in Devipuram, the ritualists are "four others," we do not find out who they are. Typically, in the final ritual movement of *purnahuti*, the entire person is offered to the sacrificial fire with the mantra *"purnamadah purnamidam."* Amritananda's narrative is also reminiscent of another Vedic hymn, the Narayana-suktam, where the space within the heart is the location for the presence of the deity Narayana. Verse nine ends with how everything is established in this space (*tasmin sarve pratiṣṭhitam*) and verse ten speaks of the great fire (*mahānagni*) at this location, and at the center of which lives the deity Narayana.[7] *Pratishtha* is a technical term in Hindu rituals meaning "establishment," and a *prana-pratishtha* means that a deity's life-force has been established in an image. In Amritananda's narrative, his heart is the site of the pratishtha. Not only is Devipuram a manifestation of the body of the Goddess, the Goddess is established in Amritananda's heart and through him, within the community he was soon to lead.

Mani Prasanna saw her body cut up into triangles, suggesting a deeper grammar, or an underlying grid. This helped her realize an equivalence between herself and the Sriyantra, also made of triangles. For Mani Prasanna, the mantra "put" into the body activated the reality of the body as a Shakti-pitham; the yantra is inside her. Don reversed this process, he is inside the yantra, and he has precise vision of the locations of the Khadgamala deities. Don locates his position within the meru, and retraces the walk up and down the meru, which is now also his body. Gopi and his wife are physically inside a yantra—the yantra dominates the floor space of their room, which is their bedroom and their puja room. Once seated inside the transformed space, Gopi continues to conduct the worship intuitively. Sitting upon the sacred seat and reciting mantras is transformative, giving him an instinctive knowledge

---

5 The Purusha-suktam is also in the Rigveda (Rigveda Samhita 2006, vol. 4, pp. 287–91).

6 Even though the cosmic 'Purusha' has been understood as a genderless, representative figure, i.e., as 'Man' rather than 'a man,' his masculinity is not to be ignored. In verse 5 of Purusha-suktam, Purusha produces the feminine principle, the cosmic egg, 'Viraj' and then unites with her.

7 Narayana Suktam is a vedic hymn that is also in the Mahanarayana Upanishad. The portions I am quoting are from mantras 9 and 10 of section 11 (p. 11) in the version edited by Jacob (1888, pp. 11–12).

of the ritual procedures. Gopi gains a specific vision with the information he is looking for, and the fulfillment of his hopes—the birth of a daughter. The motif of vision is highlighted in the very name of the Goddess—"Sahasrakshi." Devipuram practitioners see and know something beyond what they can perceive through their ordinary sensory apparatus. The experience of Srividya at Devipuram has a thematic consistency, of embodiment.

Each of the practitioners brought a unique methodology to their practice. Mani Prasanna, Don and Gopi followed the framework of Srividya practice including the appropriate mantras and the ritual placement of the mantra in the body/yantra; at the same time, their practice expressed their own individualistic ways of relating to the Goddess. It is possible to posit that the methodologies of practice and experiences relate to their personalities and even occupations. Amritananda's experiences read like those of a physicist—he notes the frequency of the sounds when describing his first experiences. Don is an architect and his narrative shows how he is able to visualize an entire three-dimensional architectural meru in such detail that he knows precisely where each Khadgamala deity is located. It seems apt that Mani Prasanna received the Bala-mantra and saw the Goddess in the form of a little girl when she was pregnant and perhaps harboring motherly emotions. Mani Prasanna realized that her own body was a temple-yantra right down to the details including the placement of syllables—she became a priestess of Kalavahana later.

Mantra plays a vital role in the experience or realization of embodiment and identification with the deity. Mani Prasanna articulates clearly how the mantra must be placed in the body of the practitioner and Don attributes his heightened cognition to mantra. Don speaks about mantra as if it were his pulse or heartbeat that continues, involuntarily, within his body. For Gopi and his wife, it is after ten million counts of the mantra that results arrive—the vision about their forthcoming child. Srividya practitioners at Devipuram experience Srividya in tangible and palpable ways, from physical sensations to optical visions, and the Sriyantra is a core element in this experience.

Funding: This research was supported by a doctoral fellowship at Duke University.

Conflicts of Interest: The author declares no conflict of interest.

References

Amritanandanatha Saraswathi Blogspot. 2018. "Guruji's Experiences." "2 Balaji temple 1979." "3 Explosion 1979." "5 Saraswati, 1981." "7 Intelligent triangles 1980," "8 Kamakhya 1981." "9 Love Power Hladini 1983". Available online: http://amritananda-natha-saraswati.blogspot.com/2016/04/gurujis-life-experiences.html (accessed on 27 December 2018).

Brooks, Douglas Renfrew. 1990. *The Secret of the Three Cities: An Introduction to Hindu Śākta Tantrism*. Chicago: University of Chicago Press.

Eliade, Mircea. 1961. *The Sacred and the Profane: The Nature of Religion*. Translated by Willard R. Trask. New York: Harper Torchbooks.

Goudriaan, Teun. 1981. *Hindu Tantric and Śakta Literature*. Wiesbaden: Harrassowitz.

Gupta, Sanjukta. 1979. Puja. In *Hindu Tantrism*. Edited by Sanjukta Gupta, Dirk Jan Hoens and Teun Goudriaan. Leiden: E.J. Brill, pp. 121–63.

Jackson, Michael. 1983. Knowledge of the Body. *Man* 18: 327–45. [CrossRef]

Jacob, George Adolphus, ed. 1888. *Mahanarayana Upanishad of the Atharva-Veda with the Dipika of Narayana*. Bombay Sanskrit Series; Bombay: Government Central Book Depot.

Khanna, Madhu. 1986. The Concept and Liturgy of the Srīcakra Based on Śivānanda's Trilogy. Ph.D. dissertation, University of Oxford, Oxford, UK.

Padoux, André. 1990. *Vāc: The Concept of the Word in Selected Hindu Tantras*. Translated by Jacques Gontier. Albany: State University of New York Press.

Padoux, André. 2011. *Tantric Mantras: Studies on Mantrasastra*. London: Routledge.

Padoux, André. 2013. *The Heart of the Yogini: Yoginīhrdaya, a Sanskrit Tantric Treatise*. New York: Oxford University Press.

Rao, Mani. 2019. *Living Mantra: Mantra, Deity and Visionary Experience Today*. New York: Palgrave Macmillan.

Rigveda Samhita. 2006. *Rigveda Samhita, Together with the Commentary of Sayanacarya*, 2nd ed. Edited by Max F. Müller. 4 vols. Varanasi: Chowkhamba Krishnadas Sanskrit Series. First published 1870.

Sanderson, Alexis. 1988. Saivism and the Tantric Traditions. In *The World's Religions*. Edited by Stewart Sutherland, Leslie Houlden, Peter Clarke and Friedhelm Hardy. London: Routledge and Kegan Paul, pp. 660–704.

Sanderson, Alexis. 2006. *Meaning in Tantric Ritual*. New Delhi: Tantra Foundation.

Woodroffe, John. 2012. *The Serpent Power: Shat-chakra-Nirupana and Paduka-panchaka—Two Works on Laya Yoga, Translated from the Sanskrit, with Introduction and Commentary*. Delhi: New Age Books. First published 1918.

Yelle, Robert A. 2003. *Explaining Mantras: Ritual Rhetoric, and the Dream of a Natural Language in Hindu Tantra*. New York: Routledge.

religions

MDPI

Article

Modern Transformations of *sādhanā* as Art, Study, and Awareness: Religious Experience and Hindu Tantric Practice

Jeffrey C. Ruff

Department of Humanities: Religious Studies, Marshall University, One John Marshall Drive, Huntington, WV 25755, USA; ruff@marshall.edu

Received: 25 February 2019; Accepted: 3 April 2019; Published: 9 April 2019

Abstract: "My first raising of the kuṇḍalinī was hearing Ma [her teacher] speak about art." The experience of the awakening of śakti within practitioners in contemporary cultures occurs both in traditional religious settings and within novel circumstances. Traditional situations include direct transmission from a guru (śaktipāta), self-awakening through the practice of kuṇḍalinī-yoga or haṭhayoga, and direct acts of grace (anugraha) from the goddess or god. There are also novel expressions in hybrid religious-cultural experiences wherein artists, dancers, and musicians describe their arts explicitly in terms of faith/devotion (śraddhā, bhakti, etc.) and practice (sādhanā). They also describe direct experience of grace from the goddess or describe their ostensibly secular teachers as gurus. In contemporary experience, art becomes sādhanā and sādhanā becomes art. Creativity and artistic expression work as modern transformations of traditional religious experience. This development, while moving away from traditional ritual and practice, does have recognizable grounding within many tantric traditions, especially among the high tantra of the Kashmiri Śaiva exegetes.

Keywords: religious experience; creativity; modern Hinduism; śākta tantra; tantric sādhanā; yoga; kuṇḍalinī; śakti; arts & religions; Tantric Studies; Śrī Vidyā

---

1. Introduction

A contemporary artist from Karnataka states, "My first raising of the *kuṇḍalinī* was hearing Ma speak about art."[1] She is not alone in establishing direct interpretive links between religious experience, aesthetic experience, and the creative arts. Among contemporary tantric practitioners, there is a blurring of boundaries between "religious" experience and aesthetic experiences (including flow, peak, and creative experiences). This blurring is self-consciously consistent with the non-dual Śaiva-Śākta philosophy, and it provides an instructive example of how religious insiders might have some particularly sophisticated—although in some ways secularized or modernized—perspectives on their own experiences. Phrased differently, for these tantric practitioners, religious experience broadens to include a greater range of other "experiences" while simultaneously retaining aspects of its "religious" character. These new articulations typically work with the conceptual building blocks of the older cultural systems. Tantra allows for a wide variety of possible experiences, which are not limited to traditional ritual practices. In this essay, I will argue that art, music, contemporary *yoga*,

---

1 Personal communication, Sanchi, India, 17 December 2018; woman from Karnataka, student of Art History and working artist. The "Ma" she was talking about was her art history professor. It is worth noting that "Ma" ("Mother") is an honorific, with divine overtones both in terms of calling a teacher by this name (spiritual mother) and the devout but also commonly used term for the Goddess (in this case, Lalitā of Śrī Vidyā).

love, and self-reflection can be understood within the paradigm of traditional tantric metaphysics and related traditions of aesthetics. This is important because from an historical perspective, tantric traditions are disappearing in the face of competition with globalizing forces and standardized forms of Hinduism: a kind of *vedānta* and conventional *bhakti* monopoly on what can *count* as Hindu. This is not the end of the story. Tantric self-reflection and creativity may be hiding in plain sight. While it loses much of its ritual and traditionally religious context, it may be reemerging in another form in arts and broadly shared sensibilities about embodied experience of life and living.

Where religious experience has often been relegated to pathology in Western social sciences, contemporary tantric practitioners (Hindus and Hindu-Buddhist inspired Western practitioners of *yoga* and meditation) are not burdened by either the conceptual history of or biases of Western religions or the Western Academy. Scholars of tantric traditions have been analyzing and interpreting the specifically religious and textual side of this issue in recent years.[2]

Practitioners' understandings of the experiences of Śakti and Śiva within their own lives occurs in traditional religious settings and within novel circumstances. Traditional situations include Śaiva or Śākta devotion (*bhakti*), through being given by one's guru via direct transmission (*śaktipāta*), through the *kuṇḍalinī* raising practices of *haṭhayoga* or similar practices, through *mantras* and *yantras*, or through spontaneous and direct acts of grace (*anugraha, prasād*) from the goddess or god. It also takes on novel expressions in hybrid of religious-cultural experiences where artists, dancers, and musicians describe their arts explicitly in terms of faith/devotion (*śraddhā, bhakti*, etc.) and practice (*sādhanā*). They also describe direct experience of grace from the goddess or describe their ostensibly secular teachers as gurus. In contemporary experience, art becomes *sādhanā* and *sādhanā* becomes art. Creativity and artistic expression work as modern transformations of traditional religious experience.

These modern embodied forms of tantric religious experience connect in predictable and unusual ways with the past. In the tantric medieval milieu (flourishing between 600–1200 CE, with roots that are older and branches reaching to the present), ascetic inspired liberation *from* the body shifts and transforms into liberation *through* the body, and this was always part of the common paradigm for Tantrism or for the *Mantramārga* and *Mantrayāna*, and especially for the earlier *Kulamārga* that gave them many of their inspirations (the historical or traditional expressions to which we refer with our modern categories of *tantra*, Tantrism, and tantric studies). The *bhuktimukti* equation of liberation through the enjoyment of the senses, or the embodied liberation of the *jīvanmukta*, or other expressions normative to the collected traditions that we call *tantra* provide a coherent basis for both the conventional, unconventional, and unexpected expressions of tantric religious experience in the modern world.

William James in *The Varieties of Religious Experience* (James [1902] 1958) argues that human beings—when confronted with a "sense that there is something wrong about us as we naturally stand" (p. 383)—seek for a solution (broadly, "liberation" or "salvation" however construed). This search, for James, is the essence of a religious life, and the solution might arise suddenly, gradually, or be enjoyed consistently throughout a life. (ibid.) James summarizes religious experience as the experience of coming to recognize one's true self as a kind of "germinal higher part of himself [or herself]" by becoming

> *Conscious that his higher part is conterminous and continuous with a* MORE *of the same quality, which is operative in the universe outside of him and which he can keep in working touch with, and in a fashion get on board of and save himself when all his lower being has gone to pieces in the wreck.* (p. 384)

2 Tantric Studies is emerging as one of the areas in the modern Academy that is moving forward in its critique and reexamination of some older ways of thinking as well as its engagement with contemporary Cognitive Sciences and Neurosciences. For examination of ecstasy, religious experience and mysticism, see McDaniel (2018) and her sources; for Cognitive Sciences and the study of *yoga* and *tantra*, see Hayes (2011); Timalsina (2015); and Hayes and Timalsina's *Religions* Special Issue (Hayes and Timalsina 2017), and the contributors to that volume.

Despite the disciplinary and methodological disagreements and debates (ongoing since the original publication of James' work) among social scientists, philosophers, and scholars of religions as to its limits and critical usefulness, one can recognize a familiar heuristic usefulness in this kind of broad characterization. For James, the human mind was the place this "MORE" connects with the life as lived (what he called the *hither* side of this MORE). He called the *farther* side of this MORE God or the divine and this has a variety of explicit and subtle connections to Tantrism's own self-reflections and articulations, especially in the high *tantra* synthesis of Abhinavagupta and the other Kashmiri Śaiva exegetes.[3] We will return to this theme in the conclusion.

1.1. Tantric Aesthetics: Artistic Experience and Religious Experience

A comprehensive exploration of Abhinavagupta's aesthetics is beyond the scope of this paper, but there are certain concepts he develops that apply directly to the kinds of religious and aesthetic experience described by the modern practitioners.[4] Timalsina (2007) introduces these concepts in the following way:

> Classical Indian aesthetics emerge from the interpretation of dance and drama performed primarily in ritual settings. In addition to analysis of the metaphoric and literal dimensions of language, this aesthetic model relies on an understanding of psychological moods that are identified as *rasa*. Select Indian philosophers advance this theory by propounding the doctrine of *dhvani*, by which the highest aesthetic bliss is experienced through suggestion. (p. 135)[5]

Rasa means tasty liquid, flavor, concoction; Indian alchemy, or the mercury used in alchemy; and, in aesthetics it relates to invoking emotions, moods, aesthetic experience, and (what the Western world has also called) having good taste (poetically, aesthetically). According to Lee Siegel, "the taste of an object, the capacity of the taster to taste the taste and enjoy it, the enjoyment, the tasting of the taste. The psychophysiological experience of tasting provided a basis for a theory of aesthetic experience which in turn provided a basis for a systemization of a religious experience." (Siegel 1991, p. 43). In this articulation of aesthetics, the ability of a poet, artist, dancer, or musician to stimulate or evoke emotions (in themselves) and in a sensitive and attentive audience, becomes a direct analogy to the religious awareness (*cid*), or a flash of insight (*pratibhā*), and bliss (*ānanda*) that arise when a perfected mystic expresses (suggests, *dhvani*) the ultimate truth to others. The mystic can through self-awareness (which is an expression of ultimate truth) evoke or point to the inexpressible and inspire an awareness of it in others through various means (*upāya*).

For Abhinavagupta, the true nature of reality (The Supreme Lord, Parameśvara) is the ultimate source of everything, and is imminent as "everything." Acts of profound self-awareness by the perfected religious seeker are ultimately a reflection of that ultimate. (Larson 1976; Timalsina 2007; Lidke 2011, 2016) Profound self-awareness is proof of and a direct expression of Supreme Consciousness knowing itself through itself, as itself. Larson, in his seminal article (Larson 1976) on aesthetic enjoyment (*Rasāsvāda*) and religious realization (*Brahmāsvāda*) expresses the essence of the teaching. He suggests that Abhinavagupta's non-dualism (*advaya*), while different from the non-dualism of *Advaita Vedānta*, ultimately maintains the distinction between the aesthetic enjoyment of embodied

---

3 Arguably, James' general familiarity with *Advaita Vedānta*, directly and through the American Transcendentalists, (and to a lesser extent, Buddhism) explains in part, the general ease with which this kind of *response to what is conceived as greater-than-human* can accommodate existential problems traditional to India, such delusion (*moha*), ignorance (*avidyā*), uneasiness/affliction (*duḥkha*), etc.; and, resonate with their solutions: *vidyā*, *jñāna*, *mokṣa*, etc.

4 For concise introduction to Indian aesthetics in the context of religion, see Schwartz (2004). For Indian aesthetics in general and relative to Abhinavagupta, see Kavi (1934); Masson et al. (1969); Larson (1976); Katz and Sharma (1977); Gnoli (1985); Lidke (2011, 2015, 2016); Timalsina (2007, 2016); Wulff (1984).

5 See also Lidke (2015) for more exploration of these concepts.

experience and the ultimate spiritual realization of the disembodied absolute on logical and linguistic grounds. However, he also recognizes the paradox inherent in the distinction:

> For Abhinavagupta the ultimate or *parama-śiva* is in its deepest essence totally transcendent—that is to say, *viśottīrṇa* and *anuttara*. It is finally an unfathomable mystery. Yet this mysterious ultimate shines in its clarity and in that shining is the presupposition or ground for all manifestation. Hence the totally transcendent (*viśottīrṇa*) is also the totally immanent (*viśvamaya*) as universal consciousness (*saṃvid, cit*), as universal joy (*ānanda*), and as *prakāśavimarśamaya*—that is to say, made up of "pure undifferentiated light and clarity" (*prakāśa*) and "pure unhindered awareness" (*vimarśa*). (Larson 1976, pp. 379–80)

It is a paradox that the ultimate is totally and completely transcendent *and* totally immanent: these concepts are mutually exclusive in terms of plain logic, but they are *suggestive*. The properly prepared mystic can express these irreconcilable truths so clearly and powerfully that such speech can evoke or kindle religious insight in others. While the concepts may be irreconcilable or incommensurable to ordinary thinking or in literal speech, the activity of various forms of *śakti* (even if in highly aesthetic and grammatical forms) mediate and resolve the paradox for Abhinavagupta such that in the lived world, the *Jīvanmukta* abides in this ultimate realization. (ibid.)[6] In the manifest world, and in reflective experience, the paradox simply fails to matter. The paradox dissolves in the experiences of beings awakened by liberating knowledge.[7]

1.2. Ecstasy and Embodied Forms of Tantric Religious Experience

There is also a less philosophical aspect of Tantrism that comes into play within the contemporary communities. Ecstasy, possession, and yogic trance are pervasive features of tantric religious experience.[8] In some cases, this ecstatic rapture grabs people directly (or is evoked or enacted through rituals and practices). The varieties of tantric approaches to religious experiences are often called *upāyas* (means, approaches, methods, etc.) that may be thought of as sequential or as alternative methods. There is also a "non-method" (*anupāya*) of direct intuition of the divine consciousness that is sometimes attributed to the most developed religious seekers. It is not my contention that today's practitioners meet the rarified expertise that Abhinavagupta was talking about, but rather that his aesthetics and his theology opens a social space for the kinds of expressions we find today.

In the sections that follow, the experiences of being Śiva-Śakti are examined from the words and accounts of contemporary practitioners to provide examples of religious experience in modern *śāktatantra* settings. The statements of artists, dancers, musicians are also described, where the act of creativity and other specifically aesthetic experiences are understood as direct experience of the living goddess.[9]

Some technical vocabulary was common to the selected informants surveyed here. Generally, *svādhyāya* was considered a required part of their practice. Sources interpreted this to mean study, especially of scriptures, but there were a variety of additional interpretations. For the more cosmopolitan practitioners, *svādhyāya* meant study and contemplation that was intended to penetrate all aspects of their lives. It was described as a kind of reflection on and awareness of all aspects

---

6 See Larson (1976) note 58.

7 For a detailed but accessible expression of the Abhinava's fluent mixing of the aesthetic and the religious (tantric) in his own poetry, see Muller-Ortega (2000).

8 Possession and ecstasy (*āveśa, samāveśa*, and in some of its uses, *mudrā*) as well as "powers" (*siddhi*) have a long association with tantric text, cult, and practices. See (Sanderson 1986, p. 169; 1988), throughout; Smith (2006), throughout, especially Part IV; Biernacki (2006); Wallis (2008).

9 Field interpreters, informants, and consultants: classical Indian musicians and dancers, artists and painters, an Art Historian, *haṭhayoga* and meditation practitioners, and Hindu *Śrīvidyā* initiates. This collection of contemporary practitioners includes Hindus of South Asian origin (both in South Asia and the Western world and Western practitioners of Hindu and Hindu-Buddhist fusion traditions. Fieldwork interviews in India & Nepal, 2000, 2001, 2008, 2018. Fieldwork with South Asian and Western practitioners in the USA: ongoing, interviews 1985, 1990–1994; 1996–1999; 2002–2009; 2015–present.

of life as expressions of the divine, and thus worthy of study and contemplation (see Sections 2.2 and 2.3). Alternatively, students in universities and informants living in traditional settings (such as their guru's ashrams) described *svādhyāya* as study of their subject matters or arts, and as study of the scriptures respectively. For practitioners whose study focused on the scriptures, *svādhyāya* was at times described as *japa* (reciting the names of the goddess or chanting aloud or silently the goddess' *mantra*). One informant suggested that repetition of the scriptures was to gain worldly benefits and to prepare a person for a deeper understanding. She also suggested the contemplation and study were habits that developed over time after one's repetition was stable and consistent.

Mantra recitation was typically described as accompanying the ritual worship of the *śrīcakra*. Two practitioners surveyed here suggested that the ritual and meditation should be practiced with *nyāsa* where the sounds are installed or visualized within the human body of the practitioner (Section 2.3). Most practitioners surveyed said that it was only necessary to recite the *śrīvidyā mantra* aloud or silently during worship or contemplation of the deity's *yantra*. Practitioners who were not Śrīvidyā devotees generally described mantra recitation as chanting *bīja* mantras and the *gāyatrī mantra*. Some devotees defined the *śrīvidyā mantra* as the true or superior form of the *gāyatrī mantra*.

Informants widely referred to their practices as *yoga* and *sādhanā*. Many employed the term *yoga* to refer to devotion and discipline in general (as used in the *Bhagavad Gītā*). In cases where devotees described their practices as Tantric yoga or kuṇḍalinī yoga, their descriptions included both conventional *haṭha yoga* and *mantra yoga*. One practitioner described himself as first learning kuṇḍalinī yoga in the United States under a teacher trained by Yogi Bhajan (Harbhajan Singh Khalsa). The Rishikesh trained practitioners differed as to their yoga schools and personal gurus, but commonly recommended the study of Saraswati's (1981) book. Sādhanā was used by informants to refer generally to all their practices. This could refer to their total religious life, or more specifically to their mantra and meditation practices.

Practitioners used the word *ānanda* or the English word "bliss" when describing their experiences of the divine. One practitioner (Section 2.4) used the term *sukha* (bliss) as a synonym for *ānanda* but this connection was unique among those surveyed. This experience of bliss was associated with practices in general and specifically to the cultivation of an awareness of the goddess (or for some the unity of Śiva and Śakti) as pervading all aspects of life and existence.

The conclusions of this essay explore some reflections on the continuity (and diversity) within and across modern practitioners who broadly identify themselves as tantric and who actively seek intense religious experiences via either aesthetic or yogic expressions of the embodied traditions of their practices.

2. Modern Practices and the Adaptability of *Tantra*

In some cases, practitioners assert that it was their academic or artistic mentors who inspired more specifically and directly "religious experience" than their devotional gurus. They often credit their devotional gurus for teaching them moral purity and good habits (through ritual, *japa*, or *yoga*, etc.), and that this was the foundation of their *sādhanā*. Many of these same practical *gurus* tended to express the meaning of what they were doing in the stereotypes of contemporary *advaita vedānta* and through Kṛṣṇa *bhakti*. The artists and university students often stated that it was their art and music teachers, and the university professors who truly inspired them.[10] Some of them went so far as to describe this inspiration as devotional bliss.

One university student says:

---

[10] Interviews: Music students in Varanasi (October 2000; August 2001); Delhi University students (September through December 2001); musicians and *yoga* students in Delhi (August 2008); university students, art students and yoga students in Sanchi University, Sanchi (December 2018).

> "I do believe that my *guru-śiṣya*, student-teacher [i.e., with my professor of Indian philosophy] relationship and meditative, thought-provoking discussions [about art, *tantra*, *yoga*, philosophy] most certainly qualify as religious experiences. After a 'session' with my professor-mentor, I feel as though I am walking on clouds, that if a bus were to hit me, I wouldn't even feel it. Journeying back to 'normal life' is so much easier and relaxed after 4, 5, 6-h discussion." (Correspondence, August 2017; edited by informant, 15 January 2019)

This characterization has some practical resemblance with Abhinavagupta's aesthetics, where the artist, teacher, or writer (like the mystic) through channeling the divine consciousness can transfer it to others or evoke it in others through suggestion. Another informant explains:

> I got my *mantra* from my family guru, but the grace of the goddess descends and fills me when I am working with my music teacher. He is my true *guruji*. Our family temple's *guru* is the power of the goddess on earth; he heals the sick. But he never really awakened any profound feelings in me. He is *guruji*. I shouldn't say this, but it has something to do with my feelings. I feel the goddess moving in the music. I feel a great respect and reverence for my tradition at the temple. I think they are both my experience of the goddess, but the driving passion is in the music. I burn with that fire. It is the *śakti*. (Interview: Geeta, student of music in Delhi, 2008)

Music, art, and dance traditions are part of the broader Hindu religious landscape where their traditions are—even in the modern world—*guru-śiṣya-paramparā* traditions, even if carried out in academies, universities or other modern educational institutions. This characterization needs measured consideration, since such relationships might or might not have any formal initiation or include *gurudakṣiṇā* (gifts or tokens of gratitude) or certain other traditional patterns and expectations.

There is one noticeable distinction. Many of the students or practitioners have directly received *mantra*s and initiation from their religious *guru*s. In this context, their practice of repeating *mantra*s occurs explicitly in the context of established religious institutions and traditions. Some report that ecstatic or religious bliss (for some) or meditative peace (for others) does arise in them relative to *mantra-japa*. Among modern practitioners, their contemporary *yoga guru*s do give *mantras*, but their arts and sciences teachers typically do not.[11]

2.1. Normative Constructions of Religious Experience

The developments and stereotypes of contemporary tantric religious experiences have a great variety but have been overwhelmingly influenced by normative concepts (broadly modern, Hindu, and somewhat tantric). One of these is the non-sectarian (*haṭhayoga*) set of modern practices and concepts broadly expressed as *kuṇḍalinī yoga*. Essentially, this is the *yoga* of the fifteen-century *Haṭhayogapradīpikā* (*The Illumination of the Forceful Discipline*) in which postures and other techniques (*āsana, mudrā, bandha*), breathing exercises (*prāṇāyāma*), and visualization exercises awaken *kuṇḍalinī śakti* that normally sits dormant at the base of the spine or floor of the pelvis. When this *śakti* force is awakened, it rises through the body as heat or energy along the central subtle pathway (*suṣumṇā nāḍī*), piercing or enlivening subtle body nexuses or centers (*cakra, padma*) until it rests in the heart, head, or exiting the cranial suture and sitting above the head in union with Śiva (*pīṭhā*).[12] This modern *kuṇḍalinī yoga* is typically described with interpretive connections of two sorts. This *kuṇḍalinī yoga* is embedded in

---

11 There were some exceptions of a secular teacher giving *mantra*s or recommending *mantra* practice and directing them to religious professionals in their community (such as the nearby temple). I think this suggests avenues for future research. In many of these interviews, I was not guiding the conversations beyond general questions about practice and devotion; and more often, I was asking them questions about *yoga*. It was only later that I saw some of these pseudo-secular patterns reflected in separate informants. I more detailed study of whether ostensibly secular or arts teacher give *mantra*s would be a worthwhile project.

12 Breathing and meditation exercises have an ancient history in India. The modern *yoga* techniques have older roots in *tantra* and were systematized into what became the model of their modern forms by the *guru*s of the Nāth Siddha lineages.

some modern vernacular understandings of the *Yoga Sūtras* of Patañjali, synthesized with modern "serpent power" interpretations of *kuṇḍalinī śakti.* These are in some cases drawn directly from the works of Sir John G. Woodroffe/Arthur Avalon (1865–1936) and some nineteenth to early twentieth century Indian gurus, but often via their local Indian gurus. In other cases, practitioners reference the World Wide Web as their source for *kuṇḍalinī yoga* and *yantra* practices. Whatever the sources, the *kuṇḍalinī* concepts and generalizations are consistently modern and often using the language of empirical science. Śrī Vidyā and Siddhayoga practitioners differ somewhat from this trend, but not significantly.[13] Some informants were aware of the field of contemporary Tantric Studies; among them the normative stereotyping was less pronounced, but the empirical science frameworks were generally stable and consistently represented. Some were quick to differentiate what they did from what they called Neo-Tantra or Western *Tantra* with New Age sensibilities, although they did not explicitly enumerate the differences.

The practitioners represented in this study all received their *yoga* training in India or Nepal: some in the competitive markets in and around Rishikesh, but others in various locations from Varanasi to Madurai (to locations all over India and Nepal). Even though their personal *guru*s emphasized a variety of practices from laughing, to hugging, devotional singing and recitations, to repeating *mantra*s, their representations of *kuṇḍalinī* and *Śaktipāt(a)* were generally of the conventional, widely publicized and shared type. Many described a variety of mystical and visionary experiences. Western converts described these as mild, dreamlike, and generally pleasant: "It was like a dream, but I was awake," but often accompanied by deep, existential feelings and meaning. Traditional Hindus described both visions and dreams as often having oracular power: they could predict the future or provide a sign to them about various decisions they needed to make.

There was a strong and stereotypical *bhakti* devotionalism common to almost all informants. This *bhakti* sometimes crossed sectarian lines. For example, one informant identified her most important teachers as Girināth and Śivānandaji (Śaivas) and she had spent significant pilgrimage travel and retreats in the Himalayan foothills but described the central teaching of all her teachers as emphasizing love of Lord Kṛṣṇa, while also requiring (the expected) Śiva or Durga Pūjā at specific times or seasons. (Shanta, a Pilgrim, personal communication, Rishikesh, 18 July 2008).

2.2. Artists, Musicians, Dancers, Writers and Their Aestheticized Expressions of Religious Experience

Despite normative Hindu expressions of practice and devotion, several practitioners specifically linked their artistic practices and performance to various forms of blissful experience that they called *kuṇḍalinī* experience. Unlike the broadly shared modern configurations of *yoga* (*cakra*s, ascent of the power, etc.), they tended to express this power as the descent of the grace of goddess more than the rise of *kuṇḍalinī*. This was pronounced among musicians and dancers, where they reported "ecstasy," "being filled up," "losing my sense of time and self" or other forms of significant blissful experience that they call *kuṇḍalinī śakti*.

Several performers repeated similar characterizations. One of them expressed this as: "when I perform, the goddess descends and pierces my *cakra*s and enters my heart, where I am filled with

---

See White (1996, p. 218ff, and throughout); Mallinson (2011, pp. 14–15); Mallinson and Singleton (2017, throughout, especially, p. 171ff); Hatley (2016).

13 These practitioners did refer to the *Yoginīhṛdaya* and the *Vāmakeśvaratantra* (which combines the *Yoginīhṛdaya* and the *Nityāṣoḍaśikārṇava*) and described their practices as illuminated in the *Tantrāloka* and other texts by Abhinavagupta and his interpreters. However, in general conversation, their descriptions of *kuṇḍalinī yoga* tend to follow the more contemporary and generic forms widely held in India and abroad. It is in their discussions of *mantra yoga* and their meditations on Lalitā in the form of her *yantra*, the *Śrīcakra*, that that these practitioners most distinguished themselves (not in terms of their descriptions of *kuṇḍalinī yoga*). Other practitioners and informants suggested a wide range of texts as the object of study, contemplation, or repetition. Several texts were indicated: *Lalitopākhyāna, Lalitātriśati, Lalitāsahasranāma*. The more cosmopolitan informants also listed the *Tripurā Upaniṣad*, Bhāskararāya's commentaries on the Lalitā texts, a variety of Classical *Upaniṣads*, and the *Bhagavad Gītā*. For the contexts and uses of these texts in Śrī Vidyā, see Brooks (1992) and Lidke (2017).

bliss." These experiences were sometimes described as trance or flow experiences. More than one practitioner was quick to differentiate this flow of the goddess into them as not the same as—what they considered "lower class" or "village"—the loss of consciousness common to possession-trance or mediums. Many of these characterizations were pejorative and dismissive of traditions that they thought of as lesser or inferior to their aesthetic-creative expressions. Although the connection was unknown to the informants, these kinds of accounts bear striking similarities to the trance and direct experience of the divine in Medieval Kashmir, but of the more *tantra* of the Right for the Trika (although typically non-dualistic) in contrast to the *Kaula*, where the "possession" by the god/goddess was required but generally tame. (Sanderson 1986, p. 169) It does not have to include loss of awareness, cataleptic feint, or radical altered states of consciousness. Like the Trika adepts, there is ecstasy and possession by Śiva-Śakti in performance, music, art, dance, and it exhibited an intensity that they described specifically as blissful and extraordinary but framed and expressed in the disciplines of their arts. Despite the mixture of these interpretations with various other modern symbols and models and a common reliance on devotional and *vedānta* modes of expression, these accounts have a strikingly tantric character. This is sometimes expressed as self-consciously tantric and in terms of traditional aesthetic categories wherein the flow of emotion is articulated as *rasa*. (See Lidke 2015).

One professional *yoga* teacher and writer from Los Angeles articulated this creative modern (but aware of tradition) re-envisioning of the traditional practice:

> Getting lost, or perhaps found, in meditative experience is commonly found among those who practice and immerse themselves in creation. This creation is found in the arts (i.e., painting, sculpting, playing an instrument, writing), in athleticism (i.e., yoga, rock climbing, serious athletes), in sex and birth, and in *svādhyāya* which can encompass all of these things and more (i.e., school and lecture halls, one-on-one interactions with teachers or mentors, formal meditation practices, reading). Through creation one literally acts as and therefore becomes God: "Haṃsa" (I am), "I am Śiva", "I am Śakti". In these acts of creation, one exchanges oneself (their time, energy, knowledge, creativity, and even emotional stability) for an expansion of themselves. This expansion can derive from the growth that comes from baring oneself emotionally to create a piece of art, from disciplining one's body to levels of extremity to reach that next peak or to break a record, from letting go of emotional and physical barriers to engage in passionate and meaningful sex, and from opening the mind to allow new information to flow in. While these are not traditional religious experiences, this does not take away from their importance in our modern-day world where more and more people are straying away from religion and finding expansion and growth in their own unique spiritual practices. Tantra stemmed from this same concept, straying away from the orthodox Brahmanical Vedantic practices and beliefs to create their own spiritual path which consisted of, at the time, highly unorthodox and profane practices. While these expressions of art, physical feats, and self-knowledge may not usually (though sometimes) have the same unorthodox connotations as tantra has had, they do stray far from the typical archetypes of religious practice and experience. Rather than search for an external answer or God, these processes of creation assert the concept that God is not without but within. (Original interviews, April 2017; Revised by the informant, personal communication, 28 January 2019)

Here we see a very modern set of sensibilities, but another self-conscious connection of her experience to a tantric paradigm. This is also consistent with the non-dual Trika in its awareness of self-knowledge is a path to God-knowledge. She connects traditional *yoga*, activities that are more mundane, art, and study to all result in awareness the Śiva and Śakti are found within oneself. This reflects both James classic definition and the sentiments of Abhinavagupta.

2.3. Signs of the Goddess and a New Kind of Secrecy

Two life-long practitioners of Śrī Vidyā expressed a deeply informed (but I think essentially modern) style of practice. Both report significant ecstatic experiences over the many years of their practices. One who performed a complex set of regular rituals, *yoga* and meditations stated:

> [What] is most important is that you find a teacher with whom you can regularly talk and even practice meditation or *yoga* if that is possible. It is most important that a bond, a genuine love and devotion develop between you and the teacher you work with. That is more important than whatever the *mantra* might be. It is in that intensity of the connection between you and your teacher(s) that the grace of the goddess will descend. *Mantras* invite the goddess to descend, but a bond with a teacher is part of what makes it "real" for you.
>
> (informant asked for anonymity, 2018)

Another (who was also a musician) related a relaxing of his practice after many years of consistent and highly disciplined work:

> I don't have a consistent practice. I did for years, but then comes a time when you leave all the details behind. You understand. Then it just being aware of your I-consciousness. Your Śiva-nature. It is almost like the Buddhist insight or mindfulness practices. Your awareness of 'I am Śiva. I am Śiva. I am Śiva . . . ." becomes stable and fixed. It never leaves you. Then when you do anything with that awareness, then you are filled with calmness and clarity. Good things can be enjoyed. Bad things can be endured. Because good and bad, it is just the unfolding dance of Śiva-Śakti. (edited compilation of interviews 2016–2018; informant edited statements and asked for anonymity, 2018)

Both these informants were steeped in the intricacies of traditional, living tantric traditions. For them the practices and the theology were normal, even ordinary. In both cases, the contemplation of Abhinavagupta and other traditional Sanskrit philosophical texts or scriptures, family devotional practices, and a living embodied reflective Śiva-awareness were the main and consistent pattern of their experiences. It was not fully expressed, but the pattern suggested that the more ecstatic experiences were a kind of pedagogy or training that would provide the stable basis for a deeply embodied awareness. With that stable foundation established after years of more rigorous disciplines, no specific practices or expressions of experiences were better than any other (and this is despite the context of their lives being full of normal ritual obligations and regular experiences of religious practice and community). Neither claimed to be saints or *siddhas*, but their deeply reflective attitudes did resonate with both the need for practices (*upāya*) and a stage of awareness in which the practices become unnecessary (*anupāya*).[14] Both men desired privacy. And, although they were not completely secretive about their practices, they were humble and had a strong desire that their friends and neighbors not come looking for advice or to treat them as *gurus*.

These accounts resonated with practitioners interviewed in Rishikesh in 2008. On several occasions, unrelated practitioners in Rishikesh suggested Saraswati's (1981) book on Tantric Yoga. Many also recommended various works of South Asian and Western scholarship. They repeated the need for secrecy, despite describing many of the secrets as included in books about *tantra*. The general theme was that experiencing the grace of the Śiva-Śakti could be readily accessed through reading, devotion, *yoga*, or powerful direct transmissions of grace through love. It was paradoxical: one needed to do serious work to experience the bliss of the divine, or just let it arise naturally through a kind of reflected awareness. This corresponds to James and Abhinavagupta in that *tantra* for them most centrally involved a kind of mystical reflection and awareness. Practices were fundamentally important, but the direct personal awareness of the divine was the true core of the practice.

---

14 See also Lidke (2005).

2.4. Unconventional Expressions of Religious Experience

A few experiences in the accounts stand out as having some idiosyncratic elements. One goddess devotee[15] described a variety of traditional ritual practices, Śrī Vidyā initiation, and he was a well read and well-travelled middle-aged devotees. He described spontaneous religious experience in the following way:

> In meditation I experienced the curious sensation of a sapling emerging from and growing through the top of my head like a plant bursting through soil. The experience was profound and unusual. I experienced such a strong physical sensation that I felt the need to break my posture and meditation and to touch the top of my head occasionally to feel if the stem were there. I'm not sure I would describe it as a vision—I suppose it was—but at the time it felt more like a dream and a feeling. I did not see it as a vision or hallucination. It felt as if the sapling grew into a tree. I thought the tree had blue buds or possibly leaves. I've dreamt the experience occasionally afterwards, and I think that those dreams have affected my memory of the original event. The dreams and subsequent memories or visualizations—just thinking about it in a focused way, and not necessarily while meditating—the feeling of tingling and hollowness return. It was accompanied by of calm, joy, and awareness. When I think of it afterward and get that feeling it works as a prompt or reminder to be aware and mindful of my breathing, emotional states, and a deep thankfulness to the goddess for working within me and my life. (Personal communication, Delhi, 2001)

This same practitioner generally identified strong trance experiences in systematic *yoga* and visualization meditation practice. He described his practice as *mantra yoga* and *yantra pūjā*. He described several direct experiences of the goddess but added that they were not from systematic *yoga-cakra* practices. Instead he reported experiences relative to his heart, throat, forehead and top of his head/above his head with visionary components or feelings. He commented as an aside that he was having difficulties with his throat and was focusing his practice and devotion to remedy that.

He additionally reported meditation states that included both profound heaviness or sinking, as well as—relative to different practices—lightness or flying. He described all these as uncanny and generally unexplainable beyond gifts of the goddess: he did not consider them essential to his practice but instead "signs" of progress and deepening awareness. He generally characterized the experiences as therapeutic, but also included that they were experiences toward which he consciously cultivated non-attachment. "You cannot *do* anything with such experiences; they do not have a purpose. They are like dreams that come true: there is no way to tell the difference between them and meaningless dreams. They are the expressions of the unfolding of one's practice, the do not have a use. As, I said before, they are signs of progress. I do not ignore them or trivialize them, but I do not obsess over them either." (Interview, Delhi, 2001).

The light and heavy states associated with yogic practices were reported by other practitioners as well. One woman stated:

> During the practice I felt my upper body (from the ribcage up) begin to descend downward, I felt so very heavy, but my lower body (from solar plexus down) felt like it was flying, so very airy. This seems counterintuitive (because the grounding chakras are the lower ones and the uplifting ones are the higher ones). It's likely I am thinking too much into it. I found the whole thing puzzling. (Correspondence, 2016)

---

15 This practitioner lived in Delhi during 2001 when I first interviewed him. He was an engineer, and originally from Kerala. My interviews did not capture a full biography, but it was clear from his accounts that he had made pilgrimages to Varanasi and made repeated pilgrimage to the Char Dhams and multiple Khumb Melas. This practitioner did not elaborate on the full range of his practices, but he did recite and read Sanskrit, and his flat included images or *yantras* of The Ten Mahāvidyās, Sarasvatī, Gaṇeśa, Lakṣmī, and multiple forms of Śiva.

Another practitioner expressed spontaneous *kuṇḍalinī* experiences as blissful, but not like what she had read about or heard others describe.

> Bliss. I sought out other teachers, both pandits and practitioners. Some older, more experienced, or more knowledgeable than my teacher. None of them provoked the intensity and presence of the goddess in the same way. Our practice, meditations, and even talking about *yoga dharm* or *tantra-mantra-yantra* were emotionally intense. These experiences gave a direct bliss. It's hard to explain. It is like being in love, but not quite like that. It certainly was an awakening in my sacral center that moved back and forth up and down my spine. It was vague, and I never learned any practices to cultivate it. (Suneela, speaking about when she was a university student; Correspondence 2018, based on interviews in Delhi, 2008)

In these accounts *kuṇḍalinī śakti* moves when true and meaningful connections are established: with the divine, with the self, or with a teacher. Coming to recognize themselves in their visionary experiences or in meaningful intense emotional connections with others is essential for these practitioners.

2.5. *Traumatic Yogic Experiences*

One informant reported disagreeable experiences from *yoga* practices. He reported gradual, direct *kuṇḍalinī* experiences, of ascent and descent through nine cakras. Initially he declined to report them as a matter of private experience. He did say that it caused him great suffering that was later replaced by joy. He reported seeking help from his Indian guru and from a Western *kuṇḍalinī* support group. He additionally reported that these were partly produced by him continuing to do practices that his *guru* had told him to discontinue. He said that he had gone to other *yoga* teachers and failed, then succeeded, and then suffered and ultimately returned to his original *guru*. He strongly insisted that his *guru* gives him the same ecstatic experience through *śaktipāt*, and that people should get *kuṇḍalinī* from their teachers because that is the only safe way to do it. In a later set of interviews, he described some of his experiences, and these followed the conventional descriptions of *kuṇḍalinī* gone wrong that can be found in Gopi Krishna or more recent *kuṇḍalinī* trauma literature.[16] He described *kuṇḍalinī* practice as likely to produce dissociative states and trauma. He explicitly wished that he had never tried the practices.

This contrasts with the unusual and unsystematic rising of bliss in the previous accounts. In this case, the practitioner was trying to provoke a mystical experience through embodied practice. Although he had experiences, he felt they were destructive. His return to peacefulness was through devotion to his *guru*. This corresponds to the non-systematic accounts in as much as it involves love and coming to recognize himself and his needs more clearly.

2.6. *The Two Poles of Practice: Scientific Descriptions and Ascetic Accounts*

Field interviews with some practitioners who identified themselves as experts (in this group, these informants often did identify themselves as *yogis* but generally avoided the term *guru*) provided a noticeable control group. For practitioners who explained their practice primarily in Western Psychological terms or scientific terms, there were only rare references to devotion, theism, or supernatural

[16] Over the several decades, I have recorded accounts of traumatic *kuṇḍalinī* experiences among South Asian Hindus and Western Hindu and Buddhist converts. These accounts are beyond the scope of this argument, but they demonstrate a general pattern of widespread and broadly inconsistent levels of training and oversight among *kuṇḍalinī* training and practice. Alternatively, the more ritualistic (*mantra-yantra*) orientations to these practices render fewer accounts of this sort, while the *guru* driven and international *yoga* movements include higher amounts. This may be a false impression, since arguably there may be many more people participating in these practices among the latter groups than the former. Additionally, these accounts are balanced by both conventional and idiosyncratic accounts of the activations of the bodily Śakti(s) that are reported as wholesome or empowering. For a broader perspective of this and related topics, see Tomas Rocha's article (Rocha 2014) on Willoughby Britton's Dark Night project, and related topics included in the Britton lab's "Meditation Safety Toolbox" (Britton Lab 2019) for the "First, Do No Harm" Meditation Safety Training. In addition to Britton, for discussions of trauma directly linked to *kuṇḍalinī*, see White (1990) and Sannella (1987).

agency. There were exceptions to this pattern. A practitioner specifically trained in medicine, psychology, holistic medicine, traditional *Āyurveda* explained tantric experiences as:

> Meditation and the various states of consciousness affect muscles, bones, glandular secretions, the gross bodily functions. Thoughts and feelings must be attuned to the inner realm of the subtle body. The subtle body is a cosmic pattern that was worked out by the ancient Vedic tradition. This pattern can be mapped by modern neuroscience. Anatomy and subtle body are connected like a network. [He went on to describe extensive body *yoga* and breathing exercises] ... We go through the flesh to the subtle body. The longer we practice, the subtler our practice becomes. It opens like a vast space. The ascension of *kuṇḍalinī*—the breath or life force—moves in any direction. It is not physical. Consciousness is bound to our body, but there is a greater cosmic consciousness that is beyond. The Rishis of the Vedas knew these truths. (Rishikesh 2008)

The modern expressions of *haṭhayoga* did have the striking characteristic of having several agnostic or non-theistic accounts. These accounts heavily emphasized the embodied nature of religious experiences, often in scientific or psychological terms. Despite ecstatic, paranormal, and visionary experiences, the explanations of their experiences are expressed in scientific or medical terms. However, in the context of participant-observer dialogue, if I were to express this sentiment these same practitioners could (while returning to scientific terms consistently and often quickly) can translate those models into *advaita vedānta* terms, via Trika concepts, or even through interpreting the *Bhagavad Gītā*. For this reason, I would be hesitant about too strongly emphasizing that accounts of highly educated and heavily Westernized Hindus as being exclusively body focused (and agnostic or non-theistic) or as needing no philosophical or theological grounding or underpinning. In some cases, these accounts seemed very cosmopolitan and like the discourses of internationalized movements of Mahāyāna Buddhism. Nevertheless, they seem to be on the pole farthest away from the traditional theological landscape.

Alternatively, on the opposite pole are ascetics and the Aghoris. Through historical and cultural developments their practices seem to be straightforwardly connected via Nāths, and other *Kāpālika*-inspired traditions (Hindu or Buddhist), back to the very *kula/kaula* roots of the shared traditions on the other pole. Where their theology and expression–although often couched in the "practice as a kind of knowledge" (*jñana*) pattern of the high tantric synthesis—represent an opposite pole as a kind of recognizable modern expression of medieval tantric values and meanings, life and practice (with understandable developments and shifts).[17] The Aghoris also engaged in conventional *bhakti* descriptions and sang devotional songs.

The two "pole" groups (the scientists and the Aghoris) are mostly not the focus of the explorations in this essay. This is because they did not really speak about their experiences in terms of "religious experience"; instead, they used medical, psychological or scientific paradigms. They tended predominantly to speak of a great depth and commitment to practice, but their explanations of experiences tended to deemphasize ecstatic bliss and god-consciousness (or similar phenomena). Their practices more closely resembled descriptions from the mindfulness movement and New Age *yoga* rather than tantric practice (and what some have called Neo-Tantra). The Aghoris were overwhelmingly tantric and relatively straightforward. Since these ascetics have been explored elsewhere, this essay has primarily focused on the middle ground between radically modernized-scientific responses and traditional ascetic expressions of tantric practice and experience.

[17] For selected scholarship that explores the concepts related to knowledge (*jñāna*) becoming the focus of all forms of practice, and how concepts and practices developed or changed over time, see Sanderson, especially (Sanderson 1995) but also throughout his many works (Sanderson 1985, 1986, 1988, 2009), White, especially (White 1998), but also (White 1996, 2000, 2003), Padoux (1990, 2017).

The main subjects for this essay are all the people in the middle. For them, the recognition of "I am Śiva" is expressed in both their conventional tantric, urban, educated practices, and in alternative approaches. In modern South Asia, non-dualism extends so far as to include their university and artistic mentors as guides, and their aesthetic practices as a direct access to the descending grace of the goddess.

3. Conclusions

Religious experience for these modern practitioners who identify themselves as *tāntrikas* shows considerable variety. In some cases, experience of the divine is tied to property and good fortune (material success). In others, there is a strong emphasis on knowledge and insight (awareness and reflection), that was deemed existentially meaningful and ultimately freeing. In others still, it is creativity, artistic expression, and experiential bliss that moves them: a kind of living in the flowing power of the goddess. The scientists and medical professions described therapeutic models, and tied their practices to wellness, longevity, and happiness. Returning to James' definition of religion, the knowledge-insight seekers would match most closely with his concepts, but that would do a disservice to many of the other practitioners. There was an earnestness and focus to many of these practitioners and a genuine joy that suggests that Abhinavagupta's concepts (or his interpreters') match better than James, although the differences are subtle in some cases.

Consider the standard *advaita vedānta* analogy of the snake and the rope, where appearance or illusion (*māyā*) of manifest reality (the snake) disappears in the clear light of day (understanding). One sees that the illusion (snake) is not real (it is only a rope). The only true reality is the ultimate void beyond all qualities or forms (*brahman*, or *nirguṇa brahman*). Despite its non-dual theology, the analogy does not work for the modern practitioners or for medieval high *tantra*. All the paths (Right, Left, ritual, *mantra*, *yoga*, aesthetic, etc.) ultimately lead to the same place within the consciousness of the practitioner: conscious recognition and embodiment of ultimate consciousness, often phrased as "I am Śiva." For most forms of tantra, embodiment is real (not illusion).[18] All of these practices have emancipatory power. For Abhinavagupta (and generally for non-dual Śaiva-Śākta high *tantra*) the Right and the Left paths were equally valid and provided powerful access to ultimate truth and direct embodied experience of the absolute source and expression of all realities.[19] The snake and the rope (if the simile works at all in this context) are both, ultimately, expressions of Śakti and Śiva in their eternal dance of expansion and contraction.

In this non-dualism of Abhinavagupta or its modern expressions in Śrī Vidyā (or the like) reality has many appearances. These are not illusions, they are both those many things (embodied experiences) and they are their source (Śiva, Lalitā, Tripura Sundarī, Devī, etc.). The more appropriate simile for modern practitioners and for non-dualistic Śaivism would need to focus on the varieties of experiences, whether they are more expanded and complex or more compressed, sublimated or refined. Ultimately speaking and in relatively straightforward ways all experiences have the same value, *if* they lead to the ultimate I-awareness of the highest Śiva or the highest Śakti.

There are problems with this characterization, but not at the theological level. Feeling aesthetic experience as religious experience, or practicing traditional worship with a *yantra* or *mantra*, or doing either traditional *yoga* or learning *yoga* from the world wide web, or even playing music or making art are all theologically acceptable if the practitioners attains reflective self-awareness of ultimate Śiva awareness.

18 I am aware that one can parse this simile in ways that match the Trika (and other ways) and make finer philosophical distinctions than I am making here. However, in the context of these ethnographic accounts, I think the line of reasoning I am pursuing holds, even if not universally.

19 There is a long history of qualifications to this recognition. Arguably, Abhinava taught that very few people could succeed at many of these practices, and that many of them were sequenced (where preliminary practices built slowly toward advance practices), and that there were a complex requirements and qualifications. Foremost of these, was practicing in a community under the careful guidance of a fully realized teacher.

According to some of these practitioners, many different experiences can provoke the unfolding of the liberating reflection or knowledge. When this kind of knowledge-connection is formed, then the practitioner can see everything experienced (transcendental, aesthetic, or other) as in the end "I am Siva." The identity is the key that unlocks any form of practice or experience becoming a form of ultimate consciousness. Therefore, one of the things that appears in the contemporary patterns of religious experience and expression, is that secularized student-teacher interactions or among art students learning from other artists, these relationships become sacralized as an experience of the absolute that is not conceptually alien to the non-dualistic Śaiva *tantra* or aesthetics (despite it being a kind of ritual/*mantra*-free reinterpretation).

It is easy to appreciate *that* the high tantra synthesis of post-eleventh century Kashmiri *Mantramārga*—especially through the multidisciplinary articulation of Abhinavagupta—includes and compresses all of *tantra* within its non-dual resolution of the simultaneity of the total absolute, the embodied subject, and the enjoyment of aesthetic experience. Ordinary urban, modernized, or cosmopolitan practitioners of contemporary Hindu *yoga* and *tantra* show a wide variety of awareness (from deeply studied to virtually unaware) of the philosophical foundations or conceptual structures of their practices and theologies. Many articulate their practice in stereotypical (modern) expressions of Śaṅkara's *advaita* or other contemporary discourses of Hinduism and the Hindu diaspora. From the philosopher's or even scholar's perspective, these expressions might be more accurately expressed if they were to rely more specifically (in an historically or philosophically grounded fashion) on the Kashmiri Śaiva aesthetic and religious sources that created the symbolic and conceptual world in which their diversity of practice and experience flourishes. In the lived experience of modern (cosmopolitan, syncretistic and scientific) practitioners, this fine distinction does not often matter. At least in some, very deeply embedded cultural, ways, the urban-educated-internationalized *Śaivas*, *Śāktas*, artists, intellectuals, and *yogis* are living out their embodied traditions in very tantric ways. These ethnographic accounts do not represent a single population of practitioners. The unifying themes of their accounts consists in their shared emphasis on experience of the divine within their daily lives and in their common vocabulary (such as their uses of *yoga* and *sādhanā*) and the way that they identify their practices and concepts as broadly tantric (using such terms as *mantra-tantra, tantra-vidyā,* and *śākta*).

The "on-the-ground" equating of aesthetic enjoyment as explicitly religious-bliss-generating-enjoyment of the dance of Śiva and Śakti, or modernistic expressions of the meaning of *yoga*, or ties to their gurus might sometimes have very little theological sophistication or awareness. In the cases that these people have awareness of the texts of non-dual Śaivism, then it is not even complicated. Their scientific materialism and neuroscience; or Hindu-Buddhist mindfulness synthesis; or their arts and music as their "true" religion are all expressions of the ultimate non-duality even without Śiva and Śakti modes of expression (although this is often present in some forms).

When one finds circumstances where there is a more demonstrable tantric awareness, then it becomes a linear and straightforward expression of the varieties of explanation present in the Kashmiri exegetes (regardless of the extent of their knowledge of the Kashmiri texts). The extent of their textual knowledge does not alter their assertions that their study is *jñāna* and acts are tantric *sādhanā*). They understand their dance, art, painting, music as aesthetic-religious experience that leads directly to the ultimate identification with Śiva through the descending grace of Śakti. Even with the pervasive and assimilating power of contemporary Hindu culture (in its universalizing, orthodox, or scientific forms), the patterns and theological structures and the expressions of religious experience, here are profoundly Śaiva-Śākta, in their various experiential expressions.

Funding: This research received no external funding.

Conflicts of Interest: The author declares no conflict of interest.

References

Biernacki, Loriliai. 2006. Possession, Absorption and the Transformation of Samāveśa. In *Expanding and Merging Horizons: Contributions to South Asian and Cross-Cultural Studies in Commemoration of Wilhelm Halbfass*. Edited by Karin Preisendanz. Wien: Verlag der Osterreichischen Akademie der Wissenschaften, pp. 491–504.

Britton Lab. 2019. "Meditation Safety Toolbox" (version 4.06.18). Available online: https://www.brown.edu/research/labs/britton/resources/meditation-safety-toolbox (accessed on 1 February 2019).

Brooks, Douglas Renfrew. 1992. *Auspicious Wisdom: The Texts and Traditions of Śrīvidyā Śākta Tantrism in South India*. Albany: SUNY Press.

Gnoli, Raniero. 1985. *The Aesthetic Experience According to Abhinavagupta*. Chowkhamba Sanskrit Studies Vol. LXII. Third Edition. Varanasi: Chowkhamba Sanskrit Series Office.

Hatley, Shaman. 2016. Kuṇḍalinī. In *Encyclopedia of Indian Religions*. Edited by Arvind Sharma. Netherlands: Springer, vol. 3.

Hayes, Glen Alexander. 2011. Tantric Studies: Issues, Methods, and Scholarly Collaborations. *The Journal of Hindu Studies* 4: 221–30. [CrossRef]

Hayes, Glen Alexander, and Sthaneshwar Timalsina. 2017. Introduction to "Cognitive Science and the Study of Yoga and Tantra. *Religions* 8: 181. [CrossRef]

James, William. 1958. *The Varieties of Religious Experience*. New York: New American Library. First published 1902.

Katz, Ruth, and Arvind Sharma. 1977. The Aesthetics of Abhinavagupta. *The British Journal of Aesthetics* 17: 259–65. [CrossRef]

Kavi, M. Ramakrishna, ed. 1934. *Nāṭyaśāstra with the Commentary of Abhinavagupta*. Baroda: Oriental Institute.

Larson, Gerald James. 1976. The Aesthetic (Rasāsvadā) [sic] and the Religious (Brahmāsvāda) in Abhinavagupta's Kashmir Śaivism. *Philosophy East and West* 26: 371–87. [CrossRef]

Lidke, Jeffrey S. 2005. Interpreting Across Mystical Boundaries: An Analysis of Samādhi in the Trika-Kaula Tradition. In *Theory and Practice of Yoga: Essays in Honour of Gerald James Larson*. Edited by Gerald James Larson and Knut A. Jacobsen. Volume 110 of Studies in the History of Religions. Leiden: Brill.

Lidke, Jeffrey S. 2011. Tablā, spirituality, and the arts: A journey into the cycles of time. In *Studying Hinduism in Practice*. Studying Religions in Practice Series; London: Routledge.

Lidke, Jeffrey S. 2015. Dancing Forth the Divine Beloved: A Tantric Semiotics of the Body as Rasa in Classical Indian Dance. *Sutra Journal: Eternal Truths—Modern Voices*. December. Available online: http://www.sutrajournal.com/dancing-forth-the-divine-beloved-by-jeffrey-lidke (accessed on 1 February 2019).

Lidke, Jeffrey S. 2016. A Thousand Years of Abhinavagupta. *Sutra Journal: Eternal Truths—Modern Voices*. January. Available online: http://www.sutrajournal.com/a-thousand-years-of-abhinavagupta-by-jeffrey-lidke (accessed on 1 February 2019).

Lidke, Jeffrey S. 2017. *The Goddess Within and Beyond the Three Cities: Śākta Tantra and the Paradox of Power in Nepāla-Maṇḍala*. New Delhi: D.K. Printworld (P) Ltd.

Mallinson, James. 2011. Nāth Saṃpradāya. In *Society, Religious Specialists, Religious Traditions, Philosophy*. Brill's Encyclopedia of Hinduism. Handbook of Oriental Studies. Section 2 South Asia, Volume 22/3. Leiden: Brill.

Mallinson, James, and Mark Singleton. 2017. *Roots of Yoga*. Penguin Classics. London: Penguin Random House UK.

Masson, Jeffrey Moussaieff, J. L. Masson, and M. V. Patwardhan. 1969. *Śāntarasa and Abhinavagupta's Philosophy of Aesthetics*. Poona: Bhandarkar Oriental Research Institute.

McDaniel, June. 2018. *Lost Ecstasy: Its Decline and Transformation in Religion*. Interdisciplinary Approaches to the Study of Mysticism. Basingstoke: Palgrave Macmillan.

Muller-Ortega, Paul. 2000. One the Seal of Śambhu: A Poem by Abhinavagupta. In *Tantra in Practice*. Edited by David G. White. Princeton: Princeton University Press, pp. 573–86.

Padoux, André. 1990. *Vac: The Concept of the Word in Selected Hindu Tantras*. The SUNY Series in the Shaiva Traditions of Kashmi; Delhi: Sri Satguru Publications.

Padoux, André. 2017. *The Hindu Tantric World: An Overview*. Chicago: University of Chicago Press.

Rocha, Tomas. 2014. The Dark Knight of the Soul: For Some, Meditation Has Become More Curse than Cure. Willoughby Britton Wants to Know Why. *The Atlantic*. June 25. Available online: https://www.theatlantic.com/health/archive/2014/06/the-dark-knight-of-the-souls/372766/ (accessed on 1 February 2019).

Sanderson, Alexis. 1985. Purity and Power among the Brahmans of Kashmir. In *The Category of the Person: Anthropology, Philosophy, History*. Edited by Michael Carrithers, Steven Collins and Steven Lukes. Cambridge: Cambridge University Press, pp. 190–216.

Sanderson, Alexis. 1986. Maṇḍala and Āgamic Identity in the Trika of Kashmir. In *Mantras et Diagrammes Rituels dans l'Hindouisme*. Paris: Éditions du CNRS, pp. 169–214.

Sanderson, Alexis. 1988. Śaivism and the Tantric Traditions. In *The World's Religions*. Edited by Stewert Sutherland, Leslie Houlden, Peter Clarke and Friedhelm Hardy. London: Routledge, pp. 660–704.

Sanderson, Alexis. 1995. Meaning in Tantric Ritual. In *Essais sur le Ritual*. Edited by Anne-Marie Blondeau and Kristofer Schipper. vol. 3, Colloque du Centenaire de la Section des Sciences Religieuses de l'Ecole Pratique des Hautes Etudes. Louvain and Paris: Peeters.

Sanderson, Alexis. 2009. The Śaiva Age: The Rise and Dominance of Śaivism during the Early Medieval Period. In *Genesis and Development of Tantrism*. Edited by Shingo Einoo. Institute of Oriental Culture Special Series; Tokyo: Institute of Oriental Culture, University of Tokyo, vol. 23, pp. 341–50.

Sannella, Lee. 1987. *The Kundalini Experience: Psychosis or Transcendence?* San Francisco: Integral Publishers.

Saraswati, Swami Satyananda. 1981. *A Systematic Course in the Ancient Tantric Techniques of Yoga and Kriya*. Bihar: Yoga Publications Trust.

Schwartz, Susan L. 2004. *Rasa: Performing the Divine in India*. New York: Columbia University Press.

Siegel, Lee. 1991. *Sacred and Profane Dimensions of Love in Indian Traditions as Exemplified in the Gitagovinda of Jayadeva*. Oxford University South Asian Studies Series; Oxford: Oxford University Press.

Smith, Frederick M. 2006. *The Self Possessed: Deity and Spirit Possession in South Asian Literature and Civilization*. New York: Columbia University Press.

Timalsina, Sthaneshwar. 2007. Metaphor, Rasa, and Dhvani: Suggested Meaning in Tantric Esotericism. *Method and Theory in the Study of Religion* 19: 134–62. [CrossRef]

Timalsina, Sthaneshwar. 2015. *Tantric Visual Culture: A Cognitive Approach*. London: Routledge.

Timalsina, Sthaneshwar. 2016. Theatrics of Emotion: Self-Deception and Self-Cultivation in Abhinavagupta's Aesthetics. *Philosophy East & West* 66: 104–21.

Wallis, Christopher. 2008. The Descent of Power: Possession, Mysticism, and Initiation in the Śaiva Theology of Abhinavagupta. *Journal of Indian Philosophy* 36: 247–95. [CrossRef]

White, John, ed. 1990. *Kundalini, Evolution and Enlightenment*. St. Paul: Paragon House.

White, David G. 1996. *The Alchemical Body: Siddha Traditions in Medieval India*. Chicago: University of Chicago Press.

White, David G. 1998. Transformations in the Art of Love: Kāmakalā Practices in Hindu Tantric and Kaula Traditions. *History of Religions* 38: 172–98. [CrossRef]

White, David G., ed. 2000. *Tantra in Practice*. Princeton: Princeton University Press.

White, David G. 2003. *Kiss of the Yogini: "Tantric Sex" in its South Asian Contexts*. Chicago: University of Chicago Press.

Wulff, Donna M. 1984. *Drama as a Mode of Religious Realization: The Vidagdhamādhava of Rūpa Gosvāmī*. Chico: Scholars Press.

religions

MDPI

Article

Sprouts of the Body, Sprouts of the Field: Identification of the Goddess with Poxes in South India

Perundevi Srinivasan

Religious Studies, Siena College, Loudonville, NY 12211, USA; psrinivasan@siena.edu

Received: 1 January 2019; Accepted: 22 February 2019; Published: 27 February 2019

Abstract: In south India, when a person is afflicted with poxes of any variety, it is believed that the goddess Mariyamman has "arrived" in the person. The Tamil term "*ammai*" means pustules or "pearls" of poxes as well as mother/goddess. Indigenous discourses, gleaned from resources, such as songs and narratives, facilitate our interrogation of the Hindu "religious experience" that underscores the immanent and eminent manifestations of the deity and the dimension of benevolence associated with pox-affliction. Asking what might be the triggering conditions for identifying the pox-afflicted body as the goddess, I problematize the prevalent scholarly characterization of such affliction in terms of "possession" of a body, taken as a "mute facticity," by an external agent, namely, the goddess. Drawing from ethnographic sources and classical Tamil texts, I argue that the immanent identification of the body as the goddess and conceptualization of her sovereign authority over the body during affliction are facilitated by an imagistic relationship of the afflicted body with an agricultural field, which is conventionally regarded as feminine in the Tamil context.

Keywords: Mariyamman; ammai; poxes; affliction; Tamil; religious experience; Hinduism; rain; agricultural field; goddess

1. Introduction

On a summer afternoon many years ago, I lay stretched out on my mother's cotton sari, writhing from excruciating pain throughout my body. I had high fever for a couple of days, and it was on the third day that round pustules of chickenpox began to erupt and spread all over my body. My mother was in two minds whether to consult a doctor, since in Cuddalore town in the southern state of Tamilnadu, where I lived then, people did not normally go to an allopathic doctor to seek a cure for poxes. After hours of discussion with my father and neighbors, my mother asked a physician to visit our house. He confirmed that *ammai* (meaning both poxes and the divine mother/goddess in Tamil) had 'arrived' in my body in the form of chickenpox, and he would not, therefore, prescribe any medicine other than Crocin (paracetamol) pills to bring down the fever, though he assured us that I would be alright within a week. Even after the doctor's visit, my mother was not fully convinced about giving me what she called "English" (allopathic) medicine. Pleading with the goddess to forgive her for treating me with allopathic medicine, and after profusely requesting the goddess to "descend" from the body—all these pleadings and requests were actually addressed to me, although a few distant abodes of Mariyamman in Tamilnadu were also mentioned—my mother finally decided to give me only a single Crocin (Paracetamol) pill. When I recall that experience of *ammai* now, even after all these years, I am still overwhelmed by a strange blend of smells: of margosa leaves, of turmeric, and my mother's sari; along with them, the smell of pustules with oozing matter that had appeared all over my body and were regarded as manifestations of the goddess herself.

Mariyamman's relationship with *ammai* is considered at three levels among Hindus in Tamil culture. First, the goddess is believed to be involved with the occurrence of *ammai*. For instance,

"The mother has played" ("*amma vilaiyadiyirukka*") is a way in which the ailment is talked about. At the second level, the goddess and pustules are one and the same, and I will discuss them early in this article. At the third level, the goddess is believed to have the power to cure poxes. Several songs of the goddess in various genres, like *Talattu* (Lullaby), *Unjal* (Swing), and *Varnippu* (Description) extol the goddess for this power. Usually, when the first "pearls" become visible on the body of a person, a bunch of margosa twigs is hung on the doorway of the afflicted person's house to indicate the "presence" of the goddess who has arrived there, inaugurating a set of customary habitual practices (*palakkavalakkam*), which are both restrictive and mandatory in nature.[1] For instance, engaging in sexual activities, sleeping on a mattress, cutting hair, shaving, entertaining visitors, seasoning the food with mustard seeds, and wearing slippers, are prohibited in the house, as they are considered offensive to the goddess. A pot of water is kept near the afflicted person, and the house is meticulously cleaned every day. Occasionally, a lullaby song to Mariyamman, available in the form of a chapbook, is sung by a family member who addresses the song to the pox-afflicted person. People do not normally visit a physician seeking a cure of poxes. Instead, a vow of obligation is taken in the name of Mariyamman, in order to persuade the goddess to "descend" from the body at the earliest. In east and south east Tamilnadu, especially in and around Tanjore, Pudukkottai and Sivaganga, when the affliction is severe, a traditional healer (*ammappillai*, meaning "child of the 'mother'/goddess") is invited to visit the house regularly and recite the goddess's songs, towards seeking the goddess's grace for curing the poxes quickly.

How can one understand the identification of a pox-afflicted body as a female deity Mariyamman? What could be the triggering conditions in which the goddess is perceived as the source of poxes, as the one who heals poxes, while she is considered poxes as such? These questions, which have stemmed from my experience of pox-affliction, increasingly occupied my mind when I started working on Mariyamman worship practices in Tamilnadu. Exploring these questions might afford us a glimpse of a specific mode of "religious experience," relating to the goddess Mariyamman, who is considered in her immanent and eminent forms in the event of pox-affliction in Tamilnadu. Here, I must clarify my use of the term "religious experience." While I agree with the argument that there is a pertinent place always accorded to "indigenous religious experience" in Hindu traditions, I also tend to understand that such "experience" is historically constituted, and it is a "correlation between fields of knowledge, types of normativity and forms of subjectivity in a particular culture."[2] In the case of Mariyamman worship and pox-affliction, some of the related "fields of knowledge" include those pertaining to illnesses and healing techniques along with those related to institutionalized temple worship. Similarly, as I have discussed elsewhere, Mariyamman worship practices related to pox-affliction are replete with two key inter-related discursive tropes, *karpu* (chastity of women) and *cuttam* (purity-cleanliness), and habitual practices, organized around these two tropes, reinforce the heteronormative power apparatus.[3] Further, I think the mode of religious experience could also be a mode of "actualization" of the divine/ deity. In the instance of pox-affliction, the religious experience could be a mode in which the goddess is "actualized" as the body of the afflicted person and as an autonomous force through various habitual signifying practices of the community.[4]

---

1 For an analysis of the habitual practices followed during pox-affliction, see (Srinivasan 2009, pp. 97–142).

2 June McDaniel, in an article, contests a range of critical perspectives that deny "indigenous value on religious experience," and draws attention to distinct terminology and specific ideas that articulate such "experience" in diverse Hindu traditions, including Dharma, Bhakti, Tantra, and folk traditions. See (McDaniel 2009). In framing my take on "religious experience," I have benefited from Foucault's discussion of "experience" in the realm of sexuality in modern Western societies. Foucault defines "experience" as that which has "caused individuals to recognize themselves as subjects of a 'sexuality,' which was accessible to very diverse fields of knowledge and linked to a system of rules and constraints." See (Foucault 1985, p. 4). Further, I think religious experience, like "experience" in the realm of sexuality, is constituted historically, and belongs to an order or "reality" than that of "truth." See (Foucault 1991, p. 36).

3 (Srinivasan 2009, pp. 209–60).

4 For a theoretical inquiry into the mode of "actualization" of the goddess through performative and signifying practices, refer to (Srinivasan 2009, pp. 14–19).

The indigenous discourses which I am analyzing in the article form part of the repertoire of such collective practices centred on Mariyamman worship and pox-affliction. Specifically these discourses are gleaned from narratives and songs of devotees and healers in the districts of Pudukkottai, Dindigul, Chennai, and Sivaganga in Tamilnadu, which I gathered during my ethnographic fieldwork (2004–2006). I also refer to my personal conversations with devotees. I employ Mariyamman songs, copied from palm-leaf manuscripts and from published books, in addition to Tamil classical literary texts for the purpose of my genealogical analysis. My concern is to interrogate the indigenous discourses in order to schematically unearth the identification of an afflicted body as the divine/goddess, and in the process, problematize the prevalent notions of pox-affliction in terms of "possession" by an external agent, namely, a spirit or deity.[5] I hesitate to buy into the academic idiom of "possession," since it amounts to considering the goddess as an *a priori* source of affliction. Instead, I engage with the task of understanding how the immanent and eminent "presence" of the goddess is "normatively" established during the instance of affliction, and in doing this, I critically engage with emic references to poxes as well.[6] In addition, I seek to bring out the creative and aesthetic investment of Tamil culture in its forging discursive connections between the body and the landscape, and between poxes, pearls, pulses and grains. This may provide a counter-narrative to symbolic and functionalist interpretations of the religious dimension of the disease as representing and serving some other external reality, such as the devotee's poverty or marginalization or fear.[7]

2. Understanding the Body as and of the Goddess

In the Tamil popular discourse and folk songs, sometimes *ammai* is portrayed as a "play" or "sport" of the goddess.[8] "The mother has played around" (*amma vilaiyadiyirukka*) is a common place expression that indicates the "arrival" of poxes on a person.[9] The Tamil term *"ayi muttu,"* meaning "mother pearl," refers to both the goddess and the lesion or pustule of *ammai*. The pus or putrid matter oozing from the lesion is called "mother's milk" (*ammaippal*). In the folk song of *Mariyamman Talattu*, sung to the afflicted person, the goddess is addressed as the mother with milk oozing from her breasts, alluding to the oozing pustules.[10] Another folk song on the goddess, *Mariyamman Varnippu* (*"Description of Mariyamman"*) also contains a similar evocation:

---

[5] Throughout this article, I use the term "discourses" following Foucault. According to Foucault, the discourses are not just "groups of signs (signifying elements referring to contents or representations) but as practices that systematically form the objects of which they speak." See (Foucault 1972, p. 49).

[6] I use the term "normative" expanding the sense in which Judith Butler uses it to mean the "norms that govern gender." For Butler, the term is indicative of "ethical justification, how it is established, what concrete consequences proceed there from." See (Butler 1999, p. xx). In the present context of discussion, I employ it to draw attention to the cultural norms that govern the association of the affliction with the goddess.

[7] For a symbolist approach to Mariyamman's association with smallpox, see (Egnor 1984). According to Margaret Trawick Egnor, before its eradication, smallpox together with its religious underpinnings served as a "convenient symbol" for grim realities, such as "the pain and stigma of poverty", "family discord", and "crowded living conditions". For a functionalist interpretation of the association of the goddess with smallpox, see (Arnold 1993). For David Arnold, religion in the form of goddess worship was a way in which local people tried to make sense of the "destructive" and "fearful" smallpox.

[8] This is one of the ways in which the pox-affliction is referred to. There are certain other phrases that may be used to refer to the affliction, which I discuss in the course of this article.

[9] (Srinivasan 2009, pp. 79, 117). Also see (D 1747, lines 93–104), discussed in this paper. The aspect of "divine play" (*"khelna"*) that underscores the theme of "parental love" of the deity for the devotee is a discernible theme in the rituals of "Goddess possession" in Panjab as well, as pointed out by Kathleen Erndl. See (Erndl 1993, p. 108). The songs of the healers, which form part of the healing performances of poxes that I have attended in Pudukkottai district, contain the repetitive address of the afflicted person as a "child", thereby emphasizing the benevolent, motherly aspect of the goddess as she was asked to be compassionate to the afflicted person.

[10] (*Mariyamman Talattu*, n.d., p. 8). When I use printed texts such as this book, I cite the page numbers. In addition to printed texts, I also cite palm leaf manuscripts. In the latter case, I provide the corresponding line numbers. *Mariyamman Talattu* is available as both printed and palm leaf manuscript versions, and I use them both for the purpose of my analysis. The palm leaf manuscript version of this song as well as other songs were copied from the Government Oriental Manuscripts Library in Chennai, Tamilnadu, and they are cited by their number, beginning with the letter "D," as per the records of the Library.

The stringed pearls dance, milk oozes from the two breasts,
Devi, you grant boons to the deserving.[11]

The body with *ammai* is not merely a "sacred" body; it is the body as and of the goddess. Also, if we look at textual sources, such as songs about the goddess, ethnographic narratives, and personal conversations, we constantly encounter portrayals of *ammai* as being a benevolent state, indicating Mariyamman's grace or affection. For instance, local healers of the affliction insist that the goddess visits the house in the form of *ammai* in order to thwart an evil or tragedy which might otherwise befall the family. According to the healers, *ammai* is a protective gesture of the goddess preempting the bad fortune, which is otherwise in store for the family. Muthukkannu, a healer I met in a village called Vagaippatti near Pudukkottai in the year 2004, explained the "protection" offered by the goddess:

> *Ammai* does not come without a reason. She comes only to save us. Only when ... planets are not placed well in our horoscope, and they show wrath toward us, then based upon our *karma punniyam* (merit of *karma* or past deeds) and *dharmam* (rightful deeds/virtue), the goddess, the mother who has begotten us would think, "Oh, these planets are going to attack my child." She would come and descend into us so that the planets run away. The planets approach a house like a stone. But upon seeing the goddess, who has already arrived there (in the form of pustules), they would be afraid of thinking she has a thousand eyes and go away.[12] Then everything would be fine.

Similarly, *Mariyamman Talattu* also emphasizes the affection of the goddess for human beings. The goddess with "compassion" is believed to arrive in the form of pearls in order to dwell in the "poor one."[13] The body with *ammai*, being described as a "golden swing" or "palanquin," seems to have achieved this state due to the "devotion" felt toward the goddess:

Has she stood as a blessing in the form of a golden swing?
Has she given this boon and protected me
Thinking that "she is a devotee," and bestowing me with this palanquin?[14]

I would like to clarify that despite such glorifying remarks, people in Tamilnadu by no means seek to 'invite' any kind of poxes upon them. In fact, in the songs, related to the goddess and poxes, we do come across allusive references comparing pox-affliction, which is attributed to the goddess, with snake-bite and poison.[15] The unbearable pain and suffering caused by poxes are vividly articulated in the songs. Poxes fall very much within the Tamil discursive ambit of affliction or illness, and when someone has poxes, it is expressed that her "health is unwell" ("*udambu cariyillai*") as one has any other kind of illness such as fever. Also, when a person is afflicted with poxes, at times, *ammappillai* healers are asked to visit their home for singing Mariyamman songs to enable a quick cure, as I mentioned before.[16] Nevertheless, the affliction has discernible positive cultural connotations, and particularly I would like to focus on them to bring out the complex cultural nuances.

---

11 (D 2164, lines 24–25).

12 "The thousand-eyed" or "*Ayiram Kannudaiyal*" is an epithet for Mariyamman. A few other healers whom I met in places such as Mukkannamalaippatti and Thayamangalam (2005–2006) expressed a similar view concerning the 'arrival' of the affliction. See (Srinivasan 2009, p. 429).

13 (D 1747, lines 95–96). One can compare this with the "traditional" perception of the disease in the Bible. David E. Shuttleton observes that the eruptive disease that Job suffered was cited by theologians of the early eighteenth century to argue against smallpox inoculation because it was the devil that gave forth the "inflammatory pustules" upon Job. See (Shuttleton 2007, p. 63). Notwithstanding the conflation between original smallpox and its antidotal inoculation, the association of pustules with the devil strikes a different tone from the south Indian perception of the affliction. I should also mention here that goddess Sitala, who is associated with poxes in North as well as Eastern India, has a more limited role compared to Mariyamman. For instance, Sitala is not connected with rains, and nor is she considered as a goddess protecting a territory as Mariyamman is considered. See (Wadley 1980, p. 57).

14 (Ibid., lines 106–8).

15 (Srinivasan 2009, p. 162).

16 For a discussion on such healers in see (Srinivasan 2009, pp. 420–34). Here I am reminded of Carla Bellamy's observations with respect to practices related to *haziri*, "a form of spirit possession." She argues even though "the categories of physical

Prima facie, the Tamil conception of *ammai* as benevolence bestowed by the goddess does not fit with the scholarly framework, which discriminates between "possession" caused by malevolent spirits and by deities, espoused in binary terms of "affliction/punishment" and "gift/grace" respectively.[17] Kathleen M. Erndl, for instance, points out such a distinction in the "theological and ritual context of the Goddess cult and popular Hinduism" in northern India, and observes that the former kind of possession is sought to be removed by "force or appeasement," while the latter kind is "usually encouraged or cultivated."[18] In the Tamil context of *ammai*, as I mentioned before, the goddess's presence is not encouraged or cultivated, even though it is perceived as a gesture of grace. Further, I also hesitate to locate pox-affliction within the "models of possession," provided by Frederick M. Smith, who engages with "the field of possession" by dividing it into "positive" and "negative" possession.[19] Even though Smith's category of "negative possession" is more inclusive since it includes "possession" by the deities as well, the benevolent dimension of the pox-affliction in the Tamil milieu, as discussed above, seems to destabilize this category.[20]

In the ethnographic literature that deliberates upon the connection of Mariyamman with poxes in terms of "possession," the affliction is often rendered in terms of "penetration" or "entry" of the goddess in her capacity as an external agent. For instance, Margaret Trawick Egnor has observed that the "smallpox goddess" Mariyamman "enters the body of a person out of 'desire' for them, love for them . . . ."[21] Going along with Egnor, Isabelle Nabokov regards smallpox as "symbols" of "forceful penetration" of the goddess, which she also reads as a form of "sexual aggression."[22] Pox-affliction is viewed as an instance of "involuntary possession" by the goddess by Willam Harman too. Harman states the goddess "enters a person's body" necessitating certain "ritual protocol" at home.[23] Such perspectives of the goddess's downright occupation during pox-affliction, entailed by her "possession," resonates with the Judeo-Christian perspectives that inform the analytical category of "spirit possession," as pointed out by Mary Hancock.[24] Hancock in her ethnographic study, which engages with "goddess mediums" in Chennai, observes that this category "tends to misinterpret the phenomena that it purports to explain," since it places the "goddess's coming to a devotee" on par with "a 'demonic' visitation," and assumes a "straightforward" claim of a person by the deity.[25] The category, she explains, "derives from Euro-Western legal understandings of property ownership

---

and spiritual" in some religious traditions may not be clearly demarcated as in "the contemporary West," a denial of distinction between the categories "eliminates a distinction that is vital to the process through which most of those afflicted with *haziri* are healed." See (Bellamy 2008, pp. 31, 35). The poxes *are* the goddess, and, at the same time, as an illness, they also need to be healed. The pain that they cause cannot be subsumed under the "sacredness" attributed to the body during the affliction.

17 (Erndl 1993, p. 106).

18 Ibid.

19 (Smith 2011, p. 4).

20 Ibid. For Smith, "positive possession" is "constituted, oracular, and invited" and is attributed mostly to deities, "negative possession is normally disease-producing and is attributed to uninvited ethereal agents," which include spirits and deities.

21 See (Egnor 1984, p. 26).

22 According to Nabokov, the goddess "lodges herself 'inside' her victims' body" by this act. See (Nabokov 2000, p. 28).

23 (Harman 2011, p. 194).

24 (Hancock 1995, p. 173).

25 In the early anthropological literature on popular religion in Tamilnadu, we come across a conflation of female deities with demons. For instance, see (Caldwell 1887, p. 94), for Rev. Robert Caldwell's derisive views on the worship of female deities (*Ammans*) in relation to pestilences:

> Notwithstanding the superior dignity attributed to the *Ammans*, I question whether they are not, after all, more diabolical than the professed devils. Cholera and small-pox, the most dreadful of all pestilences, are inflicted by them alone; and what is specially extraordinary is, that small-pox is invariably called by the common people 'the sport of the *Amman*.' When a person is stricken by small-pox the expression the people use is 'the *Amman* is taking her pastime over him.' ... There is no difference between the *Ammans* and the devils in regard to their appetite for blood.

I have discussed elsewhere how Caldwell's work "has set the tone of future ethnographies, relegate[ing] goddess worship to the discursive domain of the Dravidian," while equating it with "demonolatry," and how it carved a way for "advanc[ing] colonial civilizational rhetoric intervening in the field of 'religion' of 'natives.'" See (Srinivasan 2009, pp. 31–56).

and alienability," underscoring the idea of "individual subjectivity," which can be owned or controlled by the deity.[26] Critiquing such perspectives underlying "spirit possession," she gives a list of a range of Tamil terms, such as *"eru"* (to mount), *"kattu"* (to bind), and *"parru"* (to get attached), which inform otherwise," as these terms indicate "attachments among humans, between humans and inanimate objects, and between humans and deities," emphasizing "biomoral connectedness and/or exchanges of energies."[27]

Even though none of these Tamil verbs, listed by Hancock, are used in referring to pox-affliction in Tamilnadu, I concur with Hancock that the category of "spirit possession" implying an external agent or force "entering" and occupying the body is problematic in the context of pox-affliction as well. Especially, from what I have heard from my interlocutors, a manifestation of poxes is not always perceived so. In this regard, a Tamil expression, which is used to refer to affliction, namely, *"ammai vantirukku"* meaning *"ammai* has arrived," merits attention.[28] During my fieldwork in Tamilnadu, when I asked about the "source" of poxes, my conversationalists did not always interpret the "arrival" of poxes in terms of something emanating from the outside and ends up in the house and the body. According to some devotees of Mariyamman, the "arrival" amounts to "arriving from inside the body," and manifesting as pox-affliction externally. For instance, when I asked "Where does *ammai* come from?" Velmurugan, a singer, who plays *utukkai* (hour-glass shaped drum) at Mariyamman festivals, from Ulundurpet responded: "*Ammai* is inside the body. From inside it comes out on the body as pustules that can be seen with our naked eyes." To the same question, Kala, a devotee of Mariyamman, who resides in Vannanthurai, Besant Nagar, later explained: "*Ammai* comes from inside us." In reply to my follow-up question, "What is inside?" to her, she further explained: "Akka, *ammai* dwells in the stomach and it arrives from there."

Initially, such a complex account of the source of poxes tempted me to interpret it by employing a much nuanced interpretation of the indigenous Tamil conception of *ananku* that has been advanced by Alexander Dubianski.[29] For Dubianski, *ananku* signifies both an inner "abstract power" and "a spirit, an unidentifiable deity," with these meanings "closely interlocked in their usage . . . ."[30] Dubianski further qualifies this inherent "power" as a "natural power," which is distinct from a "supernatural"

---

26 (Hancock 1999, p. 173).

27 Ibid. In speaking of "attachments" and "connectedness," Hancock is influenced by the "transactional model" on "spirit possession," advanced by ethnosociologists, such as (Marriott and Inden 1977). In this model that emphasizes transaction of "substance-codes" and essences, "[T]he biomoral boundaries of the person are considered porous," and is prone "to the influences of place, food, cloth, and others' (including deities') bodies and their voiced and unvoiced intentions." See (Hancock 1999, p. 18). Frederick Smith also observes that the "transactional model" may be partly helpful in understanding the phenomenon of "possession," and writes, "[d]ividual persons, entities, or even concepts transfer parts or essences of themselves, in whole or in part, wilfully or by force, to other dividual persons, entities, or concepts" See (Smith 2006, p. 75). Applying the "transactional model" in his study on "possession" and citing a range of sources from classical literature of Vedic texts and Upanishads and the latter *puranas*, Smith tries to pinpoint that a transfer of "essences, akin to Marriott's coded substances," takes place in "a conscious or otherwise felt experience of possession." See (Smith 2006, p. 211). Elsewhere I have contested this model, because in this model "the body serves as a medium for the transfer of 'essences,' rather than playing an active role or having any primary significance in the process." See (Srinivasan 2009, pp. 402–4).

28 In an article, Hancock states that the transformed state of the female medium of the goddess is not described by her devotees as *"avecam,"* which she notes, is "often glossed as spirit possession" (Ibid.). She explains since the condition of the medium was perceived as a "temporary transformation" by her devotees, it was rather expressed: "'the *amman* has come' (*amman vantatu*)." This is strikingly similar to the expression used to speak of pox-affliction. See (Hancock 1995, p. 89). I have also never heard of the term *"avecam"* being used to refer to pox-affliction either. Even in the temple festivals, where Mariyamman "arrives" in devotees, the term was not usually employed to speak of such condition. Similarly, based on certain Tamil terms employed to speak of the phenomenon, Kristin C. Bloomer distinguishes between "possession" by "benevolent deities and spirits," and the one by "'lesser spirits'" such as "those of deceased humans." See (Bloomer 2018, p. 9). According to her, the term *"iranku"* or "descend" is characteristic of the former kind of "possession." This particular term is also cited by Lynn Foulston to substantiate the goddess's "tak[ing] over the mortal body" as well. See (Foulston 2002, p. 145). Even though pox-affliction is regarded as an immanent manifestation of the goddess, the verb *"iranku"* is not employed to indicate the affliction, and, this again complicates the academic notion of the affliction in terms of "possession."

29 (Dubianski 2000, p. 8).

30 Ibid.

one, and proposes that since the expression of this power is "heat or/and fire," *ananku* could be perceived as being in the same order as that of *tapas* (severe ascetic practice), which produces an "ascetic heat."[31] Since poxes are said to be caused by bodily heat in popular discourse, one may consider the pox-affliction along the order of the power, articulated by the conceptions of *ananku* and *tapas* heat. This allows theorizing the affliction as a manifestation of the localized power immanent in the body and of the power of an eminent deity from outside. However, the conceptual framework of *ananku* is hardly adequate, because in the Tamil worldview, several other ailments (for instance, stomach ache, urinary infection, and certain eye diseases) are also attributed to accumulation of bodily heat, and, thus, the conception of *ananku* is not helpful to address why pox-affliction alone is perceived to be divine.

More importantly, my issue with the category of "spirit possession" is that it assumes a "mute facticity" of the body, which can be appropriated by an agent, be it a deity or a spirit. I have contested elsewhere that such consideration of the body as a "natural template or as an "unchanging material substrate" renders it a carrier of expressions of a psyche or self, "possessed" by an agent.[32] I think that in the context of pox-affliction, the body cannot be understood as something other than that which is coded with the goddess's "presence." In advancing this argument, I follow Judith Butler's "critical genealogy" of the formulation of matter in articulating the body.[33] Butler advocates "critical genealogy" in order to interrogate the assumed "biological" facticity of the body and to emphasize the body as produced by cultural norms and practices. According to Butler, matter "only appears under a certain grammatical form ... " or under a *schema*, which she further defines as a "principle of intelligibility."[34] As the schema has always been implicated with the matter through which it "actualizes," schema and matter are discursively inseparable. "'To matter'," Butler contends, is at once "to materialize" and "to mean" and, therefore, the "indissolubility of materiality and signification is no easy matter."[35] Put simply, Butler shows how the perception of the body does not precede cultural intelligibility but always occurs in conjunction with it.

'While Butler's inquiry into schema concerns with the intelligibility of the body as a specific sex, as male or female, or as abject in general life scenarios, I think the method of "critical genealogy" of materiality is valuable and indispensable for analyzing the practices that characterize the goddess worship in connection with poxes. In fact, the Tamil word "*porul*" informs us of the epistemological indissolubility of materiality and meaning, which makes this discussion pertinent.[36] The word denotes both "thing/matter" and "meaning/signification." When I say, "*un porulaip parttukkol*," it means "keep an eye on your thing;" when I say, "*accollin porul enakkup puriyavillai*," it means "I don't comprehend the meaning of that word;" and if I say "*Aval ataip porutpaduttavillai*," it means "She did not take it into cognizance/It did not matter to her."

Earlier I brought attention to the Tamil expression that denotes "the arrival of *ammai*," which complicates the theoretical paradigm of "possession;" yet, this expression still suggests an agent. However, the corporeal manifestation of the deity, suggested by emic references such as this, are complicated by another commonly used expression, "*ammai varttirukku*," which suggests

---

31 (Ibid., p. 10).

32 For a more detailed discussion on this topic see (Srinivasan 2009, p. 402).

33 (Butler 1993, p. 13; Srinivasan 2009, pp. 14–19). Due to brevity of space, I cannot provide my entire discussion on this subject in this article.

34 *Schema* means "form, shape, figure, appearance, dress, gesture, figure of a syllogism and grammatical form." See (Butler 1993, p. 33). Butler notes that Aristotle did not make any "phenomenal distinction between materiality and intelligibility," and the entire phrase "the shape given by the stamp" is rendered in Greek by a single word—*schema*. As the *schema* has been implicated with the matter through which it "actualizes," the indissolubility, between *schema* and matter, implies that "[matter] only appears under a certain grammatical form," or under a *schema*, which she further explicates as a "principle of intelligibility." See (Butler 1993, p. 33).

35 (Butler 1993, pp. 30–32).

36 Analogous to the Western (Greek) philosophical tradition, the "indissolubility of materialization and signification" does not appear to be an "easy matter" in Tamil epistemological tradition either. I have pointed out this elsewhere drawing upon the Tamil text *Tolkappiyam*. See (Srinivasan 2009, pp. 16–17).

an occurrence without attributing any agency. This particular expression implies a conception of "schema," in its articulating pox-affliction. The verb "*varttal*" means "casting/spreading in a mold." The act of "casting/spreading in the mold" with poxes, as the phrase indicates, configures the afflicted body as a "morphological possibility" with an inalienable shape or "schema." To put it succinctly, the "presence" of the goddess, perceived as poxes, operates as the "principle of intelligibility" during pox-affliction, and, with this coding principle, the afflicted body simultaneously materializes and is made sense of through discursive practices in the Tamil culture.[37]

In the event of pox-affliction, the goddess is not simply perceived corporeally, but she is accorded a sovereign status and is regarded as a super-human force who can cause and heal the affliction. One reference that categorically asserts the goddess's authority over the body during the affliction of poxes is "*muttirai*." We come across the term "*muttirai*" in Mariyamman songs and narratives, which confirms that the pustules of poxes are perceived to be the sovereign seal of the goddess.[38] Expectedly, the religious experience, underscoring the immanent and eminent "presence" of the deity, is attuned to the predominant conception of the divine in the Tamil milieu. The Tamil term "*kadavul*" for "god/goddess" indicates the sense of both immanence and transcendence. Ki. Va. Jakannatan, for instance, writes: "God (*andavan*) is called *kadavul* in Tamil. It indicates his two traits. He transcends all matter (*ellap porulaiyum kadantu*). He is inside every matter (*ellap porulkalin ullum*)."[39] As we shall see in the next section, the "presence" of the divine feminine in these two modes are in fact constituted through specific discourses that emerge from temple festival practices, pox-afflicted homes, songs and healer's narratives.

3. Sprouts of the Body, Sprouts of the Field

The discourses of Mariyamman worship are vividly marked with a couple of common iconic relationships. By "iconic relationships," I mean imagistic correlations of a "figurative kind" that eventually circulate as meaningful understandings of the afflicted body in the socio-cultural milieu.[40] I invoke iconicity here because icons, by virtue of their likeness or resemblance to what they stand for, contribute to an immediacy of perception. Moreover, forging the relationship between different domains of experience in terms of likeness allows for poetic imagination to come into play. The first iconic relationship is the one shared between a pox-afflicted body and an agricultural field, and the other one is shared between an afflicted body and an anthill.[41] The former, which I shall explicate in this article, opens up a way to understand how the "presence" of a divine force, as both immanent and eminent, is produced, and how the benevolence of the force figures in this enterprise. I propose that with the pox-afflicted body being imagined on par with an agricultural field, figurative correlations between pustules, pulses and grains could be advanced. On the one hand, due to the dependence of the agricultural field on rain, and their relationship on a vertical plane, a sovereign force analogous to the rain comes to be established. On the other hand, with rain drops, also called "pearls" (*mazhaimuttu*) producing another equivalent set of similar "pearls" of grains and pulses, thereby manifesting plenitude of the field, a dwelling, corporeal "presence" in/as the afflicted body is also forged. A song that celebrates Muttumari (meaning both "The pearl Mari" and

37 As Butler observes concerning gender, materialization and signification of the body as the goddess is never a fool-proof and complete process. Like the ideal of the heterosexual gender, the goddess is an "ideal that no one can embody." See (Butler 1999, p. 176). One can certainly discern gaps and fissures in the process. This is a topic I think deserves some more research.

38 (Srinivasan 2009, pp. 34–36).

39 Jakannatan 1977, p. 84.

40 For an introductory discussion on Peircean iconic relationship of a "figurative kind," see (Reynolds 1995, p. 23).

41 In the proposition of the shared iconic field between the pox-afflicted body and the anthill, "a significant constitutive trait of the anthill, namely, the anthill being the home of serpents, is missing in the corresponding image of the pox-afflicted body, and consequently this missing part could have been supplied by creatively forging a dwelling presence within the body that manifests as pustules." For an analysis on the figurative association of a pox-afflicted body with an anthill, see (Srinivasan 2009, pp. 145–68).

"The rain of pearls"), a famous name of the goddess, makes these substantial connections, as we shall see. Moreover, since an agricultural field is conventionally identified with the feminine in the Tamil context, this conventional identification could have been a triggering condition for forging the "presence" as a female deity during pox-affliction.

I first thought about the common iconic field, involving the cultivated field, after I attended a performance called *mulappari*, meaning the "sprouting (tender) seedlings" or "sprouts" related to Mariyamman temple festivals in Aruppukkottai and Melur. Usually, the practice of growing and offering "sprouts" takes place as part of Mariyamman temple festivals throughout Tamilnadu, even though it is more popular in the temples in southern Tamilnadu, for instance, in the districts of Madurai, Virudunagar and Dindigul.[42] In these districts, *mulappari* is a common name for sprouts, whereas, in central and north Tamilnadu, growing sprouts is typically indicated by the names *palikai* and *navadhanya*.[43]

The practice of *mulappari* consists of planting grains or pulses in pots filled with natural fertilizer, twigs of margosa, straw, sheaths of millet and maize, and soil/earth.[44] The sprouts are grown, watered and taken care of, and after seven or nine days, the seedlings are cast into water. The event of casting away is called "*malaiyerutal*" meaning "sending off" the goddess. It is significant to note that this term is also used for the first ceremonial bath that a pox-afflicted person takes after the pustules "descend" from the body. During the period of growing *mulappari*, women perform dances called *kummi* (a dance performed with sticks in their hands or with simple clapping) and *vazhttu* (songs of benediction interspersed with ullulating [*kulavai*] sounds) going around these groups of pots with sprouts. The dances are performed either daily or on alternate days. On the last day, sprouts are taken out in a procession to the nearby Mariyamman temple, and then they are dispersed in the water resources such as tanks or rivers.

In the songs of *kummi* and *vazhttu*, the sprouts are addressed both as poxes and the goddess Mariyamman. In Tirupuvanam near Madurai, two elderly women singers Minakshi and Kaliyammal compared *mulappari* performance with pox-affliction, because, they said, "sowing" takes place in both these occasions. In Melur, I heard a female singer Dhanabhaghyam singing a *kummi* song, which reinforced the idea of poxes as sprouting seeds:

> Like the green grams, she [Mariyamman] spreads throughout the body
> Like the flat grams, she swells throughout the body

---

42 Kannan, the priest at the Aruppukkottai Mariyamman temple, observed:

> The *mulappari* ceremony in Mariyamman temples becomes more significant as one travels from Pudukkottai to areas south to it, like Kamudi, Madurai, Aruppukkottai, Virudunagar and Tirunelveli.

Although the performance of carrying the decorated pots to water resources is spectacular since they are taken out in a huge procession of hundreds in Mariyamman temples located in Tamilnadu in southern Tamilnadu (like in Madurai, Melur, Aruppukkottai, Virudunagar, Nilakkottai, Andippatti, Kamudi, Tirupuvanam, etc.), the ceremony of sprouts appears to be existent in northern, north-western and central areas of the state too. I have seen a small number of pots of *mulappari* grown at the houses of individuals and being carried in procession in Chennai (Mogappair) and in Salem (Annatanappatti, Johnsonpet and Gugai).

43 See (Hiltebeitel 1991, p. 54). Hiltebeitel describes these terms in his discussion on sprouting ceremonies associated with the Draupadi cult in the north-central parts of Tamilnadu:

> The little rite before us is known under many names, the most typical for Tamilnadu being *navadhanya* (Tamil *navataniyam*), "nine grains;" *ankurarpana*; "the casting or offering of sprouts" (Sanskrit); *mulappari*, apparently referring to the tender seedlings; *palikai*, the "little pots" in which the *navadhanya* is sown, a term that can also mean "young damsel" (Tamil lexicon) ...

44 In Melur and Kamudi, black bean (*moccai*) is preferred for growing the "sprouts" for the goddess. In Nilakkottai too, two or three varieties of pulses (such as *karamani*, *tattaippayiru* and *moccai*) are grown. Usually, "sprouts" are grown in large groups of pots in the premises of Mariyamman temples (for instance, in Melur and Aruppukkottai Mariyamman temples), but sometimes they are raised in a place common to the community. It is also common for pots from various houses to be kept in a particular house, which plays a lead role in the performance of "sprouts." In Nilakkottai, I visited one such house.

Another *kummi* song, sung a female singer called Bhaghyam, opened with addressing Mariyamman as poxes. The song asked the goddess to "descend" from the body part by part (for instance, head, neck, and shoulder etc.), and then described the *mulappari* performance.[45]

The connection between *ammai* and *mulappari* was also brought out by the healer Muthukkannu, who observed that the different varieties of *ammai* are akin to different modern rice varieties, such as IR 8 and IR 20 (modern yielding rice varieties) growing on the body. The habitual practices followed during pox-affliction and during *mulappari* are also strikingly similar. The sprouts are grown inside a closed space like a room and mostly in the dark, and entry to the room is strictly restricted. This restriction is similar to the restriction on allowing visitors in a pox-afflicted household. Further, the seedlings are grown for seven or nine days, a period that could be compared with the period of pox-affliction in the body.

Dhanabhagyam also told me that to grow *mulappari* the heart-mind should be clean (*manaccuttam*): "The sprouts should grow even and green. They should not rot in the pot, nor should the seedlings shrink. Only a pure/clean heart makes the sprouts grow well." When I asked her about sexual relationship at home during their growth, she said:

> That is what I meant by the pure heart-mind. One should follow all that is followed during *ammai*. Like, the house should be wiped with water every day; no clothes should go out of the house; especially, one should not visit the house which is polluted with death or the house where the puberty ceremony of a girl is performed. It is better to avoid going to weddings too. The food should not be seasoned, nor pulses be fried or cooked with *kuzambu* (a side dish for rice). No fire should be lent, nor can it be borrowed.

One can recall that all these practices are adhered to during pox-affliction too, and they reinforce the resemblances between poxes and the sprouts. During my fieldwork (2006), Kaliyammal, a *mulappari* singer in Tirupuvanam, also gave me an account of these practices ending her narration with the statement: "*Ammai* and *mulappari* are similar (*ore matiri*)."

The above discussion allows us to infer that the sprouts growing in the earthen pots and pox pustules manifesting in the landscape of the body form a field of iconicity. The sprouts grown in the earthen pots are transposable into a larger scenario of an agricultural field cultivated with crops. The mutual correlations of a pox-afflicted body and a cultivated agricultural field formulate an ontological realm, which contributes to the forging of the "presence" of the divine, as I try to pinpoint in the forthcoming paragraphs.

4. Poxes as the Shower of Grace

A significant element pertaining to fields and cultivation is more relevant to grasping the conditions of establishment of a sovereign deity, who is in charge of pox-affliction. The celestial rain is necessary to make the grains grow and bring forth a cultivated field; and correspondingly, in considering the crops of poxes on the landscape of the body, one can speculate that a force from above has been imagined as being on par with the rain. It cannot be a mere coincidence that the term *Mari*, the proper name of our goddess, is also the term for rain and clouds in Tamil. The term "*Mari*" meaning rain appears quite frequently in classical Tamil literature, especially in classical anthologies, such as *Narrinai* and *Kuruntokai* (c. 100 B.C–A.D. 250).[46] And the term "*Mari*" does not refer to disease in these classical texts. In contemporary Tamil as well, the term denotes rain: for instance, one can consider the Tamil expression: "There should be three rains (*mummari*) in a month." A song from the

---

[45] I have discussed this term before. One can notice the term "descend" is used only for healing or making the poxes "roll down" the body, which may take place inside the body as well.

[46] The term 'Mari,' meaning rain and clouds, appears in *Narrinai* and *Kuruntokai*. See (*Narrinai*, verses 141, 190, 192, 244, 253, 265, 312, 314, 334, 379, 381) and (*Kuruntokai*, verses 66, 91, 94, 98, 117, 161, 168, 200, 222, 251, 259, 289, 319). Although the twentieth century Tamil lexicon gives other meanings of the term "*Mari*" such as death and *ammai*, it is worth noting that "*Mari*" does not have these negative significations in the earlier classical anthologies.

Tamil film *Uzhavan* (1993) begins with the line, "Won't *mari*-rain (*mari-mazhai*) pour to end the famine of the people?" This suggests that the figurative resemblances between the body with poxes and the agricultural field could have played a seminal role in the naming of the deity as "Mari." It is possible that a phantasmatic celestial force, involving in the manifestation of poxes, is conceived analogous to the celestial rain, which is instrumental in bringing forth the cultivated field, and consequently, the name "Mari" came to be shared by the rain and the deity. The identification with rain also explains how the deity is perceived as benevolent in bestowing poxes.

A song that I heard from Rajamma, a healer of *ammai* from Nattam near Dindigul in the year 2006, equates the goddess with rain: "If you say Mari, the rains would flow; If you say Devi, honey would flow." In a palm-leaf manuscript version of the *Talattu*, the description of the goddess Muttumari ("Pearl Mari") "playing virulently" conflates the images of the pouring rain and the shower of poxes on the body, thereby bringing the goddess's benevolence to the foreground:

> Has she arrived here playfully with a poor pretext
> For dwelling in me, considering me as poor? . . .
> Is she the wealth of rain hiding the sun? . . .
> Has she arrived to play virulently?
> Is she the relentless Pearl Mari, who, for the red rice to grow
> Roared as thunder with lightning and showered as rains from the clouds?
> With the sky becoming dark and the sunlight fading
> Has she stood blessing the flow of rain (Mari)?[47]

The pearls of rain embrace the earth producing another set of pearls like grains, pulses, and pearls of other crops that bud forth. An excerpt from this text further addresses her as all these pearls:

> Is she the mother pearl, pearls of rain, pearls of *ammai*, or of sugarcane?
> Is she pearls of bamboo, or of red paddy, or the playful Marimuttu?[48]

While as pearls of rain, Muttumari metonymically stands for and ensures earthly plenitude, as the sprouting pearls of the earth, she is the embodiment of plenitude. As the sprouting seeds of crops, Muttumari constitutes the cycle of birth of crops, their growth, harvest and re-entry into the earth through sowing; and as rain, she ensures that the seeds grow. Inasmuch as pearls of poxes are located on par with other types of pearls of crops, the pearls of poxes that sprout on the body correspond with these earthly seeds and are considered as plenitude and prosperity. At the same time, since the description of the goddess "playing virulently" comes along with the description of Mariyamman as the rain, the pearls of poxes replicate and correspond with the celestial rain pearls, ensuring such plenitude and prosperity.

Further, as the deity of poxes is conceived on par with rain, the traits of rain, namely generosity and impartiality, often praised and celebrated in Tamil classical texts like *Tirukkural*, *Narrinai*, and *Kuruntokai*, mark the nature of the deity too. The goddess's throwing pearls of poxes at will and in all directions devoid of bias is a narrative pattern that one comes across in songs. For instance, "The Story of Sri Mariyamman" celebrates the goddess's taking measures of various sizes used to weigh grains and throwing pearls on people in all directions without bias.[49] The generosity and impartiality of the goddess, derived primarily from the image of the rain, is extended to her justly distributing earthly plenitude. Consider, for instance, a song of benediction rendered by a woman called Lakshmi from Aruppukkottai on *mulappari*:

---

47 (D 1747, lines 93–104).
48 (Ibid., lines 71–72). I have taken some liberty in this translation: at one place I have translated "Marimuttu" as the pearls of rain and another place I simply retain it as her proper name since both translations are relevant.
49 This song (n.d.) has been published as a chapbook by a woman's group in Aruppukkottai.

The rain pours in the north, the water flows along the fields
The ducks swim across the waterways
The crane flies, the rice is being sown
Since the low caste Pallars who have sown the rice go hungry,
The Ati Para Eswari (the primordial goddess) opens the granary
And comes to bestow the grains in measures of *padis*
Make, Make the ullulating sound of the ornament of golden gems.

The concern of the goddess for the hungry have-nots, here, the laborers of the land who are alienated from their labor, which makes her bestow the rice grains on them, is transposed into her grace and protection during the affliction. Similarly, in *Mariyamman Patam*, poxes are represented as an ornament of pearls that embraces the body and "protects" one in the face of "differences" encountered in the world:

Like an ornament of pearls, Mother
You have embraced me so that you can protect me
From differences . . . .[50]

Perhaps this is because in this world of rich and poor, the pearls of poxes show no prejudice and ensure a possibility that they could arrive upon anyone erasing all differences. The *Talattu* explains this idea better when it articulates that the goddess has taken all the pearls of the world in order to divide them [among people] equally without any bias or prejudice.[51] The text further praises her as the one who "lavishes a boon of flowing pearls even upon those who have none by their side, asking them to fear not."[52]

In the above passages, based on ethnographic materials and literary evidences, I have suggested the ways through which Mariyamman is simultaneously constituted as a corporeal "presence" as well as an autonomous force determining the fate of human beings during pox-affliction. The plenitude ensured by the rain seems to have been transformed into the benevolent attribute of the deity. A temple legend, gathered from Tiruverkadu on Karumari, confirms the association of the goddess with rain. While silent on the subject of poxes, the temple legend establishes the goddess as a sovereign deity pertaining to a sacred place (*sthalam*) through reworking the equivalence between her compassion and the benevolence of rain. In the name "Karumari," the adjective "*karu*" denotes "black/dark," and "*Mari*," as already stated, denotes "rain," and metonymically "(rain) cloud." The story was narrated by Kuttiyappa Mudaliyar, whose forefathers participated in founding the temple of Karumari in Tiruverkadu:

Our family gave the land for the Tiruverkadu temple in 1937. Before that there were Harijans (Dalits) who were fortune-tellers (*kuri solpavarkal*, meaning diviners) at this place. They used to give life sacrifices such as goats to the goddess Karumari. As my father and other neighbors were opposed to that practice, they left for another place called Perumalagaram, and from there, they continued with their fortune-telling. It so happened that my father at one point went to get his fortune told by them. The goddess said [through the fortune-tellers]: "You deprived me of my home. If you find a place as home for me, then I will save you for seven generations." On hearing that, we gave away the land, and she has kept us happy. . . . Karumari means *karumukil* (the dark cloud). She bestows compassion upon us like the rain that protects the world.

---

50 (D 1750, lines 17–20).
51 (D 1747, lines 21–22).
52 (Ibid., lines 23–24).

5. Conclusion: The Deity of Poxes as Female Power

The above discussions have mapped how the super-human, autonomous force or deity presiding over poxes and manifesting as poxes could have been imagined, but the constitutive conditions of the deity's gender have not been hitherto explored. In the classical Tamil texts we do not encounter a decisive identification of rain with any particular gender.[53] However, the figure of the agricultural field itself offers help with this enterprise. It is important to note that both uncultivated land and cultivated agricultural field are articulated as female in Tamil literary sources. For instance, expressions, such as "*nilamennum nallal*" meaning "the good woman called land/field" or "*nilam pulantillal*" meaning "the housewife that is the field of land/field" appear in the second century didactical text *Tirukkural*.[54] One can also see the explicit sexual suggestion linking a woman with the agricultural field, which is ready for cultivation in the text *Kuruntokai*.[55] Since the agricultural field and the pox-afflicted body coexist in the same ontological realm, such sharing could have paved the way for identifying the landscape of the body, sprouting crops of poxes, with the feminine. With the pox-afflicted body being identified with the feminine, this gender identity could have been attributed to the dwelling "presence" of the force forged in the afflicted body. Inasmuch as this "presence" is simultaneously perceived analogous to the rain or "*mari*" from above, the autonomous and sovereign force could be constituted as the female deity Mari.

In the Tamil milieu, the religious experience of pox-affliction, as foregrounded in songs, narratives, and temple festival and healing practices, is predicated on invoking the goddess in her manifestations as pox-afflicted body and as a super-human power. At the same time, such experience is creatively invested with figurative expressions, including metaphors, metonymies and imagistic correlations, and complex multi-layered equivalences between terms, summoning a new kind of understanding while opening the doors necessary to accomplish it. Decoding the immanent and eminent manifestations of the goddess, in the course of emphasizing how the "presence" of the goddess is discursively forged in constructing these manifestations, is taking one step in that direction, which this essay endeavors to do.

Funding: This research was partly funded by a Junior Scholar Dissertation Research Fellowship by the American Institute of Indian Studies between 2005 and 2006.

Conflicts of Interest: The author declares no conflict of interest.

References

Primary Sources

Tamil

Manuscripts (Government Oriental Manuscripts Library, Chennai)

Mariyamman Talattu. n.d. D1747.

Mariyamman Peril Patam. n.d. D1750.

Mariyamman Varnippu. n.d. D 2164.

Texts

Jakannathan, Ki. Va. 1977. *Tamil Nul Arimukam*. Chennai: Amuta Nilaiyam.

Kuruntokai. Text and commentary. 1985. Ed. Mu. Canmukam Pillai. Thanjavur: Tamil University.

Mariyamman Talattu. N.d. Erode: Mathi Books.

Narrinai. Text and commentary. 1966-68. Com. Avvai Cu Turaicamippillai. Chennai: Aruna Publications.

---

53 In classical literary texts, we find references to rain in connection with both sexes. For instance, the generosity of a male patron is compared to the generous rain. See (*Purananuru*, verse 142). In *Kuruntokai*, the cool eyes of the heroine are described as "*mazaikkan*" or "rainy eye." See (*Kuruntokai*, verses 72, 86, 222, 259, 286, 329).

54 See (*Tirukkural*, Chapter "Plough," verses 1040 and 1039).

55 See (verse 131).

Purananuru. 1967–72. Text and commentary. Com. Avvai Cu Turaicamippillai. Tirunelveli: Tennintiya Caiva Cittanta Nurpatippuk Kalakam.

Srimuttumariyamman Mulappari Kummippadalkal. N.d. Aruppukkottai: Ekadasi Women's Group.

Tiruvalluvar. *Tirukkural*. Text and commentary. 2000. Com. Manakkutavar. Edited by T. Racagopalan. Chennai: Aintinaippatippakam.

Secondary Sources

Arnold, David. 1993. *Colonizing the Body: State Medicine and Epidemic Disease in Nineteenth-Century India*. Delhi: Oxford University Press.

Bellamy, Carla. 2008. Person in Place: Possession and Power at an Indian Islamic Saint Shrine. *Journal of Feminist Studies in Religion* 24: 31–44. [CrossRef]

Bloomer, Kristin. 2018. *Possessed by the Virgin: Hinduism, Roman Catholicism, and Marian Possession in South India*. New York: Oxford University Press.

Butler, Judith. 1993. *Bodies that Matter: On the Discursive Limits of "Sex."*. New York: Routledge.

Butler, Judith. 1999. *Gender Trouble: Feminism and the Subversion of Identity*. New York: Routledge.

Caldwell, Robert. 1887. On Demonology in Southern India. *The Journal of the Anthropological Society of Bombay* 1: 91–105.

Dubianski, Alexander M. 2000. *Ritual and Mythological Sources of the Early Tamil Poetry*. Groningen: Egbert Forsten.

Egnor, Margaret Trawick. 1984. The Changed Mother or What the Smallpox Goddess Did When There was No More Smallpox. *Contributions to Asian Studies* XVIII: 24–45.

Erndl, Kathleen M. 1993. *Victory to the Mother: The Hindu Goddess of Northwest India in Myth, Ritual, and Symbol*. New York: Oxford University Press.

Foucault, Michel. 1972. *The Archaeology of Knowledge and the Discourse on Language*. Translated by A. M. Sheridan Smith. New York: Pantheon Books.

Foucault, Michel. 1985. *The Use of Pleasure*. Translated by Robert Hurley. New York: Vintage Books.

Foucault, Michel. 1991. *Remarks on Marx: Conversations with Duccio Trombadori*. Translated by R. James Goldstein, and James Cascaito. New York: Semiotext(e).

Foulston, Lynn. 2002. *At the Feet of the Goddess: The Divine Feminine in Local Hindu Religion*. Portland: Sussex Academic Press.

Hancock, Mary Elizabeth. 1995. Dilemmas of Domesticity. In *From the Margins of Hindu Marriage*. Edited by Lindsey Harlan and Paul B. Courtright. New York: Oxford University Press, pp. 60–91.

Hancock, Mary Elizabeth. 1999. *Womanhood in the Making: Domestic Ritual and Public Culture in Urban South India*. Colorado: Westview Press.

Harman, William. 2011. Possession as Protection and Affliction: The Goddess Mariyamman's Fierce Grace. In *Health and Religious Rituals in South Asia: Disease, Possession and Healing*. Edited by Fabrizio M. Ferrari. New York: Routledge, pp. 185–98.

Hiltebeitel, Alf. 1991. *The Cult of Draupadi: On Hindu Ritual and the Goddess*. Chicago: University of Chicago Press, vol. 2.

Marriott, McKim, and Ronald B. Inden. 1977. Toward an Ethnosociology of South Asian Caste Systems. In *The New Wind: Changing Identities in South Asia*. Edited by Kenneth David. The Hague: Mouton Publishers, pp. 227–38.

McDaniel, June. 2009. Religious Experience in Hindu Tradition. *Religion Compass* 3: 99–115. [CrossRef]

Nabokov, Isabelle. 2000. *Religion against the Self: An Ethnography of Tamil Rituals*. New York: Oxford University Press.

Reynolds, Dee. 1995. *Symbolist Aesthetics and Early Abstract Art: Sites of Imaginary Space*. Cambridge and New York: Cambridge University Press.

Shuttleton, David E. 2007. *Smallpox and the Literary Imagination, 1660–1820*. Cambridge and New York: Cambridge University Press.

Smith, Frederick M. 2006. *The Self Possessed: Deity and Spirit Possession in South Asian Literature and Civilization*. New York: Columbia University Press.

Smith, Frederick M. 2011. Possession in Theory and Practice: Historical and Contemporary Models. In *Health and Religious Rituals in South Asia: Disease, Possession and Healing*. Edited by Fabrizio M. Ferrari. New York: Routledge, pp. 3–16.

Srinivasan, Perundevi. 2009. Stories of the Flesh: Colonial and Anthropological Discourses on the South Indian Goddess Mariyamman. Ph.D dissertation, The George Washington University, Washington, DC, USA.

Wadley, Susan S. 1980. Sitala: The Cool One. *Asian Folklore Studies* 39: 33–62. [CrossRef]

religions

MDPI

Article

Shankh-er Shongshar, Afterlife Everyday: Religious Experience of the Evening Conch and Goddesses in Bengali Hindu Homes

Sukanya Sarbadhikary

Sociology, Presidency University, Kolkata 700073, India; sarbadhikary@gmail.com

Received: 20 December 2018; Accepted: 13 January 2019; Published: 15 January 2019

Abstract: This essay brings together critical archetypes of Bengali Hindu home-experience: the sound of the evening shankh (conch), the goddess Lakshmi, and the female snake-deity, Manasa. It analyzes the everyday phenomenology of the home, not simply through the European category of the 'domestic', but conceptually more elastic vernacular religious discourse of shongshar, which means both home and world. The conch is studied as a direct material embodiment of the sacred domestic. Its materiality and sound-ontology evoke a religious experience fused with this-worldly wellbeing (mongol) and afterlife stillness. Further, (contrary) worship ontologies of Lakshmi, the life-goddess of mongol, and Manasa, the death-and-resuscitation goddess, are discussed, and the twists of these ambivalent imaginings are shown to be engraved in the conch's body and audition. Bringing goddesses and conch-aesthetics together, shongshar is thus presented as a religious everyday dwelling, where the 'home' and 'world' are connected through spiraling experiences of life, death, and resuscitation. Problematizing the monolithic idea of the secular home as a protecting domain from the outside world, I argue that everyday religious experience of the Bengali domestic, as especially encountered and narrated by female householders, essentially includes both Lakshmi/life/fertility and Manasa/death/renunciation. Exploring the analogy of the spirals of shankh and shongshar, spatial and temporal experiences of the sacred domestic are also complicated. Based on ritual texts, fieldwork among Lakshmi and Manasa worshippers, conch-collectors, craftsmen and specialists, and immersion in the everyday religious world, I foreground a new aesthetic phenomenology at the interface of the metaphysics of sound, moralities of goddess-devotions, and the Bengali home's experience of afterlife everyday.

Keywords: Bengali home; sacred domesticity; shankh; conch; Lakshmi; Manasa; shongshar

1. Introduction

Samsara is an enigmatic term. Pronounced as *shongshar* in Bengali, it refers to the general metaphysical cycle of life-as-such, including abstract and cosmic space-time, life as handed down through generations, as well as one's immediate domestic existence.[1] So *shongshar* is not only an ontological given: it is critically enacted upon, understood, intended, and managed. So the most obvious use of the Bengali term is *shongshar kora*, or "doing *shongshar*". In this, the *shongshari* person, literally, the householder, controls a slice of abstract time and space, upon which she/he works and realizes the experience of *samsara*. This slice is the home. Thus, the home is the spatial counterpart of the temporal everyday. The home manifests with the world, not apart from it; dimensions of cosmic

[1] In the text I mostly use vernacular spellings as per pronunciation, such as, *shongshar*, Lokkhi (for the goddess Lakshmi), *mongol* (peace) etc.; and Sanskrit spellings like *samsara*, Lakshmi, *mangal* etc., when referring either to Sanskritic contexts or other people's writings. Also, I italicize *lokkhi*, when the term is used as an adjective to mean domesticated, rather than as a proper name.

space and time are folded upon this everyday home, such that the home is definitely not outside the cosmic world, but it also has an embodied independence, not fully assimilable in abstract conceptions. Thus, *shonghshar* supersedes boundaries of inside-outside, agency-existence, now and before-after.

This essay, based on in-depth ethnographic research, brings together three sacred archetypes of Bengali domestic religious experience, to reimagine the *shongshar* in ways that address continual cultural undertones. These three sacralities are: (contrary) goddess-universes of Lakshmi and Manasa, and the material object, *shankha* (pronounced as *shankh*), or conch-shell. The moment when these sacralities coalesce is dusk. Ubiquitous in all Bengali homes, irrespective of caste/class, is the daily ritual of *shondhe dewa* or performing evening rites. Women tie their hair, clean their homes, water their *tulsi* plants, perform a short *puja* in the *thakurghor* (literally, gods' room, referring to the household's sanctum), and then blow on the *shankh* three times in a long, relaxed manner. Blowing the conch primarily signifies the calling in and experience of domestic *mongol* (auspiciousness): peace, health, and fortune. Right at that liminal moment, when day is slipping into night, every Bengali household captures that short span of dusk in embodied discourse, which although shall pass, twirls through the conch's spiral folds, sounding it, and opening out into the night's expanse. The *shankh's* sound is heavy and long, yet always ends suddenly. It both reminds of the day gone, and the night's arrival. Riding precisely on this dyad of nostalgia as a reminder of dark death and invitation as a reminder of life, arrive two critical goddess figures of Bengal: Manasa and Lakshmi.

So sacred sound traveling through *shankh's* bends and apertures evokes an everyday sonic experience in which domestic space and time do not remain confined to the home's walls, but necessarily flow into an outside. Using the contours of the *shankh's* material imagination, this paper shall thus also problematize straightforward notions of interiority: of homes, women, and the nation, and argue that senses of 'inside' securities are equally vulnerable, and religious experiences also tell us other stories of expanse and magnitude. The experience of *mongol*, which is central to the discourse of Bengali households, has subtle overlaps with everyday objects like the conch and the imagination of goddesses. It addresses unobvious but entwined experiential aspects like life, death, and resuscitation.

So, understanding everyday life and ethics not simply through the European category of the 'domestic' (see Chakrabarty 1993, pp. 3–4), but vernacular discourse of *shongshar*, problematizes unequivocal notions of privacy, sanctity, and secured comforts of the home, afforded by postcolonial critique. *Shongshar* literally refers to both the home and the cosmic world, and suggests how the home also dissolves. The essay works with a folded artefact as an embodiment of *shongshar's* innermost sanctum, and analyzes its material life as a creasing of opposed ethical religious experiences: life and death, fertility and abandonment.

Shondhe dewa, all women I encountered during my fieldwork, agree, is an unspoken summon to Lakshmi (pronounced in Bengali as Lokkhi), the goddess of auspiciousness, peace, welfare, and life generally. It is requesting her to be resolutely seated in the altar/home and protecting it from the fear that is dark.[2] Yet dusk shall inevitably slither into night, and the conch-sound shall necessarily slip into an oceanic outside. And like the call of death, the sea is scarier in the evenings. Thus, our efforts (to cling to day/life) are only that, and there is also the pull towards the goddess of the dark.

So Bengali *shongshar* is equally respectful of Manasa—queen of a thousand snakes—the goddess of death. Evening is when humans don't see, and snakes are at a privilege ... they feel the touch of sundown and their hissing reign begins. Like the evening conch, the female snake-goddess is of typical Bengali specificity, distinct from the worship of male snake-gods and living snakes (Bhattacharya 1965, p. 1; Dimock and Ramanujan 1962, p. 312).[3] The coiling/uncoiling of the snakes is the twisting of the *shankh*, and thus so many Bengali snake names carry the conch prefix or

---

2 Lokkhi is imagined as a restless deity, threatening to leave, implying the always-vulnerable status of wealth and peace.

3 Associations of snakes with divine femininity began in the Mahabharata (Dimock and Ramanujan 1962, p. 313), but the serpentine goddess form is fully developed only in Bengal.

suffix: *Mahashankha, Shankhachur, Shankhanag, Shankhabora, Shankhapala* etc., and the famous puranic serpent-king is also named, Shankha.[4]

The Bengali domestic experience thus finds shelter under both Lokhhi's feet and the snake's hood. Every evening, through *shankh's* folds, the "intimate immensity" (see Bachelard 1994) of the Bengali *shongshar* invites both Lokkhi/Manasa, life/death, and reminisces the time past, and time to come. Children learn the early trick of listening to sea-waves by holding the conch to the ear. Indeed, in Hindu imaginings, the conch carries the primordial AUM sound, which, like the goddess Lakshmi and conch, emanated from the first churning of the ocean. The sea's vast equanimity and the buzzing AUM sound always remind of afterlife stillness, and that the sea shall eventually take away all belonging. Yet the conch remains seated in the kernel of the home, the quintessential domain of attachment and protection. So it is a material model of cozy interiority, whose folds also however twirl towards expanse. The conch and goddesses thus come together to define *shongshar's* religious experience fused with this-worldly wellbeing (*mongol*) and afterlife quiet.

This material allegory echoes in *shankha's* linguistic lifeworld. Its etymological breakup would be *sham* + *kha*. *Sham* implying *mongol* (goodness), and *kha* (void). So *shankha* would literally mean a 'good void', the hollow/emptiness which is a moral charter for domesticity. So, while the metonyms—home/kernel/kitchen/women/nation—are generally intrinsically associated with fullness, containment, and pure sufficiency, on the ideational basis that women are essentially tied subjects, fixed to their bodies, duties, and homes; the 'good void' idea however talks of a necessary aperture as well, like the snake's slit tongue. I try to sound the domestic through that split.

It may be objected that other gods and goddesses too are worshipped in Bengali domestic altars, and the choice of Lokkhi and Manasa may skew the analysis. However, there are critical rationales for the choice of these goddess stereotypes. A feminine modality of devotional aesthetics is the primary focus of this essay's arguments, and a stretched field of imagination where goddesses embody very opposed poles of mythic themes, is productively instrumental in unfolding such aesthetic nuances. Also for instance, while Lokkhi's consort Narayana is worshipped in these households, the goddess is much more popular, and considered especially proximate, compared to a more distant Narayana. So a significantly greater number of daily, weekly, and annual rituals, offerings, and prayers are assigned to her. Finally, there are a number of symbolic and experiential overlaps which bind the universes of gods and goddesses. Thus, Narayana himself holds the conch in one of his hands, snakes coil and adorn Shiva's neck, and Vishnu/Narayana rests on the famous serpent, Ananta. Thus, the field I explore in this article undoubtedly has many possible connections with other deity worship disciplines, but here I primarily explore the experiential extension of life and death, fertility and abandonment, woven in the conch-crafted Bengali domesticities of Lokkhi and Manasa.

The tied woman fits the Lakshmi stereotype. The *thakurghor*, which has not yet been fully explored in literature, is also a quintessential marker of interiority, peace, and health. But through imaginaries which include Lakshmi, but also Manasa, and the conch, I problematize the experience of fertility in Bengal, and ask, whether an openness to death/renunciation/freedom complicates questions of femininity, home, and the nation. Inner sanctums are also called *garbha griha*, literally, womb-room. This term is telling, since the room nests, while the womb also opens up (to give birth). The sacred conch-folds address this very experiential dyad of insideness and infinity.

In tracing the workings of the Bengali home's religious experience, I engage with ethnographic insights among conch-collectors and craftsmen of different traditional *shankh* sites, priests and devotees of Lakshmi and Manasa, and other ritual, textual and artifact material of Bengal. Although Manasa worship is definitely more popular among lower castes and classes of both west and east Bengalis, other classes of people still worship her (Bhattacharya 1965, p. 5). Lokkhi too is worshipped by people

---

4 There are many South Asian snake-conch stories, including how the North Indian snake god, Naga Devata, crept out of a sage's conch.

cross-caste/class. Lokkhi primarily represents qualities of restoration and health, and Manasa, of (cure from) disease, crisis, rupture, and disaster. At the outset it seems that Lokkhi and her model of domesticity are more relatable to all sections of society, for their mild, pure qualities. So even when a lower-caste/class household worships Manasa, she represents to them Lokkhi-like aspects. But while in her domesticated form Manasa is Lokkhi, her venomous passion also threatens the home.[5]

While the two goddesses share qualities, I argue that they primarily however represent opposite dimensions, which all different classes of people identify with. My ethnography suggests that in households which worship Lokkhi, narratives of family jointness, nuclearity, working women, housewives are all woven together through experiences of wellbeing and peace; while in those which worship Manasa, experiences of fear, death, and *niyoti* (fate) often dominate. Through such a class/caste entangled group, tied narratives of fertility, purity, death, and scare, and the conch's sound-world, I hope to intuit some common Bengali Hindu understandings of the experience of home/*shongshar*.

2. Entwined Everyday

The embroiling of the goddess of purity, goddess of poison, object-world of *shankh*, home, dusk, and the world, took effort to recognize. Connected vignettes of the Bengali everyday point to these entangled religious experiences.

Fertility is one such entangling meta-thematic. Married women wear red bordered saris, red paint (*alta*) on the feet, vermillion (*sindur*), white, red, and iron (*sh(n)akha*, *pola*, and *loha*) bangles, and for those who can afford, a lot of gold ornaments. Red is the color of fertile abundance, *sh(n)akha* made of conch-dust, a symbol of lush purity, iron, of (matrimonial) protection, and gold, of wealth. Such a woman is literally called Lokkhi, an everyday mortal embodiment of Vishnu's consort. The deity-couple, Vishnu-Lakshmi, is associated with *samsaric* preservation, symbolized also in Vishnu's conch, the *panchajanya*; and Lakshmi's *vahana* (mount), the owl, is also seated on a conch. The heavens and the mundane thus meet in the restorative home, in Lokkhi's fertile figure. Every home-altar has a *mongol-ghot*, a pot full of water, which signifies *shongshar's* fullness: bountiful grains in the kitchen and the Lokkhi wife's plentiful womb. Thursdays (and all full-moon nights) are considered auspicious for Lokkhi's worship, when her *panchali*, a ritual ode, is sung.

But the *ghot* is also Manasa's emblem. All through Bengal's rainy months (*Ashadh*, *Sravan*, *Bhadra*), the ultimate sign of tropical fertility, snakes thrive, and so does Manasa's worship. A staple shrine in rural Bengali homes is dedicated to her (the *sij* tree, which can cure poison). Bengal is most snake-infested, has innumerable references to them in songs, novels, myths, rhymes, and practices, and villagers, out of fear, do not even name the snake after sundown. Similarly, Manasa is a most popular deity, and folk narratives and scroll-paintings about her personality, feats, and worship are abundant (see R. Chatterjee 2000, pp. 9–12). Bengalis grow up with the idea that the Manasa Mangalkavya documents details of Manasa's life. Of these narratives, the most celebrated is the Manasa–Behula tryst.[6]

Manasa had an intensely sad life in the heavens. She was born of Shiva's sperm when he ejaculated imagining Parvati. She shares his sovereignty over all snakes and poison. Shiva's seed trickled to the underworld interstices on a lotus leaf, where snakes took care of it, and Manasa took form. Manasa thus embodies divine pleasures gone astray. She is beautiful, sexually irresistible, and manipulative on one hand, and kind-natured on the other. She is thus both insurmountable and believable to her devotees. She is never able to develop strong bonds of the home. Her step-mother, Shiva's wife, Chandi, is jealous of her and so she is deserted by her father. Her husband also leaves her on the wedding night. However, she has complete triumph over both life and death of Bengal's populations.

---

5 So I theorize beyond the educated middle classes that Chakrabarty (1993) and Sarkar (2001) were referring to in understandings of Bengali domesticity. Unless we involve different classes and faith-worlds of the Manasa/Lokkhi *pujas*, we cannot problematize monolithic understandings of the home or home–Lakshmi (Chakrabarty 1993). See also (Ganesh 1990).

6 For details of Manasa's story, see (Haq 2015). Scholars debate about relations among folk literature, Sanskrit *puranas*, and Mahabharata, in the tellings about Manasa (see Chatterji 2014, pp. 1–4; Clark 1955, pp. 511–12, 516; Doniger 2015, pp. 1–28).

Only, the Shiva-worshipper, merchant, Chand, refuses to worship her. She destroys all his ships and riches, kills his six sons, and then a seventh, Lakhindar.

Herein becomes important the figure of Behula, Lakhindar's wife, who through sheer dedication to her husband and Manasa, undertakes the most arduous journey with Lakhindar's dead body across riverine Bengal, travels to the heavens, prays to Manasa, and brings Lakhindar back to life. Behula, the perfect wife/devotee, forbearance, the journey across rivers, and resuscitation, have become most powerful archetypes of Bengali marital imagination. Lakhindar was bitten by *kalnagini*, the snake of time/death (*kal*). This death was foretold, and thus his father, Chand, had built an iron room for the new-wed couple. But by Manasa's orders, a small hole was made on a wall by the blacksmith, for *kalnagini* to enter. As a mythical enactment of empathy with Behula, Bengali wives traditionally stay up with their husbands on the first night of marriage, literally known as *kalratri*, or the possible night of death, and wear iron bangles, as signs of (Behula's) immortal marriage (see also Fruzzetti 1990, p. 157).

Evidently, ambivalences characterize these experiences. Behula is the reminder of Lokkhi's morality. However, Bengal has an equally powerful oppositional archetype, A-lokkhi, who is disorganized, unrestful, and a symbol of impending poverty, disease, disaster, and death. So, as Lakhindar's/Behula's enemy, Manasa symbolizes A-lokkhi. But Behula is her devotee, and it is Manasa's snakelike powers of regeneration again, which eventually bring Lakhindar to life. So Manasa is also worshipped by barren women to secure children, cure diseases, and return life. Even in her constant death-reminders, Manasa is also experienced as Lokkhi.

Thus, everyday beliefs, rituals, and objects of *shongshar* embody representations of Lokkhi/Manasa, day/night, life/death, and attachment/detachment. My informants recounted that Manasa's husband, the sage Jaratkaru, did not wish to marry, but had to, due to foretold fate. Thus, there was divine intervention in the form of *sandhya devi* (goddess of dusk), who appeared much earlier than usual one day. It is a ritual among auspicious/Lokkhi women to wake everyone before dusk to avoid *omongol/okolyan* (impurity), and thus Manasa woke him up. But *sandhyadevi* immediately vanished, the sun reappeared, Jaratkaru was angry, and deserted his A-lokkhi wife. So Manasa tried to be Lokkhi, but was fooled by the evening. She is thus forever enraged by the dusk, takes on her angriest avatar then, and ravishes in killings. She henceforth established her powers over the goddess of dusk, and the god of sleep/death, Yama, such that when snakes strike, they are silent (like sleep) and put others to sleep.

But this dreadful snake-goddess can return life, just as she can kill. She is the most dangerous combination of eros and poison. She maintains rights over her dead bodies, the snake-bitten corpses, who in Bengal, are not burned like ordinary Hindus, but floated in the river, in the hope that she may revive them. Manasa's husband deserts her, her sexual powers remain concentrated, and get activated in complete control over death and (re)birth. Unlike Lokkhi's/Behula's, her husband does not stay/return. Manasa can neither be imagined as an immaculate virgin, nor as domesticated. She stands alone (yet) as a sexualized being. The term used for her in *panchalis* and ritual texts, is *shoirindhri* (Dvija and Shastri n.d., p. 7). It carries connotations of living in another's home, and solitariness. All these goddess stories evoke powerful ideas about how Bengali women experience femininity and domesticity as both secured and vulnerable, sites of both fear and hope.

Dusk remains a critical time for both goddesses: one needs to be invited desperately to ward off the other's dangers. This is also the time to return home, the all-important abode of rest and regeneration. In Bengali imaginings, long flowing night-like black hair is a woman's adornment, but it is also the mark of unrestrained lust and death. So, *lokkhi* women tie their snakelike hair into buns before the evening ritual. But the conch's swirls remain mysterious.

Shankha is one of Vishnu's central symbols and a critical sacred object in the *puranas* and Mahabharata. Apart from its religious significance, and therapeutic usages in ayurveda and yoga, it is an insistent metaphor of fertile femininity through links with other water symbols like the snake. The most common kind of *shankh* kept in Bengali homes is Lokkhi *shankh*, the symbol of pure order. However, apart from ideas of Lokkhi's restorative conch, one of Manasa's eight major snakes is also *shankhanaga*, since Manasa too has powers over the coiled conch.

The sensory life of this artifact also tells a similar ambivalent tale about domestic religious experience. Visually, its inward coils remind of the invitation (*ahoban*) to Lokkhi to come home, while its outward-bound sound opens out to the dark expanse of the nighttime sea. This twirling of remembering and forgetting seats the depths of time in the conch-space; its concentricity weaves through a hopeful Lokkhi and feared Manasa.

Metonymic connections among the conch, snakes, and home are amply evident in South Asian discourse. The ancient text, Manasara Vastushastra, studies the science of architecture/inhabitation (*vastu*) of any construction: from a bird's nest to a palace. Following minute measurements and astrological principles, every aspect of the 'inside' is planned, including the deities'/Lakshmi's altar. Snakes are critical design thematics therein (P. K. Acharya 1942). *Naag chakras*, or coiled serpentine motifs, are also important in the 1969 *vastu* text, Vishvakarma Darpan (Sachdev 2005, p. 167). Similarly, during the *Sravan* month Manasa *puja*, alongside evening readings of Manasa tales before groups of women, a critical object of folk-art, *karandi*: model of a small house, is made, with drawings (*alipana*) of serpents on it. This is worshipped with the Manasa idol, and sometimes *in its place* (Bhattacharya 1965, p. 6). So the *karandi* is representative of the home/Manasa/snakes, which are metaphoric substitutes.

Snakes as guardians of homes and ancestral treasures (*vastu-shaap*) also feature in longstanding fables. The term 'vastu', generally glossed as house, is significant. Shulman (1978), in his analysis of a Tiruvarur anthill myth, talks about the anthill's relations with the nether world, snakes, and *vastu*. The anthill, or god's home, leads to the underworld of the dead and snakes. This anthill is also the site of the end of cosmic sacrifice. The term thus literally means remainder (of the sacrifice). So, if *shongshar's* everyday religious experience is a sacrifice to the divine altar, then what stays, the residue/habitat/resident is the home. The *vastu* is what remains, and also opens to the after-world: the lived *shongshar* of domesticity and the cosmic *samsara*.

Similar to the temporality of the conch-artifact, *vastu*, or remain, is thus also about a nostalgic past, which *remains* (in the architecture and experience of the home and mind). Snakes have been important metaphors of ancestry, antiquity, and primevalism (see Wake 1873); and it is thus in notions of both the spatial (home) and temporal (remain) depth that the idea of *shongshar* operates.

So I argue that in understandings of the Bengali domestic (religious) experience, we need to go beyond secular-historicist tropes of postcolonial literature (see Chakrabarty 1993). K. Chatterjee (2008) uses 18th century Mangalkavya narratives, including the *Manasa-mangal*, to argue that premodern cultures also had tangible imperatives in senses of history, or *itihasa*. So linear temporality here is being extended to the precolonial. But I argue that domestic experience, as especially understood through conch passages and goddess stories, offers its own senses of sacred time, which go beyond pre-/post-colonial paradigms. The conch-prism is an allegory: with its hole and swirls refracting light and sound to other spaces and times.

Everyday, afterall, is a temporal category. It exceeds; has a life beyond historicity. The goddess of death and Behula's riverine struggle with her are etched in the Bengali everyday domestic ethic. So "The Bengali past itself combines with death in the image of a dark depth from where the rivers, now constituting some kind of primeval past, send forth their primeval call. That call does not belong to the past. It comes from a future that at the same time is a return" (Chakrabarty 2004, p. 681). The conch's coils also speak about this sacred temporal experience.

3. Twists of the Conch, Folds of the Home

The conch is the material model of depth-aperture, interiority-expansion, hearth-vastness, and past-future dimensions. I argue that in the context of Bengali domestic religious experience, its sensory world embodies both fertility and renunciation, Lokkhi and Manasa.

The *kha* of *shankha* carries the subtlest message. Ananda K. Coomaraswamy explains that it is the direct metaphoric translation of empty space. It means cavity generally, and the nave of a wheel, in the Rig Veda (Coomaraswamy 1934, p. 487). Mathematically, it represents zero, with connotations of both fullness and void (ibid, p. 493). This zero is not an origin, but a potentiality: infinity of concentric movements (ibid, p. 490). In this, its cognate term is Ananta, end-less, which is also the *puranic* serpent (ibid, p. 491). *Kha* also correlates with *nabha/nabhi*, the navel (ibid, p. 487). This alludes to the potential/expansive spatiality of the human body, in its navel and heart-space (ibid, p. 490, 493). So the conch-opening (*kha*) signifies both corporeal and domestic fullness, and simultaneous emptiness; both plenum and void, security and openness. The experience of *shankh's* ontology is therefore distinct from the phenomenology of roundness, theorized by Gaston Bachelard (1994, pp. 232–41). The conch-vessel is not fully interior, but rather, spirals towards expanse.

Everyday experiences of the *shankh* narrate similar senses of body and space.

The lower caste Bengali community who collect conches from the sea, work as craftsmen on its surface, sell conches and conch-products, and play a critical role in marriages by putting on the white bangle made of conch-dust on women's wrists, are called *shankharis*.[7] A *shankhari* explained that only their caste can make the bride wear the conch-bangle since it is fragile and needs handling expertize. Thus, despite being a low-caste person the *shankhari* touches the bride irrespective of her caste, and as a mark of respect, in addition to giving him his remuneration, the bride touches his feet. In this, he said, their caste is higher than Brahmins. This marital symbol of Lokkhi, asserts folklore, was first put on Parvati by Shiva, disguised as a *shankhari* (Fruzzetti 1990, pp. 69–70). Similarly, the caste which makes iron bangles for married women, claim to be descendents of the blacksmith who made Behula-Lakhindar's marriage quarter (Fruzzetti 1990, p. 158). So all symbols of marital fortification are simultaneous symbols of Lokkhi/Manasa/conches.

Shankharis and conch-users relate to the *shankh's* anatomy through various ideas and practices concerning its interiors. Like the insides of the sea, conch-interiors are considered innately sacred, and devotees adorn their entire physical and spiritual selves and homes by using its internal parts: in *ayurveda*, sound yoga, astrology, and fertility rites. The *shankh's* sacrality is asserted by people in terms of debates on its depthful naturalness and ritual value. These ideas also connect the conch to the *vastu*: snakes/homes/women.

Through my work with *shankharis* I realized that there are three main uses of the conch: nutritional/ayurvedic, since conch dust is sold for treatment of stomach and skin diseases, fertility problems, and as fish food; in worship rituals; and in marriage rites. In ritual contexts, there are two main conch types: *jol-shankh*: ones which are used to store Ganga water and not sounded, and *badyo-shankh*: those with slit mouths for sounding. All three uses relate to the domestic experience of *mongol*: fertility, peace, longevity, and wellbeing. The *puranas* also talk about the links of conch with fame, wealth, life on one hand; and the primordial meditative calm embodied in Buddha's navel, on the other. Simply blowing on the conch is considered therapeutic, since it involves a sophisticated exercise of breath-control. Through the inhaling-exhaling rhythm experience, the mouth, breath-cavity, and body-interior become sonic extensions of the twirled conch.

It is popularly also believed that sounding the conch during floods or cyclones heal them. This is based on the South Asian homoeopathic logic that same cures same, as for snakes/Manasa, poison cures poison.

Notions of naturalness and originality are vital with respect to conches. All *shankharis* told me that an original *shankh* (and even the *sh(n)akha* which a woman wears) is never perfectly round, and every conch is distinct. Although craftsmen work on conch-surfaces and make designs, they assert that the *shankh* is a natural sacred object, and as humans, they are always less than the entity; they are subordinate to their 'creation'. They recraft it only minimally, so they don't tamper with its naturalness.

There are two significant worship conches. The *homochori Lakshmi shankh* is decorated with *sindur* and worshipped. It is the most common kind of *shankh*, and represents everything the goddess stands for. So *shankharis* explained that people buy them to "*keep Lokkhi at home*": to increase wealth, and fight

[7] I worked with *shankhari* communities in important centres of conch-work and sale in and around Kolkata: in Kalighat, Bagbazar, and Barrackpore.

a-shanti (unrest). In addition to rhetorics of wealth and peace, the rare conch variety, *Dakshina shankh* or *Narayanshankh*, with the right sided fold, is also worshipped for three days by people who want to get married, or have children. A *shankhari* said aptly, "It is of *shongshar's* use." 'Use' surely refers to the potent idea of fertility. Narayan Shankh is considered to be of greater sacred value than Lakshmi Shankh, and thus *shankharis*, to respect its naturalness, do not slit its mouth. So this *shankh* is not sounded, but only adorns domestic altars.

Given ideas of nature, fertility, and wealth, I asked *shankharis* what may be defined as a *shankh*. I received two distinct responses. One was that a *shankh* must be used in *puja*, and to make a woman's *sh(n)akha*. A *shankhari* said, "No expensive jewellery shall suffice, unless the *shankh* is sounded and the bride wears a *sh(n)akha*." In this explanation, only that which can be used for sanctifying the (fertile) home and woman is a *shankh*. Other conches, for instance, octopus-like ones which *shankharis* buy from the Andamans, or *batishankh*, *dishyashankh* etc., which are decorative and cannot be cut, are not considered sacred. In another opinion however, these too should be considered as *shankh*, since they are natural. In this view, the conch's sacrality rests with the object's naturalness, not ritual value.

These distinct representations stem however from similar experiences of conch-depth. Montagu also says about Central American conch-pottery craftsmen that they have persistent relations with conch-depths, canals, air-paths, and are "intoxicated by the exuberance of their own virtuosity" (Montagu 1981, p. 276). Bengali craftsmen's relations with conch-interiors begin with intuitions about how many folds there are inside it. The terms they use are *pyanch/g(n)it*, literally, coil/knot. Some say there are two-and-a-half folds, some three, some three-and-a-half. The *pyanch* is an interesting problem, since it can only be intuited: when intact, the inside is invisible, once opened up, the folds disappear. There are approximately three faint surface fold-lines, with which *shankharis* make sense of the inside. Correctness about the fold-number is not important. Rather, it is significant that there are senses of the intense inside, full of potential, which *shankharis* say, must be experienced fully in the home-interiors and women's bodies.

For instance, *shankharis* identify the conch's navel, *b(n)aj* or *shankh-nabhi*, a little flat portion, which is hung on children's bodies to treat stomach illnesses and ward off evil—similar to Manasa-fortified iron bangles. Children also wear conch-end pieces (*padak*) for six months after birth (Fruzzetti 1990, p. 157). In rural Bengal, the *d(n)arash* snake coils around cows' feet and sucks all their milk. Villagers say that cows cannot milk after that. So, another conch-portion, *chali*, is tied on cows' necks to ensure fertility. Here too, we find homoeopathic ideas of curing (snake)-poison with (conch-) poison. Another portion, *g(n)at*, is used to make amulets for people's *mongol*.

One may ask whether the *shankh* has sacred value because it has a useful depth, or it is put to use because it is naturally/ritually valuable. Either way, it is significant that its sacred depth is recognized, and reinteriorized (in body-homes) through notions of *mongol* experience. I argue however, that although *shankh's* obvious discursive connections are with Lokkhi, in the phenomenology of *shongshar*, it also carries other meanings.

Shankharis say that the conch's body is Vishnu's embodiment under the waters. When it is brought out from its habitat, it loses life, and emits a smell. A *shankhari* used a domestic metaphor and said, "When you break its home, it loses its power." But this home is not broken. Through establishing relations with its sacred interior, the dwelling is transposed from the sea-abode to other sacred spaces: the altar and the fertile body. In that, it reinvigorates their life-giving qualities. But when sounded every dusk, its interior echo spurts out of its shell, travels through every nook, corner and interstice of the home, and necessarily escapes into the outside. Its sonic universe approximates the profound oceanic gush (of depth, death, and renunciation), and the home opens out to the sea again. In bringing the *shankh* home, we bring nature into the domestic, but simultaneously remind ourselves (also) of nature's innate freedom as opposed to *shongshar's* bondage. So freedom's natural state dies when brought to the world, but the renunciate spirit, through the conch's primordial sound, still permeates *shongshar's* religious experience.

Montagu says that conch-acoustics is complex, and little studied (Montagu 1981, p. 274). Following logics of sensory sympathy, there is always phenomenological similitude between the perceiving organ and the perceived object. Likewise, one can posit an intrinsic relation among the ear, conch, and *shongshar.* Also, etymologically, *samsara/shongshar* refers to a circularity of being, but one which is not a perfect circle, and repeats with a difference. Like the conch, it is a spiral. The hearing part of the ear, the cochlea, or inner ear, is similarly shaped like a coil, and its Greek root literally means a spiral, snail shell. The cochlea is made of half-water, half-air; that is, it is half-full, half-empty. Air passing through it causes (sonic) waves in the water, and we can hear and maintain balance. This empty, *kha*, in the ear/conch, is thus essential for the generation of sound-experience. I argue that this empty also brings the conch/ear in sympathetic proximity with *shongshar*, the domestic experience. *Shongshar's* opening is constitutive of its everyday performance; essential to its experience of fullness and wellbeing is the simultaneous sense of relinquishment.

In a scientific reading, Shaw argues about wave-sounds that we hear in the conch: that they are produced by "successive reverberations of external sounds against the interior side of the conch" (Shaw 1875, p. 69). What we hear when we place the conch on the ear, itself coiled with air passage like the conch, is only an echo, a return. The sound returns from *shonghshar* to *shankh.* Rather than the conch itself holding the sound, if there is no 'noise' in *shongshar*, the conch will not sound. So, conch-layers are (like) folds of everyday life: only when there is life, is renunciation heard. Fullness and emptiness, order and excess, necessarily fulfill each other. By keeping the conch in the house, we do not invite renunciate possibilities; rather in hearing the sea in its shaded interiors, the householder experiences infinitude, resurrection, and genesis within domesticity.

There are thus contrary modes of phenomenological argument: that the conch's body manifests both fertility and renunciation (Lokkhi and Manasa), and the domestic is modeled after this materiality. Alternatively, the conch sounds the external world, or is a representation of its experiential possibilities. Either way, we reach an analytic of the domestic religious experience which twirls through a depthful closure of life, and possible aperture of escape.

Folds of the conch/home entail ideas of continuous regeneration, too. In this, links of conches, snakes and domesticity become significant again. In South Asian imagination, the snake's shedding off skin and gaining new life is typically symptomatic of its powers of immortality and healing. The snake can move as it wants to, curl, put off old age, regain youth, increase strength, and even, consume itself (Wake 1873, p. 380). So Shulman says, "... it is surely no accident that a serpent has come, as Adisesa, to embody the idea of the remainder ... The serpent emerges from his own aged skin; he is the remainder of himself, an equivalent of the dangerous, fiery, yet fertile and productive seed. The serpent is the *vastu*; it is, therefore, not surprising that the Vastupurusa becomes a Vastunaga" (Shulman 1978, p. 124).

In Bengal, poisonous snakes are burnt when they die, since otherwise it is believed that they can be reborn. However, *vastu-shaaps*, ones which live in homes, are never killed, since like Lokkhi's altar, they are considered as the domestic kernel. Killing them would destroy the home and all fertility. Equally powerful Bengali lores talk about dead snakes being exchanged for health and wealth; and snakes and goddesses appearing on the hearth to bless the household with unlimited grains. Like conch-dust which is used to treat illnesses, in Manasa *puja*, earthern snakes are made, which are kept at home even after the *puja*, since dried snake-earth is considered therapeutic (Bhattacharya 1965, pp. 5–6). Mating is the perfect regenerative sign, and in rural Bengal, snakes' mating-act is considered auspicious, and literally known as '*shankh laga*': joining of conches.

4. Lokkhi Pujo: Mongol and Rehabilitation

The goddess Lokkhi, and women who embody her qualities in the home, literally referred to as Lokkhi *meye* (the ideal girl) or *bou* (wife/bride), are responsible for *shongshar's mongol*: purity, health, and wellbeing (Fruzzetti 1990, p. 123). In this context, the term *lokkhichara* is a significant ethical charter, meaning without–Lokkhi, or abandoned by Lokkhi. The woman who does not embody the goddess's qualities *is lokkhichara*, and shall *be lokkhichara*, that is, without wealth/peace. So one has to be a certain way to attain a certain state; an ethical present determines a domestic/cosmic future.[8]

A critical way to understand the Lokkhi-domesticity experience and ethic is by reading *panchalis*.[9] *Panchalis* are "Pre-British folk literature" (Chakrabarty 1993, p. 8) describing the goddess's qualities, mantras, and efficacy of worship (see also Mohanty 2008, p. 6; Rhodes 2010, p. 8). These texts dedicated to all twelve months of her worship, are most popular devotional manuals in Bengali homes, and married women read them every Thursday, and on full moon evenings.

There are general guidelines for Lokkhi's worship. She is a collected deity, and dislikes restless bell-sounds; but *shankh-dhvani* (conch-echo) is indispensable, since it is the definitive *mongol* sign. The conch is specially worshipped during her *puja*, also as a symbol of Kuvera, the god of wealth (Paranavitana 1955, p. 125). After Lokkhi's *puja*, women take food-grains in their hands, and listen to the *panchalis' brotokotha* (worship-tales). Her idol is not immersed unlike other goddesses', since her leaving the home is considered inauspicious.

In the *panchali*, the Thursday *puja* experience is described as very clingy towards the goddess: requesting her to be *ochola* (resolutely seated in the home), not *nidoya* (heartless) or *chonchol* (restless), the devotee promising to serve her feet-shadow (*padachaya*), and linger around her. Lokkhi's invitation is not only to the home (*aloy*), but also other metonymic interior domains: the altar (*thakurghor*), worship pot (*ghot*), kitchen-grains (*dhan*), and devotee's heart (*hridoy*). Such an inward-looking narrative aims to ensure Lokkhi's *mongol* boons, her restiveness associated with the home's essential vulnerability. This is equally true for the rich. Thus, there are *panchali*-stories about proud traders losing their assets, and regaining them only after Lokkhi's worship. One cannot be indifferent (*obohela*) towards Lokkhi, and a lot of care is needed to *keep* her. This 'care' centrally defines the religious experience of *shongshar*.

Most *panchali* stories convey that Lokkhi reverses people's poverty and disharmony, the main causes of *dukkho* (unhappiness); and blesses with good marriage, wealth, and sons. Also, during marriages, every person (especially the woman) "becomes a deity" (Harman 1987, p. 171), and embodies the same qualities.[10] The domestic ethical universe is intriguing, such that, devotees may even be allowed selfishness and connivance, if for the sake of the home; and the goddess may even stand in for the homemaker. So (in a particular month's *panchali* story) when Lokkhi promises to take care of a woman's household during her absence, she decides to commit suicide, so that her home is blessed infinitely. In another, a woman is the goddess' embodiment, others are jealous of her, desert her in the forest, disaster falls upon the family's seven brothers, and she is eventually reinstated to bring back peace. Similarly, mothers and sons are blessed through peasantry, and the importance of bountiful grains is evident repeatedly, for instance, in the autumnal ritual of *khetro-broto* (field-rituals), and there are even narrative instances of grains transforming to gold.

Discursive relations with Manasa are also clear: in a story, Lokkhi drowns a proud man's seven ships (like Manasa), and later returns them. In the story of a dead snake restoring a king's health and a poor man's wealth, the sense is that death/disaster/Manasa can be tamed by Lokkhi's auspiciousness. In another tale, a poor woman, unable to feed her children, tries to cook a dead snake, which turns into Lokkhi on the pan. In the reverse mood, a popular belief is that unless correct rites are followed during Bengal's cooking festival (*ranna pujo*), when Manasa is worshipped, a snake appears on the pan (rather than the goddess), and that signifies the end of home-fertility.

My interactions with different classes of Bengali women revealed that these textual (*panchali*) thematics remain distilled in their religious experience of *shongshar*. Either through direct reading, or through the vibrant oral culture of listening to these *panchalis*, women are aware of the stories, and fashion and make sense of their lives, ethics, and experiences in terms of the narrative codes

---

8 For a succinct ethnographic analysis of constructions of feminine ethics and the making of women's virtuosity, which combine classical Hindu idioms with folk stories and rituals (*bratas*) in Bengal, see (McDaniel 2003).

9 See for instance, (A. Acharya n.d.; Basak n.d.; Chakrabarti n.d.).

10 Significantly, Manasa, did not have a successful marriage, and is considered essentially fearsome.

employed in these texts. So these ethical experiences help us appreciate how the home is primarily imagined as a site of building and nourishing different aspects of Lokkhi-*mongol*, which is also critically embodied by the conch.

4.1. Bose Family

The Bose household, an upper caste/class family, has been living in the same house for three generations. The house is 95 years old, with beautiful architecture, old furniture, ornaments, and well-accomplished members. Bankim Bose, a young barrister in the early 20th century, was cheated by his friend and family, shifted home, and built this one painstakingly. But his descendants give greater credit for wealth restoration, maintenance of the huge house, and management of human relations in it, to his wife. The couple had a difficult life with a cancer patient at home, and a schizophrenic daughter. Their narrative is of developing a Lokkhi-experience of the home in the first generation, a *lokkhichara* disposition of one of the daughters in the second, and restoration of the Lokkhi–full household experience in the third.

Bankim's wife, Kamala, was a living embodiment of the goddess. She had a "lot of Lokkhi-*sri*" (the goddess demeanour) and was the center of the household's *mongol*. She wore a sweet smile, was peaceful, soft-spoken, and humbly covered her head with her sari. She never spent too much and maintained careful accounts. She had few saris but maintained them so well that it always seemed that she wore new clothes. Similarly, she would carefully calculate the amount of vegetables, fish, etc., every day, and see that all 25 family members received proper food. On Thursdays she would do *Lokkhipuja* and read the *panchali*. One important altar-ingredient would be a rice-grain temple signifying the home itself.

Her daughter, Bimala, got married to a prosperous family who were moneylenders to the British. They owned a house with 66 rooms. She confessed however that unlike her mother she had no interest in homemaking; that both she and her husband were *lokkhichara*, maintained no accounts, lived lavishly, sold ornaments, and lost all wealth. Her husband died early, she was childless, and returned to one small room in her father's house. The rest of her life was about financial and social indignity.

The third generation reinstated home-Lokkhi. A daughter-in-law, Indira, performs the annual autumnal Lokkhi *puja*. Indira and her husband began life with limited money, and she was 'trained' by Kamala in the homemaking art. Indira says that punctuality, thriftiness, and justness were the important Lokkhi-traits she imbibed from Kamala, rather than "making lots of money." Chaudhuri argues similarly that although Lakshmi is the goddess of prosperity, what is really intended in her persona is "grace" and "ritual certainty" (Flibbertigibbet 1966). Through Kamala–Bimala–Indira, we find the rehabilitation of the religious experience of *mongol* in the Bose family.

4.2. Sulagna

Indira's friend, Sulagna, has a different experience of Lokkhi-ness. She was brought up in an upper caste joint family. They had a big *bh(n)arar ghor*: room where grain stocks were stored, and an idol of a golden Lokkhi. They used to perform the annual Lokkhi *puja* with aplomb. Alongside usual rituals, Lokkhi would be gifted a sari, which, after the *puja*, Sulagna's mother, as Lokkhi's direct household embodiment, would wear for a year. Sulagna and her husband are rich, and have a fancy house which she manages well. Sulagna, like a true Lokkhi *bou*, is a good cook, and completely committed to her household. She was therefore most upset when her husband decided to live with another woman. She left the house and "kept Lokkhi in her place". She said, "I told the goddess, take care of the household, and if I have been a good wife, bring me back to ... my home." Her "*being* Lokkhi" paid, and she returned in the goddess's place. So while the woman is the goddess' embodiment in the home, the goddess replaces her, if necessary, like in the *panchali* story. Bimala's *samsaric* experience of disharmony was financial, and Sulagna's, marital. The Lokkhi-experience is rehabilitated here as well, and like Behula returned with her husband, Sulagna returns to hers.

4.3. Malati

In the contemporary period, there is another narrative about the experience of the "modern Lokkhi." Malati, a relatively lower-class/caste woman, who is a yoga-instructor to Indira and Sulagna, also performs the Thursday *puja*. She had a poor and struggling early life. Like one of the *panchali* stories, she thinks one should be shrewd if for the sake of one's household, and filed and won court cases against her in-laws, to ensure that her husband gets a share of ancestral property. They have now built a small house in the city's outskirts, and Malati says it is the goddess who ensured that they live with self-respect.

Sulagna defines "being Lokkhi" as one who is able to *concentrate*. She is a school teacher, works very hard, and has limited time for *puja*. She says that unless she devotes fullest attention, she makes mistakes in both school and worship. She added that in modern times it is challenging to be the best homemaker, and feels anxious for instance, if she forgets the *panchali*. Hers is symbolic of the general working woman's anxiety about "forgetting the home," and always-possible disasters of "becoming A-lokkhi." Indira is also always "balancing" her schedule, and obsessive about *"remaining* Lokkhi." All these experiences generally point to the consistent desire to embody Lokkhi-ness in the home and the constant fear of domestic vulnerability.

Mohanty (2008) gives an evocative interpretation of the Oriya Lakshmi Purana as a modern text. In this vernacular appropriation, the text represents Lakshmi as every woman's goddess, irrespective of class/caste. She is a feminist who wins every woman's rights to the good home, mindful karma, and *shongshar dharma* (duty).

In distinction to the Lokkhi experience, a *lokkhichara* person, or A-lokkhi, is the disorderly, greedy, proud, disobedient woman (and her husband), who are responsible for poverty, decay, insubordination, absence/loss of children, and death. A-lokkhi is also an oppositional goddess-stereotype. Many women, including Malati, perform an A-lokkhi (*tarano) puja*, to get rid of A-Lokkhi on Kali *puja's* new moon night. An A-lokkhi idol is made of cow dung, kept either in the backyard or courtyard/verandah, worshipped, requested to leave the home, and the homemaker returns without looking back at her. Doniger similarly says about snakes, that they are invoked, and simultaneously requested to leave without harming (Doniger 2015, p. 3). In other instances, A-lokkhi is worshipped with the left hand, and swept with a broom, both the left hand and broom considered inauspicious (Fruzzetti and Ostor 1984, p. 243). In Manasa's story too, the defeated merchant, Chand, worshipped Manasa eventually, but with his left hand. The links of A-lokkhi and Manasa are thus clear again through symbolisms of the snake and inauspiciousness.

Lokkhi—A-lokkhi *pujas* together define the spectrum of *shongshar's* religious experience. *Mongol* (sanctity and health) is invited home, and disorder, ritually forsaken.

Dipesh Chakrabarty argues that the imagination of the ideal modern domestic woman (*grihalakshmi*) took shape with reference to the discourse of Lakshmi—A-lakshmi. Lakshmi was a suitable model of the colonial woman/home, her orderliness perfecting the disciplined modern temper. Chakrabarty also says, "However she originated, Alakshmi came to embody a gendered conception of inauspiciousness and the opposite of all that the Hindu law-givers upheld as the *dharma* ... " (Chakrabarty 1993, pp. 7–8). While Chakrabarty gives a nuanced analysis of the modern private compared to relatively simpler postcolonial understandings, he displays a distinct ambivalence with regard to the question of time.[11] While he suggests that these ritual universes hide a precolonial past, he also tries to locate a colonial origin (see also Chakrabarty 2004, pp. 666–67). Thus, although there are multiple references to A-lokkhi in popular Bengali folklore, he ascribes a suddenness in his indecisive phrase, "However she originated ... " However, elsewhere, he argues that the category of *'mangal'* (domestic wellbeing), for instance, pertains to the *kula* (community/lineage), and goes beyond the linear historical time of the nation

---

[11] Chakrabarty problematizes unequivocal oppositions of traditional and western domesticity, theorized by (Chatterjee 1990; Bagchi 1990; etc.).

(Chakrabarty 1993, pp. 28–29). Taking Chakrabarty's own cue, I argue that notions of domesticity exist in Bengali cultural memory, which exceed (post)colonial imaginations, and involve deeper senses of temporal experience.

These memories of complex goddess-domesticities, and temporal spirals of dark interiors sound in the experience of the evening conch, and *panchali* narratives. Also, besides Lokkhi, there are other goddesses who remained immediate and non-sanitized through time, as strong 'other' models of the home's experience. Manasa, particularly, remains as the critical archetypal counterpart to Lokkhi's moral universe.

4.4. Manasa Pujo: Tragedy and Fear

Snakes generally, and Manasa particularly, are insistent archetypes of Bengali religious experience and imagination. Manasa's dimensions threaten Lokkhi's calculated domesticity; and the Bengali sacred domestic includes both harmony and fear in the construction of *shongshar*. Manasa's life/death prototype draws influences from folk religion, Buddhist *tantrism*, Brahmanical Hinduism, and *bhakti* devotionalism (Chatterji 2014, p. 7).

Manasa is a combination of regeneration and destruction, desire and fear. So while she is worshipped before marriages or childbirth in rural Bengal, in her *darshan* (sight) one also views death. Lores have it that Shiva's wife, Candi, hit her out of jealousy, and so Manasa is blind in one eye, and stores poison in it. Thus, Manasa is a form of both *visa-dhara*, one holding poison, and *visa-hara*, one destroying poison (Dimock and Ramanujan 1962, p. 321; Doniger 2015, p. 2). Manasa's death-interruption transgresses Lokkhi's peaceful ethos of domestic experience.

Chatterji (2014) characterizes Manasa as a subaltern goddess since her repulsive, *bibhatsa* (disgusting) dimensions rupture Sanskritic dharma. While Mohanty (2008) establishes Lokkhi's modern avatar as a cross-class feminist goddess, Chatterji (2014) imagines Manasa as a Dalit prototype, asserting herself through disgust, fury, and humiliation. I argue however that Bengali domesticity seats both life/Lokkhi and death/Manasa, together expressed for instance in the conch's materiality. Although Lokkhi originates in the Brahmanical tradition, the discourse of her virtuosity gets domesticated in all households, irrespective of caste; and ethnographic narratives suggest that all classes of people also relate to the (desirous) fear that Manasa evokes.

I have consulted different versions of Manasa *panchalis*. The *panchali* form is typical to Lokkhi, and thus Manasa's textual representations are similar to hers. Manasa *panchalis* include *brotokotha*, *mantras* etc., and although Manasa is an independent goddess, her husband is propitiated, like Vishnu is, before Lokkhi.

Manasa is primarily described in the *panchalis* as one who fills households with bounty. Like Lokkhi she gifts pots of gold, children, and health. Indeed, the *panchali* asserts that "Lokkhi is seated in the home due to Manasa's blessings" (Dvija and Shastri n.d., p. 9).

Additionally, Manasa takes away poison (with poison), and the fear of death (with death). She destroys Chand's seven ships and six sons. But the seventh son, Lakhindar (and all others), is eventually brought back to life by her. Lakhindar remains a liminal figure in the Manasa discourse: the goddess pushes the limit of domesticity to death, but with Lakhindar, there is also always the *possibility* of return. The *puranic* serpent (Ananta, whose coils embody the same infinity as the *kha* of *shankha*/conch) eats its own tail, but can grow again. This concentric experience of life, death, and return, is also materially embodied in the swirled home-conch.

In Manasa *puja* narratives, there remains a persistent dissonance in the domesticity logic: here, like Lokkhi's devotees, people try to maintain restoration as an experiential focus, but cannot sustain it. Manasa narratives are productive enmeshes of the everyday and afterlife. A-lokkhi cannot fully be kept out, and there remain ambivalences among devotees about the deity herself—she is greeted with both affinity and hatred. This contradiction is also embodied in household women's experiences. So sometimes different women represent Manasa's contrary dimensions, and sometimes, the *grihini* (homemaker) embodies them all.

4.5. Sita

Like the conch itself, Sita's *shongshar* is a coiling of three folds: a secular narrative of mistrust of humans, Manasa's fertility, and Manasa's destructiveness.

Sita is from a lower caste and lower-middle class background. Her husband is a tailor, and they live in a dingy Kolkata neighbourhood. At her entrance hangs a poster, which is a peculiar welcome note. It says:

> Humans,
>
> if you accept them, they take you for granted,
>
> respect them, they think it is appeasement,
>
> give them advice, they do the opposite,
>
> help them, they disown you
>
> trust them, they harm you,
>
> do well, they are jealous,
>
> when sad, they take advantage,
>
> love them, they hurt you,
>
> and desert you when their need is fulfilled.

She said, "These are lessons of my life ... My home is *hazarduari* (thousand-doored). I let everyone in. But they have only harmed."

Sita and her husband's families were from Bangladesh. After her in-laws died, they were deserted by the extended family. Her husband is a hardworking man, started business with meagre money, and it was a "rags to riches" story. However, his business partner was jealous, and displaced him. He then started a tailoring shop. He gradually earned a lot, and they established a factory. Sita said these were possible due to Manasa's worship at home. These clearly were Manasa's Lokkhi-like dimensions in *shongshar*. Sita performs Manasa *puja* with great splendor for an entire month of monsoon. Like other Bengali women, she performs Manasa *puja* for *shongshar's mongol*, and considers her *puja*-offerings as auspicious also for first menses and pregnant women. On the last day, five pots—for Manasa, her two female accomplices, snakes generally, and *kalnagini* specifically—are worshipped. Sita said that the goddess, happy, bestows fertility, but when angry, destroys everything.

Sita had two sons and a daughter. Her younger son married suddenly without announcement. The bride came with no belongings. Sita said she was A-lokkhi (personified), since a Lokkhi bride brings ornaments with her. Also, she would sleep till late, and even through the evening. She was greedy, asked for new saris every day, and spent all her husband's money. She would throw away home-cooked food, and keep dirty menstrual clothes unwashed. Once while arguing with her husband, she even threw her conch-bangles at Manasa's idol. One of her children were stillborn, and she was not even sad. So according to Sita, her daughter-in-law bore all signs of A-Lokkhi (and infertility): bad routine, drain of wealth, loss of child, disregard of the kitchen, and disrespect of marriage.

In 2010 winter, on *Poush shongkranti* (last day of a Bengali winter month), considered auspicious for agriculture, it happened to be a Thursday (auspicious for Lokkhi), *omaboshya* (new moon), and the following day was *grohon* (eclipse). Bengalis consider *omaboshya* and eclipses to be ominous; and thus, this day was a strong blend of fertile and inauspicious symbols. Sita decided to perform *basti* (*vastu*) *pujo* (home-worship). She explained that the *vastu* itself is snake and Manasa. The *puja* is performed in the house's courtyard, where rice-pudding is cooked on an earthern pot. The solidified oven-earth is then preserved.

Sita's daughter-in-law was pregnant again, and so Sita disallowed her from going out with her husband that evening. She felt that the new moon and eclipse might harm the child. But the woman (A-lokkhi) was angry. Sita explained with remorse that on that *omaboshya* night, A-lokkhi should have ideally been sent away, but as fate would have it, Sita herself insisted that she stay back during the *vastupuja*. And, her son never returned. Later they found out that he was poisoned by the wife's lover. The wife then left the home with all his money and Sita's ornaments.

Sita's narrative of the experience of *shongshar* gives a story of building Lokkhi, and losing it all. The powers of *omaboshya* and *grohon* were greater than those of Thursday and *basti pujo*. Sita said, "That woman was *a-lokkhone* (inauspicious), *bechal* (of loose morals), *uronchondi* (restless), and the *kalnagini* ... My husband cried so much that he became blind in one eye." In these utterances about A-lokkhi, Sita also called her *kalnagini*, the snake which killed Lakhindar. This was a narrative slip, since *kalnagini* is Manasa's, greatest embodiment. So unconsciously, Sita also blamed her goddess, Manasa.

There were other slips. Sita said, "The domestic fate is bad." She said there are snakes in her home, and sometimes her Manasa idol lets out green light from one eye, which is poison. Before her son died, she dreamt of many snakes—she killed them, but few could not be destroyed. Here too, Sita displayed overt disgust of snakes. In her own reckoning, the *vastu* (home) itself is (like) the coiled snake, and I have argued earlier that the snake and conch are materially related through idioms of twisted death and regeneration. These joined discourses of Lokkhi, Manasa, home, and the conch thus come together in Sita's domestic experience.

Sita has further ambivalent emotions towards the goddess. She said, "Manasa is in my veins." By this she indicated her total faith in the goddess. Again, Manasa, symbolically seated herself in Sita's husband, and he became blind in one eye. Both of them say that because of Manasa's continued presence in the home, they have managed to restore some wealth and calm.

So for Sita, Manasa comes to embody both Lokkhi and A-lokkhi. Manasa as A-lokkhi manifested in Sita's daughter-in-law, and as Lokkhi, in her and her husband. In the struggle between Sita and her daughter-in-law: the two aspects of Manasa, the Lokkhi-A-lokkhi dialectic of *shongshar*, the son was sacrificed. In Sita's narrative itself, Manasa = snake = *vastu*. The Bengali term *shaap* (snake) has a homophone, which means curse. So the *shaap/vastu* is harmed by the *shhaap/vastu*, like the snake consuming itself. Again, Sita said that Manasa is in her veins—so she shall reinstate the home, the snake shall reinvigorate. Symbolically almost, for as long as she spoke, Sita's hair-bun kept unfastening, and she quickly tied it up every time.

When I was leaving, Sita said through simultaneous allusions to fertility and death, that although she lost everything with her son: her complexion, hair, beauty, and desire to live; she cannot die by will, so "she continues to convert the raw to cooked". Like the conch's coils, *shongshar* is the twirling of life and afterlife. This is what Sita calls *niyoti*, fate.

4.6. *Sadhana*

Every year, after Manasa *puja*, many women are possessed (*bhor*) by the goddess, drums are sounded, and Manasa speaks through them about birth and disaster. Once she spoke through Sadhana. Unlike in Sita's household, in Sadhana's, she herself is Manasa's ambivalent embodiment: the seat of fertility and destruction, affinity and fear. Once when she fell very ill, she underwent Manasa's *bhor*, and started Manasa *puja* for recovery. She remembered, "I (as mother) said that I would be fine, and my *shongshar* would be Manasa's own".

Sadhana, from the lowest of castes, was extremely poor, when as a five-year-old she migrated to the city. Her father played the *dhaak* (drums) in *pujas*, mother worked as maidservant, and they lived on footpaths. She started work as domestic help, since when she was seven. She got married at fifteen, her husband did not earn, and the couple eventually separated. She had six children, two survived. Finally, she worshipped Manasa, and after "taking care of one child like fire in a hurricane", she survived. Sadhana maintains the rhetoric of domestic vulnerability throughout. After years of struggle, she has made some money, and a small house. In her insistent poverty, bad marriage, and loss of children, she embodies destruction; and in hard work and regaining of health, revival.

Sadhana performs an annual Manasa *puja* at home during monsoon. This worship is also intended towards the goddess of food, Annapurna. The conch is sounded to let the goddess know that her food is being prepared. All through the night before the *puja*, Manasa's *panchali* is read, and a lot of food cooked on earthen oven. This critical act is performed with perseverance, since if the earthen pitchers break, the goddess is angry, appears as a snake in the hearth, and signifies a lifetime's loss of wealth. The cooking must take place inside the home (unlike A-lokkhi *pujo* which is performed outside). So Manasa bears A-lokkhi's marks of devastation, but demands to be treated like Lokkhi. The next morning, Manasa and her snakes are worshipped. As Annapurna too, Manasa is the fertility goddess.

Sadhana's narrative also reveals intensely ambivalent responses towards her deity; like Sita, she is the perfect seat of *critical piousness*. She says that there are snakes which stay in and protect her home (*vastu-shaap*). They are divine, and do not allow harm to fall upon her household. *Yet* she hates their sight, is very scared of them, and prays to them to not appear before her. She used to have dreams of snakes coiled together, but ever since she worshipped Manasa, the goddess found a rightful place, and the snaky dreams stopped. While Sadhana says she gets angry if anyone is disrespectful to "her mother", she herself admits to also cursing her. She said, "Just because Manasa is unhappy, she is jealous, and does not let others be happy. She is *shoitaani* (devil)". She added that snakes can bring both fortune and disaster: "*shaap-i obhishaap*" ("Snakes are curses"). She stresses that she loves Manasa, but does not enter her temple after dark—Manasa's poisonous glare scares her.

In my analysis too, just as coiled snakes are revered as embodiments of both disaster and revival, the other embodiment of a natural spiral kept at home, the conch, too, is a reminder of both Lokkhi-like restorative peace as well as a desirous fear and freedom of the afterlife.

Doniger aptly refers to the experience of the "ambivalent attitude to ambivalent snake goddesses", as *dvesa-bhakti*, or "devotion through hatred" (Doniger 2015, p. 3). This is particularly comparable to the devotional aesthetic style of *nindastuti* (worship through criticism) in Sanskrit literature. Sadhana's paradoxical relationship with Manasa also reminds of the *bhakti* poet Ramprasad's relationship with Kali. Dalmiya says about his worship that, "Praying to Kali becomes a relentless litany of her faults and misdemeanors, and these are harped upon in the very act of seeking redemption through her! So not only is Kali paradoxical herself, but so also is the *love* of Kali" (Dalmiya 2000, p. 127).

4.7. Kishore

Sita's and Sadhana's stories speak of psychological ruptures in domestic religious experiences, which affect health, fertility, and wellbeing. Kishore's narrative reveals other dimensions of loss (of property) where Manasa's ambivalence plays out in business, material holdings, and family lives. Decadence manifests in a shrinking business, and shift from a happy joint family to modern nuclear flats. Like the other two, Kishore's narrative has frequent symbolic references connecting their life with Manasa's. So, like Manasa's opponent, Chand's family, they are seven brothers. Their family migrated from East Bengal, and they form a network with other migrants in their thriving textile business. This relatively middle-upper caste, rich family used to own a big house with 30 rooms, and now live in a multistoried complex in a posh urban locality, where there is a roof-temple with a Manasa idol holding snakes, and her four companions—two holding lotuses, and two, conches.

While in East Bengal, their father, as a toddler, was once very unwell, and became almost blind. His grandmother dreamt that if they worshipped Manasa, he would recover. The priest worshipped the goddess, and the ritual water was sprinkled on his eyes. He regained sight, but thereafter bore water marks in his eyes. His mother later found a jeweled-*ghot* and conch in a pond, and a snake appeared and told her that she should start Manasa *puja* at home. She did, but also went mad after that. Kishore said that the *ghot* was *obhishopto* (cursed), and brought with it both Lokkhi and A-Lokkhi. So it was a story of tremendous economic uplift after that, but the mother lost her sanity.

Even after migrating they continued Manasa *puja* at home, and it is now 104 years old. The annual revenue of the family business was used for the worship. However, the family could not continue to live together due to incessant fights. So they sold their property to a promoting group.

So Manasa brought both wealth and decadence in the family-business dyad. Like Sita's husband, Kishore's father bore Manasa's mark in his eye, and some family members believe that he was most afflicted by her, and the domestic embodiment of her ethics. So while it is more common for women to embody goddesses and the ambivalent home, *shongshar* more generally is the site of sacred morality.

In the Manasa-Behula chronicle of the Manasa Mangalkavya, the goddess instructed the blacksmith to leave a vermillion mark as identification on Behula-Lakhindar's iron marriage-chamber's hole, for the deadly *kalnagini*, to enter (Dvija and Shastri n.d., p. 13). The snake climbed on their bed through Behula's open hair (Dimock and Ramanujan 1964, p. 314). In another telling, Behula, angry, throws her *sindur* at the snake, and snakes ever since carry red spots. Vermillion and long black hair, quintessential symbols of the Lokkhi woman, themselves thus become possibilities of death during intimacy. Like the evening conch-sound twirling out of the coiled *shankh*, and like knotted hair unfastening, Lokkhi unfastens to Manasa, and the home relaxes towards abandonment.

5. Conclusions

The Bengali religious experience of the home includes the long-drawn sounding of the conch at dusk, and domesticated deities: the *lokkhi* woman, the female snake-goddess, and persistent folklore about Behula–Lakhindar's immortal powers of marital resuscitation. The icon of ultimate *mongol* (wellbeing), Lokkhi, also anticipates senses of domestic vulnerability; Manasa and her devotion carry ambivalent messages of death and regeneration; and the conch's materiality and sensory universe twirl through these opposed sensibilities of interior attachment and renunciate slits. The home/*vastu* thus becomes the site of experiencing both security and openness. This openness could imply detachment, freedom, death, or expanse.

So the Bengali Hindu domestic space particularly (and certain South Asian Hindu archetypes more generally), involve contrary messages of sacred homemaking. The home altar is itself also the renouncing space, and the *samsaric* fertile body, the detached body. The home enacts upon its folds, which coil inward toward comforts, and disentangle outward, with A-lokkhi, and *shankh* sounds: through the interstices of conch-contours and twilight. The frictions of these folds constitute *shongshar*. There are narrative journeys from disaster to fortune and vice-versa, and the serpentine *vastu* is reborn through these performances. The symbol of everyday restoration and rebirth, the conch (*shankh*) and its sonics, open to the sea, and the sea can both kill and heal. Like the *puranic* serpent eating its tail and its growing again, this infinite concentricity does not speak of eternity, but endless life *including*, not transcending death (Wake 1873, p. 378). *Shongshar* twirls peace and fear, love and hate, Lokkhi and Manasa; and the *shankh* is the embodied kernel of this snake-folding.

However, the *shankh* is not only a spatial embodiment of the home's religious experience; its twisted depths also take us into refracted shadows of the ocean's interior and time's sacred inside. So the paper also helps reimagine temporal/historical experience: the Bengali home and its postcolonial understandings, precolonial materiality, and essential temporal archetypes.

Analyzing Home Science discourses circulating since the 1910s, Hancock (2001) argues that the home and women's experiences emerged as sites of imagining a future nation. Like Chatterjee (1993) she views the home as the location of interior traditional grammar, in distinction to the modern outside. She says however that the gendered domestic discourse and experience, carried traces of precolonial vernacular distinctions between interiority and exteriority. These distinctions were not fixed. For instance, she says, following A. K. Ramanujan, that in Tamil classical Hindu poetics, "house" simultaneously also means the self and womanhood. With the influence of Victorian conceptions of gendered spaces however, the private and public became relatively more congealed. The home became the interior feminine domain, standing against the masculine modern public (ibid, pp. 875–76). I argue however, that this discussion about political appropriations of interiority does not consider that the precolonial influences could not simply have disappeared. Everyday domestic experience is the best locale to imagine different politics of time's folds upon sacred textures of life. Mundane temporality—ingrained in senses of passage, decay, renewal, birth, and disaster, narrated in goddess stories of Lokkhi/Manasa, and embodied in artefacts such as the conch—supersedes historicity. But postcolonial theorizations of Chatterjee (1993), Hancock (2001), Sarkar (2001), and even their critique, K. Chatterjee (2008), who tries to extend history to the *puranas*, are locked only in sequential secular time.

Chakrabarty (1993) hints at alternative temporal imaginations. He says that the notion of *grihalakshmi*, "is the horizon where history "unworks", i.e., 'encounters interruption, fragmentation, suspension'. The reality of this past, to speak with Levinas, therefore 'must not only be determined in its historical objectivity, but also from interior intentions, from the secrecy that interrupts the continuity of historical time'" (ibid, p. 29). Chakrabarty also says that the sacred-aesthetic ideas of beauty ('*mangal*') that Lakshmi carries with her, are carried over from everyday performances and Mangalkavyas, in which, the divine and mortal worlds are not separate (ibid, p. 28). In another article, published a decade later, he similarly evokes senses of non-secular time, again through the Manglakavyas (Chakrabarty 2004, p. 679).

I have argued that the regenerative home and its folds address these secret interiorities of time and space, as *shongshar*: the Bengali religious experience of the everyday, where goddesses, *shankh*, and devotees meet, to understand life and death.

This paper has tried to understand the Bengali Hindu home (with the conch as its embodied kernel) as a locale where contrary religious experiences and ethics enact through worship idioms and practices of Lokkhi and A-lokkhi/Manasa. There are three major analytical functions of this understanding of the ambivalent nature of sacred domestic experience. First, it revisits and problematizes the insistent trope of the home as the secured hearth, and the protecting domain from the outside world. Second, it helps conceptualize ways in which elements of the household—people and objects—also embody the religious contrarieties of peace and fear. Finally, it reimagines the space and time of domestic experience, in the image of the conch itself, beyond dialectics of interiority-exteriority or linearity-circularity, as a *spiraling* of sacred emotional experiences.

Funding: This research received funding from Presidency University, Kolkata.

Acknowledgments: I thank Dipesh Chakrabarty, Partha Chatterjee, and Upal Chakrabarti for their very careful comments on earlier drafts of the paper. I presented parts of the essay in the Centre of South Asian Studies and Department of Social Anthropology, in Cambridge, and I thank the participants, especially James Laidlaw, Norbert Peabody, and Susan Bayly, for their critical comments.

Conflicts of Interest: The author declares no conflict of interest.

References

Acharya, Prasanna Kumar. 1942. Manasara Vastushastra: The Basic Text on Architecture and Sculpture. *Annals of the Bhandarkar Oriental Research Institute* 23: 1–18.

Acharya, Ashvinikumar. n.d. *Baromasher Sri Sri Lakshmi Debi-r Panchali O Brotokotha*. Kolkata: Shojol Pustakalay.

Bachelard, Gaston. 1994. *The Poetics of Space: The Classic Look at How We Experience Intimate Places*. Translated by Maria Jolas. Boston: Beacon Press.

Bagchi, Jasodhara. 1990. Representing Nationalism: Ideology of Motherhood in Colonial Bengal. *Economic and Political Weekly* 25: WS65–WS71.

Basak, Sri Jasodanandan. n.d. *Sri Sri Manasa Debi-r Brotokotha (Panchali)*. Kolkata: Tapan Pustakalay.

Bhattacharya, Asutosh. 1965. The Serpent as a Folk-Deity in Bengal. *Asian Folklore Studies* 24: 1–10. [CrossRef]

Chakrabarti, Shaktipada. n.d. *Sri Sri Manasa Debi-r Panchali O Brotokotha (Puja Paddhati Shoho)*. Kolkata: Benimadhav Sil's Library.

Chakrabarty, Dipesh. 1993. Deferral of (A) Colonial Modernity: Public Debates on Domesticity in British Bengal. *History Workshop* 36: 1–34. [CrossRef]

Chakrabarty, Dipesh. 2004. Romantic Archives: Literature and the Politics of Identity in Bengal. *Critical Inquiry* 30: 654–82. [CrossRef]

Chatterjee, Partha. 1990. The Nationalist Resolution of the Women's Question. In *Recasting Women: Essays in Colonial History*. Edited by Sudesh Vaid and Kumkum Sangari. New Brunswick: Rugters University Press, pp. 233–53.

Chatterjee, Partha. 1993. *The Nation and Its Fragments*. Princeton: Princeton University Press.

Chatterjee, Ratnabali. 2000. Representation of Gender in Folk Paintings of Bengal. *Social Scientist* 28: 7–21. [CrossRef]

Chatterjee, Kumkum. 2008. The Persianisation of "Itihasa": Performance Narratives and Mughal Political Culture in Eighteenth Century Bengal. *The Journal of Asian Studies* 67: 513–43. [CrossRef]

Chatterji, Roma. 2014. Folk Theatre on the Modern Stage: Manasa—Death Dealer/Life Giver. *Indian Anthropologist* 44: 1–18.

Clark, Thomas Welbourne. 1955. Evolution of Hinduism in medieval Bengali Literature: Siva, Candi, Manasa. *Bulletin of the School of Oriental and African Studies, University of London* 17: 503–18. [CrossRef]

Coomaraswamy, Ananda K. 1934. Kha and Other Words Denoting "Zero" in Connection with the Metaphysics of Space. *Bulletin of the School of Oriental Studies, University of London* 7: 487–97. [CrossRef]

Dalmiya, Vrinda. 2000. Loving Paradoxes: A Feminist Reclamation of the Goddess Kali. *Hypatia Winter* 15: 125–50. [CrossRef]

Dimock, Edward C., Jr., and Attipate Krishnaswami Ramanujan. 1962. The Goddess of Snakes in Medieval Bengali Literature, Part II. *History of Religions* 1: 307–21. [CrossRef]

Dimock, Edward C., Jr., and Attipate Krishnaswami Ramanujan. 1964. The Goddess of Snakes in Medieval Bengali Literature, Part II. *History of Religions* 3: 300–22. [CrossRef]

Doniger, Wendy. 2015. Introduction: Sympathy for the Devi: Snakes and Snake Goddesses in Hinduism. In *The Triumph of the Snake Goddess*. Edited by Kaiser Haq. Cambridge: Harvard University Press, pp. 1–28.

Dvija, Banshidas, and Sri Gopal Shastri. n.d. *Sri Sri Manasa Debi-r Panchali O Brotokotha (Puja Paddhati Shoho)*. Kolkata: Orient Library.

Flibbertigibbet. 1966. The Goddess and the Owl. *Economic and Political Weekly* 1: 484–85.

Fruzzetti, Lina M. 1990. *The Gift of a Virgin: Women, Marriage, and Ritual in a Bengali Society*. Delhi: Oxford University Press.

Fruzzetti, Lina, and Akos Ostor. 1984. *Kinship and Ritual in Bengal: Anthropological Essays*. New Delhi: South Asian Publishers.

Ganesh, Kamala. 1990. Mother Who is Not a Mother: In Search of the Great Indian Goddess. *Economic and Political Weekly* 25: WS58–WS64.

Hancock, Mary. 2001. Home Science and the Nationalisation of Domesticity in Colonial India. *Modern Asian Studies* 35: 871–903. [CrossRef]

Haq, Kaiser. 2015. *The Triumph of the Snake Goddess*. Cambridge: Harvard University Press.

Harman, William. 1987. The Hindu Marriage as Soteriological Event. *International Journal of Sociology of the Family* 17: 169–82.

McDaniel, June. 2003. *Making Virtuous Daughters and Wives: An Introduction to Women's Brata Rituals in Bengali Folk Religion*. Albany: State University of New York Press.

Mohanty, Satya P. 2008. Alternative Modernities and Medieval Indian Literature: The Oriya "Lakshmi Purana" as Radical Pedagody. *Diacritics* 38: 3–15, 17–21. [CrossRef]

Montagu, Jeremy. 1981. The Conch in Prehistory: Pottery, Stone and Natural. *World Archaeology* 12: 273–79. [CrossRef]

Paranavitana, Senarath. 1955. Samkha and Padma. *Artibus Asiae* 18: 121–27. [CrossRef]

Rhodes, Constantina. 2010. *Invoking Lakshmi: The Goddess of Wealth in Song and Ceremony*. Albany: State University of New York Press.

Sachdev, Vibhuti. 2005. A Vastu Text in the Modern Age: "Vishvakarma Darpan", 1969. *Journal of the Royal Asiatic Society* 15: 165–78. [CrossRef]

Sarkar, Tanika. 2001. *Hindu Wife, Hindu Nation: Community, Religion, and Cultural Nationalism*. Delhi: Permanent Black.

Shaw, Garvin. 1875. Note on the Sound Heard in Connection with Conches and Other Shells. *The Analyst* 2: 69. [CrossRef]

Shulman, David. 1978. The Serpent and the Sacrifice: An Anthill Myth from Tiruvarur. *History of Religions* 18: 107–37. [CrossRef]

Wake, C. Staniland. 1873. The Origin of Serpent-Worship. *The Journal of the Anthropological Institute of Great Britain and Ireland* 2: 373–90. [CrossRef]

Conclusion

June McDaniel

Hindu religious experience has been marginalized as a topic of study in the academy in recent years. We have discussed some of the reasons for this, from debates over language and access to the experience of others, to the influence of political, social and economic ideas on the culture. Yet as we see from these articles, religious experience has been a central facet of Hindu life, from ancient days to modern ones. It has been especially associated with *sādhus* (see Figure 1[1]).

Figure 1. Shiva sadhu with rudraksha beads.

[1] This portrait of a sadhu is by Leonid Plotkin, a freelance documentary photographer and the author of the photo book *Nostalgia for Eternity: Journeys in Religion, History and Myth on the Indian Subcontinent.* Leonid visited frequently and, over two decades, stayed for more than five years to study and photograph India's great religious traditions as well as its syncretic religions and numerous folk, tribal and non-mainstream practices. He may be contacted at i@leonidfotos.com.

Sādhus (as well as *sādhvīs* or *sādhikās, jogīs, sannyāsīs, vairāgīs,* and ascetics of various sorts), are people who have rejected ordinary householder life in favor of wandering alone and living lives of contemplation. *Sādhus* live in a variety of ways, from spending time in burning grounds to living in monasteries or *maṭhs,* to following pilgrimage routes and encountering their gurus and *guru-bhāīs* (fellow initiates) and members of their sampradaya groups at religious festivals. They practice their *sādhanās* or meditative rituals as a part of this life, and they have played many different roles. They have been consultants to kings and princes and have acted as warriors and defenders of the land. They have been condemned by both the nineteenth century British colonialists and the twentieth century Marxist Naxalites as homeless beggars, and they have been idealized by Indian householders as godlike people with supernatural powers. They may be actors on the modern political scene, and they may be people who reject politics and history entirely.

But religious experience in not limited to *sādhus* and other renunciants. As we have seen in this collection of essays, religious experience has been described from ancient to modern times in India and continues to be a central source of meaning for many Hindus today. These articles have described the central role of religious experience in Vedānta, Yoga, Sāṃkhya, and Sant Mat traditions. They include its importance in Vaishnāva, Śākta and Nirguṇa *bhakti,* as well as the creative roles of Hindu religious inspiration in music and the arts. Religious experience can be tied to physical illness, through the role of disease goddesses, and to insanity, through belief in spirit possession. It can be a part of daily householder life as well. The perspectives of the writers in this issue range from sympathy to skepticism, from a focus on history to an emphasis on ethnography. All of these are ways of approaching a phenomenon which is varied and diverse, linking life, death and rebirth for practitioners.

MDPI
St. Alban-Anlage 66
4052 Basel
Switzerland
Tel. +41 61 683 77 34
Fax +41 61 302 89 18
www.mdpi.com

Religions Editorial Office
E-mail: religions@mdpi.com
www.mdpi.com/journal/religions

CPSIA information can be obtained
at www.ICGtesting.com
Printed in the USA
LVHW051540201119
637827LV00005B/176/P

9 783039 21050